Practical Aspects
of Interview
and
Interrogation

Second Edition

CRC SERIES IN
PRACTICAL ASPECTS OF CRIMINAL AND FORENSIC INVESTIGATIONS

VERNON J. GEBERTH, BBA, MPS, FBINA *Series Editor*

Practical Homicide Investigation: Tactics, Procedures, and Forensic Techniques, Third Edition
Vernon J. Geberth

The Counterterrorism Handbook: Tactics, Procedures, and Techniques, Second Edition
Frank Bolz, Jr., Kenneth J. Dudonis, and David P. Schulz

Forensic Pathology, Second Edition
Dominick J. Di Maio and Vincent J. M. Di Maio

Interpretation of Bloodstain Evidence at Crime Scenes, Second Edition
William G. Eckert and Stuart H. James

Tire Imprint Evidence
Peter McDonald

Practical Drug Enforcement: Procedures and Administration, Second Edition
Michael D. Lyman

Practical Aspects of Rape Investigation: A Multidisciplinary Approach, Third Edition
Robert R. Hazelwood and Ann Wolbert Burgess

The Sexual Exploitation of Children: A Practical Guide to Assessment, Investigation, and Intervention, Second Edition
Seth L. Goldstein

Gunshot Wounds: Practical Aspects of Firearms, Ballistics, and Forensic Techniques, Second Edition
Vincent J. M. Di Maio

Friction Ridge Skin: Comparison and Identification of Fingerprints
James F. Cowger

Footwear Impression Evidence, Second Edition
William J. Bodziak

Principles of Kinesic Interview and Interrogation
Stan Walters

Practical Fire and Arson Investigation, Second Edition
David R. Redsicker and John J. O'Connor

The Practical Methodology of Forensic Photography, Second Edition
David R. Redsicker

Practical Aspects of Interview and Interrogation, Second Edition
David E. Zulawski and Douglas E. Wicklander

Investigating Computer Crime
Franklin Clark and Ken Diliberto

Practical Homicide Investigation Checklist and Field Guide
Vernon J. Geberth

Bloodstain Pattern Analysis: With an Introduction to Crime Scene Reconstruction, Second Edition
Tom Bevel and Ross M. Gardner

Practical Aspects of Munchausen by Proxy and Munchausen Syndrome Investigation
Kathryn Artingstall

Quantitative-Qualitative Friction Ridge Analysis: An Introduction to Basic and Advanced Ridgeology
David R. Ashbaugh

Practical Aspects of Interview and Interrogation

Second Edition

David E. Zulawski
Douglas E. Wicklander

CRC PRESS

Boca Raton   London   New York   Washington, D.C.

Published in 2002 by
CRC Press
Taylor & Francis Group
6000 Broken Sound Parkway NW, Suite 300
Boca Raton, FL 33487-2742

© 2002 by Taylor & Francis Group, LLC
CRC Press is an imprint of Taylor & Francis Group

No claim to original U.S. Government works
Printed in the United States of America on acid-free paper
15 14 13 12 11 10 9 8 7 6

International Standard Book Number-10: 0-8493-1153-5 (Hardcover)
International Standard Book Number-13: 978-0-8493-1153-8 (Hardcover)
Library of Congress Card Number 20001035402

Library of Congress Cataloging-in-Publication Data

Zulawski, David E.
    Practical aspects of interview and interrogation / David E. Zulawski, Douglas E.
    Wicklander.—2nd ed.
            p.   cm.
    Includes bibliographical references and index.
    ISBN 0-8493-1153-5 (soft cover : alk.paper)—ISBN 0-8493-0101-7 (hard cover : alk. paper)
    1. Police questioning—United States. I. Wicklander, Douglas E. II. Title.
HV8073 .Z85   2001
363.2'54—dc21   20001035402

Visit the Taylor & Francis Web site at
http://www.taylorandfrancis.com

and the CRC Press Web site at
http://www.crcpress.com

Dedication

To my wife, Annette, children Jennifer, Jonathan, Patrick, Katherine and Kelly, and, of course, Mom and Dad.

—David E. Zulawski

To my wife, Debbie, children Matthew, Andrew and Ann, and to my mother, Callista, O.G.M. Not enough can be said about their love and support.

—Douglas E. Wicklander

Preface

Since the first edition of this text was published a decade ago, interrogation has come under attack as its opponents focus on the possibility of false confessions. It is disconcerting to interrogators that false confessions exist. Why would individuals confess to crimes they did not commit? It boggles the mind that this could occur; however, with the advent of DNA evidence, it is clear that, in a number of capital cases, an innocent person was convicted.

Critics of interrogation point to these injustices and then completely condemn interrogation tactics without offering an alternative. If one examines criminal cases at random, it is clear that most cases are resolved by confession, not forensic evidence. Most interrogation critics have never questioned a suspect, much less tried to obtain the truth. Instead, to prove impropriety they blindly accept what the suspect says happened during the interrogation. They then point to experiments with college students to confirm their belief in coerced confessions.

There is no doubt that false confessions exist. However, common factors are present in most false confessions. The extreme level of threats, length of interrogation, or mental condition of the subject, are a few of the most common. Very compliant individuals may give false confessions — but they may also confess when they are actually guilty.

Thoughtful criticism is always of value, as it causes one to examine long-accepted positions and attitudes. Many avenues have been opened when the proper questions have been asked. Because of such questions, we have rethought our positions and tactics. We are committed to understanding why false confessions exist. Besides reviewing the literature, we have begun to talk with those who have falsely confessed to a crime. The edited interview granted by Christopher Ochoa in Chapter 4 is one example that we wanted to share with the reader. He confessed to a murder and rape, then implicated his roommate in the crime. Ochoa was exonerated by the efforts of the University of Wisconsin Law School Project Innocence, a confession from the real killer, DNA testing and the State of Texas, which re-examined the evidence in the case.

In the coming years, we intend to continue to broaden our understanding of the interview and interrogation process by examining what we do and why. We intend to encourage change where it is warranted and to defend the process against self-proclaimed experts who have never had to seek the truth in real life. Valid criticism is always welcome, but the blanket condemnation of a process without the offer of a solution should similarly be condemned.

David E. Zulawski
Douglas E. Wicklander
Downers Grove, Illinois
March 2001

Acknowledgments

Entering our 19th year in business does not happen without the help of family, friends and valued business associates. We have been fortunate over the years to have enjoyed all of the above. Sharing insights, experiences and dreams has helped us be better teachers and investigators.

When one believes that he understands it all and has every answer, he truly becomes ignorant. Fortunately, we are not there yet. Each day brings new awareness and understanding of things that we had thought we understood. We have been fortunate in the generosity of our friends, both professional and personal, who have shared their insights, concerns, and questions. As a result, we have found there is much we did not know or understand. For this, we thank them.

We have been joined in our professional adventure by a group of very special co-workers who have become our friends. Their willingness to help out at Wicklander-Zulawski & Associates in getting the job done with a smile has been the foundation of our business. These associates are the base upon which we built our reputation. We thank each of you for your efforts and friendship.

Special thanks must go to our partners Wayne Hoover, Shane Sturman, and Kate Zovnic for their suggestions and efforts to make this text and Wicklander-Zulawski & Associates a success. We especially appreciate the work Jennifer Roder and Connie Holroyd did to prepare the manuscript for our editors — almost always with a smile. We also acknowledge the contributions of Brett Ward, Chris Norris, Lou Tessmann, W. Michael Floyd, Stan Slowik, John Guzman, and Dennis Nebrich, who have shared so generously with us. Cheryl Blake contributed to our knowledge of telephone interviewing, offering experience and insights unselfishly. Again, thank you for your special efforts.

We also wish to offer a special thank you to Mark Mennis, Greg Sun, and Al Barry, who have stood by us since the beginning of our business. Each has offered invaluable skills and advice that helped to carry us to where we are today.

Last, but not least, we want to thank our families and spouses for the tolerance they have shown. Their observation that between the two of us we make one good man, was both comforting and frightening.

If we have inadvertently left anyone out, know that it was because we owe so much to so many. Thank you all.

David E. Zulawski
Douglas E. Wicklander

Cause of Crime

Hey, Mom. Why do bad people do bad things? I know! Their Moms and Dads didn't love them. If they came in my house I would tell them I loved them. And their parents were mean.

—Mitchell Zovnic, age 5

Mitchell, if it were only that simple. Perhaps one day.

The Authors

David E. Zulawski is a 1973 graduate of Knox College, Galesburg, Illinois, from which he received a B.A. degree. After graduating, he spent 2 years with the Chicago & Northwestern Railroad as a special agent. During that time, he investigated thefts from interstate shipments in transit.

Mr. Zulawski left the railroad to accept a position with the Barrington, Illinois, Police Department. As a police officer, his duties included patrol, investigations, and working as an evidence technician. In addition, he presented seminars on crime and rape prevention to groups in the Barrington area.

In 1978, Mr. Zulawski left the police department to attend the Reid College of Detection of Deception to become a polygraph examiner. He then joined the staff of John E. Reid & Associates as a polygraph examiner and later became the director of the Police and Fire Applicant Screening Division of the company. Mr. Zulawski also instructed at the Reid College and the Criminal Interrogation Seminar, which is presented to law enforcement and private security personnel.

In October, 1980, Mr. Zulawski joined Reid Psychological Systems, an affiliate of John E. Reid & Associates that markets paper-and-pencil honesty tests, as a sales representative. With Reid Psychological Systems, Douglas Wicklander and David Zulawski co-authored Reid Survey III, a paper-and-pencil honesty test to investigate theft, drug and organization problems within companies.

Mr. Zulawski is a licensed polygraph examiner in Illinois and Indiana and has personally conducted more than 9,000 interviews and polygraph examinations. He is a certified fraud examiner and member of the American Polygraph Society, the Illinois Polygraph Society, the Special Agents Association, and the American Society for Industrial Security.

Douglas E. Wicklander received his B.S. degree from Athens College, Athens, Alabama, in 1971 and his M.S. degree in the detection of deception from Reid College in 1972.

Mr. Wicklander was employed by John E. Reid & Associates from June 1971 to October 1980 as a polygraph examiner and instructor at the company's school of polygraph and criminal interrogation. During this time, he was named director of the company's Behavioral Analysis Interview Division. In this capacity, he worked extensively with the late John Reid in the development of this division. In October, 1980, he was assigned as a sales representative with Reid Psychological Systems.

Mr. Wicklander is a licensed polygraph examiner in the states of Illinois and Indiana. He has personally conducted more than 10,000 polygraph examinations and interviews. He is a certified fraud examiner and member of the American Society For Industrial Security, Special Agents Association, American Polygraph Association, and the Illinois Polygraph Society.

In May, 1982, Mr. Zulawski and Mr. Wicklander formed their own company, Wicklander-Zulawski & Associates, Inc. Through the use of interview, investigation, and polygraph techniques, the firm specializes in the investigation of internal losses. In addition, the firm conducts loss prevention surveys, pre-employment background investigations, and training seminars. It is nationally recognized as the standard of the industry in conducting seminars on interview and interrogation techniques.

Mr. Zulawski and Mr. Wicklander produced an audio cassette program entitled Interview and Interrogation Techniques. In addition, they served as subject-matter experts in the development of a comprehensive interactive computer-video-training program entitled The Art of Interviewing — The Integrity Interview. This training program instructs the loss-prevention or security professional on the complexities of interview and interrogation techniques. Furthermore, they wrote an in-house-training program that companies use to train their own staffs in interview and interrogation techniques. They also developed and wrote a VHS tape and CD-ROM review on the accusatory interview. Both have written extensively on the topics of interview, interrogation and loss prevention over the past 15 years.

Since 1982, Wicklander-Zulawski & Associates, Inc. has trained tens of thousands of individuals in interviewing and interrogation techniques. These seminars address the proper way to obtain legally acceptable confessions, and the content and form a written statement should take. They and members of their firm have lectured on these topics to professional and civic organizations throughout the country.

Wicklander-Zulawski & Associates, Inc. has been licensed since 1984 by John E. Reid & Associates, Inc., originator and developer of the method, to teach the Reid Method of Criminal Interviews & Interrogation. Since that time, the updates for the seminar have been developed by Wicklander-Zulawski using the latest information from legal, psychological and interrogation research.

Table of Contents

4   Memory and False Confessions   73

5   Interpretation of Verbal and Physical Behavior   105

6   Causes of Denials

Part Two — Interviewing

7 Interviewing 187

8 Why People Confess 241

Part Three — Establishing Credibility

9 The Accusation   251

Part Four — Reducing Resistance

10 Rationalizations   305

Part Six — Development of the Admission

13 Development of the Admission 391

Part Seven — The Statement

14 The Statement 415

Introduction — Overview of the Process

1

There's one way to find out if a man is honest — ask him.
— **Groucho Marx**

It is still appropriate that this second edition on interview and interrogation begins with a quotation from a comedian. Comedians are perceptive individuals who can see humor and truth in people — two things that sometimes are one and the same. Interrogators attempt to be as perceptive as comedians — looking for the truth in people. The following chapters follow Groucho Marx's advice and ask suspects whether they are telling the truth. The suspects' truthfulness can be evaluated by their verbal and physical behavior as well as by their attitude toward the interrogator and the investigation.

Although many readers of this book may be experienced in interview and interrogation, we hope to put into perspective aspects of the process that may benefit them as well as those less experienced. The book categorizes suspects' actions that the experienced reader may have already observed. At the same time, it identifies for the new interrogator phases and actions that can act as a foundation during the interview/interrogation process.

There are many different forms and derivations of the interrogative process. History shows that interrogation during a war has taken the route of torture and killings to elicit information from suspects. Currently, a number of nations still use this method to wring confessions from those unfortunate enough to be perceived as suspects. Narcotic interrogation using resistance-weakening drugs is also a method employed by some governments to obtain information.

Although torture and drug-influenced interrogation may have very high confession rates, they are, simply stated, illegal. The U.S. Constitution and the Bill of Rights preserve the rights of the individual during a criminal investigation, thereby rendering these inhumane techniques unlawful. The

Supreme Court, through several landmark decisions, has reinforced the rights of an accused that are guaranteed by our democratic process.

Good Guy/Bad Guy Approach

In the United States, several interrogation methods are typically used to elicit information from a suspect. One method made famous by television and Hollywood is the good guy/bad guy routine. In this type of confrontation with the subject, one interrogator plays the heartless, uncompromising role while a second interrogator, in contrast, plays the soft, understanding role. The contrast between these two individuals encourages the suspect to take the sympathetic ear of the second interrogator and confess to the incident. Depending on the role of the hard interrogator, it may verge on intimidation and coercion, which could render a suspect's statement unusable.

Factual Approach

Another form of interrogation is the factual approach. It requires an extensive investigation into the circumstances surrounding the incident and the activities of the suspect. In addition, the answers to most of the investigative questions of who, what, when, where, how, and why must be available to the interrogator.

Unfortunately, this type of interrogation lends itself only to those situations that have been intensively investigated because of the serious nature of the incident. In most instances, this factual approach is ineffective because the scope of the investigation has not been sufficient to counter the suspects' explanations or stories. Often, a factual interrogation may also lack the inclusion of "rationalization" by the interrogator, which allows the suspect to save face while making an admission.

Emotional Approach

In the emotional approach to interrogation, the interrogator confronts the subject not on the circumstances or details surrounding his involvement in the issue, but rather on the reasons that the subject did what he did. The interrogator rationalizes with the suspect by offering reasons or excuses that allow the suspect to save face while admitting involvement in the incident. This form of interrogation does not require the extensive investigation into the incident that a factual attack requires. The use of rationalization in an emotional appeal is effective on all but the most street-hardened individuals.

By allowing suspects to save face, it makes it easier for them to talk about their guilt. Rationalizations offer a means for suspects to save face and make their reasons for becoming involved appear to be understandable under the circumstances.

The emotional approach can be more effective in many cases when modified by incorporating a factual component that establishes the credibility of the interrogator's investigation before the interrogator expresses his understanding of why the suspect committed the offense. Modifying the emotional approach through the use of a factual component allows the interrogator to quickly reduce the suspect's resistance by first establishing his guilt and then offering him an easy way out that allows him to save face while confessing.

The discussions in this text focus primarily on using an emotional appeal to suspects, justifying their actions, and minimizing the seriousness of the incident under investigation. Even in situations where the factual approach is deemed the most appropriate method, the emotional interrogation, using rationalizations to justify and minimize the seriousness of the suspect's involvement, can enhance the results achieved.

Although the interview and interrogation process is an art rather than a science, it can still be learned. However, some interviewers, because of their own personality, perception, perseverance, and practice, will be better at interviewing and interrogating than others are.

Many of us have had the good fortune to learn from expert interrogators as they worked. These men and women have a natural flair for interview and interrogation of suspects. This book offers new interrogators advice and experience to which they would not otherwise have access.

Unfortunately, many things that have been learned by expert interrogators are not passed on because they do not or are not able to understand or describe how they interrogate or encourage a suspect to confess. The techniques discussed in the following chapters are not always going to identify the guilty or cause them to confess. There will always be a certain percentage of suspects who will never confess, no matter what evidence is available, or what is said to them.

The interview and interrogation techniques discussed in the following chapters are not a substitute for a good investigation. That investigation is essential to discover the factual basis behind the issue under investigation, narrow the scope of the suspect population, and learn the background of all possible suspects. The interviewer's job is made easier and produces more effective results when proper investigative techniques have developed evidence.

Certainly, the purpose of the interview and interrogation process is to identify the guilty party and obtain a legally admissible confession. This outcome, without question, makes for the most satisfying of all interrogations: the case is satisfactorily resolved with a signed statement attesting to the suspect's involvement and perhaps the development of additional evidence.

Unfortunately, in the real world, there are suspects who will not confess; therefore, the second purpose of the interview and interrogation process must then be to establish convincingly to ourselves that a particular suspect was, indeed, involved. In doing so, we have narrowed the scope of the investigation and focused the entire investigative resources of the company or department on the investigation of a single individual or group of individuals. At the same time, and more importantly, we have eliminated a very large percentage of the innocent suspects within the scope of the investigation. In private-sector investigation, it is imperative that this narrowing of focus be done to maintain the morale of the employees and their image of the company. The public sector must do this simply to have a manageable number of suspects.

The third and equally important purpose of the interview and interrogation process is to clear other related cases and recover evidence or assets of the company or victim. Whereas the security or loss prevention department is rarely viewed as a profit-making function of the company, it does not have to be that way. Restitution in the form of cash payments can be added to the bottom-line profits of the company and justify security expenditures and operations. For example, one company recently obtained several hundred thousand dollars via theft confessions from employees. Almost half of this amount was actually recovered in the form of cash repayment to the company. Certainly, recoveries of this nature can help justify some of the company's security expenditures. In any company, the ability to make a profit is paramount; security can contribute through loss prevention and restitution programs.

Public law enforcement can enhance a prosecutable case by providing a solid foundation of additional evidence of the subject's guilt. Other investigations can be resolved by the suspect's admitting involvement or having knowledge of those responsible.

Defining several terms will aid in clarifying the information in the following chapters:

Interview: a nonaccusatory, structured interview during which specific behavior-provoking questions are asked with the purpose of eliciting interpretable behavior that is typical of innocence or guilt. Additional factual information concerning the case and/or suspects may also be developed during this nonaccusatory interview.

Interrogation: a conversation between the interrogator and suspect, during which the suspect is accused of involvement in a particular incident or group of incidents. Many companies use the word *interview* as a substitute for *interrogation*. For the sake of clarity in this text, interview will be used to indicate a nonaccusatory conversation while interrogation will represent the change to an accusatory tone.

Interviewer: an individual skilled in the interview and interrogation process and in the interpretation of verbal and physical behavior. As above, the terms *interviewer* and *interrogator* will be used to differentiate between a nonaccusatory and accusatory environment.

Suspect: any individual within the scope of the case who has not yet been cleared by the investigation. A suspect under this definition can be either truthful or untruthful.

Witness: an individual who can provide direct or indirect evidence to the case. This individual may or may not be providing truthful information and may or may not be the victim.

The need to interview and interrogate victims, witnesses, and suspects encompasses both public law enforcement and the private sector. The development of information is fundamental to the process of investigations. However, it is worth noting that there are significant differences between the investigative techniques and strategies employed by public law enforcement and those of the private sector. Differences in resources and operational strategies between the public and private sectors require each to use methods and procedures specifically designed to enhance the success of the process.

Public- versus Private-Sector Approaches

A fundamental difference between the public and private sectors is the use of investigations. Public law enforcement prepares a case specifically for prosecution and trial. The private sector prepares its case to present it to the personnel department for termination of the suspect's employment or defense of the company in an unemployment or arbitration hearing, or some other form of litigation. Under certain circumstances, the private-sector investigator might also take the case to the next logical step, which is prosecution.

There are significant differences in the levels of proof needed, depending on the choice of result. Business, by its very nature, is profit oriented and clearly weighs the return on its investigative dollar. Many corporate officers who note a significant shortage after reviewing figures demand results — not today, but yesterday. They may not accept an investigation that will resolve the case in 6 months to a year. Only with major cases do police feel that type of pressure. A random murder, burglary, or robbery does not generally stir public sentiment and pressure as does a serial killing or burglarizing of an entire block of houses. With the latter, public sentiment and pressure are focused to resolve the case and can alter the interview and investigative process.

The public law enforcement officer typically has the resources and time to conduct indepth investigations of suspects to ascertain their involvement. It is not unusual for such investigations to continue for months or even years to develop the information necessary to convict in a court of law. Additionally, the vast amount of information available to public law enforcement is significantly different from that available to the private sector. Often, wiretap, surveillance, physical evidence, and other forensic techniques can independently identify the suspect as the person responsible for the incident even without a confession. Legal avenues using search warrants, subpoena, and grand jury hearings open doors to information that the private sector could never hope to obtain. Only rarely will these types of resources be allocated to a private-sector investigation.

The types of cases also vary significantly. The private sector handles primarily economic crimes such as theft, fraud, and embezzlement. Less often, drug, burglary, or other criminal activities may be investigated, but usually as part of an ongoing theft investigation. In the private sector, the goal is not only the prosecution or termination of the dishonest employee, but also recovery of company assets through restitution, civil recovery, or insurance claims. The public sector's goal, on the other hand, is the suspects' conviction, with restitution or compensation to the victim far down on its list of priorities.

Private-sector cases typically are related to incidents that have occurred within the company or at a single location. The number of potential suspects is generally already limited to any employees assigned to that location. In contrast, a public law enforcement investigator often has to deal with cases that cover multiple jurisdictions and numerous states. Thus, the scope of the investigation is broader in the public sector, perhaps encompassing thousands of potential suspects.

Private-sector investigators generally deal with cases at a single location with smaller suspect groups. The incidents being investigated may continue over a longer period of time, however, whereas public law enforcement more typically investigates single issue incidents and the circumstances surrounding them, with larger groups of potential suspects.

Legal Issues

The legal constraints also differ between public law enforcement and the private sector. The *Miranda* decision, custody, Exclusionary Rule ("fruit of the poisonous tree"), and the courts' view of the totality of circumstances to determine the voluntariness of the confession are some of the more common issues raised by the public sector when discussing interview and interrogation. Private industry must contend with management, personnel, company policy, and hearing officers when conducting their interviews or interrogations.

There are still many fundamental similarities between private and public sectors in the interview and interrogation process. For example, it is conducted in privacy, generally on a one-on-one basis, possibly with a witness present — for example, when a woman is being interviewed, when an employee requests union representation, when an interpreter is needed to conduct the interview or interrogation, or as a matter of department policy. On occasion, a novice interviewer may accompany the experienced interrogator to gain valuable experience.

Overview of the Text

This text is presented in a building-block style: Information from previous chapters is used as a foundation for subsequent chapters (see Figure 1.1).

Part One: Preparation and Strategy

This deals with the preparation and strategy that effectively counter the suspect's resistance to confessing. Here, discussion takes into account differing legal constraints facing the public and private sectors. Then, the foundation for the interrogation is laid by considering why and how people lie, a discussion of verbal and physical behavior, and, finally, the reasons for denials by suspects.

Part Two: Interviewing

Part Two considers the nonaccusatory interview in a number of ways — fact gathering, the heart of the investigation; cognitive interviewing, a method to enhance witness recollection; and the selective interview, a means to evaluate the truthfulness of a potential witness or suspect.

Neurolinguistics is also considered as it relates to the process of communication and evaluation of truth and deception. Each of these topics is discussed in light of the differences among victims, witnesses, and suspects.

The last step before interrogation is the identification of individuals responsible for incidents or the gathering of factual information from informants and witnesses using the *selective interview technique*. This technique can be used in both specific incidents or general-loss-incident investigations. It offers the interviewer a structured format using questions that elicit verbal and physical behavior typical of innocence or guilt. The techniques necessary to identify the guilty and eliminate the innocent from the investigation are also discussed.

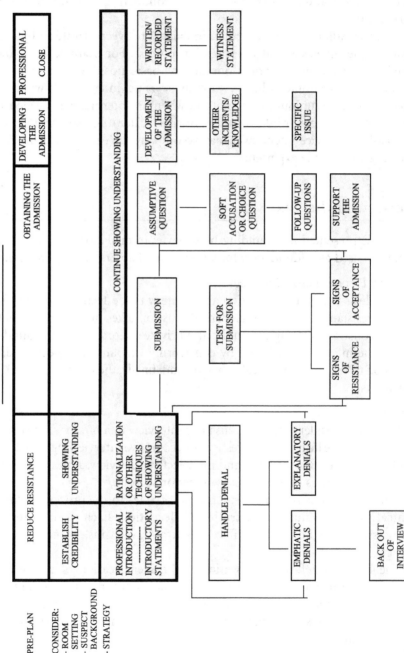

Figure 1.1 Chart illustrating the flow of information from preplanning to conclusion.

Part Three: Establishing Credibility

Part Three discusses the interrogation of a guilty suspect. Once this person has been identified through the interview or investigative process, the interrogation is ready to begin. In any interrogation, an accusation of wrong-doing must be made at some point so that the suspect understands that the interrogator believes that he is involved in the incident under investigation.

The accusation can take one of several forms, depending on the purpose of the interrogation, the background of the suspect, the factual nature of the case, and the restraints under which the interrogator must work. The purpose or direction of the overall interrogation will be dictated by the desired result and preinterrogation strategy selected by the interrogator.

In this section, the interrogator learns to establish the credibility of the investigation in the suspect's mind. The interrogator convinces the suspect that the investigation has clearly identified him as the perpetrator of the crime.

Part Four: Reducing Resistance

Following the accusation, the interrogator must use techniques that reduce a suspect's resistance to confession. The interrogator may get a denial from the suspect that can take one of two forms: emphatic or explanatory. The *emphatic denial* is where the suspect refuses to acknowledge the truth-fulness of the accusation. It can be a physical behavior, such as shaking the head, or a verbal response such as "No, I did not do it." The explanatory denial, which usually follows the emphatic denial, is any response from the suspect that offers an excuse or reason that the suspect could not or would not have been involved in the incident. A suspect's explanatory denial may be the first time that the interrogator recognizes that he is making progress in the interrogation. Examples of explanatory denials are "I wouldn't kill my wife... I loved her," or "I wouldn't take that money ... I don't need it."

Throughout the course of the interrogation, the interrogator is control-ling and directing the conversation. During this conversation, the interroga-tor offers the suspect rationalizations (reasons or excuses) for the suspect's involvement in the incident that will psychologically minimize the serious-ness and make the suspect's actions understandable. The interrogator removes blame from the suspect and focuses it on someone or something else. Thus, the suspect's attention is focused on resolving the problem rather than on any consequences for his own actions. It is during rationalizations that the subject might interrupt the interrogation with emphatic and explan-atory denials.

Part Five: Obtaining the Admission

When the interrogator is making headway in reducing the suspect's resis-tance to confessing, the suspect begins to go into the behavioral phase of submission. That is, the suspect enters a behaviorally recognizable phase of the interrogation that indicates susceptibility to making an admission. This phase is typified by a suspect who has stopped all denials and has come to the realization that he is going to admit his involvement.

Once the suspect displays the behavioral manifestations of submission, the interrogator continues with the rationalization but shortens its length and prepares to present the suspect with a choice question, i.e., a question offering two choices. One choice appears harsh and unacceptable, whereas the second seems to be understandable or more socially acceptable — for example, "Did you use the money for drugs or for bills?" or "Did you use a match or lighter to start the fire?" Although the interrogator does not care which of the choices the suspect chooses, he is encouraging the suspect to choose the more acceptable, face-saving choice. The interrogator is simply looking for the suspect to pick one of the two choices, which is the first admission of guilt.

Part Six: Developing the Admission

Once the suspect has made an initial admission by selecting one of the two choices, the interrogator prepares to develop this admission into an acceptable confession. This development can take one of two directions. In a single specific-issue case, development will first focus on the incident in question — for example, "How did you get the $1,000 out of the safe?" "What did you spend the money on?" "What bills did you pay?" "What did you start the fire with?" "Where did you put the gun?"

During development of admission in a general-theft case, the focus will also be on the total amount of the suspect's involvement in the theft of money or merchandise or on his knowledge of others' involvement in dishonesty at the company. This avenue will also be followed when a suspect has made an admission in a specific incident and the interrogator expands it into involvement in other types of criminal or procedural wrongdoing. The interrogator can also correct the choice question by confronting the subject again.

Part Seven: Professional Close

Part Seven deals with the professional close, the written statement, and treatment of the suspect. The suspect, having made admissions, puts these into writing. The discussion here deals with the form and content of the written statement and techniques to ensure the suspect's cooperation in writing it. Part Seven also discusses how to end the process, i.e., how the suspect should be treated and strategies to ensure continued cooperation.

The Process of Interrogation

Confronting the target of the investigation is one of the final steps the investigator takes in concluding the inquiry. Often the ultimate outcome of the case will hinge on whether the subject confesses. The confession of a subject is responsible for more successful case resolutions than all the other forensic techniques combined.

An investigation relies on the collection of evidence; both direct and circumstantial, along with the interview and interrogation of individuals involved in the case. These individuals may be victims, witnesses, or suspects in the incident under investigation. Interviews with these individuals answer the investigative questions who, what, where, when, how, and why. The interrogation of an individual is carried out when he is the target of an investigation or is withholding information crucial to the successful conclusion of the investigation.

Confronting the reluctant witness or suspect has a process that can be applied to increase the likelihood of engaging the individual's cooperation. Unlike the "third degree" tactics deplored by the United States Supreme Court, today's methods do not rely on the use or threat of physical force.

Types of Interrogation

The confrontation of a suspect is a complicated process made more difficult by a multitude of factors. The type of individual, age, education, job, experience with the criminal justice system, or awareness of the investigation are just a few of the variables with which the interrogator must contend when preparing to confront a suspect. Selection of an appropriate strategy, time, and location for the confrontation requires the investigator to preplan for the case close.

A number of interrogation styles are used to facilitate a confession. This book focuses on one method, but the five following avenues are also to be considered:

1. Suspect decision-making (Hilgendorf and Irving, 1981). This interrogation model relies on the premise that the suspect becomes involved in a complicated decision-making process. The suspect's decision to confess revolves around several paths or courses of action from which the subject must choose. He must also weigh the probabilities of likely consequences attached to each of these possible courses of action. The final decision is based on the evaluation of the gains or liabilities associated with each possible course of action.

In this model of interrogation, suspects must consider their options and the likely consequences. Their decision in this model is driven largely by the perceived consequences they believe to be attached to a course of action. In essence, the individual must balance the perceived consequences against the perceived value of a chosen path. Other factors, such as the individual's self image, may play a strong role a decision to confess. The strong social prohibition against lawbreakers will play a role with all individuals except the sociopathic personality.

The interrogator in this model manipulates the concept of social approval and self-image to influence the decision making suspects. The interrogator can also influence suspects by focusing on the liabilities of certain choices they may have to make. Third, the interrogator can increase the stress related to social and psychological costs suspects may face by not confessing.

2.   **Cognitive-behavioral model of confession (Gudjonsson, 1989b).** In this model of interrogation, the confession results from the unique relationships among the subject, environment, and others involved in the process — other suspects, victims, witnesses, and interrogators.

Gudjonsson argues that this model of interrogation elicits a confession that is the result of cause and effect, that is, what occurred prior to the interrogation may encourage a suspect to confess. He describes a number of factors that may be relevant to the decision to confess, such as social isolation, fatigue, stress, and feelings of guilt.

As in the previous model, consequences play a role in the subject's decision to confess. There are two types of consequences that he must consider: immediate and long term. There are also four basic areas in the cognitive behavioral model that the subject uses in determining whether to confess:

Social — The individual subject's fear of isolation from friends and co-workers may or may not increase resistance to a confession. A benefit, which is positive reinforcement and praise for taking the interrogator's preferred path, is provided by the interrogator.

Emotional — The experience of being confronted or arrested is certain to increase an individual's anxiety level. Because of the fear of the unknown, combined with guilt and shame over the violation, the suspect is likely to experience a great emotional relief when he elects to confess. When subjects are presented with a clear idea of what the future might hold, they may experience relief and abandon the shame and fear of the unknown that accompany an illegal act.

Cognitive — This area deals with the subject's thoughts and perceptions. Here, suspects interpret facts and make assumptions about what is or is not known. They might convince themselves that their guilt is known absolutely, even when it may not be the case.

Situational — This area relates to the timing of the confrontation and the circumstances surrounding it, such as where the interrogation is conducted, if the subject is allowed to wait, if the interrogation begins immediately, and who conducts the interview and when.

3. Psychoanalytic model of confession (Reik 1959). Probably the least valuable model to consider is the psychoanalytic, which postulates that feelings of guilt are the foundation of the decision to confess. According to this model, guilt after the event triggers the individual's need to punish himself and results in a confession.

This model certainly does not account for career criminals who have little, if any, guilt for their actions. However, subjects with strong ties to family and community and with little or no previous experience with the criminal system may react in certain situations with a need to be punished for their actions. In general, this model is only marginally accurate in addressing a small percentage of those who have a need to confess.

4. Emotional model of confession (Jayne 1986). This model postulates that subjects' failure to tell the truth is the result of their attempt to avoid the consequences of their actions. The consequences might be real, such as the loss of freedom, or perceived, as in the loss of self-image. The suspects in this model shift blame for their actions to some source other than themselves.

In this model, the interrogator uses the natural inclination of the subject to shift blame. Face-saving statements allow subjects to justify their actions without freeing them of the legal responsibility for their criminal acts. Suspects internalize the suggestions and show their acceptance of them through behavioral changes. The interrogator in this instance is not viewed as an opponent, but rather as a mediator between the suspect and the company or criminal justice system.

The process of rationalization is driven by the suspect's acceptance. The interrogator judges the acceptance of a rationalization by the frequency and intensity of the suspect's denials and changes in physical behavior, which is used to determine his resistance to making an admission. When the time to obtain the admission is right, the interrogator offers an alternative question that is based on the rationalization. The alternative contrasts the acceptable versus the unacceptable choice and the suspect is encouraged to select the face-saving choice, thus making the first admission of guilt.

In general, this model encourages the individual to make an emotional decision to confess, rather than a rational one. As a result, suspects may react emotionally, crying and sniffling as they relate their criminal act to the interrogator.

5. Interaction process model of confession (Moston, Stephenson, and Williamson, 1992, Zulawski and Wicklander, 1993).   This model uses the characteristics of the suspect to determine the approach and style used by the interrogator. The approach considers the suspect's background, preferences, likely responses to the confrontation, the case facts, and case development in making the decision on what methods might be useful in facilitating a confession.

The Wicklander-Zulawski approach is strongly dependent on the evaluation of the subject and his likely reaction to the confrontation. The interrogator then selects the approach most likely to be successful with the subject. It is hoped that the approach chosen encourages the subject to make a rational decision to confess, rather than an emotional one.

Decision to Confess

The suspect who elects to confess makes the decision to do so either emotionally or rationally. Emotional decisions to confess are related to the subject's guilt feelings and self-image. This type of individual needs the support of rationalization and projection to protect the framework of his or her emotional state. The emotional model of interrogation (Jayne, 1986) works well with this type of suspect because it supports individuals and their self-image while allowing them to justify their actions. It is not unusual for a suspect making an emotional decision to confess to show pronounced signs of submission, which could progress from a head and shoulder slump to tearing up and to crying.

Unfortunately, when suspects are in an emotional state, they often react in ways that benefit neither the interrogator nor themselves. Eric Byrne, an American psychologist, founded a branch of psychology called **Transactional Analysis**, which attempts to explain interpersonal relationships. In transactional relationships, individuals adopt one of three roles, depending on their perception of the other party. The three roles — parent, adult, and child — interact in the dominance and dialogue as the two parties converse.

In the **emotional model**, the interrogator takes the role of the parent and the suspect takes the role of the child. If Mom confronts her child about a misdeed, it sounds remarkably like an emotional interrogation of a suspect. The child makes a denial to the mother's direct accusation, quiets into submission, becomes withdrawn, and then finally cries and admits the misdeed.

Conflicts arise when one party, the interrogator, tries to force a role on the other party that he or she does not wish to play. The child reacts to the mother with the statement, "Well, go ahead and send me to my room for the rest of my life and don't feed me!" The suspect responds, "Well go ahead and lock me up. I don't care!" Neither of these statements is the true desire of the speaker, but is instead an attempt to change roles in the conversation.

The child no longer wishes to be spoken to as a child, and this statement is an attempt to alter the power of the other individual.

When the suspect makes a rational decision to confess, the interrogator and the suspect are in a complementary conversation. The Wicklander-Zulawski Technique (Zulawski and Wicklander, 1993) creates a complementary conversation that encourages a subject to make a rational decision to confess. In this approach, the interrogator takes the role of the adult speaking to the adult. When this approach is successful, there are many benefits for the interrogator and the suspect in the encounter that are discussed later.

The decision to confess means that the suspect has addressed the fears or concerns he had and has resolved them. This is true regardless of whether the suspect has made a rational or emotional decision to confess. The fears or hurdles that the interrogator must address to overcome the suspect's resistance to a confession fall generally into one of the following five categories:

1. **Fear of termination or financial repercussions.** Suspects are reluctant to make an admission because it might affect their ability to get or retain a job. Suspects may also focus on bills that are due or other financial obligations in their lives.

2. **Fear of arrest or prosecution.** This area is often of greater concern to those suspects who have had little previous contact with the police. Often, their inexperience will create a greater fear of the consequences of arrest than the circumstances warrant.

3. **Fear of embarrassment.** This hurdle to a confession relates to suspects' self-image — the fear that they will shock family, friends or co-workers and lose their respect. Still others are unable to face in their own mind what they have done without destroying their own self-image.

4. **Fear of restitution.** Some suspects are resistant to confession because they could not compensate the victim for the damage or loss their actions caused.

5. **Fear of retaliation.** This hurdle can often be insurmountable. Fear for one's safety or for that of a family member can often be difficult to overcome. This factor is becoming more prevalent as gang intimidation and violence increase. Child molesters are often reluctant to make an admission because of the fear of being labeled as such in the prison system.

When the interrogator considers the reasons that a subject elects to confess, it is an educated guess. Interrogators, through experience, recognize that some suspects confess to relieve guilt, others because of overwhelming proof of their guilt, and others because of the interrogator's persuasion. In our research with convicted felons, they all have said essentially the same thing: if the interrogator treats them as if they have value, they will at least consider confessing. This seems to be true regardless of the consequences. To a person, the convicted felons said that their resistance to a confession would increase if they were berated or looked down upon (Wicklander and Zulawski, 1994, unpublished research).

Suspect Denials

Certainly, the fears of the suspect play a role in the decision to confess, but the way a suspect is approached by the interrogator is undoubtedly a greater factor. Every individual has a learned predisposition to deny, which is an avoidance behavior learned as a child. This learned behavior is an attempt to avoid the consequences of an illegal, dishonest or shameful act. The interrogator must anticipate what actions or behaviors the suspect will use to counter the accusation of wrongdoing.

The role of the interrogator in the confrontation should be to avoid forcing the suspect into a position where he or she must deny guilt. Traditionally, interrogators have been trained to do the same things each time they confront a guilty suspect, a tactic that often influences the suspect to deny rather than make an admission of guilt.

The reasons a suspect might deny guilt can be divided into three basic areas: environment, suspect, and interrogator. The suspect's decision to deny is often directly influenced by the choices the interrogator makes and the strategies chosen to engage the suspect in the confrontation.

- **Environment** — The timing of the interview, location, room setting, witness selection, and other factors all may play a role in the suspect's decision to confess. The resources and flexibility of the interrogator may dictate many of these factors.
- **Suspect** — Suspects will often deny because of past experience with the criminal justice system. During a confrontation, the suspect is making decisions about what the interrogator knows and the evidence that may have been uncovered during the investigation. Suspects react to the interrogator and his strategies, either reducing resistance to a confession or increasing it. Other suspects simply use the denial to buy time to evaluate the investigation and interrogator.
- **Interrogator** — The interrogator makes the largest contribution to the suspect's decision to deny. The interrogator's word usage, plan of attack and confidence in the suspect's guilt help to define the probable response of the suspect.

The interrogator must look at the suspect's behavior in all aspects of his daily life to be able to understand how the suspect is likely to react when told that his involvement in an illegal act has been uncovered. The answer to this can often be found in how the individual reacts to conflict. Since people are creatures of habit, they tend to respond to similar problems with a preset response. The child who is disciplined by a parent may react with anger or a sullen silence. Once the parent learns the child's preferred response, the parent can create an approach that leads to a more satisfactory behavior by the child.

The suspect's choice of a strategy will be based on what has been found to be successful in the past. The identification of the suspect's likely response can often be discovered by asking previous interviewers or supervisors how the suspect reacted when disciplined or confronted.

Once the interrogator identifies the probable suspect response to a confrontation, he decides what approaches may be effective. He should devise an approach that does not encourage the suspect to use that previous strategy. For example, if the individual is generally aggressive in confrontations, the interrogator should plan an approach that will not allow the suspect to become aggressive. This might mean that the witness selection or the location of the interview would be used to control the suspect's decision-making process.

The traditional thinking in interrogation has always been to use a nonsupportive environment for the suspect interview. This approach may not be effective because of the needs of the subject. The positioning of the participants in a room might change because of the need of the interrogator to create a certain mind-set in the suspect.

Regardless of the other factors, the interrogator should make a conscious decision about forcing the suspect to make a denial. Once suspects have made a denial, they are then forced to defend it with additional denials. This situation places them in a position of having to continually deny to defend themselves. It is often easier for people to make an admission if they have not been forced into a position where they had to lie.

There are situations in which the suspect's lie can work in the interrogator's favor. In fact, a lie may be as good as a confession in some instances. Encouraging a suspect to tell lies can increase the value of the evidence that was developed during the investigation. Direct contradiction of the suspect's statements with irrefutable evidence can also be a powerful wedge in bringing out the truth, but it does not always result in a confession from the guilty. In some instances, the presentation of overwhelming evidence by an interrogator can have the reverse effect of increasing the suspect's resistance to a confession. The obvious benefit to the investigation, when suspects choose not to confess, is that they have to live with the lie they chose to tell that the evidence now contradicts.

Four Parts of Interrogation

No matter how the interrogator chooses to interrogate a suspect, there will be four distinct parts to the confrontation.

1. **Reducing resistance** — The interrogator chooses some method to reduce the suspect's resistance to a confession. Depending on the style chosen, this could be done with a systematic presentation of evidence, use of an emotional appeal, or interrogator persistence. In the case of interrogation by torture, physical pain or deprivation of the basic needs reduce the suspects' resistance to a confession.
2. **Obtaining the admission** — The second part of every interrogation is the first admission of the suspect. This is his or her first acknowledgment of involvement in the act under investigation. This admission is not a confession, but merely the first admission that confirms the interrogator's assertion that the suspect was involved.
3. **Development of the admission** — This phase of the interrogation expands the suspect's admission into a legally acceptable confession that answers who, what, where, when, how, and why. It also allows the interrogator to explore other areas of criminal activity in which the suspect may be involved.
4. **Professional close** — The interrogator reduces the suspect's oral admission to a permanent form, either written or taped, and has it witnessed.

Wicklander-Zulawski (WZ) Technique

To this point, the types of possible interrogations, causes of denials, fears of the suspect, and the common parts to an interrogation have been considered. Focus now is on the construction of an interrogation to encourage the suspect to make a rational decision to confess, in many cases without making a denial.

Preparation and Profiling

The interrogator considers the case development and goal of the interrogation. The elements of the crime or violation are defined, and the evidence indicating the violation is clearly understood. The interrogator should understand the strengths and weaknesses of the inquiry and begin to consider whether direct evidence should be used early or late in the confrontation, or if it should be revealed at all. It is at this point that the interrogator may consider what type of enticement questions or bluffs might prove useful and when they should be used.

The next consideration is special personnel or legal requirements that might be necessary to close the investigation. Is the interrogator acting as an agent of the police or working independently for an organization? Is there a union? There may be legal issues that need to be addressed based on the answer to these and other questions and also on the geographical location of the interview. Different countries and even states within the United States have unique legal aspects the interrogator should consider before beginning the confrontation. The ultimate goal, to prosecute or simply terminate, may dictate some of the case-closure methods. There are obviously many other factors that should be considered during the preparation phase, in addition to those mentioned here.

The interrogator then begins to look closely at the suspect involved in the incident. Is the suspect aware of the investigation, or has the inquiry been concealed from him or her? Knowledge of the investigation certainly may affect the individual's resistance to a confession and the methods chosen to confront the suspect. For example, a woman was killed in her home sometime during the day. The suspect's vehicle left tire tracks in the drive that showed the tires were mismatched. The investigators determined that a delivery was made to the home during the day. During the interview with the delivery driver, investigators asked him if he had returned to the victim's home a second time on the day of the killing. In response to the question, the driver turned red, averted his eyes, and delayed his response to the investigator's question. The suspect's physical response was so pronounced that the investigators asked only a few more questions and concluded the interview.

The investigators then checked the suspect's vehicle and determined that its tires matched those left by the killer's car. The investigation focused on the delivery driver, who was convicted of the murder but never confessed to the crime. In most cases, there will be a time when the interrogator has an advantage in obtaining the admission. In the case just cited, the time to begin the interrogation of the suspect was when he first realized the possibility that his involvement might have been discovered. The officers certainly did not err in waiting to gather additional evidence before they confronted the suspect, but the tradeoff was letting the driver know that he was the focus of the investigation.

In most investigations, there is a time when the suspect is more susceptible to a confession. Unfortunately for the investigator, that time might arrive before the investigation is complete. The investigator has to decide whether the value of possible additional evidence will outweigh the suspect's current susceptibility to a confession. If the investigators in the foregoing example had confronted the driver based on his verbal and physical responses even though the investigation was not complete, they might have gained a confession because of the suspect's momentary confusion and mental state.

It could be asked how interrogators could confront someone without proof. They cannot if they plan to use a factual attack, building the case for the suspect's guilt on the evidence that was accumulated during the investigation. There are several problems with a factual interrogation. First, the presentation of evidence may show the weaknesses in the investigation. Second, presenting evidence to suspects when they are still physically and emotionally strong will often result in their contradicting the evidence's meaning or relevance. Third, in the small number of cases where the possibility of a false confession might exist, the subject's knowledge of the evidence could contribute to a convincing statement from the suspect, who just repeats the facts that have been told. The WZ Technique solves these problems and allows the interrogator to confront a suspect even when the investigation is not as complete as it could be. This situation gives the interrogator an opportunity to take advantage of the "optimum moment in time" when the individual is susceptible to a confession.

Reducing Resistance

In the first part of the WZ interrogation, the interrogator has several clear goals: establish rapport with the suspect, convince him his guilt is known, allow him to save face, and avoid forcing him into a position where he has to deny.

After establishing rapport with the suspect, the interrogator begins to develop the credibility of the investigation. This is done in generalities, with interrogators talking about the work they do. This discussion also includes the types of cases that are investigated. This allows the interrogator to introduce the topic of the investigation without making a specific accusation the suspect might deny. The second benefit that the interrogator derives from this is possible behavioral reactions to other acts of dishonesty or involvement.

Building the credibility of the investigation continues with a general discussion of investigative techniques, which, if they had been used, could have developed information linking the suspect to the crime. The discussion of investigative techniques causes suspects to consider, perhaps for the first time, that there might be evidence linking them to the crime.

Guilty suspects have been rocked by the realization that their guilt is known, but they generally do not deny because no direct accusation has been made by the interrogator. The suspect also may withhold denial out of hope that perhaps his or her assessment of the situation is wrong.

The second component of reducing resistance is showing understanding for the problems that people face. The interrogator begins a discussion of reasons that people might become involved in criminal acts. The interrogator offers these reasons in a manner that is general rather than specific to the suspect. The interrogator uses "he," "she," "they," or "them" rather than "you" when presenting the rationalizations. This lack of personalization continues the suspect's pattern of no denial while listening to the reasons people make "errors in judgment."

The rationalization process is perfectly suited to the criminal suspect. Above all else, criminals are rationalizers. It allows them to justify their actions and project their own feelings onto others — the company makes a lot of money; she was asking for it; he doesn't pay us enough. These are the same rationalizations that the interrogator offers the suspect to minimize the consequences, focus the suspect's attention on the resolution of the problem, and to transfer blame to his circumstances in life.

The rationalizations are selected based on the background of the suspect. For example, if a suspect is having financial problems, the interrogator might talk about the costs of raising a family and the stress of bills. The interrogator knows that the reasons he offers the suspect may not be the real excuses that the individual became involved in the criminal act, but are simply reasons that allow the suspect to save face. The other benefit to the interrogator is that rationalizations do not usually affect the elements of the crime. Does it make a difference that a suspect says he stole the money to take care of his children or to buy drugs? What the money was used for is irrelevant to the case, but the admission that he stole the money is not. Showing understanding allows the interrogator to continue building rapport, and the interrogator becomes a mediator, rather than an opponent in the encounter. Rationalizations help the suspect overcome the fears of confessing that were discussed earlier: loss of employment, financial issues, arrest, self-image, restitution, and retaliation.

While an interrogator might suggest that there are benefits to confessing, the suspect does not necessarily see these advantages. The interrogator has to work with tangible or intangible benefits to the suspect. Tangible benefits might be the placing of only certain charges, allowing bond, charging the suspect at a later date, or any of a number of others. More likely, the interrogator has to deal with intangible benefits. These are the suspect's perceived advantages of a confession — self-image, relieving guilt, or others' understanding of his plight.

One way to hasten the suspect's recognition of the benefit of confession is role reversal. The interrogator sets up a story in which the suspect must make a decision about two people, one who is uncooperative and one who is not. The suspect recognizes that if he were in the decision-making role he would feel different about the two people. This story empowers the suspect with the knowledge that he is not helpless, but can have an influence on the decision-makers, based on his actions.

Behaviorally, suspects will move through several distinct phases as the interrogator continues his monologue. The first behavioral phase will be **rejection** as suspects recognize that their involvement in the criminal act has been discovered. This recognition will usually result in closed body posture, crossed arms or legs, which provides a defensive barrier and increases the comfort level of the suspect. The second phase of behavior, **evaluation**, generally commences shortly after the interrogator begins the process of showing understanding and rationalization. The suspect's body will begin to appear more open, the muscles will begin to lose tension, and the hand will often move to the face in a consideration pose. The final behavioral change is **submission**. The suspect's body begins to open, the arms and legs uncross, and the suspect begins to withdraw mentally to consider options. A salesman would recognize these behaviors as the "buy signs" of the customer. The interrogator comes to the same conclusion.

Obtaining the Admission

The third phase of the interrogation is obtaining the first admission from the suspect. The admission may be made verbally or with a head movement, either a nod or a shake. The interrogator observes the signs of submission and offers an assumptive question to the suspect that encourages an admission of guilt. The **assumptive question** is generally an extension of the rationalization the interrogator was offering to the suspect. If the interrogator was talking about the crime proceeds' being used to pay family bills, the assumptive question might be, "Did you use the money for bills or was it for drugs?" The interrogator offers the suspect a choice, acceptable versus unacceptable, that makes it easier to save face by selecting the more acceptable of the two.

Another type of assumptive question is the **soft accusation**. This question does not provide the suspect a choice but instead asks about some aspect of the suspect's involvement in the crime. An example of this type of question might be, "When was the first time that you took money from the company no matter how long ago?" This type of question is followed immediately with a **follow up question** such as, "It wasn't your first day on the job was it?" This exaggeration by the interrogator often brings a denial from the suspect. However, it is a denial that is an admission of guilt. The interrogator supports this denial as an admission saying, "Great, I didn't think that it was your first day on the job! When was the first time?" The suspect's admission brings us to the third phase of the interrogation, development of the admission.

Development of the Admission

This phase of the interrogation answers the questions who, what, where, when, how, and why. The suspect's involvement in the criminal act is explored fully by the interrogator, who looks for confirmation of the investigative findings. Another key purpose of this section of the interrogation is to expand the admission into other areas of dishonesty or criminal activity of which the interrogator may not even be aware. A recent study of rapists found that they had been involved, on average, in 20 additional criminal acts for which they had neither been arrested nor questioned. The development of the admission and the expansion of the individual's involvement can have a number of obvious benefits to the investigation or the organization.

During this phase of the interrogation, the interrogator may be faced with an absolute denial from the suspect: "That is all I did, and I don't care what you or your investigation say." This is the time to present evidence that clearly contradicts the suspect's statement. Even weak circumstantial evidence is often enough to break this denial and gain additional admissions. Saving evidence for this phase of the interrogation often has a greater impact on the suspect than using it early in the interrogation to obtain the first admission.

Professional Close

The final phase of the interrogation is preserving the statement for future use and witnessing it. This can be done in many different ways and formats, but each captures the same information from the admission. The final statement contains the subject's admission and covers the elements of the crime or policy violation to which the suspect has admitted. The language clearly details what was done, by whom, and in what context. The suspect's statement may be handwritten, audio/video taped, or taken by a court reporter. Regardless of the format, the information accurately portrays the suspect's admission and its voluntary nature.

Discussion

In general, suspects make the decision to confess based on their own perception of the situation and their own personal needs. With apologies to Freud, few do so as a result of overpowering guilt or desire to punish themselves. Rather, the decision to confess is probably a combination of the suspect's need to release the internal pressure of guilt by talking about the incident and rationalizing his involvement. It could also be the suspect's belief that his guilt is known or the interrogator's persuasive arguments. Or some combination of these reasons.

Gudjonsson and Petursson (Gudjonsson and Petursson, 1991a) attempted to quantify the reasons for a confession resulting from these internal, external, or proof factors. External factors, the fear of being arrested, threats, or other issues contributed to a confession less than 20% of the time. Internal factors proved to be a much stronger reason to confess. In the study, 42% of the suspects indicated that they experienced relief after talking and explaining their side of the story. Fully a third indicated that they wanted to "get it off their chests." By far, proof was the strongest factor to encourage a confession. Fifty-five percent of the suspects in the study said that they confessed because they believed that the police could prove their involvement.

The WZ Technique takes advantage of these findings by first creating a strong belief that the suspect's guilt is known. Second, it offers rationalizations that allow the suspect to save face, while building a persuasive argument in favor of a confession. Finally, it creates a winning situation for the suspect by not forcing him to lie to the interrogator in the early stage of the interrogation when he is physically and emotionally strongest.

The WZ Technique also allows the interrogator to change tactics and strategies based on the type of suspect personality or the reaction to confrontation. The interrogator who understands the suspect and his motives can create an environment and strategy that encourage a confession.

References

1. Hilgendorf, E.L. and Irving, B. (1981). A decision-making model of confessions. In *Psychology in Legal Contexts. Applications and Limitations*, M.A. Lloyd-Bostock (Ed.). Macmillan, London 67–84.

2. Gudjonsson, G.H. (1989b). The psychology of false confessions. *Medico-Legal J.* 57, 93–110.

3. Reik, T. (1959). *The Compulsion to Confess: On the Psychoanalysis of Crime and Punishment*. Farrar, Straus and Cudahy, New York.

4. Jayne, B.C. (1986). The psychological principles of criminal interrogation. An appendix. In: *Criminal Interrogation and Confession*, 3rd ed. (F.E. Inbau, J.E. Reid, and J.P. Buckley, Eds.) Williams and Wilkins, Baltimore 327–347.

5. Moston, S., Stephenson, G.M., and Williamson, T.M. (1992). The effects of case characteristics on suspect behavior during police questioning. *Br. J. Criminol.* 23, 32, 39.

6. Zulawski, D. and Wicklander, D. (1993). *Practical Aspects of Interview and Interrogation*. CRC Press, Boca Raton.

7. Gudjonsson, G. H. and Petursson, H. (1991a) Custodial interrogations: why do suspects confess and how does it relate to their crime, attitude and personality? *Pers. Individ. Diff.* 12, 295–306.

Part One

Preparation

Preparation and Strategy

2

Two minutes of preparation can save hours of interrogation.

Although interviews typically take place outside a formalized setting, proper preparation for the interview or interrogation is essential for its successful conclusion. Many field interviews taking place on the street or at a place of business outside the control of the interrogator must rely on the locations at hand to provide a proper setting. The decision to interview a witness or suspect should be handled with a careful eye toward the ultimate goal of the conversation.

Interview Goal

Key interviews can generate a considerable amount of information if the interviewer gives thought to the type and quality of information that the witness or suspect could potentially provide. When interviewing a witness for any incident, the scope of the interview should be based broadly enough to allow information that is not actively solicited from the suspect to come out. In addition, whenever possible, the elements necessary to prove the crime being investigated should have been carefully reviewed by the interviewer.

In situations where the interviewer is questioning an individual who could be a suspect, the guidelines as to what will allow for the individual's arrest or termination of employment should be considered. An interviewer who has these boundaries clearly in mind will understand the elements necessary for a criminal prosecution in the public sector, or for a termination of employment in the private sector. In public law enforcement, the actual interview may be designed simply to elicit an alibi or a sequence of events that can later be proved or disproved by an investigation. However, in the private sector, the interview is more typically designed simply to draw out the factual circumstances surrounding a case or specific loss and to establish the behavioral clues necessary to clear the suspect or focus the investigation on him.

Evidence Considerations

Another element that the interviewer should consider is the available evidence concerning the incident under investigation. In identifying the evidence and how it fits into the incident, an interviewer can preplan a suspect's plausible explanations for the evidence. These explanations, while false, still afford the suspect an opportunity to explain key damaging elements of the case. By anticipating these explanations, a skilled interviewer can have the suspect lock himself into a story or sequence of events that can later be disproved. Additionally, a suspect's lying about his or her activities increases the impact of any evidence developed during the investigation that disproves the concocted story.

Case Example

A security manager for a large national retailer was suspected of stealing $900 from the store's safe during an audit of the cash. During the investigation, it was learned that the suspect was having financial problems and had made a deposit into his account at the bank across the street from the store.

The seemingly damaging evidence of the deposit could be plausibly explained or excused by the suspect. By anticipating that he might use his girlfriend, also an employee, as an alibi to verify his story, it was decided to interview her simultaneously. She was mentally walked moment by moment through the day of the theft. By locking her into a sequence of events, her value as an alibi for the suspect was seriously diminished.

Several probable suspect explanations were anticipated by the interrogator:

1. The suspect omits the bank deposit entirely from the sequence of events he recounts.
2. The suspect explains that he won the money gambling or in another untraceable activity.
3. The suspect says the money was a loan or gift from a family member.
4. The suspect relates that the money had been saved over time and the decision to deposit it that day was a coincidence.

The suspect was asked to recount the events on the day of the theft from the time he arrived until he left work. Surprisingly, he admitted that a deposit of $900 was made into his account in the early afternoon of the day of the theft, saying, "I know this looks suspicious." His attempt to stay close to the truth was to his benefit. The best liars generally attempt to stick closely to the truth. A denial of the deposit or its omission while recounting the day's events would be incriminating. When asked where the money came from, he said that it was a loan from his mother and uncle. He said he had been saving the money at home for some time, again a good move because family members will often back up a relative's story or be uncooperative during the investigation.

Having anticipated this as a possible explanation, however, a trap was already prepared: "When your mother lent you the money, what bank was the check drawn from?" He replied, "First National of _____." Then the second trap was sprung: "Did your uncle send you a check or money order?" The reply was, "Money order." "Was it a Visa or American Express?" He replied, "American Express."

The preplanned interview, which anticipated the suspect's responses, allowed the suspect to be trapped well before any interrogation even started. There were no documents to match the story the suspect told, which, besides his confession, helped establish clear evidence of his guilt.

Background Information

Prior to any interview or interrogation, the interviewer should review the background information on the subject. During the study of the suspect's background, relevant information might develop that would assist the interrogator during the interview/interrogation. It might also allow the interrogator an opportunity to begin developing preliminary thoughts regarding rationalizations that might be effective with this particular individual if an interrogation were contemplated.

Background information is also useful during interviews where the subject may have a hidden agenda that would taint the information that he or she is willing to provide. The interrogator should also consider the order in which the subjects should be interviewed. This decision could be particularly important should the interviewer anticipate that one suspect might provide critical evidence against other suspects.

The primary suspect's knowledge that a co-conspirator is being interrogated at the same time may add stress and concern about what is being said. In the early stages of an investigation, when a primary suspect has not been identified, there may be no basis for a particular order of interviews until the investigation begins to focus on a suspect. In larger cases involving multiple suspects, such as the closure of a sting or undercover operation, the interrogation takes on as much of an administrative tone as an interrogational one.

The organization of files, choreography of the movement of suspects to and from the interview, assignment of interrogators, feeding of suspects, and establishment of an evidence-holding room all play a critical part in the successful conclusion of the process. An excellent discussion of handling large case closures can be found in J. Kirk Barefoot's book *Employee Theft Investigations*.[1]

One preliminary issue not to be overlooked is how the suspect has reacted during previous interviews or interrogations. If the interrogator could ask only one question regarding the subject's background, it should be, "How has he acted when he's either been disciplined or confronted on previous occasions?"

The skilled interrogator realizes that people tend to fall into patterns when they respond to confrontation. The suspect who has in the past reacted aggressively is likely to react exactly as he did before. This information is often available from other officers, loss-prevention personnel, the employee's supervisor, teachers, or personnel department. By knowing in advance a previous problem or a likely response from the suspect, an interrogator can anticipate tactics that will beat the suspect at his own game.

Selection of the Interviewer

Another consideration prior to conducting any interview should be the selection of the interviewer. In many cases, the individual who actually develops the case may not be the best person to conduct the interview. Although that person might have the best overall knowledge of the case, an investigator might not fully appreciate the complexities of the interview or interrogation of suspects.

Thought should be given as to whether past experience with the person to be interviewed would be beneficial. In some cases, previous contact and its resulting rapport will benefit the interviewer in getting additional admissions. However, this may not always be the case. For example, there could have been a personality conflict, disagreement, or an arrest that resulted in hard feelings against the interviewer. In situations where the interviewer would be a subordinate of the person to be interviewed, thought should be given to choosing another interviewer. A store loss-prevention manager attempting to interview a store or district manager or senior executive whose level of responsibility is far above his might present an insurmountable barrier to a confession. There may also be cultural or gender issues that must be taken into consideration before confronting a suspect. Asking a female

---

[1] Butterworth Publishers, Stoneham, Mass., 1980.

interrogator to confront a male from certain cultures is likely to result in increased resistance.

Selection of the interviewer in the private sector may be based on the suspect's job level and areas of responsibility. Whereas the public law enforcement sector has the legal system to support an investigator's right to interview or interrogate a suspect, the private loss-prevention representative does not. The relative position of the loss-prevention investigator in the company will thus dictate those he should interview. In many cases, company policy dictates who will interview upper level management. This situation is something the public sector rarely considers.

Case File and Props

In an interrogation of a suspect, the use of a case file can facilitate a confession. The case file, which may be nothing more than a file folder containing papers, is the embodiment of the investigation. It is something tangible that the interrogator can touch, look at, and review to add credibility to the idea that an indepth investigation has been conducted, regardless of whether it has in fact, been, undertaken. It is not in the best interests of the interrogator to overplay the case file with props, forms, or videotape cassettes in an attempt to add credibility to the investigation. Overplaying the file can lead to denials by the suspect, or, worse, having the suspect ask to be shown the proof of his involvement. It is preferable to keep the file simple, and let suspects reach their own conclusions regarding what it might contain.

In many instances, interrogation of suspects can be conducted with less than absolute proof of their involvement in the issue under investigation. In these situations, the case file can be used as a prop to gesture toward and review when appropriate. At the very least, the case file should contain the materials necessary to complete an interrogation without leaving the room. It should contain paper for notes, consent-to-search forms, statement forms, restitution forms, evidence to be presented to the suspect, and any other pertinent material. The interrogation of a suspect is something that should not be interrupted, and the interrogator should have all the tools necessary to complete the task so that the psychological mind-set of the suspect is not diverted from the decision to confess.

It can also be beneficial to have present any evidence that could be identified by suspects to further implicate themselves in the incident under investigation — for example, documents establishing fraud, such as fraudulent refunds or credits, forged checks, or other paperwork needed to commit the crime, weapons, articles of clothing, or pictures. Whenever evidence is brought within reach of a suspect, it should be safeguarded.

Never leave a case file or evidence unattended with a suspect. Valuable evidence can be easily destroyed or tampered with, thereby ruining an otherwise airtight case.

Privacy

Generally, interviewers and interrogators have an opportunity to preplan both the time and the location of the interview. The field interview conducted in response to suspicious behavior by suspects is generally conducted at the location of the stop. In these situations, the officer has little, if any, control of the surroundings of the interview. However, the officer should, whenever possible, attempt to establish a zone of privacy in which to communicate with the suspect. In a field interview, the surrounding distractions may interfere with the suspect's concentration on the officer's questions. In addition, the potential for danger through intervention of associates or passersby complicates the problem. During a field interview in threatening circumstances, an officer's safety is paramount.

The zone of privacy that a field officer establishes can be beneficial in eliciting information from a suspect. In certain situations, a zone of privacy can be established simply by moving the suspect a few feet into an area where the conversation cannot be overheard. This privacy can also be attained by allowing the suspect to join the officer in the squad car. However, department policy may preclude or discourage this practice unless the suspect has been searched prior to getting into the vehicle with the officer.

In a stop-and-frisk interview or a planned field interview, privacy plays a major role in obtaining information from a suspect. Consider, for a moment, that we are asking a suspect to tell something that perhaps nobody else knows — a deep, dark secret in his life, a secret that, if found out, might cost him freedom, job, or reputation. For example, consider your own preferences if you had done something that was either wrong or shameful and then decided you wanted to talk about it. Which would be easier for you to do — confide in one person about that most embarrassing moment in your life, or admit to that same embarrassing incident in front of a group of people? Secrets are disclosed in moments of intimacy. The single interviewer who has established a significant rapport with a suspect can gain the secret.

Although the noncustodial stop-and-frisk interview in response to suspicious activity is designed to elicit information concerning the reasons for and circumstances surrounding the suspicious behavior, it has several major differences from a formalized interview or interrogation:

- The spontaneity of the stop and lack of preparation for it
- The uncertainty of the guilt of the suspects being interviewed

- Uncertainty of the incident under investigation
- The necessity to broaden the scope of the interview in an attempt to identify other information that could be used as grounds to establish probable cause for a search or arrest
- The semi-arrest status surrounding a stop-and-frisk interview

In a field interview, the two keys are officer safety and a zone of privacy where the discussion between the officer and the suspect can take place without being overheard.

Location — Planned Field Interview

In many instances during an investigation, the interviewer will interview victims and potential witnesses in the field. At such times, the location of the interview is often out of the hands of the interviewer. In many cases, the interviews are conducted in the supportive environment of the witnesses' homes or places of business. Often, these interviews have multiple distractions, such as phone calls or interruptions by children, that break the continuity of the interview. These distractions often disrupt the interviewer's flow of thought and can allow a suspect time to manufacture a plausible story or explanation. For witnesses, these distractions may cloud an already uncertain memory of the incident.

The planned field interview, an integral part of the investigation, can be made more effective with preparation and preplanning. Often, calling ahead to arrange for a convenient time will reduce distractions and may make the witness more receptive to questioning.

On occasion, a suspect will be interviewed in a supportive environment either because he has not yet been identified as the primary suspect in the incident or because it is still in the very earliest stages of the investigation when it is necessary to obtain the suspect's alibi. Regardless of the reason for the interview's being conducted in a supportive environment, the interviewer should still attempt to reduce surrounding distractions and create a zone of privacy that will make the individual more comfortable in talking.

Room Setting

The privacy and intimacy that an interrogator creates in the interrogation is enhanced by a private setting. This should be arranged so that interruptions and distractions will be minimized and so that a suspect can focus his somewhat divided attention on the interrogator and his words. The interrogator attempts to build a mind-set that focuses the suspect's attention on the resolution of the problem and away from the consequences of his actions. Interruptions during a dialogue only reduce the likelihood of success.

In selecting a location for the interrogation or planned interview, the interrogator should consider several points. First, the interrogator should consider the privacy of the particular location in which to do the interview. The room should be one that will be available for the duration of the interview and that will not allow frequent interruptions by others. Second, the room should be arranged to appear as nonthreatening as possible. The days of the bleak, stark, cold interview room should have passed. Such an environment is alienating to a suspect who is already apprehensive about his presence at the interview. A cold, stark setting only aggravates the suspect's defensiveness and fear of what may happen. Instilling fear into the suspect increases the likelihood that the suspect will move into a denial phase and makes it even more difficult for the interviewer to obtain the desired information.

An office is a comfortable place that most people have either worked in or visited. It is essentially a neutral, nonthreatening environment. Although it has certain distractions that a classic interrogation room may not have, it also provides certain benefits to the interrogator. The warmth and comfort of an office tend to reduce the defensiveness of the suspect and remove some resistance to the process of communication. An essential point in the practice of interrogation is to not put suspects into a defensive posture such that they will want to dig in and defend themselves with denials. The office (see Figure 2.1) should be private and have enough chairs for all the participants. An office also has the benefit of reducing the interview's level of seriousness and gives it the appearance of a business meeting rather than a serious confrontation between adversaries, as an interrogation room might indicate.

More and more often, witnesses are present in the interview/interrogation room during the encounter. Following are a number of advantages in having a witness present:

- There is a second person to testify that no threats, promises, or coercive tactics were employed during the interview/interrogation.
- There is a second set of eyes and ears to observe what is being said and the behavior of the subject.
- The witness (who also may be the second interrogator) has heard and observed everything that has transpired, and there can be a seamless exchange of responsibility between the primary interviewer and the secondary interviewer.
- If there is a lack of rapport between the primary interrogator and the subject, there can be a switch to the secondary interrogator, who receives the benefit of any rapport established by the primary inter-

rogator while avoiding any negative feelings the subject may have for the primary interviewer.

- The interview or interrogation can continue seamlessly because the secondary interviewer can take over immediately upon a signal from the primary interrogator that he is finished.

The presence of two interviewers does not mean that both are talking to the subject at one time. There is one primary interviewer who does all the talking, while the secondary sits quietly noting the exchange. It is only when signaled by the primary interrogator that the secondary interviewer changes roles with the first, who then takes the role of the mute witness.

Note the positions in Figure 2.1. The subject has her back to the door with neither the primary nor secondary interviewer blocking her path. The secondary interviewer is positioned just to the side and slightly outside the peripheral vision of the subject. This position offers an opportunity to observe yet not be a distraction. Having the subject face away from the door gives the interviewer two advantages. First, because the subject is facing away from the door there is not a constant reminder of leaving. Second, this position makes it more difficult for an attorney to argue that the client felt she could not leave because the exit was blocked. Furthermore, many departments and interviewers find it advantageous to have the witness be a female if a male interviewer is questioning a female.

Figure 2.1 The interrogator (foreground) should establish a neutral nonthreatening environment that reduces the level of seriousness of the meeting. Note the position of the witness (center) in relation to the subject (right), which minimizes any distraction or violation of privacy between the interviewer and subject.

Although the comfortable feeling of the office has a definite impact on the defensiveness of the suspect, the office should not be cluttered. The desk should be cleared of items that the subject may use to distract himself. The room should be evaluated for items or distractions that might influence a suspect's behavior and make it difficult for the interviewer to ascertain the reason behind the certain behavior. For example, privacy not only makes it easier for the suspect to confess, it also makes it easier to read a suspect's behavior. A field interview, for example, might be conducted on an open street where the officer has little or no control over the surroundings. In such a situation, the breaking of eye contact might be the result of the suspect's lying to the officer, a car passing, or light going on in a window across the street.

Thus, the interpretation of the behavior in areas where distractions are allowed adds a variable that makes an accurate determination of the suspect's truthfulness more difficult for the investigator.

Distractions

If a suspect is allowed to smoke or is indirectly offered an opportunity to smoke by providing an ashtray, a variable has been added to the interview that complicates the interpretation of behavior. If, in response to a question, the suspect reaches into pocket and withdraws a pack of cigarettes, takes one out, and lights it, how does one interpret it? Was this act designed to buy the suspect time to concoct a response, or was it merely his desire for a cigarette? The same could be said for offering the subject a beverage. Was a sip taken designed to delay a response or was it just a coincidence? There is no way to know unless it consistently happens. Offering a beverage to a subject whose guilt is certain has less effect on the process.

Leaving pencils, paper clips, or other items on the desk where a suspect can reach them can create a similar set of variables for the investigator. Does the suspect's attention to the created job of bending the paper clip mean he cannot look at you because of lying, or is he simply playing with the item? In many cases, suspects will use these methods in an attempt to buy time after being asked a question so they can determine which answer is going to help them.

An additional source of distraction can be reminders of punishment. These reminders can take many forms, from plaques on the wall to articles of clothing worn by law enforcement officials. In many instances, the gun, badge, handcuffs, or certificates of training can create in the suspect's mind an understanding of the seriousness of the investigation and its consequences.

A detective for a Midwestern police department came into the authors' office with someone suspected of sexually abusing his 18-month-old daughter. While the authors were involved in the interview of the father, the investigator was invited to have a cup of coffee and relax while doing his paperwork. The offices were well lighted and at a comfortable temperature, so the officer kept his jacket on while he awaited the outcome of the interview. During the next hour and a half, he occupied himself doing paperwork and having coffee. One of the authors returned to report on the suspect's confession to the sexual abuse of the child and asked the investigator to come in and witness the verbal statement. The investigator immediately rose, took off his jacket; and picked up his file to walk into the interview room. This action displayed the officer's badge, handcuffs, and weapon. Whether this action was an indication that he intended to get down to work and resolve the case or whether it was a need on his part to display his authority was never ascertained. However, before he entered the room, he was asked to put his coat back on so that the suspect was not faced with the visual impact of the seriousness of his actions.

The discussion of distractions during the interview could be carried out to infinite detail. However, if interviewers merely place themselves in the position of the suspect and view the room from the suspect's vantage point, they will easily be able to determine the distractions that could influence the interview or interrogation. Closing the blinds, unplugging the phone, and removing items from the top of the desk can certainly be done without any inconvenience.

In many instances, the interviewer is not lucky enough to have a private office but has to make do with a stockroom in a store, a conference room, or other temporary facility not designed for an interview. Using those facilities requires the same planning as for private offices: prepare for privacy by putting up "Do Not Disturb" signs, take items off the desk, and arrange the furniture in such a way that the interview can begin as soon as the suspect or witness walks in the door.

The authors' least-favorite interview site is the police interrogation room. The cold, hard feel of the room and the starkness of the surroundings are alienating to a degree that even a veteran interrogator can find uncomfortable. Is it any wonder that a suspect might feel uncomfortable and perhaps defensive in this environment? Although these types of interview rooms have their place in the police environment, especially when a suspect is in custody and freedom of movement must be limited, it may be beneficial to move the suspect to another office for the actual interview or interrogation. Obviously, care should be taken to prevent a dangerous or escape-prone prisoner from gaining access to items that could be used as weapons against the interviewer. If the room is the traditional interrogation room, one can "warm it up" by putting a picture on the wall behind or to the side of the suspect so it is not distracting.

Roles of the Interviewer

An interviewer was asked, "In five words or less, can you describe what it is that you really do?" After pondering this question for a short time, the response was, "I'm a confident negotiator." The more we consider this statement, the truer we believe it to be.

In the traditional view of the interrogator versus the suspect, the two become opponents who can challenge each other. A suspect may, in fact, direct his anger or frustrations toward the interrogator. The interrogator may be frustrated by the suspect's unwillingness to confess and direct sarcastic or unkind comments toward the suspect.

The interviewer must understand that it is the suspect's job during the interrogation to omit, evade, conceal, lie, and attempt to deceive in every way possible. By understanding the roles played by the participants in an interview, it becomes evident that taking the roles as adversaries is counterproductive. The role of the confident mediator allows interviewers to direct hostile feelings, frustrations, and blame away from themselves and toward the law, criminal justice system, company, or some other entity.

Successful interrogators take on the role of the mediator–negotiator, negotiating from a position of confidence — confidence not only that they can resolve the problem, but also that they can understand the suspect and believe in the facts of the case. The mediator acts as a go-between, someone who can find common ground in any situation without appearing to take sides. Think of the interview process as a well-planned play. Interviewers have an opportunity to choreograph the movements, the setting, and some of the dialogue of the play about to be acted out. They consider and arrange the room setting and location of the interview to their advantage.

They think about personal appearance. Many interrogators have the mistaken belief that they should be dressed in a suit and tie and look the absolute professional at all times. Although this may be true in certain circumstances, they must also give consideration to the needs of the suspect. Interrogators should have the ability to change appearance, depending on the person to whom they are speaking. For example, when interrogating a senior vice president of purchasing on a kickback scheme, the interrogator is addressing someone of power and must dress as well as, if not better than the suspect, to make them equals. In other instances, such formal dressing only increases the defensiveness of the suspect and may not be in the best interest of the interrogator. On the other hand, in dealing with a younger person who is perhaps less educated than the interrogator, it might not be best for the interviewers to be dressed in formal business attire. In this situation, it might be to their advantage to appear in short sleeves with the tie loosened, or even in less formal sport clothes.

In his book *Spy vs. Spy*,[2] Ronald Kessler discussed counterintelligence activities and security breaches in the United States. It is interesting to note the preparation of the setting, demeanor, and dress of the agents as they planned for a confrontation with a suspected traitor. The Behavioral Science Unit of the FBI helped plan the interview approach that took these factors into account.

By anticipating what attitude is likely to be taken by the suspect, the interviewer can often counter him. In being prepared for behavior such as anger, suspicion, sullenness, or contempt, interviewers can plan to fit their image to the needs of the suspect.

Language

Looking at the process of interview and interrogation reveals many similarities to a sales function. In selling, the salesperson must identify the needs of the customer, which could include image, financial, or emotional needs of him or his corporation. Once the salesperson has identified such needs, those benefits of the product that answer the client's desires can now be highlighted. If the product's benefits outweigh any objections from the client, and the product meets his needs, both personal and corporate, he will make the purchase. If not, there is no purchase. Similarly, in an interrogation, if the perceived benefits of giving the information, either from a witness or suspect's point of view, don't override objections to giving this information, the witness or suspect won't talk.

Central to selling a suspect on confessing is the level of rapport and communication that the interviewer achieves with him. When we communicate with other individuals, it is imperative that they understand what we are talking about. It is always preferable to speak simply. People will never look down on another individual who talks clearly and simply. What does cause problems is when someone talks above the educational level of another person or uses words improperly during a conversation.

Interviewers or interrogators who attempt to talk above a suspect's intellect face the problem that the suspect might not understand what is being asked. This compounds the problems of an already difficult situation during which the interviewer has been attempting to establish rapport and read a suspect's behavior for deception. Should the suspect fail to understand what is being asked and therefore delay answering to consider the question, the interviewer is forced to decide whether the delay is an attempt at deception. In addition, the witness or suspect may be antagonized by interpreting the interviewer as trying to be superior.

[2] Pocket Books, New York, 1980.

Many interviewers attempt to use street language or slang to establish a rapport with the suspect. In our experience, only rarely does this strategy have positive benefits, primarily because few interrogators can successfully manage it. In most instances, when interviewers or interrogators attempt to use street language, it only diminishes their credibility in the eyes of the suspect. Suspects view this use of language as a phony front. They recognize that it is unlikely the interviewer or interrogator actually speaks in this manner in day-to-day conversations.

Suspects or witnesses have to decide on whether to talk about what they know. Part of their decision, and often the critical part, is their evaluation of the questioner. In instances where they see phoniness or dialogue that obviously does not match the person seated in front of them, they become suspicious. This undermines the role that the interviewer is attempting to achieve.

Interviewers maintain a professional role, and their language should match the level of professionalism they have attained. The use of curse words or derogatory terms during an interview/interrogation often is counterproductive. Even if a suspect repeatedly curses and uses vile language, the interviewer should refrain from doing likewise. The suspect's behavior is often an attempt to provoke a similar response in the interviewer, to which the suspect can then take exception and become angry. If the suspect can draw the interrogator into making such a response, he has then succeeded in making the interviewer an opponent rather than a mediator.

A final note on language and communications with a suspect: Consider the process of interview and interrogation as psychologically reducing the seriousness of the incident under investigation and justifying the actions of a suspect. This allows suspects to perceive a reduction in the seriousness of their violation. The interrogator can unwittingly reinforce the seriousness of the incident by tone of voice and word selection. In any conversation, the tone of voice can transmit to the other party an underlying meaning that may be totally opposite to the words used.

Consider the example in which a husband comes home and asks his wife, "How was your day?" She responds, "Fine."

The word she has chosen indicates that her day has been successful and nothing out of the ordinary has happened. If the tone of voice chosen by her was lilting and lighthearted, it substantiates the fact that she has, in fact, had a good day.

That same response, "Fine," used in a short and clipped manner, however, contradicts the meaning of the word itself. She has given an appropriate response that her day was fine, but the tone of voice accompanying the word was a contradiction that would lead us to believe that her day has not gone well. This initial conclusion may be further validated by other physical gestures and behaviors accompanying the response. Sharp, jerky movements and rattling of pans would support the conclusion that all has not gone well.

In the same way, interviewers can be seen by the suspect as being accusatory, rude, or frivolous in a serious situation when they have no intention of being any of those. Since a vast amount of human communication occurs below the surface of the actual words through the tone of voice, speed of delivery, and physical behaviors, an interviewer can convey meanings both intentional and unintentional along with the spoken word. In some instances, these tones can provide a valuable communication tool for the interviewer, who can convey another meaning without actually having to say the words that might otherwise inflame a volatile situation.

Think for a moment about how you speak to another person when you want to display disbelief, ask a question, make an accusation, or restate a fact. A valuable exercise in communication, which can be done quite simply by the reader, is to speak into a tape recorder and listen to the tone of voice, speed of delivery, and word selections that are used. Often people are surprised to hear their own voices and may at first not recognize themselves. Imagine for a moment that it is not you speaking, but an interviewer. Ask how the voice sounds and what meaning is actually being conveyed. One of the finest learning tools available to an interviewer is to tape actual interviews and interrogations. The review of these tapes provides valuable insight into the ways that the interviewer can improve. Before doing this, however, the interviewer should review department policy and state law to ascertain whether taping is permitted.

Consider also the choice of words used by the interviewer. Harsh words that attach connotations of punishment recreate the seriousness of the incident under investigation. Words like kill, rape, embezzle, fraud, and theft remind the suspect, victim, or witness of the seriousness of the issue. When interrogators personalize the rationalization, they invite denial and defensiveness. Using a nondirected third-person approach, the interrogator avoids conflict, yet effectively conveys the message to the suspect.

The process of rationalization is designed to minimize the seriousness of the incident in the suspect's or witness's mind. An interviewer who repeatedly uses harsh words defeats this purpose. Interrogators should take a lesson from the suspects and reduce the seriousness of the incident by using less descriptive terms. They might, for example, use terms such as "this thing," "it," "took," or "did him."

A cardinal rule is to attempt to communicate on the same level as your suspect. If the suspects are, in fact, attempting to minimize the seriousness of what they have done through the use of these words, it benefits the interrogator to follow suit and attempt to minimize the crime's seriousness as well.

The guilty tend to use words that justify what they have done: "borrowed" instead of stole; "done" instead of killed. The media does the same thing when describing an incident. During a war, to make the losses of human life more palatable, a "body count" was reported rather than the death of human beings. If the media wants to highlight the viciousness of the crime, they use words such as "massacre" or "brutalize" — words that highlight the seriousness of what has actually happened.

Taking Notes

Commonly, during the interview and interrogation process, the interviewer takes notes. In the earliest stage of an interview, notetaking is generally not in the best interest of the interviewer. It is essential that the interviewer gain a rapport with a suspect, victim, or witness before attempting to record any of the information obtained. Most people, through TV and media exposure, expect an interviewer to take some notes during the interview. It is generally preferable to have gained the information first, then go back and create your notes during a second review of the facts with the suspect.

The notes taken during a nonaccusatory interview may have evidentiary value and should be comprehensive in reporting what was said. During notetaking, the interviewer should record who was present, the correct spelling of their names, and the time and place of the interview. The correct spelling of names and addresses should be obtained at the conclusion of the interview. Writing witnesses' or suspects' names and addresses when they are first given might reduce their cooperation.

Should an interview turn into a situation where the interrogator is attempting to elicit information of an adverse or incriminating nature from the suspect, the notetaking should cease and the pen and paper be put away. Taking notes at this point can remind the suspect that everything said is on permanent record. Instead of notetaking, the interrogator focuses on offering the suspect face-saving rationalizations. Notetaking can resume after the confession has been gained and the interrogator has developed it into the full story surrounding the incident(s) in which the suspect was involved.

Strategies

The person responsible for conducting any interview or interrogation should have the overall responsibility for establishing a strategy for it. This strategy should consider the order of interviews, their timing, and the plans for handling simultaneous multiple interviews.

One of the most difficult types of interrogation is that of a single suspect who has no co-conspirators because single suspects alone are fully aware of their exposure based on what they have or have not told others. In collusion cases where multiple suspects are acting together, it is usually easier to interrogate because the interrogator can play one suspect against another, none of whom has the full knowledge of what has or will be said. Collusion cases tend to be similar to knocking down a row of dominoes. Once you are able to push one over, the others generally follow by falling in order.

Deciding who should be interrogated first is usually approached by two separate strategies. The first consists of identifying the individual who, based on background and personality, appears most likely to confess. By initially confronting the weak link in the chain, the interrogator hopes that information this suspect provides can be used against the stronger personalities or more streetsharp individuals. The second strategy consists of identifying the most difficult suspects, the ones the interviewer feels will be least likely to confess during an interrogation.

Case Example

During an undercover operation at an electronics and appliance warehouse, a number of employees were identified as being involved in a theft ring. These employees, working with drivers, would move merchandise onto the dock. At the end of the day, they would load the merchandise that was to be stolen onto the now-empty trucks for delivery to an apartment that had been rented as a storage facility.

Based on the information available, it was decided that the investigation would be closed at a time when two opportune investigative objectives could be achieved: first, that one of the more difficult primary suspects would be caught in the act, and second, that the apprehension would take place at the apartment being used for storage. This way, two results would be achieved: first, the initial resistance of a difficult suspect would be overcome, and second, an opportunity would develop either to look into the apartment or to establish the grounds for a search of it.

The apprehension was made as the primary suspect and helper attempted to carry a 25-inch color TV into the apartment. At that time, the suspect and the driver's helper were separated and returned to the warehouse to be interviewed.

The primary suspect's first words were, "The paperwork is in the truck." The other stolen merchandise — a freezer, washer, and dryer — were recovered from the truck. When the suspect was unable to produce the paperwork for the stolen goods, he immediately denied stealing anything.

Shortly thereafter, he admitted that he had stolen these items and stated it was his first time. He also stated that the other individual with him had no knowledge of what was transpiring.

During a subsequent interview at the warehouse, the suspect acknowledged additional theft activities and implicated other employees in the warehouse. The two suspects were turned over to the local police for prosecution. During the remainder of the investigation, approximately 12 other employees were interviewed regarding their involvement in theft activity at the warehouse. These interviews resulted in six additional felony prosecutions and termination of 12 employees.

Anticipating a suspect's response to an accusation and planning for it as a preinterrogation strategy will often allow an interrogator to obtain a confession from people who would not ordinarily confess.

Legal Aspects

3

Legal precedents change and interviewers must constantly be aware of decisions that have an impact on their jobs.

This chapter reviews the key areas of law that define the boundaries of how an interview or interrogation must be conducted. It is not meant to cover all the details of law, but rather to highlight general principles applicable to the process. Legal precedents change and interviewers must constantly be aware of decisions that have an impact on their jobs. The interviewer should regularly ask for interpretation and direction from prosecutors or corporate counsel. Asking for clarification is preferable to proceeding without direction although it might make life more difficult for the investigator if the answer is different from what is expected. Textbooks cannot remain current with the ever-changing court decisions, so professional interviewers must constantly update themselves on local and federal laws and company policy.

Who Are You?

The first step in determining which rules an interviewer is to play by is to define what, in fact, the job is. Traditionally, individuals employed by local, state, and federal agencies are deemed to be in the public sector and are required to follow the rules and regulations set down by the laws relating to arrest, search, seizure, and interrogation. In most cases, these same rules and court decisions apply to private-sector employees who have been granted special powers of arrest, which applies to railroad police officers, university campus police, or any private employee who has been empowered with special police powers by the local jurisdiction. Also bound by these rules are private-sector employees who act as agents for the police during an investigation; this would entail performing some type of action at the direction of a law enforcement officer. As an agent of the police, the employee is required to follow the arrest and search-and-seizure decisions of the courts and legislature.

Individuals employed in the private sector who have no affiliation with a public law enforcement agency typically need not concern themselves with the issues of *Miranda*, right to counsel, or most search issues. Private-sector interrogators who intend to prosecute cases that they develop should contact the local prosecutor to determine any special requirements for case preparation. Some local prosecutors require private-sector interrogators to "mirandize" a suspect even though it is not required under the *Miranda* decision. However, off-duty law enforcement officials "moonlighting" in the private sector generally must still comply with the restrictions placed on public-sector employees. There can be confusion in this area when public policy dictates that the officer is on duty and available at all times. Private-sector employee investigations may be less concerned with the ultimate prosecution of an individual and focus instead on the termination of the suspect's employment and recovery of the company's assets. The private-sector interviewer must be concerned with the policies and procedures established by company management, personnel department, and collective bargaining agreement, as well as the rulings of labor arbitrators in conducting interviews and interrogations with employees.

Some private-sector investigators, such as railroad police officers, special agents for the post office or utilities, and campus police, have the public law enforcement officer's power of arrest, search, and seizure. However, they are also directed by the policies and procedures of their employers and potentially by the contracts with the unions servicing the company's employees. Thus, they may have the additional responsibility of presenting a case to a labor arbitrator regarding a policy or procedural violation of company rules. For example, railroad special agents might present evidence gathered during an investigation into an employee's drinking alcohol during working hours. Discipline, as a result of the investigator's findings, could result in suspension or termination of the employee's employment. Because of union contracts, any discipline might later be appealed to an arbitrator for review. Interviewers employed by the private sector, while having the powers of arrest granted them by statute, may face a conflict in objectives due to their special status.

The scope of the case also differs between the public and private law enforcement sectors. Generally, public-sector law enforcement is specifically focused on a particular act or group of acts that are clearly defined by the investigation (i.e., the victim was raped and murdered on January 29). In the private sector, the scope of the investigation may be equally well defined, such as the theft of a $7,000 deposit on a specific date; or be less clearly defined, such as looking into acts that are committed in violation of a number of company policies (i.e., a store has an inventory shortage of 5.2% since the last inventory — this means that 5.2% of its inventory in relation to its sales at that location are missing for any of a variety of reasons: paperwork errors, shoplifting, or employee theft). There may also be issues that are not necessarily criminal in nature but violate company policy, such as a sexual harassment claim made by one employee against another.

Constitutional Amendments

The basis for legal decisions in the United States is the Constitution and its amendments. The United States Supreme Court reviews cases in light of the guarantees granted by the constitution and legal precedents. The following excerpts from the Fourth, Fifth, Sixth, and Fourteenth Amendments provide an understanding of some of the court's basic rulings relating to interview and interrogation.

- *Fourth Amendment*
  The right of the people to be secure in their persons, houses, papers and effects, and against unreasonable searches and seizures, shall not be violated, and no warrant shall issue, but upon probable cause, supported by oath or affirmation, and particularly describing the place to be searched, and the person or things to be seized.

- *Fifth Amendment*
  No person ... shall be compelled in any criminal case to be a witness against himself, nor be deprived of life, liberty, or property without due process of law ...

- *Sixth Amendment*
  In all criminal prosecutions, the accused shall enjoy the right ... to be confronted with witnesses against him, have compulsory process for obtaining witnesses in his favor, and to have assistance of counsel for his defense.

- *Fourteenth Amendment*
  All persons born or naturalized in the United States, and subject to the jurisdiction thereof, are citizens of the United States and of the state wherein they reside. No state shall make or enforce any law which shall abridge the privileges or immunities of citizens of the United States; nor shall any state deprive any person of life, liberty, or property, without due process of law; nor deny to any person within its jurisdiction the equal protection of the laws...

These four amendments provide the basis for the courts' rulings in many landmark cases. The Fourth Amendment is the basis for the Exclusionary Rule, which excludes evidence that has been improperly or illegally seized. The Fifth grants the citizen the right to remain silent, and the Sixth gives the right to counsel to represent a person in proceedings against him. The Fourteenth Amendment grants each citizen the due process of the law.

Public-Sector Rules

One of the earliest cases that related directly to the interrogation of a criminal suspect by police was *Brown v. Mississippi*.[1] In this case, the United States Supreme Court found that the police had obtained the confession from Brown through the use of "third degree tactics." The Court ruled that the resulting confession was inadmissible as evidence in the case. In its decision, the Supreme Court applied the Fourteenth Amendment Due Process Clause, ruling that a confession is admissible only if it is voluntary. Therefore, to admit an involuntary confession into evidence is to deprive a citizen of his liberty without due process of law. This decision does not deal with the trustworthiness of the suspect's statement, but whether it was voluntarily given. *Brown v. Mississippi* was the first state confession case that used the federal constitutionally guaranteed rights and made them applicable to the states and, thus, to state and local investigators. An accused is deprived of due process if conviction rests partially or completely on an involuntary confession, as in *Lego v. Twomey*.[2] The deprivation of due process can occur even if the suspect's statement is true, as in *Rogers v. Richmond*,[3] and even if there is substantial corroborating evidence of the suspect's guilt (see *Payne v. Arkansas*[4]).

Once the United States Supreme Court applied the Fourteenth Amendment Due Process Clause to the states, the Fifth and Sixth Amendments to the United States Constitution were also made applicable to the states. This application created decisions that were especially pertinent to the public law enforcement officer. These rulings related to the suspect's privilege against self-incrimination and the right to counsel. Today, the landmark decisions of *Escobedo* and *Massiah*, both Sixth Amendment right-to-counsel issues, and *Miranda*, the Fifth Amendment right against self-incrimination, are all applicable to state and local law enforcement officers as they interview and interrogate. In these three landmark cases, the court set down specific rules and

---

[1] *Brown v. Mississippi*, 297 U.S. 278 (1936)
[2] *Lego v. Twomey*, 404 U.S. 477 (1972)
[3] *Rogers v. Richmond*, 365 U.S. 534 (1961)
[4] *Payne v. Arkansas*, 356 U.8. 560 (1958)

guidelines that a public law enforcement officer had to follow to protect the rights of a suspect.

Voluntariness

Although *Escobedo*, *Massiah*, and *Miranda* overshadowed the voluntariness rule for testing the admissibility of a confession, it is still the voluntariness of the confession that is the fundamental issue in determining the admissibility of a confession. Unfortunately, although the courts have provided guidelines for the officer in the *Escobedo*, *Massiah*, and *Miranda* decisions, determining the voluntariness of a confession is much less clear. To determine whether a confession is voluntary, there are no specific rules to follow or apply. Rather, the court has used as a test the "totality of circumstances." Here, the courts view the circumstances and environment surrounding a suspect who gives a confession. The courts take into account the methods employed in obtaining the confession, the suspect's physical and mental condition, the length of time over which questioning took place, and the suspect's age, education, and previous experience with law enforcement agencies, before making a determination of whether the confession was voluntary.

The courts have made it very clear that the use of physical force or physical abuse or even the threat of this type of conduct on the part of police will render a confession involuntary. Depriving a suspect of sleep, rest, food, or drink for substantial periods while being interrogated would make any resulting confession highly questionable.

However, the courts have also ruled that the use of trickery or lying by an officer to obtain a confession does not necessarily invalidate the confession. In the case of *Frazier* v. *Cupp*[5] the court upheld a conviction based on a confession elicited by the officer's trickery and lying. The defendant was suspected of a homicide and was told that his accomplice had confessed. This was completely untrue. The Supreme Court ruled in its opinion that the mere fact that the police had misrepresented a statement, i.e., that the suspected accomplice had confessed, was insufficient to make the confession involuntary. The court also stated that the voluntariness of a confession must be decided on a case-by-case basis, viewing "the totality of circumstances" surrounding the confession made by a suspect.

The danger to a prosecution in obtaining an involuntary confession goes past its exclusion at trial. Evidence developed as a result of the confession may also be inadmissible because of the Exclusionary Rule. As a "fruit of the poisonous tree," evidence developed as a result of an inadmissible confession may also at times be excluded. The primary difference is found in the Fifth

[5] *Frazier v. Cupp*, U.S. 731, 89 S.CT. 1420 (1969)

Amendment privilege against self-incrimination and the Sixth Amendment right to counsel. The suppression of statements as a result of a Miranda violation is based on a simple failure to follow the rules proscribed by the cases, rather than a due process violation of the Sixth Amendment.

The *Miranda* Rule

Simply described, *Miranda* could be said to be warnings to a suspect administered during a custodial interrogation. For *Miranda* to be applicable to an interrogation, it must meet two criteria. First, the setting must be custodial in nature. The court has defined custodial to mean that the suspect's freedom of action has been curtailed in some significant way. Second, the individual conducting the interrogation must be a law enforcement officer or acting as an agent for a law enforcement officer.

Should a custodial situation arise, the suspect must be advised of the following: the right to an attorney, right against self-incrimination, and his right to remain silent. If a suspect is taken into custody by police and questioned without having been advised of his *Miranda* rights, the suspect's responses cannot be used in evidence against him to establish guilt.[21] However, the court ruled in *Harris v. New York*[7] that statements made by a suspect after questioning, without being advised of the *Miranda* warnings, may still be used later to impeach a defendant's credibility should he elect to testify at trial.[22]

Some states have chosen to broaden these rights either by legislation or general practices to include the administering of rights when a suspect becomes the focus of an investigation. Texas requires that *Miranda* warnings be included as part of the audio- or video-taped interrogation. Failure to include the warnings on the tape will result in suppression of subsequent admissions or confession regardless of whether the rights were read prior to the interview or interrogation. Washington requires that suspects be told of their right to counsel even if no interrogation is taking place. Failure to do so might result in the suppression of any spontaneous utterances made while in custody. New Jersey has a state constitutional rule, known as the "Sanchez Rule,"[8] preventing police from questioning defendants without the consent of defense counsel.

California officers used a method of interrogation the courts termed *Beachheading* or *questioning outside Miranda*. This practice entailed the interview and interrogation of suspects in custody without advising them of

[21] re J.C., 844 P.2d 1185, 52 CrL 1468 (Colo. 1993)

[7] *Harris v. New York*, 401 U.S. 222 (1971)

[22] *Note*: the exact wording of the warnings should be read from a card or form approved by the Officer's department or prosecutor. Because local variations in wording, as well as the inclusion of other warnings by some departments, the exact wordings have been omitted.

[8] *State v. Knight*, 283 N.J. Super. 98, 661A.2d 298 (App. Div. 1995)

their *Miranda* rights or continuing to interrogate suspects who invoked their rights under *Miranda*. Once the statement was obtained, the suspect was read the *Miranda* rights and another statement was obtained, this time after proper warnings. The purpose of the statement was to impeach the suspect's testimony if he elected to testify at trial, (*Harris v. New York*[9]). The argument made by supporters of this tactic is that the Supreme Court has repeatedly ruled such statements may be used to find other evidence or to challenge the credibility of the suspect at trial (*Oregon v. Elstad*[10]). This practice came under increasing attack by the courts and defense counsel, but as long as the resulting statements were voluntary, the prosecution could continue to use them to impeach the suspect and help locate evidence and witnesses in the follow-up investigation. California, at the time of this writing, was reevaluating police academy training in the practice of "questioning outside of Miranda. *Edwards v. Arizona*[11] created a bright-line rule that once a suspect invoked the right to counsel, all further interrogation must cease and may not be resumed unless the accused effects a valid waiver or renewed communication with the police. Any statements made after a request for counsel would be suppressed, except for possible impeachment purposes.

In *Oregon v. Bradshaw*, the courts speak to the opening of the interrogation again when the defendant reinitiates the conversation. Bradshaw was arrested for drunk driving and the death of a passenger after he crashed his truck. He immediately invoked his right to counsel and the interrogation ceased. He later asked what was going to happen to him and detectives informed him that he did not have to speak with them. He indicated his understanding and ultimately confessed. The court held that the confession was admissible because he initiated the conversation and the officers stopped all questioning when Bradshaw invoked his rights.

In 2000, the United States Supreme Court considered a case that focused on a 1968 law passed by Congress that effectively overruled the *Miranda* decision. Act 18 U.S.C., 3501 basically made the admissibility of any non-Mirandized statements dependent on whether the custodial statements were made voluntarily by the suspect. At issue was whether the Miranda warnings or something similar to the warnings are required by the Constitution or whether they are they a procedural safeguard that Congress can modify. This law was never formally sanctioned for use by the Department of Justice and effectively remained unused for decades. The United States Supreme Court was asked to decide in *Dickerson v. United States*[12] on just this issue. In a 7–2 decision, the Supreme Court held that the Fifth and Fourteenth Amendments require the

---

[9] *Harris v. New York*, 401 U.S. 222 (1971) Oregon v. Hass 420 U.S. 714 (1975)
[10] *Oregon v. Elstad*, 105 S. Ct. 1285 (1985)
[11] *Edwards v. Arizona*, 101 S. Ct. 1880 (1981)
[12] *Dickerson v. United States*, 67 Cr.L.472 (Case # 99-5525)

language and procedures that are contained in the *Miranda* warnings. This ruling effectively extended the rights and warnings to all state, federal, and local law enforcement regardless of the jurisdiction. Thus, the failure to Mirandize a suspect in custody will result in the suppression of the confession and possibly other incriminating statements resulting from the non-Mirandized confession.

There are exceptions to the *Miranda* decision. The use of the statement to impeach a suspect's testimony at trial is one already discussed. Another is the public safety exception where statements made by the suspect relating to the officer's or the public's safety may be admitted at trial.

In *New York v. Quarles*, the court adopted an exception that covers situations where the concern for public safety must override the officer's adherence to the rule of *Miranda*. *Quarles* dealt with a rape suspect's being questioned about the location of a gun that the victim said he had. Because there was an immediate need for the police to locate the gun to protect themselves and the public from harm, the court ruled that this overrode the failure of the officer to immediately administer *Miranda* warnings before he asked questions regarding the location of the weapon. In this ruling, the court determined that no matter what the officer's actual intent in asking the question might be, if the question could reasonably be prompted by a concern for his own or the public's safety, then the response would be deemed admissible by the court. This exception allows the street officer to respond to the needs of public safety when circumstances warrant, but still protects the suspect's rights with an objective test the courts can apply. It would be a mistake for the officer to use this case as a crutch to avoid the administration of a suspect's rights.

Custody

The issue of custody becomes important as an officer moves into less traditional settings for the interview or interrogation. *Miranda* deals with custody when the suspect has been "deprived of his freedom in any significant way." *Miranda* does not make all police questioning custodial, as noted in the following:

> General on-scene questioning of citizens in the fact finding process is not affected by our holding. It is an act of responsible citizenship for individuals to give whatever information they may have to aid in law enforcement. In such settings the compelling atmosphere inherent in the process of in-custody interrogation is not necessarily present.[13]

The IRS conducted a standard tax compliance investigation of Mathis, who was serving time in the Florida Penal System for a state violation. The

---

[13] 384 U.S. at 477-78

interview was conducted in Mathis' cell without *Miranda* rights being given. During the interview, Mathis made some incriminating statements that helped to convict him of filing false tax claims. In *Mathis v. United States*[14] he challenged the admissibility of those statements because of the environment of the interview. Mathis has since been severely undermined. In 1990, *Illinois v. Perkins*[15] addressed this issue with a far different result. Perkins had allegedly told an inmate that he had committed a murder and provided enough details to convince the police the confession was real. Placing an undercover officer in Perkins' cellblock, the police hoped to overhear details of the murder. During jailhouse conversations, Perkins recounted the murder with enough details to convince authorities that he had, indeed, committed the murder. The confession was suppressed and the government appealed. The Supreme Court reversed the trial court, stating that conversations between suspects and undercover agents do not require *Miranda* warnings. Most courts currently follow the *Perkins* finding that most prison interrogations are not custodial unless there are some added constraints beyond those they would find in ordinary confinement. In Florida, a similar situation arose where an undercover officer posed as an inmate to elicit incriminating statements, but these statements were suppressed because they violated Florida's due process clause. The court held that the gross deception used violated the defendant's right against self-incrimination.

In *Orozco*, four police officers arrived at Orozco's room at 4 a.m., suspecting him of being involved in a shooting. One officer testified that Orozco was under arrest as soon as he identified himself; however, the man was allowed some freedom of movement in his apartment. Orozco made some incriminating statements and turned over a gun, all without *Miranda* warnings. Texas argued that Orozco was not in custody because he was in his own room in familiar surroundings, but the court held that when an individual is in custody the prescribed warnings are required. Clearly, it depends on whose eyes one looks through to determine whether there was custody.

Cervantes v. Walker[16] set forth a four-part test to help determine whether custodial interrogation is taking place:

(1) The language used to summon the individual
(2) The physical surroundings of the interrogation
(3) The extent to which officials confront the prisoner with evidence of guilt
(4) Whether officials exert any additional pressure to detain the individual

[14] *Mathis v. United States* (1968) 391 US
[15] *Illinois v. Perkins* (199) 496 US 292, 110 L Ed 2d 381, 88 S Ct 2394
[16] *Cervantes v. Walker*, 589 F.2d 424 (9th Cir. Cal. 1978)

In 1976, there was further clarification of custody in *Beckwith v. United States*.[17] In this case IRS agents met with Beckwith in his home, told him that he did not have to speak with them, but did not advise him of his formal *Miranda* rights. Over a period of several hours, he made admissions and offered some documents to the agents. Beckwith, traveling in a separate car from the agents, then took them to his place of business, where the incriminating papers were kept. Beckwith turned over the additional documents and was later charged. The U.S. Supreme Court affirmed his conviction, stating that while an adversarial interrogation had taken place, he was not under arrest. Just because the meeting resulted from the "focus" on Beckwith as a suspect it did not mean that he was in custody. The difference between *Orozco* and *Beckwith* clearly stems from the officer's decision to arrest and the police-dominated environment of four officers during a 4 a.m. confrontation.

In *Berkemer v. McCarthy*[18] the court also has determined that traffic stops are non-custodial when probable cause exists and the stop is limited to the initial roadside conversation. The court's opinion was that traffic stops are short lived and take place in the public eye where there is much less of a police-dominated atmosphere. When the questioning takes place in a police vehicle it is noncustodial unless the suspect has been placed there in formal custody. Likewise, an interrogation at a suspect's place of employment is generally also noncustodial unless a police-controlled and -dominated atmosphere exists. This was further clarified in *Florida v. Bostick*, where the court held that questioning during random vehicle stops and consent to search luggage was permissible without the *Miranda* warnings. The courts have also ruled that some evidence would not be suppressed when it could be shown that there was inevitability of its discovery independent of the suspect's statement. The court further ruled in *McNiel v. Wisconsin* that statements about other crimes for which the defendant was not charged or under arrest are admissible so long as *Miranda* warnings were given on the custodial offense.

Telephone Interviews

Telephone interviews have also been found to be noncustodial because the suspect can simply hang up the phone (*State v. Mahoney*[19]). Another case that mixed custody and telephone interviewing was *State v. Tibiatowski*.[20] A juvenile on the run from detention was suspected of committing crimes while at liberty. After being caught, he was held in a juvenile detention facility where he received a call from his caseworker, who asked if he "had anything he wanted to tell her." The juvenile then admitted he had committed an

[17] *Beckwith v. United States* (1976) 425 US 341, 48 L Ed 2d 1, 48 L Ed 2d 1, 96 S Ct 1612
[18] *Berkemer v. McCarthy* (1984) 468 US 420, 82 L Ed 2d 317, 104 S Ct 3138
[19] *State v. Mahoney* (1995) 80 Wash App495, 909 P2d 949
[20] *State v. Tibiatowski*, 590 N.W. 2d 305 (Minn. 1999)

armed robbery. *Miranda* was not required because the caseworker was not a law enforcement officer and this was not a custodial interrogation.

In another case, an officer called a 12-year-old boy on the phone at his home. During the call, the boy made incriminating statements to the officer. The court held that the interrogating officer was not in the youth's presence and thus could not exert immediate physical control of him. The court further stated that even a 12-year-old would not feel restrained in this type of encounter.[21]

The courts have limited the need for *Miranda* warnings to those situations where there has been such a restriction on a person's freedom as to render him in custody. It is the totality of circumstances surrounding the interrogation and environment that must be considered to determine the question of whether there was sufficient restraint of the suspect's freedom of movement to constitute an arrest.

From a practical standpoint, an officer must determine the local prosecutor's and court's preferences in applying *Miranda*. Many prosecutors encourage *Miranda* warning even when not necessary because they believe it will make their job easier.

The Warnings

After each warning, the officer must determine whether the suspect has understood what he has been told. *Miranda* states the following:[22]

1. He has the right to remain silent.
2. Anything he says may be used against him.
3. He has the right to an attorney.
4. Should he not be able to afford an attorney, one will be provided for him without charge.

Only upon the waiver of these rights by the suspect can an interrogation occur. Awareness of these rights will help to assure the courts that the confession is a knowing and intelligent decision by the suspect.

The Supreme Court ruling in *Miranda* also found that a suspect could waive these rights at any time during the interrogation. As a result of this portion of the decision, many agencies added a fifth warning that was not required by the court. This fifth warning basically asked the suspect to acknowledge that he understood the rights and that he could stop talking to

---

[21] re J.C., 844 P.2d 1185, 52 CrL 1468 (Colo. 1993)
[22] *Note:* the exact wording of the warnings should be read from a card or form approved by the officer's department or prosecutor. Because local variations in wording, as well as the inclusion of a fifth warning by some departments, the exact wordings have been omitted.

the officer at any time and demand a lawyer at any time. Many departments also have taken the stance that the suspect should sign a written waiver on which he initials each of the warnings, signifying his understanding of them. This, however, was not required by the court, but rather is an attempt by departments to help show that there was a knowing and intelligent waiver by the suspect.

A commonly held misunderstanding is that the mere focusing of suspicion on a suspect requires that the *Miranda* warnings be administered. In *Beckwith v. United States*,[23] the court found that the issue of custody was the test and not merely the focus of suspicion on an individual.

The focus-of-suspicion issue was carried a step further in *Oregon v. Mathiason*,[24] where a suspect was invited into a police station to discuss his involvement in a burglary. During the course of this discussion, he was told that he was not under arrest and could leave at any time. Subsequently, the suspect made a confession to the burglary. He then left the station after making his damaging admissions. The detective later obtained a warrant and arrested Mathiason for the burglary. In this case, the court ruled that since the suspect was not in custody at the time of the confession, the need to give *Miranda* warnings was not present. However, if the suspect had been arrested when he elected to leave, it would generally have required that the *Miranda* warnings be given.

In the strict sense, if suspects are not under arrest, there is no need for an officer to advise them of their rights. However, from a practical standpoint, it may be advisable to warn the suspect. Defense counsels often use *Miranda* as a smoke screen to confuse the issue once in court. Also, the interrogation of a suspect on a serious issue such as homicide might make it preferable for the officer to advise a suspect because of later advantages it might give the prosecutor. In serious crimes, the prosecutor should be consulted if there is a question as to whether to advise a suspect of his rights before questioning.

Suspect Waiver

As a general rule, it is preferable that the accused verbalize his or her understanding of the *Miranda* warnings. The nodding of the accused's head *might* also be acceptable, but a verbal response is usually preferable. Depending on the suspect's age, education, and experience with the criminal justice system, it might also be beneficial to ask additional questions that will help satisfy the court's need to establish that the suspect understood his rights prior to the waiver and knowingly waived them.

---

[23] *Beckwith v. United States*, 425 U.S. 341
[24] *Oregon v. Mathiason*, 429 U.S. 492 (1977)

At any time during an interrogation following the reading of the waiver of the *Miranda* rights, a suspect can make a demand for counsel or assert the right of silence. Once either of these rights is invoked, all questioning must cease. The officer can make no attempts to convince the accused to give up the constitutional rights that he has elected to exercise. Some officers in the past have, at a later point, asked a suspect if he has changed his mind about talking; however, this is dangerous ground and could easily result in a confession's being ruled inadmissible. In *Edwards v. Arizona*,[25] the court made it abundantly clear that, once a suspect invokes the right of counsel, all questioning must cease unless the suspect's attorney is present or the suspect initiates subsequent conversation. In December 1990, the Supreme Court extended the protection of *Miranda* even further in its decision of *Minnick v. Mississippi*.[26] Minnick was arrested for murder and his interrogation ended when he requested an attorney. He was allowed to meet with his attorney two or three times. He later confessed to a deputy sheriff, was convicted, and sentenced to death. The court held that, once counsel is requested, the interrogation must cease and may not begin again until counsel is present. Even after the suspect has had an opportunity to consult with his attorney, no questioning can resume without the attorney present. This new rule makes it almost impossible for the police to urge a suspect who has invoked *Miranda* to change his mind. Once a suspect invokes the right to counsel, a permanent prohibition against interrogation begins unless the attorney is present.

Failure to administer a *Miranda* warning will not always result in the suppression of a confession. Currently, there is only one public safety exception to the *Miranda* rule. As described earlier, this exception is in *New York v. Quarles*.[27] Here, the court adopted a public safety exception that covers situations where the concern for public safety must override the officer's adherence to the rule of *Miranda*.

The *Massiah* and *Escobedo* Rules

The difference among *Massiah*, *Escobedo*, and *Miranda* lies in the right to counsel. In *Miranda*, the right to counsel is significant in that it assists a suspect in exercising the right to silence. However, in *Massiah* and *Escobedo*, the suspect's right to silence is secondary to the suspect's right to counsel.

Massiah concerns the right to counsel after the suspect has been indicted; however, this has expanded through other cases that make it clear that *Mas-*

---

[25] *Edwards v. Arizona*, 451 U.S. 477 101 S. CT. 1880 68 L. ED. 2d 378 (1981)
[26] *Minnick v. Mississippi*, 89-6332, Cited 51 CCH S.CT.BULL. p. B313-336
[27] *New York v. Quarles*, U.S. 104 S.CT. 2626 8 IL.ED.2d 550 (1984)

siah is now applicable any time counsel has entered the picture in defense of a suspect. Based on the *Massiah* and *Escobedo* rulings, it is evident that law enforcement officers must take extreme care when questioning any defendant who is represented by counsel. The waiver of rights made by a suspect after counsel has been retained will be difficult to show, unless it can be clearly established that the waiver was done at the instigation of the accused and not the police (see *Minnick v. Mississippi*[12] expansion of *Miranda* protection).

Youths and Incompetents

When can young people or mentally incompetent individuals give a knowing waiver of their constitutional rights? This question addresses two issues. The first is voluntariness, and the second is the mental capabilities of the individual. The courts have generally ruled that a person of young age can give a voluntary confession and knowingly waive his constitutional rights. However, the actual age of the suspect is not necessarily the critical factor. In determining whether the waiver was voluntary, the court looks at prior experience with police or the judicial system. This prior experience can overcome the suspect's young chronological age. Age does, however, become a factor when there is a lack of experience with the criminal justice system. Immaturity and the lack of experience bring into question whether the youth can adequately evaluate the ramifications of a confession.

Although many youths will not have had any experience with the law enforcement community, their education can take the place of contact with the law. Given a school-acquired understanding of the governmental process and the rights that can be exercised under the Constitution should allow the youth to make the same competent decision an adult or delinquent would under similar circumstances.

Many states have legislated juvenile acts that require public law enforcement officers to notify the parent or legal guardian, without any unnecessary delay, when a juvenile has been taken into custody. In many instances, the juvenile acts also require the officer to turn the minor over to an officer who has been specifically designated to handle juvenile problems. A confession by a youth prior to either of these circumstances' taking place may bear on the voluntariness of the confession given by a juvenile.

Whether a suspect is mentally incompetent is a decision for the court to judge during a competency hearing. The suspect who is judged mentally incompetent cannot knowingly understand or waive his constitutional rights. If, in fact, he was mentally incompetent, it would also be unlikely that he would be able to participate in his own defense prior to and during trial. The officer has no choice but to go through the *Miranda* procedures. The officer should

---

[12] *Dickerson v. United States*, 67 Cr.L.472 (Case # 99-5525)

maintain a detailed record of what was said to and by the suspect, along with notes concerning his condition and demeanor at the time the confession was given. The ultimate determination of mental competency and whether a person was legally insane during the commission of the crime, yet later competent to give a voluntary confession, is up to the court. The officer's sole responsibility is to gather evidence and accurately report that evidence to the court.

Alcohol or Narcotics Intoxication

Intoxication is not generally a defense, although it may speak to the lack of a specific intent to commit a crime. The real question addresses the mental competency of the suspect. Simply because an individual is more likely to confess if intoxicated does not mean he is mentally incapable of giving a valid confession. The burden falls on the suspect to show that the confession was involuntary and untrue. The defendant also must prove intoxication to the point of being unconscious of the meaning of the words he used when confessing. For example, in *People v. Sleboda*,[28] the defendant was able to stand and answer questions following an automobile accident. In addition, he was concerned for other family members and showed an awareness of the accident that had taken place.

The suspect attempted to use the defense that he was so intoxicated that he could not knowingly waive his rights. The court found that, for the defendant to be able to use this defense, he would need to have been so grossly intoxicated that he could not waive his rights. However, in light of the factual testimony relating to concern he showed for family members and his awareness of the circumstances surrounding the accident, the court found that the defendant's statements were knowingly and voluntarily given.

A suspect should *never* be given any alcoholic beverages or illegal drugs prior to or during the course of an interrogation. Administering alcohol or illegal drugs to a suspect is unprofessional and may open the department and officer to litigation as a result. Typically, the administration of any medications should be done only on the instructions of competent medical staff.

Tricks and Promises

All interrogators should avoid doing or saying anything that might cause an innocent person to confess. The deception must be intrinsic to the case but not involve the creation of fabricated evidence that might corrupt the later hearing or trials.

An officer's promise to a suspect of more lenient treatment or sentence, based on cooperation, could provide an innocent person an opportunity to

---

[28] *People v. Sleboda*, 166 Illinois APP. 3d 42, 519 N.E. 2D512 116 Illinois DEC.620 (1988)

confess when there is strong circumstantial evidence. The courts have established a general rule that the promise of leniency to a suspect will nullify any subsequent confession. However, a promise by the interrogator to discuss the suspect's cooperation with the prosecutor is permissible.[29] In *McLeod* the detective promised to make the defendant's cooperation known to the prosecutor and judge. This statement did not form a promise of leniency but was judged on whether this statement overwhelmed the defendant's free will and caused a confession. Viewed in total with the defendant's background and length of interrogation, it was not found to be a promise by the court.

Other examples of promises that would not make a confession inadmissible would be an interrogator's promise to seek psychiatric treatment for the suspect or recommend a lower bail for the suspect. However, it is often the context and the way the statements are made by the interrogator as well as the totality of circumstances that will determine if a promise of leniency was made to the suspect. In *U.S. v. Pierce*,[30] an officer on the way to the station told the defendant that he could "get off pretty easy" if he cooperated with the police. When read his *Miranda* rights at the station, the defendant acknowledged he had received no promises in exchange for the statement. This, along with the totality of circumstances, negated the inference by the officer.

Some states have enacted specific statutes regarding the use of promises during an interrogation. These statestatutes would supersede any other court rulings for that locale. Still, most courts view the deceptions in their totality to decide whether they effectively removed the voluntariness of the confession. Trickery and deception are also not permissible when trying to obtain a waiver of *Miranda* rights from the suspect. To use deception in this way clearly violates not only the law, but its spirit as well. A waiver can not be "tricked or cajoled" from a suspect in custody.[31] If trickery, such as the misrepresentation of the amount of strength of the evidence, is to be allowed, it must, as a minimum, be preceded by an effective *Miranda* waiver that must be free from any constitutional taint.[32]

Public Employers

The United States Supreme Court, in a series of decisions, has forced public employers to apply the Fifth Amendment right against self incrimination to their employees. Public employers cannot force employees to choose between their Fifth Amendment rights of silence and losing their jobs.

---

[29] *McLeod v. State*, 718 So. 2d 727 (Ala 1998)
[30] *U.S. v. Pierce*, 152 F. 3d 808 (8 Cir. 1998)
[31] *Miranda*, 384 U.S. at 476
[32] *Jones v. State*, 57 CrL 1062 (Fla. App. 1995)

The first case relating to this issue was *Garrity v. New Jersey*.[33] In Garrity, police officers were subjected to dismissal if they refused to answer questions on the grounds that the answers to those questions could tend to incriminate them. The police officers answered the questions and were subsequently prosecuted for conspiracy to obstruct the administration of traffic laws. At trial, they sought to exclude the statements that they had made from any criminal proceedings on the grounds that the statements had been coerced in violation of the Fifth Amendment. The United States Supreme Court found that the statements were, in fact, coerced, and, as a result, should be excluded at trial.

In 1968, the United States Supreme Court once again looked at the Fifth Amendment and the coercion of a statement from a public employee. In *Gardner v. Broderick*,[34] a police officer was to appear before a grand jury investigation, but refused to sign a waiver of immunity from prosecution. As a result of this refusal, he was subsequently discharged from the force. The Supreme Court saw a significant difference between this case and *Garrity*. The primary difference between the two was the officer's refusal to testify after he was told that he would not be subject to prosecution for any incriminating statements he made to the grand jury, as opposed to the circumstances in *Garrity*, where the threat of termination coerced the officer's statements.

Determining whether the Fifth Amendment right against self-incrimination is applicable is directly related to whether a prosecution is contemplated. In instances where the officer is to be disciplined administratively rather than through the criminal justice system, the officer has no right to remain silent without its affecting his employment. Once the decision has been made to approach the case from a criminal prosecution standpoint, the public employer must advise the employee of his rights. Therefore, the officer should be aware that any incriminating statements he makes can be used against him at trial.

Private Employers

Under common law, the private citizen has a limited right to arrest and question a lawbreaker. The primary rule applied in these types of cases is the voluntariness of the statement and the resulting trustworthiness of the confession. The courts have consistently ruled that the trigger for *Miranda* in a private interrogation is that there must be some government involvement. Only when private interrogators are acting as an agent for the state are they bound by the rules of a government agent.

---

[33] *Garrity v. New Jersey*, 385 U.S. 493, 17 L Ed 2d 562, 87 S Ct 616 (1967)
[34] *Gardner v. Broderick*, 392 U.S. 273, 20LEdid 1082, 88S Ct1913 (1968)

In general, school officials, social workers, and counselors are not public law enforcement and an interrogation by them is not the functional equivalent of a police interrogation. However, in the event that they are acting as an agent of the state or are working with the police, then *Miranda* warnings are likely to apply. Similarly, correctional officers are considered law enforcement officers for *Miranda* purposes. The issue of a suspect's custody by being in jail was discussed earlier in this chapter, but the question of custody is related to how the suspects were summonsed and whether there were additional restrictions placed on their movements after being summonsed.

The United States Supreme Court has made a distinction between public and private employers in the application of the Fifth Amendment. The Supreme Court has ruled that, as long as the private employer or its employees are not acting as agents for public law enforcement, the Fifth Amendment generally does not apply to private employers. In the first case relating to this issue, *Gardner v. Broderick*,[34] the court clearly distinguished the difference between a public- and private-sector employee. The court ruled that there are few employment situations where the employee does not agree to take the employment on the terms that are offered him; thus, the constitutional rights are generally not protected when dealing with a private employer. However, the Supreme Court has clearly set up the guidelines under which *Miranda* warnings are required: (1) questioning is begun by law enforcement officers and (2) the individual has been taken into custody or has been deprived of his freedom in some significant way.

A landmark case relating to the nonapplicability of *Miranda* warnings to the private sector came in a California case, *People v. Deborah C.*,[35] In this case, a plainclothes store detective detained a 15-year-old female after observing her leaving the store without paying for some jewelry. She was taken to the loss prevention office and placed under a citizen's arrest without being given a *Miranda* warning.

The California Supreme Court distinguished in its decision between the state involvement created when a loss prevention investigation acts in the law enforcement sector and when that same loss prevention investigator is interrogating someone. The interrogation of someone is an action that in and of itself is not illegal. The California Supreme Court looked upon the *Miranda* decision as the U.S. Supreme Court's response to "third degree" tactics used to obtain confessions. Third degree tactics are considered physical abuse or the threats of physical abuse, duress, coercion, and length of the interrogation. The court found no evidence of abusive techniques by loss prevention agents that would require *Miranda*.

---

[34] *Gardner v. Broderick*, 392 U.S. 273, 20LEdid 1082, 88S Ct1913 (1968)
[35] *People v. Deborah C.*, 30CAL3d 125, 177CAL RPTR852, 635P2d446 (1981)

The court concluded that the private loss prevention or security function was not required to follow the *Miranda* warnings before eliciting an admission that could be used in a later trial. The noncustodial setting and the differences in psychological advantages between law-enforcement and private-sector investigators allowed the California Supreme Court to conclude that private and public employers who interview their employees about job-related events in a noncustodial setting need not administer the *Miranda* warnings.

Sixth Amendment: Right to an Attorney

The employer, public or private, conducting an interview in a noncustodial setting need not advise the employee of his right to counsel. However, if the employee is protected by a collective bargaining agreement, the right to a representative may include the implied right to select an attorney to represent him during the subsequent grievance proceedings. The public employer who is faced with questioning an employee who potentially may be charged criminally must provide for due process, as must the private employer with a union agreement that may require an attorney or representative to be present. Private employers can force an employee to choose between having an attorney present or discontinuing the interview. If the interview is discontinued, the employee should be advised that any decision relating to employment will be based on the information available to the company without his cooperation. However, the interrogator and the company should be aware that there may be some potential liability with this tactic, because an employee may file suit for negligent discharge, alleging that the company incompletely conducted its investigation.

Federal Statutes

Under certain circumstances, other federal statutes will come into play concerning the interviewing or interrogation of the public or private employees. Some of the provisions of the National Labor Relations Act, Title VII of the Civil Rights Act of 1964, or other discrimination laws may be applicable.

For example, the National Labor Relations Act prohibits an employer from questioning an employee about his union affiliation or sympathies, organizing efforts, bargaining, or other union-connected activities. In addition, an employer, either public or private, cannot single out for interviews or interrogation a protected group under Title VII without risking a claim of discrimination. This is not to say that an employer cannot question a group of employees who are all of the same age, race, or sex regarding wrongdoing, but merely to point out the potential allegation that could later be raised.

In addition, the public and private employer may face a violation of federal or state statutes should they fail to fully investigate and discover the wrongdoing of an employee. The activities that the employer failed to uncover may have violated the Occupational Safety and Health Act (OSHA), which requires the employer to provide a safe environment for work. Finally, the public or private employer might violate the Fair Labor Standards Act if the employee is not paid for the time spent in the interview.

Unions/Weingarten Rights

The United States Supreme Court, in reviewing *NLRB v. Weingarten Inc.*,[36] has given employees the right of union representation during certain interviews. *Weingarten* concerned a union retail employee who was suspected of dishonesty. The employee was interviewed and, during the course of the interview, requested that her union steward be present. The interviewer denied this request, and, following the interview, the employee filed an unfair labor practices charge with the National Labor Relations Board (NLRB). The NLRB found that the employer had, in fact, violated the contract. On appeal, the United States Supreme Court agreed with this finding.

The *Weingarten* rule is applicable only if the employee *requests* representation and only if the employee reasonably believes that the interview could result in disciplinary action against him. The employee representative can act as an observer and advise the employee regarding his rights under the collective bargaining agreement but cannot act as an investigator. The union employee can waive the right of union representation during any interview. Generally, the offer of union representation does not have to be made to an employee prior to the interview, unless it is required by company policy or the collective bargaining agreement.

At one time, the NLRB had ruled that the *Weingarten* rule was also applicable to nonunion employees. It later reversed itself and then, in the summer of 2000, did another about-face to make the decision applicable to all employees again. The position of the NLRB left many questions unanswered, such as who could act as a witness. While the union's collective agreement clearly sets forth the procedures and support system for the accused employee in a union environment, the NLRB made no such guidelines for the employer to follow in its current ruling. It is likely that issues will be addressed on this and other topics in the coming years. Because the NLRB has fluctuated on its position relating to *Weingarten*, the company's

---

[36] *NLRB v. J. Weingarten, Inc.*, 420 U.S. 251, 43 L Ed 2d171, 95 S CT 959 (1975)

corporate counsel, Human Resources Department, and investigators should monitor any changes in the NLRB's position.

State Law

Most states have constitutional provisions that follow the U.S. Constitution. In many cases, the restrictions imposed by the state constitutions will be similar to those imposed by the U.S. Constitution. Interviewers should familiarize themselves with any specific state laws or regulations relating to the interview and interrogation process.

Common Law

The following are common-law causes of action of which employers or interviewers must be aware before conducting any interviews. Even though the employee has common-law rights, the public or private employer has the right to investigate and to expect loyalty from the employee.

False Imprisonment

This cause of action generally requires that an employee be detained without his consent or a legal justification for restraint. False imprisonment is a detention where no arrest warrant has been issued, or, if one has been issued, it is void. For employees to prove a case of false imprisonment, they must prove the following: first, an arrest or forcible detention took place; second, the arrest or imprisonment was caused by the company; third, the detention was unlawful or made without a warrant; and fourth, there was malice on the part of the company.

An employer is entitled to interview an employee on its premises about violations of company policy without liability for false imprisonment, as in *Faniel v. Chesapeake & Potomac Telephone Company*[37] and *Lansburgh's Inc. v. Ruffin.*[38] Although an employee may have a fear of losing his employment through an interview, and though it might seem coercive, the situation will not make an employee's submission to an interview become involuntary.[37] In viewing whether false imprisonment has occurred, the courts look to the length of the interview and the manner in which it was conducted.

In a number of cases where false imprisonment was found to have occurred, the employee was physically restrained from leaving. In other cases,

---

[37] *Faniel v. Chesapeake & Potomac Telephone Compnay*, 404 A2d174 (DCAppl979)
[38] *Lansburgh's Inc. v. Ruffin*, 372 A2d561 (DCAppl977)
[37] *Faniel v. Chesapeake & Potomac Telephone Compnay*, 404 A2d174 (DCAppl979)

the interrogator yelled, beat on the desk, or made threats that the suspect would be sent to the penitentiary or would never be let out of the room.

The company may be further insulated from a claim of false imprisonment by not having the employee arrested immediately. Instead, company investigators present the evidence to prosecutors, who later make a decision to pursue criminal actions, having an arrest warrant issued after review.

Defamation

The allegation of defamation of character is the common allegation made by a suspect regarding an incident of misconduct. Defamation of character may occur in the form of a slander or libelous statement. Slander is a false statement that was not written but was spoken to one or more individuals. Libel is an untrue statement that was written and was communicated to others.

For employees to establish that they have suffered defamation of character, they must first prove that particular words were actually spoken, including proving both the time and place that the activity took place. Second, employees must also prove that these words were spoken or published to third persons. The third proof that employees must show is that the words written or spoken were actually false. Finally, employees must also show other facts that prove that the words were libelous or slanderous. This would include that there was malice on the part of the company or investigator and that the libel or slander was not privileged in any way.

For an allegation of defamation of character, the truth is always a complete defense regardless of the motives of the person saying it. A comment made by an investigator or company is fair when it is based on facts that have been truly stated and is free of motives, either real or imagined, by the employees. There is also a defense against defamation of character if the company can establish that it had a qualified privilege to communicate the information to third parties. An employer has a qualified privilege to communicate allegations during an investigation. However, this qualified privilege is lost if false communications were made out of spite or malice with knowledge that the statements were, in fact, false. In addition, these knowingly false statements must have been communicated to an excessive number of people. The interviewer, during the course of investigative interviews, should avoid repeating to third parties any information or allegations of which he is uncertain. As a practical matter, the interview process is one of gathering rather than giving information to the interviewee.

An investigator should limit communicating allegations to those who have a need to know as part of the investigation or decision-making process relating to the consequences of the suspect's actions. An investigator can establish the qualified privilege by noting on investigative reports that the document is privileged for counsel. This establishes an attorney-client privilege and protects many documents during an investigation. However, allowing attorney-client privilege is a complex issue and should be discussed with the corporate legal counsel. Certain work product documents may be protected, as well as others not depending on the actions of the team.

The interviewer should understand that a qualified privilege exists to express oral charges to superiors, police, prosecutors, or other persons having a need to know within the company. Care should be taken that the report of what happened during the investigation, interview, or interrogation is fair and that statements made are fairly reported and done without malice to the suspect.

Malicious Prosecution

Companies investigating employee theft, illegal drug use, or other illegal activities within a company must decide whether it is in their best interest to contact a law enforcement agency. A number of factors may come into play relating to the decision to contact a law enforcement agency, including an assessment of the investigative abilities of the company, a decision on whether a prosecution is desired, and any legal requirement to make a report with a public law enforcement agency. Certain businesses, such as financial institutions, are required to report thefts to the FBI. Illegal activities such as the theft of firearms or controlled substances are also closely monitored by federal and state agencies. Since most companies do not have a requirement to notify public law enforcement of problems within their company, they generally do not do so because of the cost of prosecution and the difficulty of proving circumstantial cases. A corporation's bonding company may also need to be made aware of loss to keep the insurance contract in force.

Once the company has decided to prosecute an employee, it can be opening the door to potential liability for an allegation of malicious prosecution and false arrest. Malicious prosecution involves the use of a legal authority, such as the police or prosecutor's office, to have a person arrested and brought to trial. For an employee to establish a malicious prosecution claim against the company, the employee must prove that (1) the employer instituted or continued a criminal proceeding; (2) the proceeding was terminated in the employee's favor; (3) no probable cause existed for initiating a proceeding; and (4) the employer's motive in initiating the proceeding was malice or purpose other than to bring the employee to justice.[39]

By the action of simply informing a prosecutor or law enforcement agency of the facts of the case and leaving the decision to prosecute to them, a company reduces potential liability. An exception to this would be if the company or its agents knowingly provide false information or attempt to influence the prosecution of the employee. Thus, if the company obtains a legally authorized arrest warrant for an employee, it cannot be held liable for the arrest by police unless it misused the legal process.[40] If the employee is found guilty, the company has a complete defense against liability for a malicious prosecution; however, any termination of criminal proceedings in the favor of the employee can create a potential for liability. Liability can also be created if the company files a complaint against the employee and later withdraws it. This action on the part of the company, without a waiver from the suspect, establishes one of the elements necessary for a malicious prosecution claim. A commonly contested issue is whether probable cause for a criminal proceeding existed when it was initiated by the employer. Probable cause is a reasonable belief in the guilt of the employee. Probable cause is determined by evaluating the information available to the company at the time a complaint was made.

Private sector investigators can limit their own and the company's potential liability for a malicious prosecution allegation by allowing the prosecutor or police officer to make the decision to prosecute. The fourth element in a malicious prosecution claim is malice, which can be differentiated from an employer's having probable cause. Malice on the part of the company or an employer may be shown through personal animosity between the person making the accusation and the accused employee. It can also be inferred from the lack of a complete investigation on the part of the company. Furthermore, the company may show the element of malice if it conveys facts that are untrue or withholds facts that might mitigate the conclusion reached by police investigators or prosecutor.

Assault and Battery

Although assault and battery are related, they are fundamentally different. Battery is bodily contact that either causes harm or is offensive to a reasonable person's sense of dignity;[40] assault is words or actions that place the employee in fear of receiving a battery. Actual physical contact is not an element of assault, but violence, either threatened or offered, is required. An assault can occur when the person uses threatening words or gestures and has the ability to commit the battery.[40]

---

[39] Prosser 8 Keeton on Torts (1977)
[40] Prosser 8 Keeton on Torts (Fifth Edition 1984)

Intentional Infliction of Emotional Distress

In this tort, the company or its agents must deliberately and outrageously conduct activities toward a person that would inflict emotional harm. The elements incorporated in this claim are

1. Outrageous conduct by the defendant
2. Intent to cause emotional injury to the employee
3. The occurrence in fact of emotional injury to the employee

This conduct on the part of the employer or its agents must be outrageous and extreme. This would include any activity that would not generally have been tolerated by society. It also must have been meant to cause severe emotional distress to the suspect. This action against the employer is also often combined with alleging a wrongful termination. However, the termination of an employee's employment is not outside the reasonable bounds of conduct and this alone does not result in an intentional infliction of emotional distress.

The employee alleging intentional infliction of emotional distress must also prove that he suffered from severe emotional distress. This must be shown in some way other than simply by his own testimony. In addition, the employee must prove malice. In many investigations, an employer may make accusations based on reasonable suspicion. Once an employer is able to show reasonable suspicion, the burden of proof to prove malice or disregard of the employee's rights shifts to the employee.[41]

Courts frequently have rejected these suits based on the fact that simply firing an employee is not extreme and outrageous conduct beyond what would normally be found in society. However, when the courts or juries have found that employees were abusively treated, the damages awarded have been considerable.

Use of the Polygraph (Lie Detector)

Significant restrictions have been placed on the use of the polygraph, also commonly referred to as a lie detector. The United States Congress passed the Employee Polygraph Protection Act in the late 1980s, which largely prohibits requiring or requesting employees or job applicants to take a polygraph test. Investigators in the private sector should also avoid asking if an employee would be willing to take a polygraph examination during the behavioral

[40] *Prosser 8 Keeton on Torts (Fifth Edition* 1984)
[41] *Aerosmith v. Williams*, 174 GA. p. 690, 331 S.E.2d30,33 (1986)

interview, as this might violate the act. In addition, there are significant prohibitions regarding discharging or disciplining employees or prospective employees for refusing to take a test or for exercising their right not to take a polygraph examination under the rights afforded under the act.

Prior to the Employee Polygraph Protection Act, numerous states and some cities had instituted legislation relating to polygraph testing or the licensing of polygraph examiners. Legislation varies significantly from state to state in both licensing of examiners and the rights afforded the employee or prospective employee. Many states also prohibit police departments from testing the victims of a crime, when the subject is a victim of the sexual assault.

A number of exemptions in the Employee Polygraph Protection Act, as well as state laws, are applicable. In general, federal, state, and local governments are not affected by the law. The law also does not apply to polygraph examinations administered by the federal government to private individuals engaged in national security-related activities. The law permits polygraph testing to be administered in the private sector subject to certain restrictions. These restrictions provide that the employer must set forth the circumstances and reasons an employee is suspected of involvement in a workplace incident that resulted in an "economic loss" to the employer. These reasons must be provided in writing to the employee ,along with the questions to be used in the examination, 48 hours prior to any scheduled polygraph examination. The employee has the right to refuse to submit to a polygraph examination or to discontinue a test being conducted. The law also restricts the disclosure of test results to unauthorized persons and prohibits employment decisions based on the polygraph results alone.

The Employee Polygraph Protection Act permits using polygraph examinations with certain job classifications in the private sector. Some employers are permitted to use pre-employment polygraph testing as part of their selection process. These private-sector employers are restricted to armored car companies, nuclear facilities, certain alarm and guard companies, and pharmaceutical manufacturers, distributors, and dispensers.

Enforcement of the Employee Polygraph Protection Act falls under the auspices of the U.S. Department of Labor, which can assess civil penalties up to $10,000 against violators. Employees or job applicants who have their rights under the Act violated may also bring their own court actions to obtain a remedy for damages, in addition to any fines assessed by the U.S. Department of Labor.

Private-sector investigators, prior to using the polygraph as part of an ongoing investigation, should ascertain any specific federal, state, or local prohibitions against its use. The investigator should also determine that the polygraph examiner has the necessary educational and training qualifications to administer the test. These qualifications might include completion of a certified testing program, state licensing, insurance, and membership in a state association or membership in the American Polygraph Association. The polygraph can be an effective tool in eliminating suspects from an investigation or focusing the investigation toward a specific person; however it must be used judiciously.

Sexual Harassment

Federal statutes forbid the harassment of employees because of their protected group status: race, color, national origin, religion, disability, age, or gender. The most common form of harassment is based on gender: sexual harassment. Sexual harassment takes two common forms:

1. **Quid pro quo** — involves an explicit or implicit demand that the employee provide sexual favors to obtain or retain a tangible job benefit. This might be getting a raise, obtaining a new position, or getting hired. This type of sexual harassment can be committed only by someone in a position of power over the individual being harassed.
2. **Hostile environment** — refers to when the sexual harassment does not affect tangible job benefits but affects the individual's performance by creating a hostile, offensive, or intimidating work environment. This type of sexual harassment can be created by co-workers, supervisors, customers, or vendors.

The unwelcome conduct can fall into one of three categories: (1) unwelcome sexual advances; (2) sexually demeaning conduct toward individuals because of their gender (i.e., hazing or gender baiting); and (3) a sexually charged workplace even if the individual is not the target of the conduct. This type of conduct might be sexual favoritism or the display of suggestive photos or cartoons or a variety of other activities.

The law is a fluid process that depends on precedents. No textbook can remain current with all the legislative and court rulings; rather, the purpose of this chapter gives a sense of the court's direction in deciding cases. Interviewers must constantly review changes in the law that might affect approaches and strategies currently in use. Each state has its own statutes that determine which investigative and interrogation tactics are permissible. When working outside the United States, investigators must carefully explore the legal aspects of the country in which they are working. Failure to do so might subject the investigators and their organization to civil or criminal actions.

Memory and False Confessions

4

Truth is an elusive companion.

In any human encounter, the truth is an elusive companion. Even when the situation is most favorable, the interviewer has to contend with differences in perceptions, personal needs, and biases. Witnesses have grudges, faulty memories, and preconceptions, all of which alter their perception of the facts.

What is a fact really? In many instances, it is merely an observation that is subject to the individual's rationalization or personal interpretation based on a desire for a particular outcome. This is further complicated by the listener's interpretation of the individual's word choice and nonverbal nuances.

For example, a buyer purchasing records and tapes admits receiving money from a vendor. This is a fact; however, the buyer describes the money as a loan made to purchase property. This description, while accurate, conveniently ignores the rest of the kickback scheme, which allowed the buyer to launder this loan and convert it to cash for his own uses. In this instance, the fact, receiving money from the vendor was conveniently renamed by describing it as a loan rather than a kickback, to minimize its seriousness.

This reframing of the situation allows an individual to minimize its seriousness while relieving the anxiety he feels internally. This lie of omission allows a subject to "toss a bone" to the interrogator in hope of ending the conversation without making a full admission. Lawyers call this "creating an argument." Take a given set of facts, rename them, and re-emphasize or reorder them to create a plausible explanation to support the attorney's "argument" or theory. Statistics provide another convenient way of twisting perceptions to support a particular point of view. Politicians of all persuasions use the same set of facts, and, by presenting them in ways favorable to themselves, create the illusion of a positive position on an issue.

False Confessions

False confessions are completely different.

"I killed her," the suspect stated. He said this even though he had no involvement in the crime. Or, "I committed about eight burglaries." The suspect said this when, in fact, he had really been involved in a different number of burglaries. Both are false confessions in their own way.

One is completely false because the individual had absolutely no participation in the crime, while the other person's confession either exaggerated or minimized his involvement. In one case, a young woman confessed to stealing about $40,000 worth of company merchandise. She related that she arrived at that figure "by her memory." Did she actually steal merchandise from the company? Undoubtedly she had, based on the evidence. However, did she really steal $40,000 or is she involved in stealing a lesser amount? Her lawyer would have people believe that this was a totally false confession, but in reality it is much more likely that she is a thief, but not of $40,000. Unfortunately, investigators have and will continue to wrestle with development of admission problems whenever there is a long pattern of criminal activity. How many times and how often can be difficult for a subject to reconstruct. Confessed murderer Henry Lee Lucas claimed to be involved in hundreds of murders across the country. Is he a murderer? There is no question about it, but he voluntarily confessed to murders that he did not commit. Whether we can give any credence to his reasons for confessing remains to be seen, but the fact is, he repeatedly confessed to murders he did not commit.

While any admission that is either exaggerated or minimized by the suspect is disconcerting to everyone involved, it is the totally false confession that stretches people's belief system. What must be going through people's minds to confess to a crime of which they are completely innocent?

Example

Consider the Phoenix Temple murder case, which occurred just outside Phoenix, AZ. This is one of the more bizarre examples of false confessions to occur, if for no other reason than the severity of the crime. Nine Buddhists were savagely murdered at a temple. The victims, six monks, a nun, and two others were killed execution style. The case created international attention because of the religious aspect of the crime and the number of victims killed. Any investigator can imagine the public and political pressure to solve such a case.

The case languished until the police received a phone call from an individual in a psychiatric hospital in Tucson, AZ. Unfortunately for police, the individual was not an employee, but a patient at the facility. The patient confessed to the nine murders and implicated in the crime five other people he knew from the Tucson area. The patient was making a "voluntary false confession," but also implicating other innocent people. These types of voluntary false confessions are often encountered in high-profile cases. Police departments usually hold back evidence to test the confessions against the evidence, thus eliminating those people who falsely confess. The sheriff's department apparently accepted the confession even though the patient knew virtually nothing about the circumstances surrounding the crime.

While the patient was predisposed to make a voluntary false confession, what happened to the five others named as being involved in the murders? Police interrogated the five and obtained confessions to the Temple murders from three of them — three false confessions, as it turned out.

Within weeks of claims that the case was solved, the real murderers, two young boys from the local Air Force base, were arrested. The murder weapon, items from the murder scene, and their confession conclusively proved that the young boys had participated in the murder.

So what about the one voluntary false confession and three obviously false coerced confessions? One is certainly understandable since the individual was a resident in a psychiatric facility. The other three had to have been the result of inappropriate interrogation techniques or threats, which resulted in coerced false confessions.

Certainly, in the preceding case, there can be little doubt that the confessions obtained were false. This chapter discusses the characteristics common to people willing to make a false confession and the circumstances surrounding false confessions. By understanding the types of people and characteristics common to individuals making false confessions, interrogators might avoid making the mistakes found in the Phoenix Temple case. The false confessions in that case appear to be the result of fundamental errors in interrogation of the suspects and a failure to test the subjects' confessions against the crime scene and investigation.

How often do false confessions actually occur? This question is beyond the scope of this book and the abilities of current researchers. Some critics suggest that false confessions occur frequently, but they lack a scientific basis for these assumptions. Most people have difficulty understanding the reasons that a person would make a false confession, but the real danger to society lies in the false supposition that confessions are frequently unreliable and coerced. This is clearly untrue. Crimes are committed by individuals who are able to rationalize their actions or see no other options available to themselves at the time they choose to commit the crime. These people are then placed in a position of self-protection, where they willingly and convincingly lie to protect their freedom and self-image.

In our experience, using proper interview, interrogation, and investigative efforts, false confessions are relatively rare. However, any time an individual has a marginal personality or is subjected to physical torture, threats of violence, threats against loved ones, lack of food, water, or toilet, or is interrogated for an extended period of time, there exists the possibility of a false confession.

Types of False Confessions

Recognizing that false confessions do exist is the first step in protecting against obtaining one. In any discussion of false confessions, it is important to understand the different types and the circumstances surrounding them when they occur.

Definition

Creating a definition of what constitutes a false confession is helpful in understanding them. For the purposes of this discussion, we define a false confession in two ways. The most obvious false confession is when the suspect is totally innocent of the crime or incident to which they admit. The second form of false confession, and probably the more common variety, is when the individual over- or understates his or her involvement in the crime or incident or refuses to reveal the true motivation behind the crime.

Ofshe (1989) more simply defines a false confession:

"A confession is considered False if it is elicited in response to a demand for a confession and is either intentionally fabricated or is not based on actual knowledge of the facts that formed its content."[1]

In light of the previous definitions, consider the following portion of a transcript of a murder suspect's interrogation, published in the *Washington Post.*

Shelton: "Did she tell you to tie her hands behind her back?"

---

[1] Ofshe, R. (1989). Coerced confessions: the logic of seemingly irrational action. *Cultic Studies J.,6,* p. 13.

Vasquez: "Ah, if she did, I did."

Carrig: "Whatcha use?"

Vasquez: "The ropes?"

Carrig: "No, not the ropes. Whatcha use?"

Vasquez: "Only my belt."

Carrig: "No, not your belt ... Remember ... Cutting the Venetian blind cords?"

Vasquez: "Ah, it's the same as rope."

Carrig: "Yeah."

Later in the transcript the detectives asked Vasquez to talk about the actual murder:

Shelton: "Okay, now tell us how it went, David — tell us how you did it."

Vasquez: "She told me to grab the knife, and, and, stab her, that's all."

Carrig: (raising his voice) "David, no, David."

Vasquez: "If it did happen, and I did it, and my fingerprints were on it..."

Carrig: (slamming his hand on the table and yelling) "You hung her!"

Vasquez: "What?"

Carrig: (shouting,) "You hung her!"

Vasquez: "Okay, so I hung her."

Based on the suspect's verbal responses in the transcript and the fact that the detectives spoon-fed Vasquez with crime scene information, this confession is clearly suspect. Vasquez later pled guilty to second-degree murder and burglary. Five years later, police found the real murderer and Vasquez was pardoned.

An interrogation, like an investigation, is a search for the truth; a confession is not the ultimate aim. Obtaining a false confession creates two wrongs. First, an innocent individual suffers unnecessarily, and second, the guilty go free.

We also need to consider the difference between a false confession and one that is retracted by the subject at some later point. Almost every confession is disputed in a suppression hearing prior to trial or at a subsequent administrative hearing. The lawyer for the defendant alleges that the statement was coerced and is therefore false or involuntarily given. The fact that the confession is disputed or was retracted does not necessarily mean that the statement was false or coerced. Unless the confession was recorded, it is difficult to determine the circumstances surrounding the giving of the confession. The mere fact that a confession is retracted does not necessarily mean that it is untrue. Many individuals faced with the reality of punishment will retract their confession in an attempt to avoid jail, termination of employment, or embarrassment. This creates a profound difficulty for the justice system in that both an innocent person who gave a false confession and a guilty individual may retract confessions. It seems reasonable that a confession alone without supporting or corroborating evidence should be insufficient to convict an individual.

Kassin and Wrightsman[2] offer three types of false confessions. They call these voluntary, coerced compliant, and coerced internalized.[2]

Voluntary False Confessions

A voluntary false confession occurs when a subject admits to an act without any external pressure from an outside source such as the police or loss prevention. Kassin and Wrightsman offer three plausible reasons that an individual might make a voluntary false confession. The first reason they offer is a "morbid desire for notoriety"(p. 76). One has only to look at high-profile crimes to see this occur. Police departments recognizing this phenomenon commonly hold back information from the public about certain aspects of the crime so that a voluntary false confession can be identified. The individual attempting to make a voluntary false confession lacks those specific details of the incident that were withheld from the public, helping the police identify this type of individual.

The second reason offered is a person's "unconscious need to expiate guilt over previous transgressions via self-punishment" (p. 77). The guilt to which Kassin and Wrightsman refer could be related to a real incident or one that is imagined. It is the need for self-punishment that causes these individuals to come forward and admit to a crime they did not commit.

The third reason people make voluntary false confessions is an inability to tell fact from fantasy. This type of thinking is usually associated with major psychiatric illnesses, such as schizophrenia. With these types of mental illness, the individual is unable to tell the difference between things that really happened and those only imagined.

There may also be another plausible reason for a voluntary false confession: to protect someone else. Where peer pressure or social relationship is especially strong, it is not unheard of for an individual to accept blame and the punishment for something he did not do to protect another.

---

[2] Kassin, S.M. and Wrightsman, L.S. (1985). Confession evidence. In *The Psychology of Evidence and Trial Procedure* (Eds. S.M. Kassin and LS. Wrightsman). Sage: London, 67–94.

Coerced Compliant False Confessions

Kassin and Wrightsman[2] identify coerced compliant false confessions as resulting from the subject's obtaining some immediate gain. The primary gain obtained by the subject in this type of false confession could be to escape from a difficult social situation. The individual confesses in exchange for being allowed to go home after the interview, thus avoiding being detained in jail, or he may simply confess as a way of getting out of a difficult situation. The subject views the immediate situation as more important and may confess to obtain release while minimizing in his mind the long-term effect that the confession may have on the case.

These types of confessions are generally retracted as soon as the immediate pressure of the situation has been relieved. Upon leaving the stressful situation, the subject immediately retracts the admission, often in the first contact with a relative, friend, or lawyer.

Coerced Internalized False Confessions

The third type of false confession might occur when individuals come to believe that they, in fact, did commit the crime of which they are accused. This type of confession may occur even when the subject has no memory of participating in the event. An example is someone who has large memory gaps because of drug or alcohol use. Because the person has no independent recollection of the event, he relies on the real or fictitious evidence presented by the interrogator and comes to the conclusion he must have been involved in the incident. This conclusion then becomes a surrogate memory of the incident absorbing the details from those provided by the interrogator into the fabric of a personal memory. Most of us have met people who have had too much to drink and the next day do not remember or only partially remember the previous evening. They then rely on others who were at the party to fill in the details of the evening, thus creating memory of events that may not have happened the way in which they were related.

Another form of the coerced internalized false confession is when individuals do not initially believe they were involved in the incident but over time come to distrust their memory of the event. This form of false confession is generally the result of interrogation tactics that create self-doubt about the reliability of the suspect's own memory. This self-doubt might be easily accomplished in individuals with a history of drug- or alcohol-induced amnesia when the interrogator refers to past instances of which they have no recollections.

Individuals giving an internalized false confession might not retract it for a significant period of time, because they actually believe that they have committed the crime. It is only later, when they become convinced from other sources that they did not commit the crime, that they will make a retraction.

Ofshe[1] suggests some tactics that he believes might increase the likelihood of a coerced internalized false confession:

- The interrogator repeatedly and confidently expresses belief in the subject's guilt.
- The interrogation is lengthy and emotional.
- The interrogator claims incontrovertible scientific proof of the subject's guilt.
- The interrogator reminds the subject of his blackouts and memory problems.
- The interrogator creates fear within the subject about the consequences of continued denials.

It is overly simplistic to believe that the mere use of some of these tactics guarantees a false confession. Quite the contrary — it is much more common that these tactics help the guilty accept that their guilt is known and their continued denials will be fruitless and unconvincing.

Some common characteristics are often associated with verified false confessions. When these characteristics are present, the interrogator must be especially careful to test the resulting confession against the investigation and recovered evidence. Use of a factual interrogation might hamper the interrogator's ability to test the confession against case facts — facts were revealed to the suspect and, when repeated by the suspect, make a plausible-sounding confession to the crime.

Factors Contributing to False Confessions

A number of characteristics often accompany subjects who give false confessions. The mere presence of these factors, however, does not mean that the subject is incapable of giving a reliable confession. These factors should cause the prudent interrogator to watch for clues that the confession is not real. Certainly, holding back evidence that could be known only to the perpetrator is one excellent method of assuring the reliability of the confession. This strategy has been practiced for years by investigators to establish the reliability of a suspect's confession. Experienced interrogators recognize that suspects, for reasons sometimes known only to them, refuse to acknowledge some of the evidence or some aspect of the crime — the suspect acknowledges the burglary but denies defecating on the floor of the bedroom, or he acknowledges the murder but not the rape of the victim. In situations like this, even withholding from the subject evidence located at the crime scene will not necessarily confirm the reliability of the confession if the suspect refuses to discuss or admit that point.

Age of the Subject

The age of the subject is often an issue in false confessions. The relative youth of a child indicates a lack of experience in social encounters and conflict resolution. For this reason, many states have enacted special legislation to protect the rights of a youthful offender. These rights might include the presence of a juvenile officer or parents during the interview, contacting parents prior to an interview, or recording the encounter.

Children are not simply miniature adults who have the same thought processes and emotions as an adult. Children will often answer questions that they do not understand or answer a question without knowing they are mistaken. The child in a confrontation with an adult is certainly more susceptible to the environmental control and status of an adult. When questioned in unfamiliar surroundings and with no adult support system at hand, children will often try to please the adult who is questioning them.

Children are adept at reading moods and body language to determine the adult's preferred answer to a question. Another problem when dealing with children is their suggestibility, which is strongly related to their compliant behavior. Answers that are suggested through the adults' questioning can influence the response from the child. The child's response to the adult's question repeated in a number of different settings can become a memory that the child actually comes to believe. As a result, the child may appear to be truthful, credible, and reliable because, for him, it is a story he has come to believe strongly.

If one considers the accusations made by children in some of the better-known day-care sexual abuse cases, there seems to be a natural evolution of the stories. The initial statements made by the children are relatively simple, but as questioning continues, the alleged sexual activity and surrounding adult behavior in the stories becomes more bizarre and horrific. Many of these cases began with claims of inappropriate touching and after numerous finished interviews, adds stories of satanic rituals, group sex, and murder. Well-meaning interviewers who believe the physical abuse is real often influence these resulting stories through their questions and attitude. The adult who believes the child's story will, often unwittingly, question the child in a way that shapes and molds statements about abuse. The leading questions posed by the adult encourage a particular response from the child, who is predisposed to please the adult. The bias of the interviewer when dealing with the child can influence what information is obtained and what is recorded:

Interviewer: Isn't it true that he put his hand in your underpants?

Child: Yeah.

Interviewer: How many times did he put his hand there? More than 3?

Child: Yeah.

Interviewer: More than three times?

Child: Yeah.

Children are especially susceptible to adult influence during questioning because they perceive pressure to perform to the adult's expectation. Children who do not give the answer preferred by the adult may be subjected to a withdrawal of the adult's pleasure and to verbal chastisement. The interviewer must constantly be aware of the unique position of power that he holds. An adult interviewer has the ability to dominate the child both physically and psychologically. In every interview with a child, the child learns what is expected and what is positively reinforced from his interviewer adult.

Actual situations faced by a child witness cannot be reproduced in any laboratory study. For example, in a typical laboratory study, children are presented the misleading information once and maybe given two or three leading questions or misleading information, while, in real-life interviews, there may be multiple interviewers and interviews that take place over a considerable span of time. Add to this, counseling sessions, parents, family, and prosecutors, and there is a tremendous amount of influence on the child and his memory. Underwager and Wakefield's[3] research suggests that leading questions and other types of error-inducing questions will occur from one-half to four-fifths of the time in the typical interview of a child witness.

If this research is even close to representing the amount of false information potentially being obtained from child interviews, it should have a sobering effect on even the most experienced interviewer. When one considers the number of adults interviewing a child during a sexual abuse allegation, it becomes even more frightening that the possibility of false information is being generated. Much of children's play, especially in the early years, involves their imagination and pretending. In fact, it is generally accepted that children consistently have some difficulty telling the difference between fantasy and reality until they are about 11 years old, although some research suggests that

---

[3] Underwager, Ralph, Wakefield, Hollida (1990). *The Real World of Child Interrogations*. Springfield, Illinois: Charles C. Thomas. 29.

children over 6 years old are similar to adults in their ability to discriminate between imagined and experienced events.[4] When fantasy elements appear, they are often the result of improper questioning, such as asking the child to pretend, or the use of props during the interview. Many of a child's language skills do not even come close to matching an adult's until the child enters the early teens, and even then it is not until the late teens that a child's language fully matches that of an adult.

When a child is asked to pretend or imagine during an interview, there might be significant confusion between reality and the created fantasy. Part of this confusion might be the interviewer's, because he has introduced imagination to the interview, and the child might confuse this with reality. Because it is difficult for adults to remember this time in their lives, they interpret the child's responses as reality even though this is not what the child is doing.

Children might provide an accurate account of an event that they experienced, but these accounts may be briefer than those of an older child or an adult.[5] The major difficulty with the younger child is the brevity and lack of detail in the retelling of the event. When there is a repetitive event, children, like adults, tend to blur the distinction between specific incidents and instead bring forth a collective memory of them. This is often seen in the private sector when the adult suspect is attempting to recount a series of thefts of cash or merchandise when there was no unique aspect to any of the thefts. Children may also be somewhat brief in recounting the event because their life experiences are relatively limited.

Consider the following portions of a transcript of an actual interview[3] with a child, Danny age 5, in light of the difficulty a child has between distinguishing reality from fantasy. Also, think about this example in terms of the questioning style used by the detective. Can you anticipate what the child will say?

Detective: Let me talk to you about what happened Friday, Friday morning when you went to...

Danny: I don't ... I don't remember.

Detective: Okay, let's pretend then. Did you have a dream the other night about Friday? You were telling your daddy about a dream, yeah? Okay. In your dream, what happened? Can you tell me?

Danny: I can't remember.

Detective: Okay, well, let me ask you this. In your dream you were here at school, and you were with your friend, yeah? Did you go to the

---

[4] Johnson and Foley, 1984; Lindsay and Johnson, 1987; Roberts and Blades, 1995.
[5] Foley, 1984; Oates and Shrimpton, 1991.

bathroom and see a man inside the bathroom? In your dream now. Yeah? Okay, can you answer? This ... I ... See, this only records talk. When you do this, when you do this the recorder doesn't pick up. So, yes, you saw a man in the bathroom ...

Danny: Uh huh (yes).

Detective: In your dream ... Uh Uh. Okay, that may put this right over here. What was the man doing in the bathroom?

Danny: I don't know.

Detective: Where was he when you saw him?

Danny: I don't know.

Detective: Okay, but he was inside the bathroom, yeah? And you went to use the bathroom, and you got scared, yeah. And you walked from the bathroom and who did you see when you walked from the bathroom?

Danny: I don't know.

Detective: In your dream now. Pretending in your dream. Okay? Didn't you see Chrissy Miller and Dawn O?

Danny: Dawn O'Malley!

Detective: Right. Dawn O'Malley. And Chrissy Miller. You seen them ...? Tell me about the man, Chrissy Miller, and Dawn O'Malley and you.

Danny: They went with the man.

Detective: They went with the man. Yeah?

Danny: I don't remember them going in the car!

Detective: But he had a car, yeah? Was it a new or an old car?

The detective makes an assumption that there was a vehicle present even in light of the denial of one by the child. This then introduces information into Danny's story from the bias of the investigator's point of view.

Danny: I think an old car.

Detective: Do you remember what color it was?

Danny: Yellow.

Detective: It was yellow, the same color as your hair? It was kinda color of your hair? Your hair is blond.?

Danny: (laughs) My hair isn't yellow. It's blond.

Detective: Real blond. Was it almost the color of your hair?

Danny: Yes.

Detective: It was. And where did you sit in the car? In the front seat or in the back seat?

Danny: Back seat.

Detective: In the back seat. And who was in the back seat with you?

The detective in this case is making the assumption that someone was in the back seat with Danny. Based on this question is it more or less likely that Danny will acknowledge someone was in the back seat with him?

Danny: I don't know!

Detective: Both girls? Were both girls in the back seat with you?

Danny: Dawn O'Malley.

Detective: Only Donna O'Malley? And Chrissy Miller, she was in the front seat?

Danny: She was in the front of the back of the back.

Detective: Okay, and how many men were in the car?

Danny: One.

Detective: Only one man?

Danny: Yeah.

Detective: You sure it wasn't two men?

Danny: Yeah.

Detective: It was two men inside the car.

Danny: No! One!

Detective: Only one man and where did the man take you? Is it close around here where the man took you?

Danny: I think it would have been.

Later in the interview the detective returns to using a pretend approach with Danny. He uses the pretend approach whenever Danny becomes reluctant to talk about the sexual aspects of the incident.

Detective: Did the man or the woman touch your penis to Chrissy Miller or Dawn O'Malley's vagina?

Danny: No!

Detective: Only pretend now, we're only pretending, okay? Now, if we were to pretend, did they make you do that? Pretend. They did? Can you answer yes or no for the tape?

Danny: Yes.

Detective: Okay! Did, pretend now, did the man or the woman, the man or the woman make you do anything else you didn't want to do?

Danny: Uh Uh. (no).

Detective: They only made you touch the two girls with your penis on their vagina, that's all they made you do, and the man was taking pictures when you did that. Okay. I, Danny, can you speak inside this, the man was ...

Danny: Yes.

Detective: Okay, now let's see how really smart you are. And I think you're really smart. Do you cameras? Do you know much about cameras? Do you know cameras take pictures?

Danny: Yes.

Detective: The camera in our pretend, was a big camera or a little camera?[6]

Danny: Big.

This transcript clearly indicates the suggestibility of a child in answering and incorporating information from the adult's questions and investigative bias. When we consider that there may be multiple interviews over time, it is no wonder that there are distortions and changes in memory of the child.

The Dent[7] study observing the interrogation of children found that the belief or bias of the interrogator about the truth of the allegation was predictive of the outcome of the interview. The interviewer's bias and questions used during interview helped frame the responses of the child. Essentially, children figured out what pleased the adult based on his or her interpretation of the adult's body language, questions, tone, and voice inflections.

When adults interview a young child, they must recognize that children might answer any question that is asked even if they do not know the answer. The suggestibility of children may be due in part to the large number of people who have authority over them, and that children need to get along with these people. When an interviewer attempts to clarify information with a question that includes information for the child to agree with or deny, the resulting response might simply be a fabrication that both are willing to believe.

Example

---

[6] Underwager, Ralph, Wakefield, Hollida (1990). *The Real World of Child Interrogations.* Springfield, Illinois: Charles C. Thomas. 198–206.

[7] Dent, H.R. (1982). The effects of interviewing strategies on the result of interviews with child witnesses. In A. T. Trankell (Ed.), *Reconstructing the Past.* Deventer, The Netherlands: Kluwer, 279–298.

A 12-year-old Chicago girl was murdered and raped. She was last seen riding her bike in the area where her body was found. Suspicion focused on two young boys, ages 7 and 8. They had also been in the area during the time the young girl was riding her bike.

During questioning with five detectives, both boys admitted to the crime. Autopsy results indicated that the girl had been raped and semen had been ejaculated into her vagina. According to doctors, it is anatomically impossible for boys of this age to produce semen. Subsequent investigation identified an adult male as a DNA match to the semen found at the crime scene. When confronted with the results of the investigation, the adult male acknowledged sexual activity with the girl, but denied the murder.

The false confessions of these two boys to a rape and homicide underscore the sensitive nature of questioning young children. This case was pivotal in the Illinois legislature's decision to introduce legistlation to provide additional protections for juveniles during interviews and interrogations.

Memory and Intelligence

Poor memory is another common characteristic found in subjects offering a false confession. In adults, it is generally related to drug or alcohol abuse or below-average intelligence. In many instances, because of drug usage or binge drinking, significant gaps exist in the abuser's memory. Because they have no independent recollection of the events during the time period in question, they accept the fact that they might be involved in the incident because of "evidence" to which the interrogator refers and the interrogator's level of confidence in their guilt. If the interrogator offers facts relating to how the subject committed the crime, the subject then only has to repeat the interrogator's statements, which present a plausible, yet false, confession. This situation certainly is one of the pitfalls of presenting evidence early in an interrogation in an attempt to convince the suspect that his guilt is known.

Suspects with below-average intelligence also present difficulties for the interviewer. These individuals, because of their lower intelligence, might not adequately communicate or understand questions that they are asked. In many instances, they might fail to understand the abstract meaning of certain terms, which may add to their confusion. Some individuals with lower intelligence attempt to mask this confusion by displaying greater confidence in their answers than they actually possess. Mentally handicapped individuals (this term will be used to differentiate from an individual with mental illness) often are successful in concealing their incompetence in this way.

Two common methods used by the mentally handicapped to survive in a world that they do not often understand is smiling and compliance. Many people who are mentally handicapped use smiling as a means to gain acceptance from those people whose help they need. In an effort to survive in society, the mentally handicapped also become extremely compliant, especially with authority figures. Their compliance has been reinforced because over the years they have been repeatedly told that they are wrong and have been redirected in the correct method of accomplishing the task. Another fundamental component of the mentally handicapped is a quickness to accept blame. This quick acceptance is probably the result of being told repeatedly they have done things incorrectly and their belief that someone must be blamed for an error. Still others may accept blame for something they did not do in order to make their interrogators like them.

Memory problems are also present in the mentally handicapped individual and are, in fact, one of the characteristics looked for when diagnosing brain damage. Children of normal intelligence are consistently accurate in memories, but inconsistent in what they recall. Young children often rely on the adult's questions to guide their recall of an event. Memories recalled by the mentally handicapped individual can be shaped in the same way depending on the questions asked and the behavior of the interviewer. Another difficulty often encountered with both the mentally handicapped and younger children is the lack of a sense of time and its passage. Because of the abstract nature of time, it is only as children grow older that they understand time and the related relationship of events.

Many mentally handicapped people and children listen carefully and even copy the person with whom they are speaking to get the "correct" answer. The use of leading questions can clearly shape such an individual's responses and lead the conversation toward the interviewer's bias. The interview then becomes a self-fulfilling prophecy when the interviewer leads the subject to the interrogator's foregone conclusion. The mentally handicapped often will simply take the last choice presented them. The same can be observed in individuals diagnosed with Alzheimer's disease. The lack of short-term memory in the Alzheimer's victim makes it easier to pick the last thing said than to admit they have no recall of the event or even the earlier part of the conversation. Many people can conceal this memory problem with smiles and jokes at first until even the most basic conversation is beyond their ability.

Failure to Understand Abstract Thought

Much of human communication is done in an abstract framework built from years of interactions with others. It is only by understanding the nuances that full communication can take place. With lesser intelligence comes a lack of grasping the full scope of the meaning of the language, and, perhaps, the underlying message. There will be an understanding of the literal meaning of the word, but not the abstract meaning of the conversation. Often the mentally handicapped will miss the sarcasm in a conversation while focusing on the literal meaning of the words.

Are you in school?

No, I am here with you.

Children, as well as the mentally handicapped, can be extremely literal in their interpretation of the language. They may also miss multiple meanings of words, "right" as in right hand, or right, such as that given by the constitution. Or they may be incapable of understanding the process and potential problems facing them. This confusion could certainly play a large role in whether the subject waived his right to remain silent. When this confusion is considered with the bluffing that is necessary for them to exist in everyday life, it would not be unusual for a child or mentally handicapped person to not question the meaning of some word or concept not understood. This lack of understanding could certainly contribute to poor decision-making by the subject.

Behavioral Differences

Another characteristic found with people making false confessions is the differences in behavior from the general population. These differences in speech and mannerisms can often lead to misinterpretation by the interviewer. There may be a general lack of impulse control and short attention span. Children will often jump from one thing to another in both their play and conversation, as will the mentally handicapped. Speech patterns may be different because of a lack of muscle control or speech problems that have gone uncorrected. There may also be differences in gait or movements because of muscle problems or simple latent development of the body that causes them to move in an ungainly fashion.

Sometimes lacking a response to the question or situation causes these types of individuals to take an inappropriate body position, such as defiance, when challenged with a question they do not understand. They may also provide undecipherable and confused responses to questions from an authority figure. Still others might mimic the behavior and language style of people they have encountered previously, adopting their street language and behaviors to appear confident in an unusual situation. Any of these responses might trigger suspicion in the interviewer because of their apparent differences from the "normal" population.

Suggestibility and Compliance

To this point, the discussion has centered on the intelligence and memory issues relating to false confessions in children and the mentally handicapped. The next germane issue is the level of suggestibility and compliance of the average individual. While authors and researchers differ on the definition of these terms, we will use the following for the purposes of this discussion.

A definition is provided by Gudjonsson and Clark,[8] who define suggestibility during an interrogation as

> ... The extent to which, within a closed social interaction, people come to accept messages communicated during formal questioning, as the result of which their subsequent behavioral response is affected. (p. 84)

This definition closely approximates the interactions occurring during an interview or interrogation. The subject and interviewer are generally alone with minimal interruptions. The subject of an interview, or a suspect, during an interrogation agrees to cooperate and ultimately makes a confession, even though his initial instinct was to not cooperate or confess. We should note that being suggestible does not necessarily mean that the suspect or subject is giving a false confession or statement. It simply means that, based on the interaction with the interviewer, the subject came to the conclusion that a particular behavioral response — cooperation — was in his best interest.

The suggestibility of particular individuals depends on the strategies that they employ when coping in an uncertain situation. The uncertainty of suspects means that they do not know the correct answer to the question. Their level of suggestibility can also be influenced by the amount of trust subjects have in the interviewer. Whenever suspects or subjects are suspicious of the questioner, they are less likely to accept suggestions from the interviewer, and there will be a resulting increase in resistance to the interviewer. Experienced interrogators recognize that suspicious ex-convicts are generally more difficult to interrogate because they distrust the interrogator.

Compliance differs from suggestibility in that compliance means the individual behaves as others wish him to behave without necessarily believing in what he is doing. However, with suggestibility, the subject actually incorporates the interviewer's biases or information into his memory. Compliant individuals generally avoid conflict or confrontation with people and have a desire to please others, and may, in certain circumstances, relent even when they know that they are not involved.

---

[8] Gudjonsson, G.H. and Clark, N.K. (1986). Suggestibility in police interrogation: a social psychological model. *Soc. Behav.*, 1, 83–104.

Language of the False Confession

Interviewers and interrogators should listen carefully to the language of a subject giving information or making a confession. The language of a false confession is laced with uncertainty and wrong information. False confessions often sound as though they are being created on the spot by the subject. Words such as "might have," "I guess," "Well, I probably would have done…" and other similar phrases may offer a clue that the statement is false. Unfortunately, these same types of words may also be used by a guilty subject who is attempting to minimize his involvement in a crime.

The danger that attorneys will attempt to find a psychiatrist to testify in support of a false confession even when the testimony lacks foundation or credibility already exists. After the O. J. Simpson case, it became fashionable for lawyers to attack the police and the"rush to judgment" in identifying a suspect. There is no question that certain cases cry out for the confession to be questioned, but attempting to suggest that confessions in general are false is just as much of an injustice to the victims of the crime. The interview and the interrogation is a search for the truth and the goal of the process is not just to get a confession.

Certain people are more likely to give false confessions or information than others. Interviewers and interrogators should make themselves aware of the potential pitfalls in dealing with these types of people. Certainly holding back evidence from the subject is one method of testing the resulting statements or admissions.

Moreover, just because a subject is highly suggestible and compliant does not necessarily mean that he or she is giving a false confession. The highly suggestible individual can be guilty and give a reliable confession. Interrogators recognize that the more experienced the criminals, the more suspicious they generally are of their interviewer, resulting in elevated resistance to giving a confession.

The danger lies with the highly suggestible individual who has a poor memory and is of low intelligence. These types of individuals are generally more suggestible because they are not assertive, have low self esteem, and an overall high level of anxiety when dealing with social situations. In many instances, these individuals use conflict avoidance as a coping strategy, which ultimately results in an increase of suggestibility (i.e. following an interviewer's suggestions to reduce their level of anxiety in the situation).

The following is an edited transcript of an interview conducted with Christopher Ochoa, who was released from prison after falsely confessing to a murder in Austin, Texas in 1988. Ochoa moved to Austin from El Paso, where he grew up with his family. At the time of the murder, Christopher was sharing an apartment with his roommate, Richard Danziger. Both men were in their early 20s and worked at Pizza Hut, Ochoa as an assistant manager and Danziger as a pizza maker.

The victim, Nancy DePriest, was a 20-year-old mother working as a manager at another Pizza Hut location. DePriest was opening her store for business on October 24, 1988 when she was raped and murdered sometime between 8:30 and 9:30 AM.

Richard Danziger and Christopher Ochoa came to the attention of police after they visited the store and asked questions about the crime. Two days after their visit to DePriest's store, the interrogation of Ochoa began. After two days of constant interrogation, investigators took statements from Ochoa, who implicated himself and Danziger in the murder. Richard Danziger never confessed to the crime but was convicted after a trial.

Almost 12 years after he pled guilty to murder to avoid the death penalty, Ochoa was released from prison. The case was reinvestigated by the Texas Rangers and prosecutors along with students from the University of Wisconsin Law School Project Innocence Program. The case was reopened after another imprisoned inmate, Achim Marino, wrote authorities confessing that he had committed the murder and rape. However, it was not until the Project Innocence Program reexamined the evidence that the investigation was reopened. Further investigation revealed that Achim Marino's DNA matched that recovered from the crime scene and his gun was tested and found to be the murder weapon. In statements to investigators, Marino confirmed that he acted alone and that both Danziger and Ochoa were innocent.

Transcript of Interview with Christopher Ochoa
University of Wisconsin Law School
Madison, Wisconsin
March 3, 2001

Dave: The restaurant where Nancy actually worked was …

Chris: (Pizza Hut) on _____ Street (Austin, TX)

Dave   Had you ever had an opportunity to meet her before?

Chris: I'd seen her at management meetings, but I never talked to her.

Dave: So she would have been a manager?

Chris: Yeah, she was a manager.

Dave: And, the relationship then between you and she was you basically worked at the same company…

Chris: There was no relationship at all.

Dave: So it was just at a manager's meeting …

Chris: Yeah, I'd seen her once or twice.

Dave: When did you first hear about the incident where she had been murdered?

Chris: It was on the news. They didn't mention any names, but later on that night they mentioned it.

Dave: So they identified at least the location.

Chris: Yeah, that same night.

Dave: Now, had there been any communication from anybody at Pizza Hut about the incident in terms of what had actually happened, the details surrounding it, anything like that?

Chris: Hmm, there was rumors going around, but I really don't know, don't recall.

Dave: OK, so nobody came and said "Here's exactly what happened."

Chris: Oh, no.

Dave: When were you then first contacted by the police?

Chris: I believe it was the … it might have been the 9th. (November 9, 1988). Richard (Danziger) was driving me home, taking me home. He was driving his car and he wanted to stop by the Pizza Hut (where the murder had taken place) … it was after it all happened. And he was curious about going in there, and I didn't want to … I was tired, told him I want to go home. He insisted, plus he was driving, we went out there, over at, outside the car for a while, over at the parking lot, and I told him I don't want to go in, I was tired. He still insisted, so we went in and he wanted to order a beer and I didn't want to, it's against policy, it's how I am basically, I try to (garbled), but he insisted and I ended up, we did anyway, and he toasted to the memory of Nancy DePriest right in the restaurant. And then we went outside and he was asking questions, asking the security guard questions, and uh I guess that raised their suspicions or whatever. Because I think before, and I didn't know this, cause I read the transcripts, that the guy who murders may come back on these things, so when they saw that, they got suspicious so they called the cops. And a couple days later they come, one of the first officers, he came to the Pizza Hut, and he asked me if I minded coming down to the station and answering questions, and I said sure why not.

Dave: So …

Chris: I said sure, I asked him if I could take my car down there, and he said "You can take your car or we can drive you." He says "It's gonna be a couple of minutes or an hour, and we can drive you back." So I said "Sure I'll go down with you."

Dave: And what time is this about now?

Chris: 10:30, 11:00, I don't remember.

Dave: Evening or morning.

Chris: Morning. So I go down to the station, and I was so…I'd never been in custody, I don't know, I was straight basically. And he had mentioned questions about a burglary, and I know the difference between a burglary and a robbery, and I knew that this murder and whatever, and I assumed that they were asking questions, asking was this about the robbery. And he said "No, it's about another burglary," and I wrote it off at that, he puts me in this cubicle or office, whatever, and he asks me some questions about a burglary that happened at North _____, earlier in the month, couple of months earlier. About 10 minutes later, I think it was about 10 minutes, I'm not too sure about the time, he gets up and he comes back after a while and he said "Would you mind stepping into this room?" I follow him. It was, what I know now it was an interrogation, but I didn't know that at the time. Uh, he starts asking me questions then, sits down and said "Why were you asking about the robbery?" I said "I was just curious." and he said "I see you're upset, so you must know something about it. Nobody's just curious." I said "No, I'm just wondering." He said "No you must know something about it." I say "No I don't." he said "Are you sure nobody asked you, nobody told you, you didn't hear anybody talking about it?" and so forth, and he walks out. In comes another detective, a Hispanic detective. He walks in and looks at me, and I guess he was pretty friendly at first, but he came in and he introduced himself, "I'm Sergeant B_____." He said in Spanish, "They call me the bogeyman on the streets," that's what it translates to. I don't know maybe, he may have said before that "Do you know who I am?"

But I do remember those words in Spanish …"They call me the bogeyman." He starts asking questions and I tell him "I don't know what you're talking about." He said "Well, nobody's just curious, somebody must have told you." This went on over a period of hours, this interrogation, and at one point he would leave and another detective came into the room, playing the good cop role. He said "Look, this guy's ready to charge you" with stuff like that, I don't know exactly, but Sergeant B_____ he comes back in and says "You know, I just looked at your record, I know you have a clean record. You're not the type of person that would do this crime, so if you know something about it, let us know, 'cause if you do know something about it and you don't say anything, we could charge you." I said "How can you charge me?" He said "It doesn't matter, we can charge you." I tell him I don't know. So this goes on through a period of hours and he's yelling and screaming, all this time pounding his fist on the table and getting in my face and yelling. And this guy's a pretty big guy and all this going on, I'd never been in this situation. And this is a heinous crime.

So he leaves, and at one point this Hispanic detective comes in, female, and I ask her if I could get an attorney, and she said, "Not until you're officially charged." And I didn't know at the time if she was right or not. And she leaves, he comes back again. He talks to me, yelling at me. He said, "Look, if somebody told you, just give us a statement and you'll go home." I think it was 6 or 7 hours I'd been there. "If somebody told you, get it over with." I tell him "I don't know what you're talking about." He starts yelling and screaming, he leaves, they go outside, they come back. He said, "You know the DA is ready to charge." When he comes in and he shows me a picture of death row, a cell. He tells me "This is where you'll live the rest of your life." Kind of shook me up a little bit, but I still tell him "I don't know what you're talking about." And he leaves, and he comes back says at one of these points the DA's outside ready to charge me with capital murder. He said' "You talk to me right now, you tell me who it was, somebody told you." He leaves, he comes back and he brings a picture of the autopsy of the victim where the bullet wound was. He said, "Don't you feel sorry for her, don't you want to help her?" I said "I do, but I don't know what you're talking about." He left and then at one point he told me that my co-defendant (roommate Richard Danziger) was in the next room ready to talk, ready to implicate me. I said "I don't know what you're talking about." Of course, that was a lie too (garbled). But he came and at one point he said, "You know the white guy (Danziger was white) always gets the deal and the Hispanic always gets the rap. I don't want you to take the rap. Why don't you just talk now?"

So he comes back and he yells at me, coming in and out, saying the same thing, the DA's ready to charge me. At one point he comes in and he's hollering and screaming and he says, "Look, I'm getting sick and tired of your BS," not his exact words, but to the effect. He said "Look, I'm gonna charge you, I'm gonna put you in a jail cell," where he said something to the effect of "You'll be fresh meat, you've never been in trouble before."

And to me this shook me up a little bit 'cause I thought, they gonna rape me, they gonna put me in a cell. And he leaves and at this point I'm tired, been there a long time.

Dave: How long had you been there by this point?

Chris: Oh, God, I must have been in there about 12 hours, 11, 10$^{1}/_{2}$. At this point, I say ..."You know who talked to me"... I told them about a black man that I heard, they never even wrote that statement down. I was just saying whatever they wanted, whatever, just to go home. Then they asked me about Nancy (victim) and then they tell me about her, you know about, and I didn't know at the time that I was even a suspect, and I was at all times a suspect. Anyway, he tells me, "Do you think Danziger was involved?" He starts taking a statement and then that's when he wanted me to implicate Danziger, and I didn't say in those words. I would say something, Danziger said he did it? did he come home? did he tell you this? and I would just agree with it and he would type it.

Dave: Now how long had you been with them at this point?

Chris: Oh, it was about 10 and a half hours.

Dave: OK, so this is at the latter part?

Chris: The latter part, yeah. And so that's how we ...I don't know, I don't recall, it's kind of difficult for me to recall everything, but that's how he would ask his questions, asked "Did he do this, did he do this?" Sometimes he'd give me two or three (choices) and whenever I would guess it right then he would type it. They did read me my rights right before the statement; that was way into the interrogation.

So when I did that, they told me to sign the statement and I signed it. And then they asked me if I would give a semen sample and blood sample, they said to make sure you weren't part of it. And I said sure, I would be more than happy to. And we did that and I thought I was gonna go home at that point, and I said, "Can I go home?" He said, "No we're going to put you up at a Holiday Inn 'cause we think Danziger might get to you." And I was OK. At this point I don't know if I'm free to go or not, but I know they told me to stay in the Holiday Inn, don't call anybody. So the whole time I'm at the Holiday Inn, I'm new to all this thing, I didn't know that I could have left, but I stayed there 'cause I trust cops, I trust the officers, I was brought up to trust police officers.

Dave: How else did you know about what had happened at the crime scene?

Chris: He would ask me "Did this happen, did that happen, was it this color of a certain item, wasn't this here, that's how he ...."

Dave: OK, so that's how that statement was taken.

Chris: Yeah, he was just giving me leading questions like this.

Dave: And what would happen if you said the incorrect thing?

Chris: Well, you know, Monday, they took two statements, one on tape. He wanted me to be an accomplice, and he went through it all and then once he was satisfied, then I just repeated what we had done on tape. Then he wasn't satisfied with that. If I wasn't answering the way I was supposed to, he would stop the tape and start it and then there was a lot of stopping 'cause I was stuttering a lot, and it started and stop and started and stopped. At that point, one of the officers got very frustrated, he threw the chair at me, he threw it at my head and it hit the wall, just missed my head, and this guy's a pretty big guy, I mean these guys are big, I was really small at the time.

He caught it right before it fell to my head and that's when the Sergeant said, "Well, here let's just type it and we'll help you out." And that's exactly how, and he typed it and I have never to this day read the statements. I signed it, he brought witnesses to sign it, and I was terrified, when he threw the chair. I thought these guys were gonna hurt me bad. But this was terrifying for me, he was giving me a choice, death or...

Dave: So basically, at this point, had you implicated Richard?

Chris: Yeah, he made sure I implicated Richard.

Dave: What did you tell him that Richard had done?

Chris: He wanted me ... He asked "Did Richard pull the trigger?" Richard did this, and he would type it. Richard told you he did this and he did that, whatever, and at this point I just wanted to get it over with. He kept on saying "We'll give you, you'll do your time and go home 'cause if you don't, you're gonna get the death penalty. You'll die for something you didn't do. Do you want to die for something you didn't do? I don't want you to die for something you didn't do," stuff like that.

Dave: So if you were gonna describe the change of emotions that you had, let's start with Friday. You first come in, what are you feeling at that point?

Chris: Well, kind of like why, not that concerned, then it gets interrogational, but then when they brought up the murder, and when Sergeant B started getting in my face, my heart went (gestures).

Here's this woman that died a horrible death, my worst nightmare come true. I didn't know what could happen, my emotions were so, it's very hard to describe, very difficult. (garbled) When he threatened to put me in a cell, it terrified me. (garbled) I had never been in that situation before. I had always trusted officers. (garbled)

Dave: Did he tell you that he had evidence?

Chris: I don't recall if he did or not. All he was concerned was for me to tell him what he wanted, and hey I just wanted to go home. I was very tired. All I thought was let me go home, I want to go home. Looking back on it, that was the most exhausting day of my whole life.

Dave: I think probably the biggest question that everybody has, that they don't understand, is why would you say that you were involved if you weren't.

Chris: I used to talk to a lot of convicts in prison and some went over to Vietnam and they were very gung ho and what they were going to do when they got into combat. Some of these same guys talking about I'm gonna do this in this situation. As soon as the bullets start firing they wouldn't fight and they run.

          That's very easy to say I wouldn't do this in a situation, but when you get into the situation it's a whole different ballgame. The man is threatening my life; I know that he's trying to murder me, so the natural instinct is to survive sometimes. Everybody has to survive. It's like somebody putting a revolver — to your head, you don't know, you just say whatever the hell comes into your mind. How would I know, I've never been in that situation, I don't know that he doesn't have the power to charge me, so what do I do? And that's the best way I can explain it.

Dave: Did you think to ask for a lawyer?

Chris: I did, I asked that lady, I asked for an attorney and she said, "No, not until you're charged." Struck me as kind of strange. Matter of fact, I wasn't even there that long before I asked for an attorney.

Dave: Now when you say that he's yelling and screaming at you, from a seated position?

Chris: No, he'd get up and get in my face.

Dave: Talk again briefly about the pictures he showed you. He showed you autopsy pictures and then pictures of death row? What's the autopsy photo, what impact did that have?

Chris: Shocked, can't explain the emotion. The one that impacted me was the one of the death row cell.

Dave: So what's your emotion then?

Chris: Scared out of my mind, terrified, what the hell is going on, terrified, and when they told me I couldn't have an attorney, I thought what the hell's going on. Very difficult to put into words, but sometimes I see him in the night. I don't know if I'll ever get over it. Maybe I didn't go to Vietnam, but maybe that's my Vietnam.

Dave: Now I want to go back to the tape, the making of the statements again. This is now Monday; you've spent the weekend at the Holiday Inn.

Dave: So then you come back in on Monday, and how is Monday different from Friday?

Chris: That I have two officers in the room. Whereas Friday just one, I have two, and whereas Friday one officer was what I know now was the good cop, whereas Monday he gets upset and throws a chair. Now I feel I've got two of them coming at me, not only that guy but this guy.

Dave: So the one that was the good cop…

Chris: Yeah, now he throws a chair at me.

Dave: So he's changed roles.

Chris: Now I've got two of them that could hurt me in there, so that was how it changed.

Dave: But did they ever physically do anything to you?

Chris: They threw the chair at me.

Dave: So there wasn't any physical abuse, striking you …

Chris: No, it was more mental.

Dave: And then they moved you when they were ready to take the statement?

Chris: Oh, no they took it right in that same room.

Dave: So did they bring a typewriter in?

Chris: Yeah, they brought a typewriter in.

Dave: How did they take this statement again, was it a question and answer kind of a thing, or did it wind up being a narrative statement?

Chris: They would ask me questions, "Was this object this color?" and I would say no, but I was trying to take a stab and I'd say it was this color, and he'd say, "No, it was this color." Or could it have been this color, and I'd say yeah. That's how through the whole statement we went through. It was actually his statement, not mine.

Dave: So then when that statement is finished, they witness it at that point?

Chris: Yes, they brought the witnesses afterwards.

Dave: Who are they, do you know?

Chris: Just some people.

Dave: At that point, do they read the statement out loud to you, do you read the statement?

Chris: No, I know I didn't read it.

Dave: So then the next thing that happens is an audio or an audiovisual statement. Is there a camera as well or just a tape recorded statement?

Chris: No, the tape recorded statement was before. But that was just when he wanted me to say he had went through the statement. He now wants me to take part in the crime, so now he's asking me questions on tape and I don't know what the hell he's talking about, I don't know no details, so he gets up and he starts and stops and gets frustrated and throws the chair. That's why with the tape they don't even use it, they go to the typewriter.

Dave: So that was the same thing that was happening on the audio tape as well.

Chris: On the audio tape, yeah I was stuttering, it was start, stop, start, stop. When I would reply and they didn't like the story, they would stop it and reverse it and start it again.

Dave: There never was a video tape, just an audio tape.

Chris: Just an audio tape.

Dave: Is that still in existence?

Chris: I don't think so, they destroyed it.

Dave: So your participation in this is not as the killer then.

Chris: No, as the rapist. Later on, right, I think they took me to meet the DA, months later, to take a polygraph. Then the DA says "I want you to be a trigger man."

Dave: So now you've gone from being a lookout to being inside to months later to being the trigger man.

Chris: Yes.

Dave: How does that happen? Do you have a sense of how that occurred?

Chris: No.

Dave: Are you represented at this point by counsel?

Chris: At that point I was, but the guy wasn't much.

Dave: Was he a public defender or did you retain him?

Chris: He was appointed by the court, court-appointed attorney. When he first saw me, I told him I am innocent, but I told him what the cops did to me, and he said "No they couldn't have given you all these details." I told him I'm innocent and he suggests I plead guilty. He said "Even though you're innocent, this is a high publicity case." He comes and sees me and then he starts calling my mom and telling her I'm going to die. She gets nervous and she gets sick. Her blood pressure shot up. My grandma wasn't supposed to tell me, but I found out about it, and I can't put my mom through this, I can't, can't do that to my mom, even though I'm not doing it to her, she can't go through it. I didn't see my attorney much after that.

Dave: So essentially when you went and saw the district attorney a couple of months it was essentially to plead guilty?

Chris: To plead guilty I'd say essentially.

Dave: You're totally aware as I understand it that the statement that you've given up to this point is false, right. It's not like you're deluded at this point that you believe you actually did it.

Chris: No, I'm totally aware that I didn't do anything, it was a false statement. And I told my attorney and my family as much. My family believed me. An uncle said this sergeant has a reputation (garbled).

Dave: So basically you're at the point where your mom's health is deteriorating as a result of this, and you just decide to avoid the death penalty you'll plead guilty.

Chris: Yeah.

Dave: What was the end result that you pleaded to?

Chris: First degree murder.

Dave: What about the rape?

Chris: Rape, they said I had to testify against Richard, so basically he was charged and convicted of rape.

Dave: So in your original statement then you told them that Richard had done the rape?

Chris: They told me that that's what they wanted.

Dave: And then you repeated that?

Chris: Yeah.

Dave: What happens with Richard?

Chris: He gets convicted.

Dave: Does he confess to this as well?

Chris: No he doesn't. He pleaded innocent.

Dave: So you've never seen him since, talked to him?

Chris: No, that's something for the attorneys to deal with. I forgot, I did see him in jail. He attacked me.

Dave: I suspect he was probably upset.

Chris: Yeah, I don't blame the guy.

Dave: In terms of, other than physically getting in your face, yelling, screaming, you said they never really presented evidence to you that you were guilty. So at no point here are we talking about you not knowing that you're innocent. You knew all along that you were innocent, so it's not like all of a sudden you become convinced that "I might have done it, I just don't remember at this point."

Chris: No.

Dave: How long between breaks, where they would let you have a cup of coffee or a coke or something?

Chris: That first day there was no breaks at all. When I was interrogated on Monday, there was no breaks. They would bring me a Coke, but there was no break. They would come in and out, yeah.

Dave: So what were they doing while they were with you?

Chris: Yelling and screaming.

Dave: Do you have a sense of how he decided that you were the murderer and Richard was the rapist? How does that happen?

Chris: No, I don't know what the DA said, if they wanted me to take the murder. All I know is that the DA said that's the only way you're gonna get out of the death penalty.

Dave: Now up to this point you'd had no contact with the police at all?

Chris: No, you know tickets for underage drinking but never in custody.

Dave: So, no juvenile problems, never had any real experience with anything other than tickets essentially.

Chris: No, I was basically a good kid, a real good kid, I wanted to make my parents proud, played baseball, sports, did everything that an American boy is supposed to do, normal kid.

Dave: So you're kind of essentially caught off guard with the initial conversations, surprised?

Chris: Yeah, never had that kind of experience before. I was taught officers would never do you wrong, they'd protect and serve.

Having sat with Christopher Ochoa at length, the interviewer saw several things that were readily apparent:

1. He was unlike most convicts, who display a zealot-like devotion to the case that caused their incarceration. Repeatedly, he was unable to recall details or exact dates. He seemed as though he was simply being pushed through the process, rather than struggling against it.
2. Christopher seemed not to have spent the time or effort to review transcripts even though he was wrongly convicted. Many of his responses were that we would have to ask his attorney.
3. Christopher, even after all that he had been through, displayed very little overt anger regarding the situation or his interrogators.
4. Christopher did display emotions, tearing up at various points when talking about the interrogation and interrogators. However, it was a quiet emotional display that might have been the result of having talked about the ordeal over a number of weeks.
5. During our interview, he was soft spoken and difficult to hear.

Christopher's confession was a coerced complaint form of false confession. His soft-spoken nonaggressive nature had difficulty coping with the aggressive actions of his accusers. Having never been in contact with the police he was outside his experience when he was threatened with the death penalty if he did not confess. Faced with the length of the confrontation he eventually gave the interrogators the answers that they wanted. The interrogators fed Christopher the details of the crime because he could have had no other way of knowing them.

Interestingly, Richard Danziger does not confess to the crime. We have no way at this time of knowing the circumstances surrounding his interrogation but can imagine it would have been similar in nature. Assuming similar tactics were used, the primary difference between him and Christopher would have been their personalities. Reportedly, Richard is more savvy and worldly, which could account for his being able to hold up under the pressure of an interrogation. Christopher, on the other hand, is a quiet, soft-spoken, trusting individual. At his young age and with limited experience with the police, he was in a situation he neither understood nor had experienced before.

If there is anyone to blame here it seems that the interrogators failed to search for the truth and instead created two injustices. First, two innocent men went to prison and, second, the real killer walked free. Interrogators have a responsibility to society to work for the truth.

Interpretation of Verbal and Physical Behavior

5

All behavior is meaningful; it is only the true meaning that may not be evident to the observer.

The seasoned investigator often refers to "gut feelings" when identifying a suspect. "I've got a feeling that it's him" and "I know in my gut that it's him" are phrases used often by investigators. The investigators have identified behavioral characteristics or investigative similarities that allow them to make an often accurate determination that a particular individual is responsible for an incident. The discussion of behavior symptoms and of detecting lies from a suspect's words, actions, and attitude is the next step in the professional interviewer's pattern of growth.

The purpose of this chapter is to take the seasoned interviewer from the level of the gut feeling to the next level of being able to articulate the behavioral clues that lead him to believe that the suspect or witness is truthful or untruthful. By being able to articulate the behavioral clues and their meaning, an interviewer can begin to use other investigators in a more systematic way. By being able to recreate an interview with a suspect both verbally and physically, the investigator can elicit opinions from other similarly trained interviewers. The ability of interrogators working as a group to recognize deception allows for the input of others into the interview.

In discussing behavior, it is important that the interviewer recognize that behavior symptoms do not occur by chance. All behavior is meaningful; it is only the true meaning that may not be evident to the observer. Each time a victim, witness, or suspect manifests a particular behavior, it is caused by something, has a reason, or has an objective. In many cases, victims, witnesses, or suspects are not even aware that they are reacting and providing the interviewer with behavioral clues.

This discussion considers two styles of behavior:

- **Verbal:** Verbal behavior encompasses the words that are actually spoken, the choice of words used, tense of the language, tone of voice, and speed of delivery.
- **Nonverbal:** Nonverbal behavior consists of facial expressions, body positioning, posture, and movements used to express the words that were chosen. In some cases, movements or gestures (emblems) take the place of words.

Studies vary in the percentage of communication that takes place in each one of these channels. However, the dominant communication channel between individuals is the nonverbal channel, accounting for 55% to 65% of the communication between individuals. Between 30% and 40% of communication is done using the tone of voice. Less than 10% of communication between people actually is the result of the words that are spoken.

Simply listening to an everyday conversation should quickly convince anyone that the above percentages are true. The pauses, movements of the hand, and shifts of the body at certain points in a conversation tell a story that adds depth and fullness to the words that were spoken.

Common Terms

The following are some commonly used terms that are necessary to understand prior to a discussion of the meaning of behavior.

- **Leakage** occurs when the true feelings or attitudes of an individual leak out through uncontrolled body language. In the deceptive individual, the behavior leaked may be contrary to the attitudes and words the individual is attempting to portray.
- **Emblems** are nonverbal gestures that can be directly translated into or substituted for words. The following are some common examples of emblems: shaking the head "no," nodding the head "yes," shrugging the shoulders with the hands turned up, index finger touching the thumb forming a sign for okay, palm extended out for stop.
- **Illustrators** are hand and arm movements that are used when speaking to illustrate or additionally describe what is being said by the individual. An example of this would be a movement that adds emphasis to the words that are spoften.
- **Congruence** means equal or the same — for example, truthful verbal behavior corresponding with truthful physical behavior. Verbal and physical behaviors are thus in congruence.

- **Incongruence** refers to words that do not match the nonverbal behavior. Truthful verbal behavior spoken in conjunction with untruthful nonverbal behavior is incongruent or not equal.

Several excellent texts are available to individuals who wish to acquire an indepth scientific view of verbal and nonverbal clues to deception: *Telling Lies* by Paul Ekman,[1] *Face Language* by Robert Whiteside,[2] and *Reading Faces* by Leopold Bellak and Sam Sinclair Baker.[3] Investigation into the study of deceit and how people lie is still in its earliest stages of evolution. Although people have been studying behavior for years, it has been only in the last ten years or so that it has received intense laboratory study. As the scientists search for scientifically acceptable parameters that will identify a lie, they are reviewing ground covered by interviewers over years of talking with suspects. Many of the research paths currently being explored hold promise for the future successful identification of lies or truth telling by suspects, victims, and witnesses. The difficulty of many of these paths is their application to the field investigator. It is extremely rare for an investigator to have the ability to measure or time facial movements or photograph expressions that last less than a quarter of a second to evaluate whether the subject is telling a lie or the truth. However, this research has only scratched the surface and may yet provide the field interviewer with methods as yet undreamed of.

The real difficulty lies in the fact that there is not a single behavior, verbal or physical, that accurately reflects whether an individual is being truthful or attempting to deceive. There is not even consistency within a single individual. Behavioral variations may be caused by the type of lie chosen, the time to prepare, the interviewer's strategy, past successes, or any of a number of other possible explanations.

The interviewer is faced with a complex situation. In an interview or interrogation, the interviewer must assess an abundance of information. In fact, the information received during the interview and interrogation is often so overwhelming that the interviewer cannot observe everything. The skilled interviewer realizes that there is no single behavioral clue that is always a reliable indicator of truth or deception in all people.

Each individual may have different behavioral norms and methods of lying. In most cases, the interviewer must assess behavioral clues over a very short interaction with the suspect or witness, making it difficult to know where to focus his attention.

---

[1] Berkley Books, New York, 1985.
[2] Fell, Hollywood, Florida, 1984.
[3] Holt, Rinehart, and Winston, New York, 1981.

Faking Behavior

Can individual in an interview successfully fake truthful behavior? The answer to this is generally that they cannot, because the suspect must pay attention to too many different signals, behaviors, and emotions. The timing of the behavior must also keep them congruent to the behavior a truthful person would utilize. Although individuals might be able to create certain behaviors that appear to be truthful, they are just as likely to allow a leakage of other behaviors that contradict the truthful behavior. Witnesses or suspects who are attempting to lie to an interviewer are generally more successful when the interviewer or interrogator is unobservant or wants to believe the story being told. It is also easier to fake behavior when the body can be hidden from the observer. The use of a desk, a wall, or an interview by telephone allows untruthful suspects to conceal all or significant parts of their bodies that may leak behaviors not congruent with their words. It is also more likely that an experienced liar, a professional actor, or politician will be more difficult to assess. These individuals consciously practice how they look when they talk and eliminate the gestures that do not help convince the listener of their truthfulness. It is generally easier to catch people who rarely lie than those who lie as a matter of course.

It is also difficult for the guilty to fake behavior successfully because the subconscious mind acts independently of the conscious mind. Because of this, the nonverbal behavior is often in stark contrast to the words that portray innocence.

Likelihood of Detecting Deception

Any number of factors can affect an interviewer's ability to detect deception.

Interviewer

The interviewer has the fundamental task of observing the subject looking for clues to the individual's true status. One distinct problem is whether the interviewers are able actually to observe behaviors that might lead them to a correct determination of the individual's truthfulness. There seems to be distinct differences in interviewers' abilities to identify correctly a subject's true status during research projects. The ability to recognize deception ranges from mere chance, 50 percent accuracy, to, in some cases, over 80% correct decisions about the individual's true status. So what are the differences among interviewers that cause this wide distribution of accuracy?

There has been significant discussion among academics about this very question, with no single answer seeming to be the final solution. There seem to be a number of reasons that untrained college students and trained law enforcement officers do not differ greatly in the research studies of recognition of deception. First is the construction of the studies, which are, by ethical constraints, limiting in the fear of detection a participant can feel when attempting to avoid detection during the study. The loss of several dollars or an extra credit grade hardly compares with the loss of one's reputation, termination of employment, or incarceration, thus the fear of detection is limited. Second is the inability of the interviewer to question the subject for extended periods or at all. When a deceiver has to conceal a deception for only a short period of time, and faces limited or no questioning, the interviewer is put at a severe disadvantage attempting to detect a lie. Another possible factor is not allowing the observer to establish a behavioral norm with the subject during the studies. It is well established that the better one knows the subject, the more likely he will leak incongruent behavior that will be picked up by the interviewer, allowing the detection of the attempted deception. A fourth factor limiting an investigator's ability to correctly identify truth or deception is not being able to force the subject from a lie of omission into a lie of fabrication, which puts considerable stress on the person's mental and physical abilities to conceal a deception. During a real investigation, evidence that allows the investigator to test the veracity of the subject's story against facts developed during the inquiry may be present.

While we have no hard data to dispute the research findings, anecdotal evidence suggests that the field interviewers' real accuracy may be higher than currently suggested by the research. However, it is intriguing that there are interviewers who have a "sense" that there is deception present in a story even with all the difficulties we have suggested. What is it that they are seeing, hearing, or feeling that allows the accuracy they have achieved? The current teaching of behavior to interviewers could be significantly enhanced by identifying those personality characteristics, that allow those interviewers to make a correct determination of the individual's status.

Finally, it is more difficult to deceive an individual who is suspicious than one who is unaware. There exists a danger here, the self-fulfilling prophecy. If an interviewer believes a subject is truthful, then he will interpret the subject's behavior as truthful. Conversely, interviewers biased against a subject may see corresponding deceptive behavior.

Environment

Another possible factor in determining the correct status of a subject might be the result of where the interview occurs. Conducting the interview at a location where the subject is comfortable may limit the autonomic nervous system arousal. Subjects can then mask their true emotions with another emotion to cover the behavioral changes. Certainly in field interviews, distractions can play a large role in distorting or concealing leaking deceptive behaviors. Passing traffic, noises, and other people combine to give plausible reasons for movements and breaking eye contact with an interviewer. However, it may be that the environment offers an interviewer a distinct advantage as well when the subject has an increased fear of detection resulting from concealed evidence or proximity to a crime. Traffic stops, where the subject must unexpectedly create a lie and worry that the interviewer might uncover concealed evidence, are a clear example of how environment can increase a fear of deception.

The Liar

The last point addresses the difficulty that a subject has when forced to create an extemporaneous lie. A planned interview in which subjects know that they are going to be interviewed about an incident allows them time to prepare a lie which, rightly or wrongly, permits them to believe that they can successfully conceal their deception. That initial belief in success reduces the fear of detection and makes the subject more comfortable in the interview. Only when the interview begins does the shallow lie begin to collapse and the fear of detection accelerate. Whether the liar will be able to carry off the lie depends on his memory, inventiveness, and practice. The more often someone lies, the less emotional weight there is when doing it. A problem with this strategy is that the individual who lies often has a tendency to do so even when it is unnecessary. Liars do this because it gives them a sense of power, but they do not realize that the unnecessary lie exposes them to detection. The less effective liar lacks a good memory and is not inventive when confronted with contradictions. These contradictions in the story increase the fear of detection and cloud the liar's rational thought process, increasing even more the likelihood of contradictory details.

The liar who can lie by omission is probably going to be significantly more effective than one who must create a story on the spur of the moment. A lie of omission is essentially the truth with the incriminating parts left out of the story.

Thus, the liar's success depends on a number of factors:

- Can the liar anticipate the need to lie?
- Can the liar use a lie of omission or must he create a fabrication?
- Is the liar inventive and does he have a good memory?
- Does the liar lie often?
- Is the liar an adept actor, capable of concealing emotions?
- Has the liar successfully lied to the interviewer before?
- Does the interviewer have a good behavioral norm for the liar?

The more factors a liar has in his favor, the less likely it is that the deception will be detected.

Rules for Evaluating Behavior

To successfully evaluate an individual's behavior, the interviewer uses guidelines that put the behavior in context.

Evaluate the Suspect Against Himself

The interviewer must recognize that verbal and nonverbal behavior are very individualized. Although generalizations can be made about behaviors that are more likely to be truthful or deceptive, each individual is, to a certain extent, unique when attempting to deceive. As people grow, they each have a unique environmental, financial, and parental situation that gives them a significant diversity of experiences. We may generalize and formulate hypotheses regarding typical behaviors that indicate deceptions, but they may not be true when read against the individual suspect himself.

The interviewer should attempt to identify a behavioral norm for the victim, witness, or suspect. This provides a baseline for individuals and corresponds to how they react in situations where they are not under stress. Observing individuals while gathering background information and during the rapport-building phase will give the interviewer an average behavior baseline that will serve as a reference point for comparison. This comparison will be made when the interviewer later discusses the incident under investigation. Does the witness or suspect significantly change when the incident is dismissed, and is the change consistent over time?

The interviewer should recognize that, in any situation that is unusual or potentially threatening, an individual's stress level may rise. Consider the reaction of most people when stopped for a traffic violation — the level of nervousness, quivering in the voice, etc., become apparent because of the stress of the situation. Simply being in this type of position causes an individual to undergo some behavioral changes. However, the observant investigator will recognize that, although people who are being interviewed or questioned may be nervous, this nervousness may have nothing whatsoever to do with deception. It may be simply their uncertainty because of the situation.

In assessing an individual's reaction to the interview, the observant interrogator knows that truthful suspects may be nervous at the beginning of the interview, but as soon as they sense there is nothing to fear, they become more relaxed. Untruthful suspects or witnesses recognize that they are in a dangerous position, and their fear of detection increases, thereby increasing the stress level that they are under during the interview. As a result, rather than becoming more comfortable as the interview proceeds, the untruthful individual tends to become more nervous or maintain the nervousness that shown at the beginning of the interview. This assumes that the interviewer has not expressed doubt in the subject's story. The greatest fear of a truthful person is the fear of being disbelieved. If truthful subjects perceive they are not being believed, that may well result in significant behavioral changes.

Evaluate the Suspect's Behavior Against that of the Population

In addition to evaluating the individual's behavioral norm, reading the suspect's behavior against the average of the population is often successful. In these situations, the interviewer assesses the normality of a behavior as it relates to the population as a whole. By this, we mean looking at what most people of that culture or race would do in a similar set of circumstances.

The interviewer commonly introduces himself and shakes hands with the witness or suspect. The interviewer should evaluate the handshake of the witness or suspect compared with all the other people to whom he has been introduced. Does the hand tremble as it is extended? Is the suspect reluctant to extend the hand? How does the hand feel? Is it warm and dry or cold and clammy? Although none of these particular responses means absolute deception, any could be the first indication for an interrogator that something outside the ordinary is happening with the suspect. Often, an individual will react in an unusual attitude toward the interviewer. Take, for example, the case of the homicide of a small child in a suburb of a major metropolitan area. The child was allegedly abducted from her home overnight while the parents were asleep. Shortly after the parents reported their child missing, she was found dead in a wooded area several miles from her home. As the investigation progressed, the parents were reluctant to cooperate with the police investigation of the homicide. This reluctance included refusing to give police access to the residence and child's room. In addition, did not want to talk with police investigators.

It is highly unlikely that any parent whose child was abducted would fail to cooperate totally in a police investigation into the incident. However, in this case, the parents refused to cooperate with the investigation, and the police ultimately had to obtain a search warrant for the residence. The parents obtained counsel and they refused to talk to police. The father was subsequently convicted of the homicide and is currently incarcerated in a state penitentiary.

Interviewers should ask themselves how they would react if their own child were abducted and killed. Certainly not as these parents did. In certain situations, however, this reluctance might not be at all unusual. If the parents had had numerous brushes with the law or had repeatedly been questioned about crimes in which they were not involved, they might legitimately be reluctant to talk with the police or cooperate in the investigation. When a parent who has had no previous brushes with the law acts differently from what most of us would consider normal behavior, the interviewer should suspect deception. The individual's own behavioral norm now should take precedence over the responses of the average population.

In another example, a woman's body concealed in some bushes was discovered by a man walking his dog. Responding officers determined that the woman had been murdered and probably raped. The crime scene was located behind a home at the far rear of the lot. Officers decided to interview the residents and went to the back door and knocked. The door was answered by a husband and wife who were told that a murder victim was concealed at the rear of the lot. Sitting in the family room a short distance from the back door was the couple's teenage son. The investigators noted that he showed no interest in the conversation or crime scene unfolding in the backyard. Instead, he busied himself watching television. After his confession to the rape and murder, his lack of interest became understandable because he was the one who had placed the body there.

Evaluate Behavior in the Context of the Situation

The behavioral clues presented by an individual can be read only in the context of the situation. For example, the eye contact of a young boy meeting older friends of his parents might be somewhat limited. This lack of eye contact is ,in all likelihood, due to the shyness he feels at meeting older adults. However, in another situation, it could mean that he is lying. Another twist of this scenario could be that, the day before, he had been caught ringing the doorbell and running away from his parent's friend's home. The boy's lack of eye contact could be for many different reasons. Thus, the exact same behavioral clues may be judged differently based on the circumstances surrounding the interview.

Behavioral Clusters

The behavior that is observed during the course of an interview or an interrogation are more likely to be valid when clusters of different types of behavior occur. For example, in a deceptive individual, the interviewer could observe a lack of eye contact, closed body posture, and grooming gestures. At the same time, there may be deceptive verbal behavior with delays in the speech pattern. The clustering of similar behaviors when evaluated globally leads the interviewer to conclude whether the individual is truthful or deceptive.

Rarely is it sufficient for a single behavior to be interpreted as truth or deception. The accuracy of the decision is enhanced when the behavior can be read in clusters that support each another, leading to the conclusion of truthfulness. Much like deception, truthful behavior can be read using clusters of behavior, such as direct spontaneous responses, good eye contact, open posture, and related fluid movements.

The interviewer should recognize that, on occasion, an innocent person may do or say something that would be more likely to come from a deceptive individual. In the same way, the deceptive individual may on occasion respond in or appear to assume a truthful manner. The clusters of behavior occurring over time during the interview/interrogation will form a pattern that will enhance the likelihood of a correct decision about the suspect's truthfulness or untruthfulness.

Interviewer Behavior

The interviewer also must be concerned that he in no way projects his beliefs or disbeliefs to a suspect. By projecting his feelings to the individual being interviewed or interrogated, the interviewer can effect a change in that individual's behavior. For example, the truthful suspects who fear that the interviewer does not believe them because of the behavioral clues the interviewer has shown, may display behavior that is incongruent. The fear of being disbelieved might, in fact, cause innocent people to alter their behavior because of this stress. Conversely, guilty suspects may reduce their fear of detection simply because they perceive that they are believed by the interviewer. As the fear of detection diminishes, guilty suspects are less likely to give themselves away through the leakage of untruthful behavior.

Additionally, the interviewer should be careful to avoid undue pressure on the suspect by sitting too close. This could cause the suspect to feel uncomfortable and modify his behavior. This discomfort would be due to the interviewer's proximity rather than any type of deception.

In the same way that the interviewer evaluates the behavior of a suspect, so too does the suspect evaluate the behavior of the interviewer. In normal conversations, eye contact between two parties ranges between 40% and 60%. When an interviewer looks too much at a suspect, the suspect may recognize that the interviewer is acting beyond the normal and accuse the interrogator of disbelief. In each of the aforementioned situations, the positioning and behavior of the interviewer have modified the behavioral clues given by a suspect. In these situations, the behavior is not related directly to the incident under investigation but rather to the interaction between the interviewer and suspect.

The interviewer should also refrain from identifying a suspect's particular deceptive behavior to him. For example, an interrogator tells a suspect that he knows he is lying to him because he cannot look the interrogator in the eye. What happens next is a staring match between the suspect and the interrogator, with the suspect rarely, if ever, breaking eye contact. This change of behavior by the suspect is a result of the interrogator's statement. The suspect consciously alters and modifies his behavior to conceal a particular deceptive response from the interrogator. Interviewers should never call attention to evidently deceptive behavior. This is the interviewer's "ace in the hole" and will allow him to effectively interpret and steer the interview/interrogation using the suspect's unmodified behavior. Once suspects recognize that their behavior is being evaluated, they may begin to modify it, which creates additional difficulty for the interviewer.

Timing and Consistency

Every suspect and witness will exhibit verbal and nonverbal behavioral clues to some extent. The interviewer must evaluate these behaviors based on their timing and consistency. For example, one common gesture of people who wear glasses is to push the glasses up or make an adjustment of the glasses on the face. This common gesture is done because the glasses are loose or because the face has become oily and the glasses have slid down. Thus, the adjustment of the glasses can be a common necessity for those individuals who wear them. This adjustment, however, can be interpreted differently depending upon the timing of the movement in relationship to a stressful question. For example, consider the following dialogue:

> *Interviewer:* Larry, let me ask you this. Did you steal that missing deposit from the safe yesterday?
> *Suspect:* (Pauses, hand over the face, adjusts glasses) No, I didn't.

A second example with different timing of the movement:

> *Interviewer:* Larry, let me ask you, did you steal that missing deposit from the safe yesterday?
> *Suspect:* No, I didn't. (Good eye contact. Direct spontaneous response. Ten seconds later suspect adjusts his glasses.)

In both of these cases, the movement to adjust the glasses was accomplished in exactly the same manner, with only the timing of the movement changing. In the first example, the suspect, Larry, uses the movement of the glasses to screen his face and eyes from the interrogator while he decides how to respond. In the second example, the suspect directly responded to the interviewer's question and only at a point of limited stress elected to adjust his glasses. In evaluating these two movements, an interrogator would assess the first as probable deception because of its timing, and the second less likely to be deception.

The suspect should consistently use a pattern of behavior that increases the likelihood of the accuracy of interpretation. In the above dialogue, the interviewer might see Larry repeatedly put his hand to his glasses to conceal his eyes and face at points when he is attempting to lie or when the stress of the questions is high. In the second example, the truthful Larry might make adjustments to his glasses, but these adjustments are not directly related to the stressful questions and lack the consistency or timing necessary to judge them as being deceptive.

Cautions in the Evaluation of Behavior

In interpreting a suspect's verbal and nonverbal behavior, the interviewer must be conscious of pitfalls in the process of evaluation. There are many individual, cultural, and environmental circumstances that can cause suspects to change their behavior. These changes might have nothing to do with deception on the part of the suspect.

Role of the Environment

The interviewer must be conscious of the environment in which the interview or interrogation is conducted. The distractions surrounding a suspect may cause behavior unrelated to the question being asked. For example, if an interviewer is asking a question and the suspect breaks eye contact, it could mean one of two things in a situation where the environment was not controlled: deception or distraction by a vehicle that drove past or someone who walked by. Ideally, the environment should reduce outside distractions so that the behavioral responses can be attributed directly to the questions being asked by the interviewer. In less controlled environments, such as field interviews or interviews conducted in a less formal setting, the interviewer must consider whether the behavior has some cause other than the question.

Interviewer–Suspect Attitudes

The interviewer must also consider any personal biases for or against the individual being questioned. In situations where the interviewer has a bias in favor of the person, it is likely that the bias may cloud the interviewer's observation of deceptive behavior. Many times during an investigation an investigator has heard, "I just can't believe Bill did it." The individual who has a personal relationship with Bill does not want to believe that Bill was involved in the incident. This personal bias allowed them to overlook information and behavior that would have been indicative of Bill's guilt. This bias may also be reflected as a result of a physical resemblance to someone the interviewer likes or dislikes. We all probably have an Aunt Marie who makes the best chocolate cake and always had an ice cold glass of milk for us whenever we stopped by. Now, whenever we see someone who reminds us of our Aunt Marie, we feel positive toward her. Conversely, when we encounter people who physically resemble somebody we do not like, we have negative feelings toward them simply because of that resemblance.

An interrogator must also take into account the attitude of the suspect when assessing his behavior. When interviewers are dealing with somebody who does not like the law enforcement function, they typically receive negative feedback from that individual. None of us likes to be disliked and individuals tend to treat others the way others treat them. Thus, when we are dealing with a person who does not like us, we are more likely to judge the person to be deceptive based on behavior owing to the bias we have against the subject. The interviewer must constantly be aware of personal biases for and against individuals and recognize that these can jeopardize the accurate evaluation of a suspect's behavior. Just remember, if you look hard enough for truthful or untruthful behavior because of a bias, you will probably find that behavior.

Mental Capacity of Suspect

A suspect's mental capacity may affect both the type of behavior and behavioral clues. When a suspect is of low intelligence, we may find that he delays before responding to the interviewer's question. This delay typically would be interpreted as deceptive. However, because of the relatively low intelligence of the suspect, the interviewer must consider the possibility that the pause was a function of intelligence rather than deception.

An individual's educational level may also play a part in determining the gestures that are used during a conversation. Research in linguistics has shown that people of a higher social status or who are better educated tend to be more verbal and use fewer gestures. The suspect who has a lower mental capacity or who is less well educated tends to rely more on gestures.

Medical Condition, Drug and Alcohol Usage

Individuals can respond in a behaviorally suspicious or noticeable manner because they are being treated for a medical condition. The symptoms of the medical condition may result in actual changes in the body's physiology. These changes in physiology could also result from the side effects of prescribed medications. For example, an individual with a dry, "clicky" mouth may be lying or may be taking a diuretic to relieve water retention. A side effect of the diuretic is a dryness in the mouth that results in a dry, clicky sound. The dry, clicky mouth is also a recognized sign of deception. Other individuals may have a tremor in the hand because of a muscle strain or even as a side effect of chemotherapy. The physical behavior observed has nothing whatsoever to do with deception but is simply a reflection of the individual's medical condition. These medical conditions or medication side effects can cause behavior symptoms similar to those of a deceptive individual.

Other individuals will be under the influence of drugs or alcohol at the time of an interview or interrogation. The use of behavior to identify their true status is unlikely because the behavioral responses may be due to the drug and alcohol ingestion alone. The pattern of slurred speech, unsteadiness on the feet, confused thought process, and the inability to stay on the topic are common side effects of someone under the influence of drugs or alcohol. An individual in a significant state of intoxication is generally unsuitable for a behavioral assessment relating to truth or deception.

Cultural, Ethnic, and Geographic Differences

The interviewer must also be aware that cultural, ethnic, and geographic differences can cause behavior variations in people. In an Asian population, eye contact may be significantly less than among Caucasians because, in Asian society, it is inappropriate to make eye contact with someone in authority. Gestures and behaviors may also be typical for specific cultures and very appropriate for their ethnic group.

There also may be geographical differences in speech patterns and social norms. By recognizing that these differences occur, the interviewer can take them into consideration when evaluating an individual's behavior for truth or deception.

Professional Criminals, Actors, and Politicians

The interviewer must always be conscious of the skill with which people interact with others. Criminals, actors, and politicians are people who are typically conscious of their behavior. To be successful, each of these individuals must have a knowledge of human behavior and the ability to mimic. These types of individuals can be extremely difficult to catch in a lie because of their ability to mask and cover their incongruent behavioral leakage.

The professional criminal (not necessarily someone in organized crime, but rather someone who has actively pursued a criminal career) can also be difficult to assess behaviorally. These individuals generally began lying at an early age. They began with their parents and teachers and continue with their employers and the police. Because of their success in deception and their practiced ability to deceive, their behavioral characteristics are often unreliable.

The difficulty with experienced criminals is that they often look truthful when, in fact, they are involved in the incident under investigation. An additional difficulty that the interviewer can face with this type of individual is that he may appear deceptive when truthful because of past involvement in similar situations. This can be especially relevant in crimes that occur repeatedly, such as burglary or theft. In addition, this type of conflicting behavior may be displayed because the individual has no respect for law enforcement and "doesn't care."

Con men who ply their trade through their ability to deceive can be extremely difficult to assess behaviorally. These individuals have often successfully beaten the system and so view the process as much as a game as a serious encounter. Because they consider it a game, they often take great delight in lying and showing their cleverness at fooling an investigator.

Many actors and politicians can successfully create emotions. They do so by recreating in their minds a past moment in their lives and allowing their bodies to display the appropriate behavior of that emotion. As a result, the emotion shown in the circumstances tends to look extremely real because it is directly related to past experience. Many actors are trained to show emotion by this very method. Consider the TV evangelists who can cry at the drop of a hat to show their sincerity.

Fear of Detection

The behavior displayed by a suspect in an interview or interrogation is often directly related to the fear of detection. The greater the fear of detection an individual has, the greater the likelihood that a behavioral slip will occur or leakage will show his true status. The investigator should not assume that the fear of detection is directly related to the seriousness of the incident. In many cases, the seriousness of the incident has little or nothing to do with the fear of detection. For example, an employee steals five dollars out of the register and nobody catches him. He continues to steal in any number of ways for a period of a year before finally deciding to steal a large amount. At this point, he is questioned regarding the theft. Does he have a fear of detection? In all probability, the fear of detection is greatly diminished because he has been successfully involved in theft over a long period without being caught. Why should he be concerned now? On the other hand, the individual may show significant behavioral changes simply because, for the first time, he did steal a large amount, using a method to which he was not accustomed. It is the perception of the individual of the likelihood that he has been detected that comes into play in assessing whether there will be significant behavioral changes.

In certain instances, as when questioning a suspect about multiple criminal acts, there may be significantly different patterns of behavior in each different act. Take, for example, an individual who has been stealing from his company using fraudulent credits. The deceptive behavior associated with stealing using fraudulent credits is significantly more threatening to the suspect than asking about biographical information. Thus the behavioral change should occur on the more emotionally stressful issue.

Suspects often react to different crimes. For example, some suspects view a rape preceding a homicide as significantly more serious than the killing itself. Thus, the fear of detection is greater on the rape than it would be on the homicide. As such, it would be likely that the individual would show more significant behavioral changes in the rape inquiry than in the homicide inquiry simply because it has a greater emotional impact and stimulates, as a result, a greater fear of detection. However, it might be easier to obtain a confession from a suspect by concentrating on the less emotional issue. The fear of detection may also be increased when there are larger punishments for one rather than another issue. In the previous instance, while the homicide is significantly harsher in terms of punishment than the rape, the suspect could still view the rape as the more emotionally volatile issue.

Although the behavioral changes observed by the interviewer may give an indication that the suspect is untruthful, they do not necessarily tell the particulars of the untruth. In some instances, the deceptive behavior may be related to a side issue, such as the theft of other money or the knowledge of who actually perpetrated the crime. The behavioral changes could also be a result of the fear of not being believed.

A lie fails because the suspect allows the attendant emotion to leak out and be observed. The stronger the emotion felt by the suspect, the greater the likelihood of a behavioral leak. The fear of detection can also be directly related to a suspect's beliefs about the circumstances of the crime. The interviewer should remember that a lie that is told over and over can actually become the foundation of a belief on the part of the suspect.

Fight or Flight

Self-preservation is one of the primary needs of an individual. The body, as it evolved, developed a system of self-preservation called the autonomic nervous system. It is the body's defense mechanism. When the mind recognizes a danger to its well-being, the autonomic nervous system changes the body's physiology to prepare it either to fight or flee the perceived threat.

Consider walking down a dark street and having somebody step out of the shadows in front of you. Without having to think about it, the body's autonomic defense system kicks in and begins to prepare the body to fight or flee from the threat. Adrenaline is pumped into the circulatory system, which increases the heart rate. As the heart rate increases, the body needs to put more oxygen into the system. The respiratory pattern of the individual changes, becoming deeper and more rapid.

The body begins to build up heat with all the movement occurring in the heart and the lungs. To dissipate this heat, the body begins to perspire and diverts the blood from the digestive track in the abdominal cavity to the surface of the skin. As the blood is diverted to the surface of the skin, a flushing begins to occur. The perspiration begins to evaporate from the surface of the skin, thereby cooling it. As this happens, the blood now begins to cool and release its heat. The body is a dynamic system that is not consciously controlled by the individual in these types of situations.

In the same way that the body protects a person who feels threatened, similar physiological changes occur when an individual has a fear of detection. The body undergoes physiological changes of which the individual is not consciously in control. The corresponding behavioral changes are often observable to the interviewer. The pulsation of the carotid artery on either side of the neck or the blood vessels in the temple are directly reflective of increased blood pressure. The flushing or blanching of the skin may be related to the body's diversion of the blood from the digestive tract to the surface of the skin. The change in the respiratory pattern can also be noted. These physiological changes in the body tend to be relatively uncontrolled by the individual and thus make excellent indicators that show a suspect's stress or strong emotion, such as the fear of detection.

Emotion

The stronger an emotion felt by a suspect attempting to lie, the greater the likelihood of significant leakage of behavior. The difficulty for the interviewer is that emotions are rarely in their pure form. The emotions may be several different types. For example, on a roller coaster ride, an individual may have the emotion of fear of being killed on one of the high speed turns and at the same time excitement and laughter as a result of the fun of having lived through the turn. Suspects feel these combined emotions also. On the one hand, they have the fear of detection, but, on the other, in many cases they enjoy the game of conning their adversary into believing their noninvolvement. The problem the guilty face is that they want to conceal the emotion associated with the fear of detection. The easiest way to do this is to mask that emotion with another. They may use anger or a smile to conceal their emotions. Often, the interviewer will notice a suspect's attempting to win him over with a smile. This is often accompanied by inappropriate laughter. The use of the smile is an attempt by the suspect to conceal one emotion with another and use it as a mask. The suspect may also commonly use anger to mask other emotions.

Probably the technique used most often to mask emotions by the suspect is the smile. It is relatively easy for the suspect to smile and it is socially appropriate. In addition, studies have shown that people who smile are judged to be more trustworthy and honest, whereas those who scowl or frown were judged to be less so.

Using the mask of emotions will help confuse the interviewer and make the true meaning of any leakage questionable. The difficulty the interviewer has is in differentiating which emotion is in play at the current time. Is it fear of detection or fear of being disbelieved? Is it embarrassment or anger? Regardless of the emotion, the stronger the emotion felt by the suspect, the greater the amount of leakage likely to occur for the interviewer's observation.

There are six basic human emotions that are recognized across all cultures: surprise, happiness, sadness, fear, disgust, and anger. (see Figure 5.1) Very often, emotions are mixed, making them difficult to interpret or letting one emotion mask another. The face is largely made up of involuntary muscles that move in response to the emotion, not the individual's conscious thought. When people attempt to create emotions that they do not feel, the muscles of the face do not move correctly, often giving the facial expression a phony appearance.

Typical Attitudes Displayed by Suspects

The interviewer should remember that extremes in behavior are often indicative of deception. At the very least, the observant interviewer should recognize that the stress of lying often causes changes in attitudes and verbal and nonverbal behavior. These changes should be compared with what is normal for the individual and the population in general.

The Truthful Suspect

Truthful individuals generally are calm, relaxed, and cooperative while being interviewed by police or loss prevention. Even though innocent, suspects may be concerned that they are being questioned, and this concern may cause some stress. However, as they become more comfortable with the situation, this stress typically reduces and their behavior becomes more comfortable and relaxed with the situation.

The truthful suspect generally is sincere in both word and action. Smiles look genuine because they are sincere. The truthful individual is inflexible in the stories told. However, the interviewer does need to be careful about

Figure 5.1 Emotions are a human characteristic that are cross-gender and cross-cultural and are easily recognized anywhere in the world. Many times one emotion may be used to conceal another, such as a smile to cover fear.

truthful witnesses and victims who may embellish or add to a description to be even more helpful. Overall, the truthful individual is cordial, friendly, and relatively easy to handle.

Knowing that these observations are generally true, experienced investigators have often interviewed individuals who were innocent but were less than friendly because of their dislike for the police or loss prevention personnel. The experienced interviewer can recognize this attitude and still make considerable inroads in establishing information.

The Untruthful Suspect

The attitude displayed by untruthful suspects may be impatience, both in word and action. The guilty will often look at their watches and suggest that they need to be somewhere else. They also are tense and defensive. An example of defensiveness is illustrated in the following dialogue. A store manager was interviewed regarding the theft of several deposits. The interviewer greeted the manager and introduced himself: "Hi, I'm Dave Zulawski. How are you today?" The manager's response was, "What do you want to know for and why are you asking me all these questions?"

Comparing the response from the manager to what one might expect from the population as a whole, this certainly is an inappropriate response and indicates an unusual amount of stress and defensiveness. This unusual response and her defensiveness were the first indications of the manager's guilt.

Some guilty suspects will attempt to portray an outwardly unconcerned attitude. They attempt to convince the interviewer that this meeting between themselves and the police or loss prevention is nothing out of the ordinary and absolutely no threat to them whatsoever. Although this surface attitude is generally supported by their casual posture, inwardly they are in a state of panic.

Guilty suspects often attempt to take an overly friendly, polite, or cooperative attitude toward the interviewer. The guilty suspect uses this tactic in an attempt to keep the interviewer as a friend rather than as an enemy. The guilty hopes this cooperative attitude will get them a break or even that they will be overlooked as suspects. Excessive friendliness and politeness by the suspect should immediately alert the interviewer to the probable deception of the suspect. Even when the guilty employing this attitude are confronted about involvement in the incident, they will remain extremely friendly. In fact, often an individual will apologize for not being involved in the crime. "I'm sorry, but I really didn't do this" is a typical guilty response to the interrogator.

Another attitude that is commonly used by the guilty suspect is that of being defeated. The suspect has done the hard work for the interrogator and reduced his own resistance to giving an admission by believing that he has already been detected and caught. Individuals with this type of attitude typically confess fairly rapidly because they already believe that their guilt is known for certain.

Some guilty suspects will attempt to take the offensive by portraying a surly, nasty, aggressive attitude toward the interviewer. This surly attitude is designed to put the interviewers on the defensive and cause them to back off from the confrontation with the suspect. The suspect's belief that a good defense begins with an aggressive offense is true if it causes the interviewer to back off. The interviewer should consider whether this individual may only have an extreme dislike for the police or loss prevention functions. If the suspect has an extreme dislike for the police, then the surly behavior may not necessarily reflect untruthfulness.

Attitudes Common to Both Truthful and Untruthful Suspects

In certain situations, the interviewer may find that some attitudes are common to both the truthful and untruthful suspect. For example, nervousness might be evidenced by a truthful person who has been put into a position of being questioned by someone in authority. The uncommon aspect of this interview might, in fact, cause nervousness in a truthful suspect. The guilty suspect, however, is nervous because of involvement in the incident and belief that the interviewer has focused on him as the primary suspect. Whereas the truthful individual will become calmer as the interview continues, the nervousness of the guilty will continue or increase.

Anger is another attitude that might be common to both the truthful and untruthful suspect. Truthful suspects might be angry because of their perception of being railroaded or because of a past experience with the police or loss prevention. The guilty suspect may use feigned anger in an attempt to take the offensive and force the interviewer to back off from any confrontation. It has been the experience of the authors that anger displayed at the beginning of the interview/interrogation is typical of a guilty suspect. However, if anger is displayed later in the interview or interrogation, it might in fact be from a truthful suspect who has now become annoyed.

Case Example

An example of anger based on the perception of the investigation can be seen in the case of the theft of $20,000 in rings from a jewelry counter in metropolitan St. Louis.

> The jewelry counter was attended by two sales clerks, a Caucasian female and an African American female. The latter sales clerk went on a break and left the area to get coffee. Behind the counter, on top of a safe, was a tray of rings valued at approximately $20,000 that was supposed to have been secured in the jewelry case. Shortly after the clerk left the department for

her break, two male African Americans entered the department. One occupied the Caucasian sales clerk with questions while the other reached across the counter and took the rings. The sales clerk observed the theft and called for loss prevention and the police. The two offenders left the area, taking the rings with them.

An investigation into the theft was initiated by police and store loss prevention. The rings had been left in a place where they were not supposed to be and this was in complete violation of company policy relating to the handling of high-value merchandise. Investigators elected to interview the African American sales clerk first because of the possibility of collusion along racial lines. The investigators made an investigative assumption that if there was help from one of the employees to commit the theft, it would have occurred along racial lines. However, when the female African American sales clerk was asked to be interviewed, she was extremely upset because of her perception of the investigation. She felt that she was being singled out for the interview simply because she was African American and the two offenders were also African American. This anger, which was legitimate, created significant problems in interpreting her behavior. The African American sales clerk was subsequently cleared of any involvement in the incident, but the order in which the interviews were conducted created investigative problems.

In other cases, the truthful and untruthful suspects might just quietly wait and listen for the interviewer to lead them. The quiet behavior is to the benefit of the guilty because they do not have to do any talking unless they are asked. Quiet truthful suspects might be quiet simply because it is their personality trait.

Interpretation of Nonverbal Behavior

The interviewer should remember that the entire body must be considered when observing nonverbal behavior. For the purpose of discussion, the body is divided into zones. In addition, behaviors are divided into those that are typically truthful or untruthful. Remember that no single behavior, either verbal or nonverbal, is always indicative of deception. The interviewer must look for differences from the suspect's normal behavior and from the population, and then put the behavior in the context of its occurrence.

Trunk, Shoulder Position, and Posture

One of the first behavioral indications that an interviewer is likely to observe is how the suspect sits in the chair. The interviewer's chair is positioned three to four feet across from the suspect's chair. After introductions, the truthful suspect will usually, without hesitation, walk in and sit down in the chair that is offered. The guilty, however, often walk to the chair and then move it. This movement will provide one of several benefits to them. First, by pulling the chair slightly away from the interviewer, suspects will reduce some of the stress they feel. Second, the movement of the chair often changes its alignment so that the suspect no longer has to directly face the interviewer. This position allows suspects to protect the abdominal region of the body by turning away from the interviewer so their shoulders are no longer parallel to those of the interviewer. In some instances, the guilty will not move the chair but will sit side-saddle, which takes the shoulders out of the position parallel to the interviewer and provides a defensive area for the abdomen. Some younger males may, in fact, turn the chair and straddle it, using the back as a barrier to separate themselves from the interviewer. This position is generally interpreted as indicative of deception.

Truthful Individual.   Usually, the truthful individual will have good posture (see Figure 5.2). When they seat themselves in the chair across from the interviewer's chair, they sit in an upright position with their shoulders squared and parallel to the shoulders of the interviewer. They are relaxed and keep their arms loose and away from the body. Imagine a small cone starting at the suspect's waist and moving up to encompass the shoulders. The truthful person generally will stay within this imaginary cone. As a result of remaining within this cone, their posture tends to remain good and any movements that they make during the course of the interview tend to be minimal.

Untruthful Individual.   Because untruthful suspects are uncomfortable and fear detection, they will often attempt to take a defensive posture that makes them feel more comfortable and conceals vulnerable parts of the body (see Figure 5.3). When individuals feel uncomfortable, they tend to protect the abdominal region of the body, which is the most vulnerable. The shoulder blades, rib cage, and collarbone protect the upper body, but it is in the abdominal region where most people feel uncomfortable. This discomfort translates into movements and a posture or position that covers this portion of the body.

An untruthful person might position his shoulders in such a way that it turns the trunk of the body so it is not exposed to the interviewer. This positioning reduces the discomfort felt from the fear of detection.

Untruthful individuals will also posture themselves in a slumping position (see Figure 5.4), extending the feet and legs toward the interviewer to put a greater distance between themselves and the person they fear may detect their deception. Recall the imaginary cone extending from the waist to the shoulder of the truthful person; it is helpful in understanding the attempted

Figure 5.2 Truthful individuals usually have good posture and appear relaxed while talking with the interviewer.

deception. The deceptive individual is not restricted by this cone and can engage in huge body shifts that may span several feet of space and take several seconds to actually complete. These large, gross shifts of the body are not in any way restricted by the cone, and, as a result, the trunk will lean excessively. Suspects who are in a position to lean on a desk or table may slump over and put all their weight on the table, supporting head in hand.

The guilty also may perspire excessively, particularly in the area of the trunk of the body. This perspiration should be considered in context with the actions immediately before arrival and the temperature of the room. In a comfortable room, where the suspect has not engaged in any physical exertion immediately prior to arrival, perspiration will be indicative of the autonomic nervous system's psychological responses in the body. The perspiration may not be a relevant clue if the suspect has engaged in strenuous activity or come from an extremely hot environment just prior to the meeting.

There may also be significant changes in the respiratory pattern of the deceptive individual. Most people at rest breathe between 18 and 22 cycles

Figure 5.3 Untruthful individuals will often position themselves in a defensive posture that makes them feel more comfortable by protecting the abdominal region of the body.

per minute. The respiratory pattern in guilty suspects often changes dramatically as a result of their fear of detection. In about a third of the cases, the suspect's respiratory pattern increases and takes on almost a panting, labored look. Contributing to this labored respiratory pattern is the tension of the large upper chest muscles. Once they inhale, they are rarely able to take the full volume of oxygen that they need. As a result of this lack of oxygen, they increase the respiration pattern until it almost becomes a pant. Because of the need for additional oxygen, the suspect also may take large breaths to build the oxygen level in the blood up to the necessary levels and compensate for the muscular tension.

More commonly, the guilty individual's respiratory pattern tends to slow and become shallow or irregular. This irregularity may be highlighted by the taking of deep breaths periodically during the course of the interview and then releasing the breath slowly through a sigh or a cough.

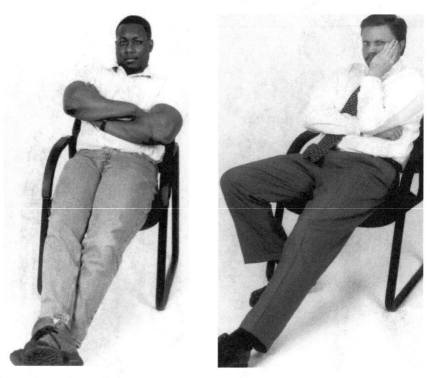

Figure 5.4 Untruthful individuals might posture themselves in a slumping position, extending their legs toward the interviewer.

Hand and Arm Positions

The hands and arms are used for a number of purposes by truthful and untruthful suspects. The hands and the arms may provide the guilty with a barrier to protect the abdominal cavity and relieve the stress of sitting across from an interviewer. The hands and the arms often are used to perform "created jobs" or grooming gestures. In Paul Ekman's book *Telling Lies*,[4] he refers to the grooming gestures and created jobs as *manipulators*. The grooming gestures and created jobs, such as picking lint, are part of our everyday life. Again, the context and, more importantly, the timing of these grooming gestures are critical in evaluating whether they are related to deception. Ekman argues that these manipulators can be a sign that someone is upset, but an increase in the manipulator activity is not necessarily a reliable sign of deceit. He believes that the prevailing belief among laymen is that they erroneously believe grooming gestures do indicate deception.

Although the manipulators may not be a reliable sign of deceit, these grooming gestures and created jobs are often used by guilty suspects in an

[4] Holt, Rinehart, and Winston, New York, 1981.

effort to cover their uncertainty when asked a question they had not considered or prepared an answer for. The suspect's uncertainty requires a pause to consider which response is truly in his best interests. This pause is often awkward, and the guilty will use the created job or a grooming gesture to cover the delay while formulating a response. It is not the gesture itself, but rather the context and timing of the gesture that need to be evaluated. We all, at one time or another, have picked a piece of lint off our clothes or smoothed our hair; however, these gestures can be considered as deceptive when they occur at certain times or cover a suspect's delay. For example, the hands and the arms are an extremely important part of any conversation. The movement of the hands and arms helps to relieve the stress of a situation. The movements may reflect the emotional turmoil of the individual or they may cover the guilty person's fear of detection. The hands and arms illustrate the conversation and expand the meaning of the actual words.

Truthful Individual.   During conversations with the interviewer, truthful suspects will generally have comfortable, relaxed movements. Truthful individuals generally have no impairment of fine motor coordination. Their ability to write, gesture, and easily control the movement of objects remains essentially normal. The hands usually are warm and dry and remain that way to the conclusion of the meeting. In some instances, because of the autonomic nervous system, a truthful person's hands may be cold and clammy, but at the conclusion of the interview, after the person becomes more comfortable, the hands return to their normal warm and dry state. The truthful individual who holds his head during the interview tends to do so very lightly. The hand merely rests lightly on the chin or on the cheek. The trunk of the body remains upright and, as a result, the weight of the head is held directly on the neck.

Untruthful Individual.   The deceptive individual tends to hold extensive tension in the muscles. This creates movements that appear jerky and abrupt. Such movements also may be inappropriately timed to the words spoken by the suspect. Movements used to emphasize words arrive early or late, thus appearing awkward. When extending the hand to make a gesture, the guilty must overcome the muscular contraction of the arm. As they overcome the muscle's contractions, they overcompensate, which causes the arm to move more rapidly than normal. As a result, the guilty often have difficulty with fine motor coordination.

Truthful and untruthful subjects may illustrate their stories using movements of the hands and arms. These movements and gestures are a natural part of talking. Generally, these illustrations are confined to an imaginary box, from belt line to the top of the shoulders to width of the shoulders.

Truthful people will more often confine their illustration to the interior of the box unless they are very emotional. The guilty will often let the illustrating gestures exceed the perimeter of the box while telling their deceptions.

The interviewer should observe the movements, judging their extent and fluidity. However, it is also likely that an individual attempting to deceive another may be unusually stiff. Locking down the movements and gestures simplifies the attempt at deception. It is much easier for the interviewer to notice movement by the subject than it is to note an unnatural lack of movement.

This loss of fine motor coordination can be observed in a number of places during an interview or interrogation. The interviewer who uses a Miranda or other release form often notes that the signature of the suspect differs from times when the suspect was not under stress. The guilty suspect's signature often becomes illegible or has a spiky appearance. The muscular tension is also evidenced in the movements a suspect may make during the interview. The quick shift of the body, jerky head movements, or difficulty in simply taking a pen out of his or her pocket and putting it back illustrates the tension.

Figure 5.5 Untruthful suspects often put a hand over their mouths to muffle the words and to conceal their facial expressions.

The deceitful suspect may also have cold and clammy hands. Although this might not always be a reliable indicator, it is a behavior that is controlled by the autonomic nervous system. The interviewer may find that the suspect has warm, dry hands at the beginning of the interview and upon shaking hands at the close, he discovers that the suspect's hands have become sweaty and cold. This change may be the result of fear of detection and the engagement of the autonomic nervous system. The suspect who has cold, sweaty hands will attempt to wipe them off on their clothes, lap, handkerchief, or tissue. Many suspects who attempt to use a handkerchief or tissue turn it into a created job — not only wiping the hands, but also rolling it into small balls or playing with it. The change in the warmth of the hands is but a small piece of the puzzle in determining if the suspect is deceptive. In the search for truth and deception, the interviewer must look at the context of the behavior, habits of the suspect, and the timing of the events.

The hands also can be used to cover the mouth. Generally, it is the guilty who cover the mouth when they put the hand to their face (see Figure 5.5). The hand over the mouth serves two purposes. First, it muffles the voice and makes it difficult for the interviewer to hear what the suspect has said. This benefits suspects by helping them to avoid saying things clearly that may not be in their interest. Second, this gesture may be an unconscious attempt to stop the mouth from actually making inappropriate statements.

In one case, the hand over the mouth was done purposely by the guilty to avoid detection. The company lunchroom had been the location of repeated thefts of the food brought by employees for their lunch. The per-petrator simply consumed another's lunch, which created turmoil among the employees. In an attempt to identify the perpetrator, a bait lunch containing a nontoxic dye was placed in the refrigerator. This dye turned purple on contact with moisture. After the lunch was stolen, it was readily apparent who was responsible. However, the suspect attempted to avoid detection by concealing her stained lips, gums, and teeth behind her hand.

Besides deception, suspects might put their hands over their mouths for other reasons. The individual may have braces or think he has bad breath, or the teeth may be in need of dental care.

The movements and gestures used by the guilty tend to diminish when they lie. In attempting to control their behavior, the guilty tend to diminish their movements and eliminate those that do not easily cover the deception.

Consider the sixth-grade book report. The child who has not read the book or practiced for the oral report tends to stand very stiffly at the front of the class, whereas students who read the book and are prepared are con-fident. As a result of the confidence in their knowledge, they react in a much more comfortable manner. This analogy applies to the criminal case. The guilty have read only the dust jacket of the book and, as a result, are prepared to talk about the high points of their alibi. The truthful read the entire book and are confident of all the details because they know the story completely.

The hands may also be used to screen the eyes during deception. Suspects often are uncomfortable looking at the interviewer while they lie. In an effort to conceal their eyes and prevent the interviewer from noting the lack of eye contact, the guilty will use their hands to cover the eyes. Scratching the nose, rubbing the brow, or adjusting glasses could also be used as a ruse to cover the actual purpose of the hand movement.

General Considerations.   The hands can also convey other messages to the interviewer. The drumming of fingers often indicates the impatience of the suspect. Clenched fists may show the suspect's frustration or a negative attitude toward the discussion or interviewer.

The hand's holding the head may indicate boredom, either real or feigned, or evaluation. If displaying boredom, the suspect holds the weight of the head up because the trunk of the body has slumped out of the upright position. In a position of evaluation or consideration, the hand is lightly held on the chin or cheek and there may be some stroking of the face as he considers what is being said.

The hand may also be used to scratch portions of the body. Many guilty individuals undergoing an autonomic nervous system response have a need to scratch. As the blood is diverted from the digestive tract it is rerouted to the surface of the skin. The capillaries expand to take this additional volume of blood and the nerve endings located on the skin's surface are sensitized, creating a tingling. Many guilty individuals begin to itch and scratch immediately after the introduction of a stressful topic. Desmond Morris, author and behavioral observer, noted that telling a lie often causes a tingling in the face or neck that must be scratched. This is especially evident in the nose, because of the large number of capillaries and its sensitivity.

This scratching can be observed in areas of the body that contain large volumes of blood — the scalp, nose, arms, and upper trunk. It is interesting to note that people usually scratch an itch five times. It is rarely more or less than five times. However, a pretend itch used to cover discomfort may be done fewer than five times. The fake itch designed to cover a delay or break of eye contact may be scratched much lighter than a real itch. Women often scratch the face more lightly than men because they do not want to smear their makeup.

The hands may also be "steepled," where the tips of the fingers of each hand are touched together (see Figure 5.6). This steepling displays a generally confident attitude on the part of the individual. The rubbing of the hands together can indicate a positive expectation such as one would do when anticipating a good meal. A slower movement is usually judged as an indication of dishonesty, such as the con man who slowly rubs his hands together and says he has a great deal for you.

Finally, the suspect may use the thumbs to indicate a defensive or superior attitude. Generally, when a suspect takes this posture, he will be leaning back

Figure 5.6 The steepling of the hands generally accompanies a confident, balanced attitude.

in the chair, arms crossed and fingers tucked underneath the armpits with the thumbs extended upwards (see Figure 5.7). This posture is often taken by young males as they sprawl out in the chair, feet extended to show that they are not in any way intimidated by the interviewer. Although the positioning of the thumbs does not necessarily indicate deception, it may be an indicator of the attitude the suspect is going to attempt to use during the course of the interview/interrogation.

Arm Barriers. A deceitful suspect may use the arms as a means of providing a barrier to protect the abdominal region. Crossed arms often indicate negative thoughts or displeasure with the conversation. This arm positioning may also be used in situations where an individual feels uncertain or insecure. The crossed arms are also used when an individual feels cold. The positioning of the hands often helps in the interpretation of crossed arms. If an individual is cold, the hands are flattened and placed under the armpits and the trunk

Figure 5.7 The individual with arms crossed and thumbs extended upward often displays a defensive or superior attitude.

of the body is hugged, whereas anger may be displayed by crossing the arms and clenching the fists under the arms. Sometimes, the hands will not be tucked but will instead be used to grasp the biceps of the upper arm. Generally, this can be interpreted as a negative posture. The suspect displaying this position is usually very resistant to changing his mind.

The crossed-arm barrier may be modified by an individual to conceal defensiveness. Public speakers, when they are asked questions or challenged, use a modified barrier to defend themselves. Rather than positioning themselves with a full arm-cross barrier, they will use a less obvious barrier that still allows them some protection. For example, the hand may come across to touch the watch or a ring on the other hand. This still provides a barrier protecting the abdominal cavity and reducing the stress that the individual feels. These types of gestures are often used to cover nervousness or apprehension without having to go into the full arm-crossed position.

Leg and Feet Positions

Legs and feet are often used to provide a defensive barrier for the suspect against the threat posed by the interviewer. This behavior has more validity with men than with women. Women are taught to sit with their legs crossed.

Their mothers and fathers taught them that this was an appropriate position socially. Younger women, with the advent of slacks, do not always use the crossed leg position. Some individuals will not cross their legs because their clothing is too tight or they are in pain from arthritis or an injury. Often, the crossing of the legs is done in conjunction with a crossing of the arms. Women often show displeasure by crossing both the arms and the legs when talking to a husband or boyfriend who has displeased them.

There are two basic methods of crossing one's legs. The first, generally used by women and older men, is the knee-over-knee (see Figure 5.8). The second type of leg cross is the ankle-over-knee (see Figure 5.9). Although many people say that sitting with their legs crossed is comfortable and that is why they sit that way, the interviewer should remember that it is comfortable because of how they feel emotionally at the moment. Crossing the ankles or legs typically provides a defensive barrier against the interviewer. As a general rule, the more defensive an individual becomes, the higher the knee rises to protect the abdominal region (see Figure 5.10). In the ankle-over-knee position, the knee rises to screen more of the abdominal region and may even have an arm draped across it to provide an additional barrier for a suspect who feels threatened (see Figure 5.11). In the knee-over-knee crossing of the legs, it is the positioning of the foot that indicates an increased defensiveness (see Figure 5.12). The foot, rather than being held off to one side, is pointed directly at the interviewer to keep him even farther away, and reduces the suspect's stress level.

The leg and arm barriers can be seen in everyday interactions between people. These barriers are used when people are dealing with strangers or with others who they do not know well. Take, for example, the positioning of people in elevators. Typically, they position themselves with their back to the wall, cross their ankles and their arms. This posturing shows the discomfort of the individual in this environment. By observing the interactions among small groups, the keen observer can begin to identify relationships among the groups in terms of who is dominant and whether people know each other well.

The guilty will often extend the legs and feet toward the interrogator to keep him physically at a distance (see Figure 5.4). This may be done using an ankle lock, where the feet are crossed at the ankles, indicating a negative attitude, nervousness, or fear. By increasing the distance between the interviewer and themselves, suspects reduce the tension and discomfort that they feel.

Changing posture in response to an emotionally significant question in many cases will cause suspects to cross or uncross their legs. When interviewers ask a witness if he knows who is responsible for a crime, and they observe the witness shift the upper body, turn the shoulders, cross the legs, and drape an arm across the abdomen, they recognize that this question has

Figure 5.8 The knee-over-knee, crossed-leg position is often used by women and older men.

caused a significant amount of stress in the suspect. The conclusion, in all likelihood, is that the suspect knows or has a strong suspicion of who is responsible for the crime.

The positioning of the feet may also indicate to the interviewer when a suspect is ready to leave. The suspect positions both feet in a runner's starting block position, twists, and leans toward the door. The hands will move to the arms of the chair or the suspect's knees to help move him into an upright position (see Figure 5.13).

This is commonly used by the host when guests have overstayed their welcome. Once interviewers observe these behavioral clues, they should not be surprised when the suspect begins to leave.

Some people will circle or tap their foot during the course of the interview. This is more commonly observed with female suspects or witnesses. Sometimes, this is done as a sign of impatience on the part of the suspect. Some individuals use this as a signal that they need to use the washroom. However, in certain circumstances, this activity can signify something in terms of a suspect's truth or deception. Many times, this activity will cease completely when a suspect has been asked a particularly stressful question. However, the activity can also start at the point where a stressful question was asked. Thus, the cessation of this activity or the beginning of this activity may in fact indicate that the individual is under stress as a result of that question.

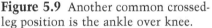

Figure 5.9 Another common crossed-leg position is the ankle over knee.

Truthful. Truthful people may use some form of a barrier because they feel uncomfortable about being asked about involvement or knowledge of a particular crime. However, a truthful individual's crossing of the legs tends to provide less of a barrier than those individuals who are deceitful. The truthful individual often positions the ankle over the knee with the calf almost parallel to the ground. In deceptive suspects, the knee typically rises to provide even more of a barrier for the abdominal cavity (see Figures 5.10 and 5.11). Truthful individuals comfortable with the situation often use no barrier whatsoever and simply place their feet flat on the floor with their legs open. This position is somewhat unusual for women, but when they do use it, the feet are placed close together. The positioning of the feet flat on the floor is also very likely to occur when a suspect decides to confess.

This positioning of the feet on the floor appears to provide some emotional stability for the suspect or anyone making a decision(see Figures 5.12 and 5.13). Studies of negotiations in major corporations have shown that when the ultimate deal was agreed upon, well over 90% of the key participants in the negotiation had their feet flat on the floor. The feet-flat-on-the-floor position then can take one of two meanings: an openness to discuss and come

Figure 5.10 A defensive individual might use the knee to screen the abdominal region of the body from the interviewer.

to an agreement, or a behavioral indication of a suspect's willingness to confess.

Head and Neck Positions

The head and the face are probably the most expressive part of the body. The face is capable is displaying hundreds of different expressions and movements to illustrate and add depth to the words that are spoften. Although the face is capable of giving significant information to the interviewer, it is also where most guilty suspects attempt to focus their deceit. In preparing their lies, the guilty often work on the words and the facial expressions that will accompany the words. The authors on numerous occasions have had an opportunity to observe suspects attempting to prepare lies. The facial expression planned by suspects played a keen role in the attempt to deceive. Generally, the guilty would begin by practicing the words they intended to use and the way they would sound. Then, the guilty suspects incorporate facial expressions and finally some minor hand movements in an effort to convey the message of truthfulness.

Figure 5.11 An arm draped over the knee can provide an additional defensive barrier along with the crossed legs. The arms might also be used to hold the leg barrier in place.

Figure 5.12 The position of the foot helps keep the interviewer farther from the defensive suspect. Note also the closed upper body position, with crossed arms and twisted shoulders providing additional comfort to the untruthful suspect.

Figure 5.13 The positioning of the feet in a starting block position, a leaning trunk, and the hands on the knees indicate that the individual is ready to leave.

Head Positions

Truthful.   There are general positions in which the head may be held (see Figure 5.14). The first is upright, held straight with its weight supported on the neck. This is generally a neutral position. Tilting the head to either side shows interest. This tilting of the head is similar to the positioning of the head of an animal who is interested in something. Puppies often do this when they hear their owner whistle or hear a sound about which they are uncertain.

Untruthful.   The head down can indicate a negative attitude or submission on the part of the suspect (see Figure 5.15). Finally, the fourth position is the head back with the suspect looking down the nose. This posture is a dominant or superior position taken often by guilty suspects (see Figure 5.16). The untruthful individual tends to put the head back or forward

Figure 5.14 Truthful individuals generally hold their heads upright. A slight tilt of the head might indicate listening or interest.

out of the plane of the shoulders. The head also may be held up by the hand in the event the trunk of the body has slumped off to one side. The movements of the guilty's head are jerky or abrupt. Many times the guilty individual will roll the neck to loosen the tension in the muscles of the neck and shoulder. In some cases, it is easier for the guilty suspect to nod his head by moving the entire trunk of the body forward and back than it is to move the head because of the muscle tension held in the shoulders and neck. By contrast, the truthful individual tends to nod very gently and fluidly.

Eye Movements

Truthful. The truthful individual will generally have good eye contact with the interviewer. Good eye contact is defined in two ways. First, the eye contact is appropriate for the individual or falls within the 40% to 60% range that is normal in most conversations. Second, the suspect maintains eye contact with the interviewer when asked questions of emotional weight. Although the eyes may offer a significant amount of information to the interviewer, it is wise to be cautious because most liars recognize that poor eye contact is an indicator of deception. Therefore, many deceitful individuals will attempt to maintain eye contact even though it is uncomfortable. Generally, the

Figure 5.15 The head-down position can indicate a negative attitude or submission on the part of the suspect. In this photo, it is more likely to be submission because of the openness of the body and lack of overall tension in the muscles.

Figure 5.16 The head back, with the individual looking down the nose, often accompanies a dominant or superior attitude on the part of the person.

truthful suspect's eyes also have warmth and depth to them and allow the interviewer to look below the surface of his eyes (see Figure 5.17).

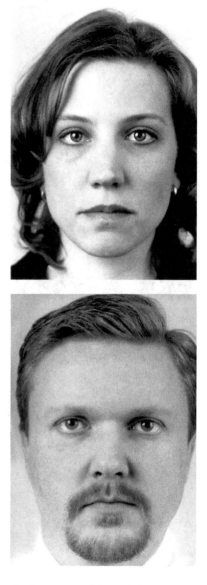

Figure 5.17(a) Note the similarity of eye and facial characteristics of the three individuals in each figure and then again when they change expression. Wide open eyes invite a deeper gaze, indicating interest

Untruthful. Often the deceptive individual's eyes will be cold and hostile (see Figure 5.17B). They have a flat look that does not allow the interviewer to look beneath their surface. The movement of the guilty's eyes can also take on a hunted look that may include rapid eye movement or the "bug-eyed" look commonly associated with fear. This bug-eyed look will usually allow the interviewer or interrogator to observe the whites of the eyes. These types of eye movements are similar to those observed when surprising a rabbit in the yard — the rabbit's eyes bulge to give it additional peripheral vision, and the rapid eye movement searches for an escape route.

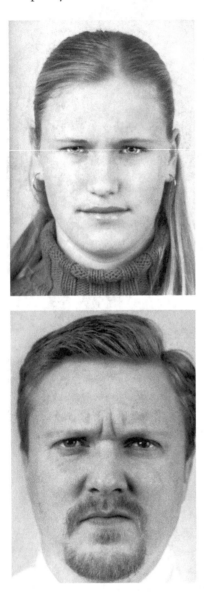

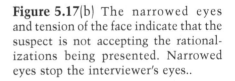

Figure 5.17(b) The narrowed eyes and tension of the face indicate that the suspect is not accepting the rationalizations being presented. Narrowed eyes stop the interviewer's eyes..

The guilty suspect may fail to maintain eye contact with the interviewer in several ways. The first type of poor eye contact is failure to look at the interviewer during stressful questions. Suspects may break eye contact by looking away and then look back, or they look away to supervise a created job or grooming gesture. Then, they may return to look the interviewer in the eyes. Other forms of poor eye contact are (1) nonexistent and (2) too dominant. This dominant eye contact appears aggressive or overly intense. The guilty whose eye contact is nonexistent are extremely uncomfortable meeting the eyes of the interviewer. This extreme lack of eye contact is an excellent indicator of deception. Nonexistent eye contact, with a corresponding emotional withdrawal, can also be an indication that the guilty suspect is in submission and ready to confess.

Eye contact may also be broken by the guilty by closing of the eyes when a denial is made or by placing the hand over the face covering the eyes. Additionally, some deceptive suspects may actually turn the entire head and look away to avoid eye contact with the interviewer at moments of deception.

It is the eyes that will help the interviewers ascertain during the interrogation whether they are making headway with a suspect. The eye muscle tension, softness of gaze, and the amount of eye contact help the interrogator determine whether the suspect is accepting the rationalization being presented.

Many facial muscles are involuntary and can be moved only when an appropriate emotion is felt. Often the muscles around the eyes and mouth do not follow the feigned behavior. For example, suspects who attempt a phony smile have difficulty doing so believably because they are not feeling the emotion of happiness or joy. Although the smile is partially there, it lacks the movement of certain muscles around the eyes and the mouth to make it appear genuine. Instead of appearing genuinely happy, the face has a forced expression appearance.

Mouth Positions

The mouth also gives behavioral clues that can help the interviewer determine if a suspect is deceitful.

Truthful.   The truthful individual generally has a sincere smile. Although there are any number of smiles an individual is capable of making, the failure to feel the emotion accompanying that smile will cause it to look phony. Usually, the face will have a comfortable, relaxed look, and the smile will be spontaneous and last for only a short period; genuine smiles tend to be short. The jaw line of the suspect will typically be relaxed and not holding tension.

Untruthful.   With the guilty, the mouth plays a much larger role when the suspect is attempting to deceive the interviewer. Initially, the suspect may attempt phony smiles or smirks to show sincerity or disbelief at what is being said. The mouth may also be used to perform created jobs, which might be anything from picking teeth to chewing fingernails. Because these activities may be done at times unrelated to stress, their timing is extremely important in determining if they are related to deception.

The mouth of deceptive individuals is often dry. This dryness results from a change in the saliva due to a natural diuretic being released into the circulatory system as a part of an autonomic nervous system response. This dryness causes the saliva to take on a tacky, stringy appearance and causes the tongue to stick to the roof of the mouth. As the tongue is extricated from the roof of the mouth, it often makes a dry, clicky sound. This particular physiological phenomena was observed hundreds of years ago by the Chinese and native American Indians. Although there are other explanations in addition to deception for dryness in the mouth, such as a side effect of medication, it is much more likely to be associated with deception if the dryness has its onset following the introduction of a stressful issue.

The dry, clicky mouth may also cause suspects to continually lick and wet the lips during the interview. The stickiness of the saliva may also require suspects to clear their throats. In evaluating these behavior symptoms, the interviewer should have observed whether they started prior to questions about the significant incident or were a result of questions only recently posed. Saliva changes also can cause a slight foaming at the corners of the suspect's mouth.

Although any of these behaviors alone is insufficient to determine deception, in combination with other behavioral indicators they can increase the likelihood of ascertaining the suspect's true status in the investigation.

Nose

Deceitful suspects often use the nose for created jobs. The hand-to-nose gesture is often used to screen the eyes and face during the course of a lie. In addition, physiological changes due to the autonomic nervous system may result in an itching or increased nasal discharge. These typical behaviors are event-oriented responses to particularly stressful questions in contrast to actions of a suspect who comes to the interview with a stuffy nose.

Neck

The neck can also give behavioral information to the interviewer. The larynx or Adam's apple can be observed most clearly in men. In some suspects, a quivering Adam's apple is from muscle tension in the shoulder and neck. This quiver may also be reflected in the guilty suspect's voice.

The large arteries and veins on either side of the neck or in the temple often show an observable pulse. The interviewer should recognize this physiological response of increased heart rate and blood pressure as an autonomic nervous system response to stress or the fear of detection.

Verbal Behavior

The difficulty in assessing verbal behavior is that the words spoken to an interviewer may be exactly the same for both the truthful and the untruthful suspect. It is only the differences in the nonverbal behavior, tone of voice, loudness, and speed of delivery that may differentiate truth from deception. The interviewer must, at the onset of any interview or interrogation, begin by establishing both the suspect's normal verbal and nonverbal behavior. Establishing a normal tone, loudness, and speed of delivery will allow the observant interviewer to note differences in the suspect's responses.

Truthful

Truthful individuals generally respond directly to questions and make timely responses. Because they are responding with a truthful answer, it is rarely necessary for them to delay to consider their answer. Truthful individuals speak understandably and use realistic terms when discussing the incident. They are not afraid to say "murdered," "killed," "stole," "raped," "fraud," or other terms that connote punishment. They are able to do so because the punishment does not apply to them, but rather to another individual.

Untruthful

Deceitful individuals are vague and stammering in their responses. There may be long pauses in speech, or answers that are too quick, too short, too long, or too elaborate. The guilty talk softly, mumble, and, in many cases, talk through their hands.

Although, on the surface, it seems that there is a significant difference between the dialogue of the truthful and untruthful, the interviewer must look at the suspect's behavior in terms of both what is normal for the individual and what is normal for the population as a whole.

The deceitful individual and the truthful vary in a number of ways in their use of verbal ploys. One that frequently comes up is complaints. A complaint may be voiced by both the deceitful and truthful; however, the timing of the complaints may be significantly different. If a truthful person does complain, he usually waits until the latter part of the interview when the interviewers have completed most of their tasks. At that point, the truthful will voice any complaints that they might have. Not so with the deceitful. They tend to form their complaints early in the interview, alleging violation of rights, the inconvenience of the interview, the discomfort of the environment, or any other complaint that seems appropriate in the least.

Case Example

Investigators were called to investigate a $100,000 diamond shortage in a jewelry store. The loss had occurred over the 6 months prior to its discovery at inventory. An analysis of the case facts led the investigators to conclude that the theft was most likely to have been perpetrated by the manager or assistant manager because it required the inventory count to be manipulated. This manipulation was necessary because the diamonds, because of their value, were counted each day. Therefore, any diamonds that were missing would have been discovered during the evening count unless company documents had been altered. The most likely individual to carry out the manipulation was either the manager or his assistant.

Prior to beginning the interviews, the interviewers were standing in the store waiting for the assistant manager to arrive. While doing so, they noted a male enter the store. He looked at the authors and the regional manager and quickly turned his back. The regional manager was questioned as to his identity and identified him as a full-time sales clerk at the store.

Because of the clerk's unusual behavior when he observed the regional manager and investigators, it was decided to interview him first. The suspect was greeted by one of the interviewers, who introduced himself. The employee immediately began a tirade. In a loud voice, he asked who the investigators were, what they thought they were doing, how they could bring him in on his day off. He demanded identification and attempted to control the early portion of the interview. His complaints ranged from his displeasure at being there on his day off to complaints about the violations of his rights as an employee. This behavior was extremely unusual for this individual, who was normally quiet and reserved.

The onset of the complaints met the criteria for a deceptive individual. Additional behavioral clues during the interview led the authors to believe that he was responsible for the $100,000 loss. His explanation for his animosity toward the interviewer was the fact that he had been brought in on his day off.

The next interview conducted was with a female employee, also brought in on her day off. She was cooperative, pleasant, and allowed the interview to go to its conclusion. Once the interview concluded, she related that she thought it was unfair that she had to come in on her day off, with no notice, to be questioned. She said that she understood the reasons for it but hoped that, in the future, arrangements could be made to do any interviews during her regular hours.

Thus, there were two suspects with the same complaint, both of whom voiced it, but the suspects' timing and attitude were significantly different. By looking at the timing of the complaints in this case, it is evident that the first individual did not want the interview to continue. Subsequent investigations revealed that the first salesman had been able to manipulate the inventory documents by deducting rings from the inventory log count. Nobody had been checking the register to determine if the ring was from the count, indicating it had been sold. When the count of the diamonds was done the same evening, the log matched the diamond pieces still present.

Unsolicited, Premature Excuses or Explanations

Often, the guilty will attempt to get their story out before they are asked. They attempt to prove their innocence through a premature explanation that typically highlights the reasons they could not or would not do anything like the incident being investigated. This explanation might be totally unsolicited or may be in response to a question such as, "Did you steal the car?" The response begins with a denial and immediately goes into a dissertation of why the suspect could not be involved. The truthful response to this question is more likely to be very direct: "No, I didn't." At that point, truthful individuals wait to have another question directed toward them. The guilty suspect will often use this method to discount, in advance, any evidence that is contrary to their claim of innocence.

Uncheckable Sources

Truthful individuals rarely rely on an uncheckable source to substantiate their story. They often do not even realize that they are a suspect or potential suspect in the case. Instead, they view themselves merely as someone who has been asked to help out. The guilty, however, view themselves as much more than a witness — they see themselves as someone upon whom the investigation may focus. As such, they feel it is necessary to add credibility to their statements over and above the words themselves. Statements made by deceitful individuals often rely on an uncheckable source to back up their story:

- If my mom were alive today, she would tell you ...
- You could ask my [priest, rabbi, minister, social worker]; they would tell you ...
- You can ask my parole officer. He'll tell you I didn't or I wouldn't ...

These uncheckable sources are intended to bolster the credibility of the suspect's statement. In reality, if investigators were to check these sources, they would generally not find any derogatory information, simply because these would be the last people in the world to whom the suspect would confide wrongdoing.

Focusing on Irrelevant Points

This tactic is often employed by the guilty in an attempt to convince an interrogator of their innocence. In this technique, the guilty identify some irrelevant point of information that can be verified by a named third person. The suspect offers the interviewer an opportunity to verify his truthfulness on this specific point because it is in fact true. The suspect then uses this irrelevant known truth to tie together the pieces of the deceptive story. The interviewer is asked to believe the alibi because the suspect has offered an incident that can be checked and found to be indeed truthful. Therefore, the suspect would like the interviewer to believe that everything else he has said is also the truth. A suspect who uses this tactic typically returns to the irrelevant known truth a number of times to tie the deceptive story together.

Suspects may also focus on petty issues that are insignificant to the major investigation. Often, rather than talking about the primary incident under investigation, suspects talk about how they were treated, or rather mistreated, by the officers during the course of the arrest. They will attempt to discredit their accuser through his alleged improper behavior. By discrediting the accuser, suspects attempt to discredit any allegations that he has made. For example, suspects will attempt to discredit the victim of a rape by calling her a "lying whore." By alleging that she is a prostitute and a liar, the suspect casts doubt on any allegations she may have made concerning her being raped. Suspects often accuse an interrogator or interviewer of mistreating them during the interview or interrogation. By casting a cloud over the propriety of the interviewer's treatment of them, suspects shift attention away from their admission and the facts of the case.

Suspects may also use irrelevant points to prove their innocence. The driver in an suspected arson case discounted the witness's description of the vehicle and recollection of a partial license number because the witness did not observe a "For Sale" sign in the rear window of the truck. The suspect's argument was that if the witness did not see the sign, it was not the suspect's vehicle.

Excessive Politeness or Respectfulness

Many guilty suspects attempt to win over the interviewer by being overly polite and respectful. This politeness often seems quite out of place — for example, the 17-year-old street gang member who talks in a respectful tone of voice and calls the police officer "sir." This attitude is out of character for this type of individual and is probably an attempt to deceive the officer or gain favor. It has one of two aims. First, suspects hope that by being polite and respectful they will predispose the interviewer to believe their lies because the interviewer likes them. Second, suspects hope that if their deception is discovered, the interviewer may give them a break because they were not a troublemaker. The overly polite and respectful manner of speech is a tip-off to the interrogator that the suspect is attempting to predispose him favorably.

However, individual differences might indicate that this is the suspect's normal behavior. Whereas the 17-year-old gang member would be unlikely to call an officer "sir" except sarcastically, a suspect recently out of the military might do so as a matter of course. Certain areas of the country also encourage the use of "sir" and "ma'am," as part of the respect shown to elders. Obviously, in these cases, the interviewer should consider that these may be appropriate geographic responses rather than a individual's attempt to attain favor.

Helpfulness

In some instances, the guilty attempt to deceive the interviewer by being overly helpful. Generally, their helpfulness is an exaggerated attempt to give the interviewer anything that he or she needs, but the helpfulness is a guise to lull the unwary interviewer into complacency about the suspects. Suspects hope that they will be overlooked because of their cooperation.

Observing suspects following the interview is often beneficial in making a determination of their truth or deception. This observation may be conducted by police, loss prevention personnel, or the employee's immediate supervisor. Often, what will be observed is an employee who is overly helpful. This overly helpful employee is overzealous in performing his work, cleaning and caring for the tasks at hand. This overzealousness is generally out of character for the employee and should be noted as an indication of deception. The suspect may also return in a sullen or despondent manner in response to the realization of his predicament.

At other times, suspects will return to talk to the interviewer to test the water and see how their story was accepted. Suspects return with a question, a minor bit of information, or to ask for directions. Using these as a ruse, they can evaluate the interviewer's attitude toward them. The suspect is looking for behavioral changes that indicate belief or disbelief. For example, the suspect may ask for directions back to his house. This is hardly necessary since, in most instances, simply reversing one's tracks is adequate. At other times, the suspect will come back to correct irrelevant information, something as simple as the suspect's starting date of employment. By correcting this information, the suspect can evaluate the interviewer's behavior, plus show his helpfulness and cooperation with the investigation. The suspect who manifests this behavior is often deceptive.

Delays

As a general rule, a delay in response to an interviewer's question is a good indicator of a suspect's guilt. Innocent individuals rarely need to think about a response. They simply answer the question posed directly and promptly. The guilty, however, often pause or delay a response while they consider: what the truth is, what type of response is appropriate to deceive the interviewer, and what the potential result of their response might be.

Ask yourself this question: "Did you have breakfast this morning?" Your response to this question has little or no emotional impact on you. Your response is generally an immediate "yes" or "no." "Did you drive to work this morning?" Again, the response is an immediate "yes" or "no." The truthful suspect does not have to delay to consider the answer. It is obvious to the truthful and they have no reason to delay. It is possible, however, that an innocent person might delay because of the wording of the question, a significant time delay between the incident and the interview, or mental confusion. As a general rule, the interviewer should recognize that a delay or pause in a speech pattern is very often related to attempted deception by the guilty suspect.

The interviewer must also recognize that a failure to delay by a suspect or witness could also be an indication of deception. Some of the questions asked of suspects require that they give some thought prior to making a response. For example, consider all the jobs that you have held and your immediate supervisor at each position. Out of those supervisors pick who was best and why. This compound question should legitimately result in an individual delaying before giving a response; it is not a simple yes or no question either in terms of the span of time covered or of its complexity. A delay to this question is appropriate and typical of an innocent individual. If the individual responded to this question immediately with an answer, the interviewer should suspect deceit. The guilty spend time anticipating questions that they think might incriminate them.

Another explanation for an immediate response to the best supervisor question would be that the individual was looking for a job and had been just recently asked the question. It could also be that they are considering looking for a job and are anticipating interview questions or could have had only one job and one supervisor.

It is usually the extremes in behavior that indicate deception. Answering a complex question without thought is just as likely to be deceptive as delaying in answering a very simple question. Many deceptive suspects use a series of verbal and physical ploys to cover the awkward pause while they decide what to say.

Physical Behavior

The suspect might use any of a number of physical behaviors to cover a delay in response. These could be coughing, taking a deep breath, clearing the throat, or sighing. The suspect also might use created jobs or grooming gestures, such as picking lint, to avoid an awkward appearance of the delay before they respond. Although these behaviors in and of themselves are not necessarily deceptive, when combined with a delay in response to a direct question, (such as, "Did you rob Marty's gas station last night?") they would be indicative of deception.

Repeating the Question

Another tactic employed by the deceitful is repeating the question before responding with the answer. For example, an interviewer asks the suspect, "Did you ever just think about breaking into a drug store even though you didn't actually do it?" The suspect responds by saying, "Did I ever just think about breaking into a drug store even though I didn't?" The suspect then pauses and answers, "I would say no."

Repeating the interviewer's question gives suspects a moment to consider their response and its implications. Simply repeating the question requires little or no work on the part of the suspect's conscious mind. While slowly repeating the question to the interviewer, the suspect can easily consider alternatives and make an appropriate choice of a response. This is a conversational tactic used between people every day while considering a response. For example, if you were asked, "Did you ever consider returning to college to get a degree in psychology?" your response might easily be, "Return to school to get a degree? Well, yes, I have thought about it." Repeating the question allows you to consider your response and attempt to identify the asker's motivation. However, in an interview/interrogation, questions often do not require thought because they are simply factual recollections. Thus, the suspect who repeats the question, "Did I kill John Jones?" or "Did I steal merchandise?" before making a denial, is in all probability deceptive.

Responding with a Question

Another ploy of the guilty is to respond to the interviewer's question by asking a question, thereby avoiding giving an answer that might incriminate them. This evasiveness is accomplished by diverting the interviewer's attention when the suspect responds with a question. In conversations, individuals often use this tactic when they perceive that the conversation is moving in a direction that is potentially embarrassing or threatening to them. Change of topic is often accomplished through a question. The evasive device might be as simple as, "Did you hear what happened over in the Fourth District last night?" The speaker hopes to pique another's interest, causing him to forget about probing an area potentially threatening or embarrassing to the individual. Suspects use the same method in attempting to evade particularly intrusive or threatening questions.

The suspect might also use this type of response in an attempt to draw the interviewer into a direct accusation. Questions such as, "Are you saying I stole?" "Are you saying I killed her?" or "Are you calling me a thief?" are ploys by the suspect to force the interviewer to take a position and defend it. If the interviewer says "no," suspects can reasonably believe that the interviewer does not know their guilt for sure. If the interviewer responds affirmatively to these types of questions, they can now make a denial and begin to defend their position. Dealing with this tactic is discussed in a later chapter.

Hanging Sentences

Often, an interviewer's question will confuse the suspect, resulting in hanging sentences. Suspects attempt to develop a response to the question the interviewer asked; however, as they begin talking, they realize that their response is inappropriate. Once they realize the inappropriateness of the response, they change the direction of their answer and attempt to continue. The interviewer hears, "Well ..." "You know ..." or "It could be that ..." Often, suspects will look sheepishly at the interviewer in hope that they will not be required to complete the answer, or they finish the partial response with a shrug of the shoulder.

Hanging sentences are an excellent indicator of mental confusion. The suspect's inability to answer the question directly and the display of a confused thought pattern should be of particular interest to the perceptive interviewer. It may be to the interviewer's benefit to explore this particular area immediately. He should, however, recognize the hanging sentence as a point of confusion and stress and, therefore, probably a point of deception by the suspect.

Nonresponses

Nonresponsiveness can take one of two forms. First is evasiveness. The evasiveness by the suspect is simply interjecting some other statement and directing the conversation away from something that he did not want to talk about. Politicians use this type of response to avoid answering questions that they do not want to answer. Instead, they turn the conversation to points that they feel make them look better or about which they want to talk. A nonresponsive answer fails to answer the interviewer's question and instead leads into areas that are either less threatening or more positive. The truthful, however, are less likely to respond this way since they tend to answer the question directly.

The second form of nonresponsiveness occurs during the interrogation of a guilty suspect. During the submissive phase of the interrogation, guilty suspects withdraw emotionally and begin having an internal conversation with themselves while weighing their options. In many instances, this withdrawal is so complete that the suspect actually does not hear the question posed by the interrogator. This requires that the interrogator repeat the question several times. It is not an unwillingness to answer but rather the emotional withdrawal that causes the delay in answering. This nonresponsiveness is discussed in more detail in the sections on submission and obtaining the admission.

Giving a Minor Admission

Another tactic utilized by the guilty is to make a minor, less threatening admission in an attempt to convince the interrogator of their truthfulness. In the private sector, the suspect may make an admission to a policy violation in an attempt to cover involvement in a theft. For example, suspects might make a minor admission to drug use in an attempt to convince the officer of noninvolvement in a rape.

The minor admission by the suspect is supposed to convince the interviewer of the suspect's truthfulness and candor. Usually, this revelation is a very minor admission that is not likely to result in any serious action being taken against the suspect. "Yeah, I tried grass," and "Maybe I didn't ring up the correct price," are examples of minor admissions that might be made by the suspect.

Gallows Laughter

Inappropriate or "gallows" laughter by a suspect is an attempt to make the interviewer's question seem petty. Generally, this gallows laughter is inappropriate and fails to have the ring of authenticity. It usually has a forced and uncomfortable sound. The laughter can also be used to cover the deceptive suspect's delay. In some cases, suspect will use gallows laughter and then mockingly admit that they did the crime and exaggerate circumstances surrounding it.

Interviewer: Did you have sex with Mary Smith?

Suspect: (gallows laughter) Have sex with Mary Smith? I did it 12 times with her and then we laid on the beach naked drinking champagne.

The gallows laughter, mocking tone, and exaggeration by the suspect are designed to humiliate questioners and ridicule them for the foolishness of the question. The interviewer is supposed to be embarrassed at having posed a foolish question. If the tactic is successful, the interviewer might fail to follow up on the question because of the suspect's mockery.

Political Answers

Political answers are attempts by a suspect to respond to the interviewer's question without telling a complete lie. The political response allows the suspect to hedge against potential evidence that the interviewer may possess. They are qualifying phrases used by the suspect to evade, to avoid having to falsify and lie directly. Some examples of political answers would be:

- To the best of my knowledge ...
- I believe ...
- If I recall correctly ...
- Kind of
- Sort of
- Not really ...
- At this point in time ...
- If my memory serves me correctly ...

These types of responses are typically used by deceptive individuals. The guilty may use these qualifiers when an interviewer's question was not exactly on target. For example, the interrogator asks the suspect, "Bill, did you break into the house on Derby Lane?" The suspect responds, "No, not really."

The suspect's response leaves open the option that he did burglarize the residence but did not break in. The suspect may have just walked into the house through an unlocked door. The response is a qualified denial which is generally indicative of a deceptive individual. Truthful suspects respond directly and deny the crime generally: "I didn't steal any money." The guilty respond by denying specifically: "I didn't steal that $300." This tactic leaves open the opportunity for the deceptive individual to evade the specific incident without confessing to a secondary involvement in a crime.

Emphasis on Truthfulness

Often, deceptive individuals attempt to convince the interviewer of their veracity by continually referring to how truthful they have been. They will use phrases such as "Honestly," "Honest to God," "Trust me on this one," or "I swear on a stack of bibles" to increase their credibility.

In addition, the guilty might point out how helpful they have been in previous investigations. They might even vaguely identify incidents in which they helped the police or loss prevention resolve a crime. The guilty might also point out the times when he has turned in lost or stolen property. These instances may or may not be true.

However, truthful individuals who have cooperated in the past generally do not find it necessary to highlight this cooperation with the police or loss prevention. They believe that this past behavior is already known by investigators. Moreover, truthful individuals usually do not consider themselves suspects, and therefore, they have no reason to enhance their believability. The guilty, on the other hand, believe that all eyes are turned on them and they will make every effort to make themselves look better.

Memory Problems

Memory problems are often indicative of the deceptive suspect and can take one of two forms: selective forgetfulness and selectively good memory. To forestall any interrogation, suspects use a selective inability to remember: "How can I tell you that I did it when I just don't remember?" or "I might have taken something, but I just don't remember what it was."

Many interrogators find that the "I can't remember" defense is difficult to overcome. The interrogator is put into the position of having to prove that the suspect does remember. The difficulty here is that the interrogator has little chance of proving to guilty suspects that they do recall their dishonesty. Even factual evidence that indicates the suspect's recollection can be overcome by the suspect's feigning a memory loss.

With a selectively good memory, suspects have the ability to recall specific details that support their noninvolvement in the incident, but they are unable to recall information that may not be helpful to their case. This selective good memory can also be found in instances where a guilty suspect is able to recall information from a previous date with great detail. The recollection of this particular incident is recalled because it favors the suspect.

In general, the recollection of an event is predicated on a "hook" in the memory — there has to be some significance to the event (hook) that causes a suspect to recall the details. For example, most people asked what they were doing on July 1, 1989 would be unable to remember. However, people involved in a significant event, such as an accident, death in the family, or vacation, or having some other memory hook tying the event to the date would probably be able to answer. Often, the ability to remember is affected by the significance of the event and the amount of time that has passed before the event has to be recalled.

With the passage of time, memory can also become distorted. Usually, the truthful individual who is able to recall an event does so repeatedly with only minor changes. Deceptive individuals who are manufacturing a story to enhance their believability are often likely to retell the story with significant changes in the details. They are often reluctant to repeat their story to other investigators or to the same one for fear the details will not match.

During the investigation of a burglary, a suspect was questioned regarding the details of his whereabouts prior to, during, and after the crime. As he recounted his alibi for the third time, the interrogator began to point out the repeated changes and discrepancies in his story. The interrogator told the suspect that he couldn't keep changing his story, and the suspect responded, "I can if I want." Suspects who change their story repeatedly do so because they fail to recall the details they manufactured, perhaps only moments before. The adage "a liar needs a good memory" is never more true than when one attempts to recount the details of an alibi repeatedly.

Finally, some suspects attempt to use the "I don't understand" tactic to discourage an interrogator from attempting to elicit a confession or information. Here, an otherwise intelligent suspect claims to not understand questions or their meanings and thus avoids responding to the interviewer. Failing to understand a question might be acceptable if the suspect were of especially low intelligence and the interviewer was not speaking to that level. However, this tactic is usually used by the guilty to evade a direct response to an interviewer's question. Suspects who speak English as a second language frequently hide behind this ploy to avoid answering questions.

The tenacity with which suspects will stick with their story is also dependent upon their truthfulness. Truthful suspects are able to recount their story repeatedly with only minor changes and will rarely change significant details of the story. In evaluating a suspect's alibi, the interviewer should look for subtle, minor differences that are likely to be found in a truthful suspect's story. It is the guilty who vary significantly in the details of the story and are willing to change them to fit real or fictitious evidence presented by the interviewer. For example, the suspect claims to have been home for the entire evening watching TV. When the interviewer questions him regarding his being identified near the location of the robbery, the suspect suddenly recalls that he did run out to get a pack of cigarettes. This change in the suspect's alibi is typical of the guilty person's need to explain away seemingly damaging evidence presented by the interviewer. Techniques to offer the suspect a chance to change his story can be found in Chapter 7, in the section "Questions of Enticement."

The Admission of Guilt and Offer of Restitution

Innocent suspects usually refuse to admit involvement in an incident to which they were not a party. Their denials are generalized, and they refuse to admit any guilt or make restitution for a loss in which they were not a party.

As a ploy, the guilty are much more likely to admit guilt if it makes the interviewer "happy." The guilty also may say, "Okay, if that's what you want me to say, I'll say it." This is said with a sarcastic voice and is rarely a genuine offer by the guilty to confess. The guilty, however, use this ploy in an attempt to make the interrogator back off. It is a childlike approach to a difficult situation in which the individual attempts to blame others for his difficulty.

The guilty might also offer to pay for things that they deny having stolen. Generally, they do this "just to be fair." In certain instances, a truthful suspect might offer restitution, such as when the individual is a long-term, conscientious member of the community who, because of a misguided feeling of responsibility, feels obligated to pay for the loss. The interrogator should view such offers of restitution carefully. They must always be tested by the interrogator to determine whether they are from the truthful or deceptive individual. To test such an offer, the interrogator offers a fictitious second amount or incident to see if the suspect is also willing to pay that amount back, even though we know that it was not stolen. The following dialogue illustrates the testing of the offer to make restitution.

> *Interrogator*: We're glad to hear you say that you're willing to pay this money back even though you didn't take it. That shows a lot of effort on your part and I think we're a long way toward getting this cleared up.
>
> *Suspect*: Yeah.
>
> *Interrogator*: Now I'm not sure if you are aware, but besides the $151 loss, there was an additional $30 shortage that came up in the funds about a day later. Can we count on you to pay that back too?
>
> *Suspect*: No!
>
> *Interrogator*: Why not?
> *Suspect:* Because I didn't take that money.

In many cases, the guilty suspect realizes what he just said. He is willing to pay back $151, but not an additional $30 because he didn't steal that. Thus, some suspects are tricked into an admission or they give a vague refusal to pay the money.

A truthful individual, however, may also reluctantly agree to pay the fictitious $30 loss. If the individual agrees to pay a fictitious amount, the interrogator should view the agreement to make restitution cautiously. The suspect might simply feel responsible but not in having stolen the money. On the other hand, the suspect might have been involved in other thefts, which was the reason for the offer to pay the fictitious loss.

This procedure can also be used in other cases, such as vandalism to property. For example, if the suspect agrees to pay for damage to the property under investigation, the interrogator should ask the suspect if he is willing to pay restitution for another act of vandalism that never occurred.

Verbal Slips

Another excellent indicator of deception is a verbal slip — mental errors by the guilty suspect. While suspects recreate the image of involvement in their mind and attempt to formulate a deceptive answer, their verbal response becomes confused. In the confusion, they actually acknowledge their involvement in the incident. The interviewer should consider the odds that a truthful person would respond in this way.

> *Interrogator:* Mark, let me ask you, did you rob the Union 76 station in Des Plaines?
>
> *Suspect:* Yes … I mean no …

The suspect has spoken the truth unconsciously. Before his conscious mind can take over with the contrived story, the mouth speaks the truth. Probably more common is the verbal slip that occurs during the phase of developing the admission. In these types of slips, the suspect is repeatedly attempting to minimize the seriousness of his involvement. Often, these verbal slips come when the suspect is asked how many items he has taken. Up to this time, the suspect has said a shirt, coat, jacket, VCR, and a radio. When asked later in the interrogation to tell again the items he has stolen, several items now are spoken pluralized, such as jackets and radios. There are really two issues at play in this example. First, the unconscious mind's selection of the truth before the concocted story takes over, and, second, the inability of the suspect to recall what he has previously told the interviewer.

The guilty will also be particularly interested in what the punishment for the incident under investigation is going to be. They will often question the interviewer regarding what is going to happen to the person responsible. Truthful suspects rarely do this because they have a good idea of what the end result will be: termination, prosecution, and embarrassment.

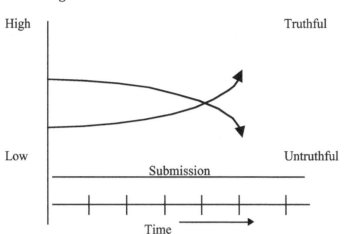

Figure 5.18 This chart illustrates the resistance of truthful and untruthful suspects. The suspect's resistance to a confession increases as time passes in the interview, whereas guilty suspects' resistance lessens until they are ready to confess.

Strength of Denials

If interrogators confront a truthful suspect, they usually receive initial denials that are direct and spontaneous. As the interrogator presses the interrogation and time passes, these denials get progressively stronger, and the truthful suspect becomes more and more dominant. Ultimately, the truthful suspect is able to stop the interrogator from making any headway and begins to convince the interrogator of his truthfulness.

The guilty suspect, on the other hand, may start off with denials that are equal in strength or even significantly stronger than those of the truthful suspect (see Figure 5.18). The feigned initial strength of denial may be coupled with contrived emotional acts that are overacted and unbelievable. The difference between the truthful and untruthful denials is that, as the interrogator begins to offer rationalizations that allow the suspects to save face, the guilty's denials tend to diminish in strength and frequency. As the rationalizations begin to have their desired effect of reducing the suspect's resistance to a confession, the suspect becomes quiet and slowly moves behaviorally to a submissive posture and, ultimately, a confession.

Causes of Denials

6

The greatest cause of denials is often the interviewer.

Lying and the use of denials is a daily occurrence in many individuals' lives. Many people find that it is easier to lie than to tell the truth. Lies and denials vary in their seriousness from the "white lie" to the very serious. Denials are usually the guilty person's attempt to protect his deception from being uncovered by another. Although there are other forms of denial, this text concentrates on those used to protect a deception.

An individual's use of denial is essentially a defensive or avoidance behavior. From childhood, we learned that an admission of wrongdoing generally results in unpleasant consequences. Young children easily learn that if they admit the damage to a fallen lamp, it will result in their being punished. After several incidents, the child has learned to deny involvement to avoid the unpleasantness of a consequence. The punishment or consequences may be as minimal as a parent's disapproval or causing pain to another by telling the truth.

Opposing an individual's perception of the helpfulness of the lie in avoiding consequences is society's moral disapproval of lying. An individual's desire to avoid the consequences conflicts with religious, parental, and societal imperatives to tell the truth in spite of the consequences. On the one hand, parents, teachers, and religious leaders encourage truth telling and appropriate moral conduct, but, on the other hand, they punish the child when inappropriate behavior is discovered. The inability of the individual to reconcile the two sides leads to a mental state called *dissonance*. Psychologists use dissonance to describe a stressful state in which the mind is not in equilibrium. The stress is created by the knowledge of what is right versus the attempt to deceive, which violates society's moral and ethical codes. The emotional stress resulting from these conflicting views is guilt. Guilt is sometimes so overpowering that it alone can overcome an individual's fear of consequences.

When individuals begin to tell lies, they discover that, on occasion, they may be successful in their deception. Thus, the successful perpetration of the lie becomes a learned behavior and is used repeatedly to overcome situations of risk. The successful liar soon learns that this deception, if successfully carried out, gives him power. Gradually, the lies begin to accompany forms of wrongdoing, such as theft, murder, or some other act.

However, lying to others has an effect upon an individual. First, the successful liar discovers that lies are becoming easier to tell and begins to perceive them as less harmful to others. Second, the liar's perception regarding the chances of being caught begins to alter. Liars begin to believe that they cannot be caught lying. This changing perception skews the individual's judgment and they begin to lie more frequently. The liar believes that lying frequently reduces the chances of getting caught. Although this is completely untrue, it remains the perception. The third effect lying has on liars is their belief in their own reasons or good motives for committing the crime under investigation. The suspect believes that to kill or steal is justified because of this altered reasoning.

Thus, socialized individuals develop a *benefit versus consequence* scale. The decision to lie is based on the individual's assessment of whether the benefits of telling the truth outweigh the consequences resulting from an admission. The suspect's fear of consequences typically falls into one of five areas:

1. Fear of prosecution
2. Fear of termination
3. Fear of embarrassment
4. Fear of restitution
5. Fear for their own or another's physical safety

The following thought process illustrates the development of a denial:

Fear of consequences → fear of confession → defensiveness → denial

Youngsters often make decisions using the fun coefficient: the amount of fun that they will have doing something, divided by the amount of trouble they will get into if discovered. If the amount of fun outweighs the amount of trouble, the decision is easily made. In the event that the likelihood of discovery seems minimal, then the immediacy of the fun will outweigh discovery, and they will elect to follow the wrong path. Very young children are not even this sophisticated and often do not even consider the possibility of a consequence. As individuals mature, the consequences, or their perception of the consequences, take on a greater role in the decision-making process.

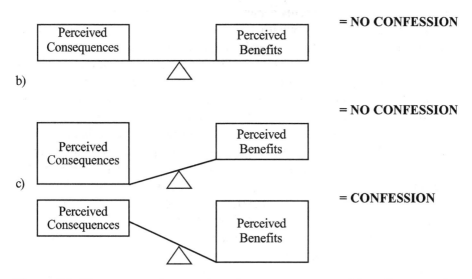

Figure 6.1 The suspect who perceives the consequences and benefits as equal generally takes the path of least resistance and does not confess. The suspect who believes the seriousness of the consequences outweighs any benefits of a confession also will not confess. It is the suspect who perceives a benefit that outweighs the consequences who confesses.

In making a decision to deny, individuals weigh the consequences to themselves and to others, as well as the benefits. These benefits, however, may not necessarily be real or tangible. The benefits may simply be the individual's perception of how he will be perceived by others. The belief that he will be favorably perceived by others may not be true; however, it might overcome his fear of embarrassment.

The decision to confess, therefore, is to a large extent determined by the benefits perceived by the individual. This decision-making process is illustrated in Figure 6.1.

Denials occur daily in each of our lives in the form of concealment, misrepresentation, avoidance, minimization, exaggeration, or falsification. Interviewers face the possibility of denials in both interviews and interrogations. During an interview, an interviewer must overcome the witness's resistance to giving information. The witness's or victim's resistance to giving information is a result of his perception of the consequences. The consequences of cooperation may be retribution from the criminal, having to testify in court, which takes time away from work or family, embarrassment, or simply being viewed as an informant. Any of these may be a sufficient consequence to cause an individual to resist giving information. On the benefits side of the equation is helping catch and punish the person responsible, doing one's civic duty, publicity, and feeling important. The perception of consequences and benefits depends on the individual but can be generalized across different types of witnesses and suspects. Each witness and suspect has his own set of needs that may influence the level of cooperation.

In an interrogation, suspects see consequences in a much more personal way. They recognize that prosecution, personal embarrassment, or loss of their jobs are directly related to their involvement in the issue under investigation. To a lesser degree, there may be a fear of having to return or pay for what was stolen or of suffering physical retribution from others involved. Even though the suspect internalizes these consequences in a much more personal way than a witness, benefits can be presented to overcome the perception of the consequences. For some suspects, simply the reduction of guilt that they feel as a result of having been involved in the incident may be sufficient to overcome the process of denial. This is occasionally seen when individuals turn themselves in after discovering they can no longer live with the guilt of knowing that they killed someone or stole from another person.

Some suspects simply cannot withstand emotionally the overwhelming weight of evidence presented to prove their guilt, so they confess. Other suspects perceive that there may be a benefit in how others will think of them. For them, it is important to be allowed to save face with family, friends, or co-workers. This face-saving provides the suspect a sufficient benefit to overcome the consequences.

Thus far, only the causes of denials as a result of learned behavior have been considered. The fear of consequences results in defensiveness, and that defensiveness manifests itself as a denial of involvement. Recognizing that consequences can sometimes be an overwhelming concern for the suspect, the interviewers must consider the suspect's view of three primary factors that can cause denials: environment, interrogator, and suspect.

An interrogator should consider the suspect's perspective as it relates to the cause of denials. The interrogator must look at the suspect's moral and ethical value system to understand the suspect's reasons for denial. How the suspect perceives the consequences, investigation, interrogator, environment, and himself can all affect the likelihood of denial.

Environment

Recognizing that the environment can play a major role in whether a suspect might deny or resist a confession is important to the interrogator. Any number of environmental considerations might precipitate a denial.

Privacy

During the discussion of setting for the interview or interrogation, privacy and the perception of privacy were equated to the emotional impact that it has on a suspect. In an environment without privacy, the suspect might feel increased fear of embarrassment, which will result in a denial. The selection of the witness might also result in increased likelihood of denials. When the witness has an emotional bond with the suspect or has developed a friendship or trust, increased likelihood of denial might result because the suspect does not want to admit that he has violated another's trust. Remembering that an individual prefers to be perceived in the best possible light will enable the interrogator to anticipate situations where a witness might cause a denial because of a relationship with the suspect.

Supportive Environment

Selecting an environment that is supportive to a suspect might also increase the likelihood of the suspect's denial. In these situations, because the suspect is in a familiar, supportive surrounding, he might feel emotionally secure and strong, which results in failure to understand the difficulty of his position completely. The higher the level of comfort, the more likely the suspects will discount evidence against them with a denial. The supportive environment might also lead to denials because suspects vividly see the impact that a consequence will have on their normal life. The supportive environment of home or office also affords suspects the day-to-day distractions that they may use to avoid thinking about their guilt.

Interviewers generally avoid interviewing or interrogating a suspect in a supportive environment, but it often is not the case with victims or witnesses. In many cases, seeking a supportive environment for a victim or witness will assist them in building a greater rapport with the interviewer. A supportive environment can be especially important when interviewing a small child. Emotionally insecure with adults, and frightened because of the situation, children are often uncooperative and denying. The interviewer who uses a supportive environment reduces the likelihood of the denial and increases the child's cooperation.

Positioning

Finally, consider the positioning of the interviewers in relation to the victim, witness, or suspect. Interviewers should avoid positioning themselves in ways that increase the subject's defensiveness, such as standing over or sitting too close to him. Individuals have elliptical behavioral zones surrounding their bodies in which they interact with others. The intimate zone is the innermost zone, which generally extends out from the individual 1 to 2 feet. Into this zone, individuals typically allow family, close friends, lovers, and small children, people with whom they are particularly comfortable. The second zone is the social zone, which generally extends from 2 to perhaps 6 feet. In this zone, the majority of an individual's social interaction takes place. It also is here that the person conducts meetings, makes purchases, and holds discussions with others. The third zone is a public zone extending 6 to 10 feet, in which the individual will react to others, but to a lesser degree.

Studies of violent criminals have postulated that their intimate zones may extend farther than normal. This would explain why these violence-prone individuals often claim that the violence was sparked because, "He was in my face," or, "He was crowding me," even when the eyewitness evidence suggests otherwise. Significant internal pressure can be felt simply by standing face to face with someone. The closer one moves forward, the greater the pressure or discomfort experienced. This discomfort is more pronounced when there is not a close personal relationship between the two individuals. When an interrogator invades a victim's, witness's, or suspect's personal zone, without allowing the individual to become accustomed to his presence, it will directly translate into an emotional discomfort. This discomfort can cause defensiveness and ultimately a denial by the individual.

Interviewers standing close or moving too quickly toward a suspect or witness often cause in a suspect's corresponding movement away. The emotional pressure caused by the proximity of the interviewers can result in a suspect's or witness's even feeling physically threatened. This certainly could increase the likelihood of a denial or a failure to cooperate further.

Interviewer/Interrogator

Not surprisingly, the greatest cause of denials is often the interviewer himself. Denials are often not fully understood by interviewers and interrogators. Interviewers often blame denials only on the suspect's fear of consequences. Although the suspect's fear of consequences and personality play a significant role, the interrogator may have caused denials because of strategies or tactics employed during the interrogation. The suspect's perception of the interrogator and his strategy can often dictate whether the suspect will deny.

Interrogator's Personality

The suspect's perception of an interrogator's personality can play a large part in determining whether the interviewers will be able to overcome a suspect's fear of the consequences. Interrogators who are overbearing, aggressive, or nonempathic toward a suspect often increase the suspect's defensiveness, resulting in denial. An interrogator who displays this type of personality is judged by the suspect to be an opponent. The suspect then counters the interviewers's attitude with defensiveness, which leads to denial. The adage that you attract more flies with honey than with vinegar is especially applicable in interviewing or interrogating.

When an interrogator is disliked by a suspect, the dislike often culminates in distrust and denial. Part of the suspect's decision to trust the interrogator is based on the interrogator's sincerity and certainty in the suspect's guilt. An interrogator's lack of sincerity encourages suspects to deny because they fail to trust the interrogator.

Interrogator's Attitude

The interrogator who appears to the suspect to be too matter-of-fact, passive, robotic, or rushed in handling the case might cause a denial. In each of these cases, suspects might determine it is in their best interest to deny as a result of their negative perception of the interrogator. Where interrogators are too passive, suspects may view them as weak and exploit the perceived weakness with denials and aggressive behavior. Where an interrogator attempts to rush suspects into a confession, they might elect to deny simply because they believe the hurried demeanor of the interrogator is a weakness they can exploit. Here, the interrogator's weakness is the lack of time to complete the interrogation. By making denials and waiting out the interrogator, the suspect believes he can win the encounter.

Interrogator Reputation

In some instances, an interrogator's reputation may foster the suspect's denial. If the interviewer has a reputation of being uncaring, rough, or unfair, it might encourage a suspect to deny because of increased fear of having to deal with a nonempathic individual.

Denials also often occur when the interviewer has previously had unsatisfactory encounters with the suspect. Personality conflicts resulting from earlier encounters, interviews, or interrogations are often sufficient to cause denials by the suspect.

If the interrogator has previously been fooled by the suspect, or the suspect has not confessed during previous interrogations, the suspect is likely to deny involvement because of those past experiences. The suspect has successfully held off the interviewer previously and fully expects to be able to do so again. The presumption that this investigation is not conclusive is supported by the past experience, when the suspect was neither arrested nor terminated. Failure of the termination or arrest to materialize after the last confrontation bolsters the suspect's ability to hold out during future interrogations. If a suspect is able to stand firm against a competent interrogator the first time, it is unlikely that other interrogators will gain an admission without strong conclusive evidence of the suspect's guilt in later interrogations.

Tentativeness and Unconvincing Behavior of the Interrogator

The interrogator's verbal and physical behavior during the interrogation can also directly affect a suspect's decision to deny. When the interrogator is perceived to be unsure, inconsistent, or weak, suspects will often make a denial to test the interrogator's assertions. Suspects seeing a lack of confidence in the interrogator deny because they do not believe the investigation is as conclusive as the interrogator would have them think. Therefore they deny involvement to continue to avoid detection.

An interrogator's uncertainty of the case facts, misquoting of commonly known facts, or unprepared appearance can also encourage a suspect to deny. The suspect's decision to deny is based upon the belief that he has not been identified. The suspect is gambling that the interrogator's bumbling of the facts is directly related to the competency of the investigation. Most suspects recognize that an incompetent investigation will be unlikely to result in their being proved guilty of the offense.

The interrogator's tentativeness, evidenced by a lack of preparation and understanding of the case evidence, might convince suspects that they are in a winning position. The interrogator's tentativeness might be reflected in his or her tone of voice. A voice that is insincere, uncertain, or lacking confidence might bolster the suspect's belief that he has not yet been discovered, and it contributes to the decision to deny.

A suspect consistently evaluates the language used by the interrogator to determine the viability of continued denials. An interrogator who uses tentative words, such as "might," "could," "perhaps," "usually," or "maybe," when describing the suspect's involvement encourages the suspect to believe he has not been caught. Consider the difference in emotional impact of the following two statements:

1. "With our investigative techniques, we can sometimes identify the person responsible for the incident. In this case we think that it is probably you."
2. "There is no question about the results of our investigation. It clearly indicates that you are responsible for the incident."

The tentativeness of the first statement encourages a suspect to attempt to evade detection by using a denial. The second statement may also result in a denial, because of its directness, but the suspect can also observe the confidence the interrogator displayed in the suspect's guilt.

Perception of Interrogator

Suspects' initial evaluation of the interrogator may cause them to deny simply because they believe that the interrogator can be fooled. Suspects are encouraged to lie and deny their involvement in the incident because they believe that it is unlikely that the interrogator can or will detect their dishonesty or lies.

Inspector Columbo is television's answer to this type of interrogator. Columbo is portrayed as a bumbling, incompetent investigator. His incompetence is perceived by the suspect who denies and makes up lies to cover his tracks. The suspect's downfall, of course, is his own lies, as he discovers the bumbling inspector is merely a role played by the sharp, intuitive Lieutenant Columbo.

Suspects are encouraged to lie because they believe that the investigator is just another individual who can be successfully fooled. Suspects' belief that they can fool others began when they successfully duped parents, teachers, and employers. Their perception of the interrogator's competence might be derived from their knowledge of the system and having previously beaten other incompetent interviewers and interrogators.

Recognizing the interrogator's bumbling ways, suspects believe they will, in all likelihood, be successful in this deception as well. Therefore, they deny involvement.

Wrong Rationalizations Used by the Interrogator

Chapter 10 discusses the use of rationalizations to overcome a suspect's resistance to confessing. At this point, it is sufficient to say that a suspect who has not been offered an acceptable face-saving option will be more reluctant to confess than one who has. In some instances, a suspect can be encouraged to confess simply because of the overwhelming evidence of guilt. However, the confession could be more easily obtained if the interrogator transfers the suspect's guilt and minimizes the seriousness of the incident through the use of rationalizations.

It is the interrogator's job, during the interrogation, to establish the credibility that leads suspects to believe they have been identified as responsible for the incident. Developing the suspect's belief that he has been caught is critical to the suspect's making an admission. However, factually overwhelming suspects without allowing them to save face or failing to convince them that their guilt has been absolutely detected is likely to result in a denial. An interrogator who fails to allow a suspect to save face is really asking for multiple admissions from the suspect — that the suspect did it and that the suspect is a horrible person for having done it.

When the interrogator fails to offer suspects a way to save face, they deny because they cannot emotionally accept the negative image of themselves and the consequences they face. The lack of justification for the suspect's actions only increases the emotional weight of the incident in the suspect's mind and encourages a denial.

Offering suspects a rationalization that they do not accept can also increase the likelihood of denial. The suspect may feel that economic reasons would justify the acts, but the interrogator talks instead about job performance. The interrogator's failure to meet the emotional needs of the suspect with a proper rationalization increases the probability of denial because the suspect has not adequately been given the opportunity to save face.

Rationalizations are always individualized for each suspect. A suspect might not accept a particular rationalization or justification for his behavior. For example, a suspect may rationalize and believe that economic reasons were a contributing factor for his committing a particular crime. If the interrogator fails to use that justification, however, he will find increased denials and resistance by the suspect. Once the interrogator discovers the reason favored by the suspect, the level of denials will decrease dramatically as the suspect accepts the face-saving strategy. An interrogator faced with recurring denials should shift rationalizations in an effort to find one more acceptable to the suspect.

Personalizing Rationalizations Too Early

In the early stages of a confrontation with the suspect, an interrogator can cause the initial denial by offering rationalizations coupled with the second-person pronouns "you" and "your" or using the suspect's name. When the suspect has not yet accepted the rationalizations, the use of those personal pronouns or name is more likely to encourage a suspect to deny because the interrogator's words are hitting too close to home. During the early stages of an interrogation, when the interrogator has not yet directly accused the suspect, the use of third-person pronouns (them, they, he, she) discourages the suspect from denying. The suspect listens to the rationalizations and allows them to have an effect but is not threatened by the rationalizations because they lack directness.

Highlighting Consequences

The interrogator can also cause a suspect's denials by highlighting the seriousness of the consequences. This is done by the interrogator's using realistic words that recreate the seriousness of the incident in the suspect's mind. An interrogator who uses words such as "steal," "theft," "murder," "rob," or "rape" encourages the suspect to reconsider the consequences. During the interrogation, the interrogator uses rationalizations to minimize the seriousness of the suspect's actions. However, by using words that attach consequences, the interrogator is encouraging the suspect once again to build his fear of detection, become defensive, and deny.

Some interrogators highlight the consequences in the hope of scaring a suspect into a confession. Only rarely does this tactic work. More often, it merely encourages additional resistance from the suspect, whose fear of detection and the resulting consequences has increased.

Interrogator Silence

The interrogator's word choice can cause denials, as can long pauses or silences. The use of silence by interviewers rarely enhances the likelihood of a confession. To the contrary, it allows suspects an opportunity to think and assess other possibilities that might convince the interrogator of their innocence. In an interrogation, silence invites the suspect to join the conversation. Especially in the early stages of the interrogation, when the suspect is still emotionally strong, this invitation will almost always result in denials. Although pauses by the interrogator have their place in highlighting a particular statement or word, pauses that extend beyond the need to emphasize a point or word invite a denial from the suspect.

Silence in an interview can sometimes be an effective tactic. Since victims or witnesses are talking much more, they tend to fill silence with more conversation, often resulting in development of additional information. By contrast, in an interrogation, the suspect will deny or lead the interrogator astray.

Interrogator Strategy

The interrogator's selection of a particular strategy in the interrogation can also increase the likelihood of denials. Interrogators who immediately confront the suspect without establishing rapport or building the investigation's credibility often force the suspect to protect a position and deny. In this case, the initial cause of denials is not complicated. The directness of the interrogator's approach catches the suspect off guard and the suspect's first instinct is to lie. Now the suspect has not only committed the crime but also has lied by denying involvement. The interrogator who forces the suspect into a position of having to lie about an incident typically encourages him to lie and deny further in order to protect what he has already said.

The interrogator who elects to use the strategy of interrogating suspects on their strongest defense might also face denials. In beginning the interrogation by focusing on a single specific incident or moment, the interrogator encourages a suspect to mount a defense. Suspects perceive that their exposure is minimal, and they can protect themselves with a denial.

Once suspects are able to discern the target and direction of the interrogation, they can build their defenses. When interrogators focus attention on a single issue, they limit the suspect's exposure and make his defense easier to construct. If the interrogator cannot prove, to the suspect's satisfaction, that he is involved, the suspect will continue to deny. Often, because the interrogator lacks the necessary proof, the suspect's denials grow in intensity when he recognizes the investigation's weakness.

Because the interrogator has confronted the suspect only on a single specific incident, the effects of denials can be very difficult for the interrogator to overcome. Once suspects discover that denials cause the interrogator difficulty, they will continue with additional denials.

Wrong or Incomplete Evidence

In many cases, an initial attack on a suspect's story is based on incomplete or inconclusive evidence. Once an interrogator uses incorrect facts to establish the credibility of the investigation, suspects will gamble that the investigation is not conclusive in proving guilt. If suspects believe that the investigation is inconclusive, they will use denials to defend themselves and their position.

Investigative errors shake the suspect's belief that they have been caught and encourage them to take a chance that the interviewer does not really know they are responsible. These errors in investigative facts might lead the suspect to deny specifically: "I didn't kill her with the bat." The suspect is denying the weapon, not the crime. In a theft, the suspect might say, "I didn't take those 20 VCRs." It might be that he took 15, and the victim inflated the loss to obtain a larger insurance claim.

These specific denials by the suspect often precede the confession if the interrogator recognizes that the suspect is not claiming innocence but just denying incorrect details. Recognizing a suspect's specific denial often allows the interrogator to correct the wrong information that caused the denial and delayed the admission.

Perceived Lack of Proof

Another cause of denials by guilty suspects is their belief that the interrogator cannot prove the allegation. The interrogator who fails to establish the credibility of the investigation promotes the suspect's belief that his guilt is not certain, which will certainly cause a suspect to deny. Suspects, in evaluating the risks and benefits, believe that they have not been clearly identified. Suspects who believe their guilt is uncertain will continue to deny until the interrogator presents sufficient evidence to prove their involvement.

Liars believe that others have the same value system as they do and believe that others would attempt to deceive them. For this reason, they are unlikely or unwilling to believe the interrogator's statements regarding their involvement in the incident. Because they fail to believe the interrogator, they are likely to continue to make denials until they can evaluate the interrogator's proofs.

Compromised Investigation

Denials are also likely from people who have had time to prepare for the interview or interrogation. Sometimes the interrogation of a suspect has been compromised by third parties. The third party might be a co-conspirator previously interrogated or a well-meaning individual who gives the suspect information, leading him to believe that he will be interrogated. The suspect, having had time to develop a story and think through the probable questions to be asked, believes he is likely to be able to convince the interrogator of innocence — the suspect believes he has concocted a plausible sequence of events that can answer all aspects of even a thorough investigation.

Also because the suspect has had time to prepare, his behavior can appear more truthful because of a reduced fear of detection or more time to practice the lie. Having time to prepare also reduces the level of emotion the suspect feels about the incident and the lie, making it easier for the suspect to limit the leakage of deceptive behavior. An interrogator should be cautious when evaluating a suspect's behavior if the suspect had prior knowledge of the likelihood of an interview or interrogation.

Similarly, interrogators who fail to pin down a suspect in his alibi or story before presenting evidence may find that they have encouraged the suspect to deny involvement because he has the latitude to invent incidents or circumstances that explain away the damaging evidence. The interrogator's failure to lock the suspect into a story allows him the freedom to make up lies more easily. Since it is easier for the suspect to lie than to tell the truth, he denies and then fabricates supporting alibis.

Questioning Techniques

The questioning techniques used by an interrogator can also prompt denials from a suspect. The use of direct accusations almost always results in a denial by the suspect, especially if used in the very earliest stages of the interrogation. It often begins the cycle of denial as the suspect uses more denials to protect himself and the original denial. An interrogation beginning with a direct accusation — such as, "Our investigation indicates that you killed John Jones," — will almost always result in a denial by the suspect because the interrogator has neither offered the suspect an opportunity to save face nor established the credibility of the investigation in the suspect's mind.

Denial to Stall for Time

On occasion, guilty suspects will use denials as a means of stalling for time while they evaluate their situation and weigh their alternatives. Suspects who have been directly accused will often make denials while they decide how to handle the situation. This is often used as a first line of defense by suspects who have been surprised with a direct accusation by the interrogator. They use a denial that refutes the interrogator's allegation simply because it requires little or no thought and buys them the time necessary to plan and evaluate further action.

An interrogator also can cause a suspect's denial by presenting evidence of the suspect's guilt too early in the interrogation. Presentation of evidence without providing a face-saving rationalization for the suspect encourages him to deny because otherwise he would be admitting involvement and being a horrible person for having participated in the incident.

Generally, interrogators who present their evidence early in the interrogation are attempting to bring the suspect quickly into submission. However, contrary to this widely held notion, it is more likely to encourage a suspect to deny, or at least to question the validity of the evidence presented by the interrogator.

The suspect is usually physically and emotionally strongest at the beginning of the interrogation. Because of this strength, even strong evidence will often be questioned by the suspect. This is particularly true when the evidence is circumstantial. Circumstantial evidence is even more susceptible to attack by a suspect than direct evidence because, when viewed separately, it may seem weak or inconclusive to the suspect. Many a suspect believes that if there is no direct evidence, such as a witness or video of involvement in the crime, then he has not been caught. This belief reduces the emotional impact of the circumstantial evidence against the suspect and increases the likelihood of a denial.

In the earliest stage of the interrogation, suspects will often look for the interrogator to offer them a question or statement that they can deny. When this question or statement is not forthcoming, suspects will often attempt to elicit it by asking, "Are you accusing me of stealing?" or "Are you saying that I did this?" The suspect has now laid a trap for the unwary interrogator. Should the interrogator respond, "Yes, that's exactly what I'm saying," the suspect has now drawn an interrogator into a direct accusation to which the suspect can appropriately respond with a denial. The suspect now has drawn the lines of engagement and will continue to protect this position with additional denials.

The stalling tactic is also employed by suspects who have used aggression and denials to get out of trouble in the past. It allows a suspect to attack. The saying, "The best defense is a good offense," certainly applies with this type of individual. The aggressiveness that the suspect had used in the past often forced weaker or uncertain opponents to retreat from even strong positions. The success of the past experiences encourages the suspect to return to this pattern of behavior.

Poorly Timed Question

Asking a poorly timed multiple-choice or assumptive question can also cause a denial. The choice question offers the suspect an acceptable versus unacceptable reason for having committed the crime, for example, "Did you use the money to buy drugs or was it for bills?" The interrogator will encourage the suspect to select one of the choices. In an interrogation in which the suspect has not stopped denying, the choice question will only encourage additional denials. The interrogator may have asked the suspect, "Did you plan on doing this or did it happen on the spur of the moment without thinking?" The suspect who is not emotionally ready to confess responds with a denial such as, "I didn't do anything." If the interrogator follows up with another direct question, such as, "Well, has this happened a lot of times or just a few?" it only encourages another denial from the suspect. The failure by the interrogator to recognize the level of the suspect's resistance will result in poorly timed questions that cause the suspect to deny.

Waiting Too Long

In some situations, an interrogator might wait too long in an interrogation and pass the suspect's point of emotional susceptibility to confess. The result is that the suspect once again becomes emotionally strong and likely to defend himself with denials. Some suspects become emotionally stronger after crying and then return to denials.

Failing to Reaccuse

Finally, a suspect's denials can be encouraged if the interrogator does not reaccuse a suspect after the suspect makes an initial denial. Once a suspect makes a denial and it goes unrefuted by the interrogator, he suspects that the case might not be as solid as alleged. The suspect thinks, "If the interrogator really did have what he says he has, he would reaccuse me. The fact that he didn't might indicate he's bluffing." This situation increases the suspect's perception that the interrogator might not be working from a position of strength and increases the likelihood of resistance.

Suspect

Seriousness of the Lie

Suspect might also evaluate the necessity to deny based on the perceptive seriousness of the lie or denial. Often, the liar is persuaded by his own rationalizations that no real harm was intended — people often evaluate the seriousness of a lie based on how much harm it does. A lie that does not do much harm is less serious than one that causes significant problems. The liar also sees a single lie as less serious than numerous lies. Similarly, planned lies are generally viewed as much more serious than lies told on the spur of the moment.

Regardless of the degree, all lies, in some way, cause damage to the suspect and violate the trust of others. Initially, the damage to the suspect might simply be the personal dissonance caused by guilt feelings. However, the need to lie might increase because the suspect has told one lie and now is required to support it with others. Thus, the individual also suffers from a diminished resistance to telling lies as he becomes more practiced and comfortable in their use.

In many cases, suspects' moral and ethical guidelines justify their telling a lie. In many cases, they actually believe such justifications. For example:

- They excuse a lie by stating that it was not a lie but simply a joke, an evasion, or an exaggeration.
- They claim that they were not really responsible for their actions and never meant to mislead, or that they were incompetent (mentally or under the influence of drugs or alcohol) at the time the lie was told.
- They admit the lie but offer excuses for it.

Finally, the interrogator might focus the interrogation on what the suspect considers the most emotionally significant issue. If an interrogator attempts to obtain an admission to what the suspect perceives as the most threatening issue, it will often increase resistance and result in a denial by the suspect.

This perception is illustrated in a case in which a security guard was suspected of stealing women's high-heeled shoes from desks at a bank card facility. Investigators also suspected that the shoes were being worn by the security officer during his shift. The interrogator could elect to confront the suspect on any one of three levels, with each level having a greater emotional weight for the suspect. The greatest emotional weight in the suspect's mind would be an interrogation regarding a sexual deviance. Of lesser emotional weight, but still threatening, would be his wearing of the women's high-heeled shoes. The third and least threatening direction the interrogation could take would be to question the suspect on his having taken the shoes without reference to his wearing them or his sexual proclivities. The case was resolved when the suspect admitted removing the shoes from the women's desks.

The interrogation was conducted beginning with the issue of least emotional weight, that the guard had removed the women's shoes from the desk. When he admitted the removal of the shoes, the next level, wearing the shoes, could be addressed. By looking at the emotional weight of the incident, the interrogator can pick portions of the issue to which it will be easier for the suspect to confess and therefore be less likely to elicit a denial.

The emotional weight or seriousness of the issue is evident in many cases, such as the rape-homicide case in which the suspect admits killing but not raping the victim or the case in which the burglar admits the burglary but denies defecating on the hall floor. The suspect's view of an issue's seriousness will often result in denial when the interrogator attempts to obtain an admission in an area that the suspect perceives to have the greatest emotional weight.

Lack of Rules

In certain instances, suspects will make denials and justify their actions because of the "lack of rules" for their behavior or job. These procedural gray areas are perceived by the suspect as not being "wrong." Suspects' perception that they have not violated rules or regulations or that they are acting within the group norm allows them to justify their behavior. The belief that they are correct causes the subjects to make a denial.

This denial is often fostered by the suspect's knowledge of the ins and outs of his job or the criminal justice system. Interrogators should remember that each person they interrogate is an expert at his own job, be it stockboy, cashier, bank president, or professional criminal. Knowing the rules, regulations, policies, and procedures of the position allows suspects to hide within gray areas to maintain their innocence. The suspect's ability to justify actions, based on his or her perception of the work, legal, or cultural environment, affords an opportunity to explain away seemingly damning evidence. As he attempts to explain away damning evidence by using the gray areas, he utilizes denials to protest his innocence.

Cultural Differences

Cultural differences can also play a role in precipitating a denial by the suspect. The cultural background and beliefs of suspects might make it likely for them to deny. In certain cultures, the practice of lying to others during business is accepted. This culture-based form of denial, and even the perception of right and wrong, might even dissuade suspects from believing they have done wrong.

In some cultures, the necessity for revenge on someone who has dishonored the family outweighs any legal prohibitions against killing. In other situations, suspects' perception of social status might preclude admission of guilt if the interrogator is perceived as being socially below them. This certainly is evident in Arab and Middle Eastern society and their treatment of women — a female interviewing or interrogating a male is likely to result in denials. Their role of women in Middle Eastern society is markedly different from that in the western world.

Drugs and Alcohol

Suspects feigning drug or alcohol intoxication at the time of the crime might deny knowledge or involvement because they "just can't remember." This denial might be real, but it is more likely to be fabricated. The denial justified by intoxication is often used by victims of prostitutes who will claim they were "drugged" or "slipped a mickey" without their knowledge. Such an assertion allows the victim a face-saving device that explains how he was robbed but saves him from having to reveal what he was doing when the incident happened. The denial is tempered by his inability to remember what actually happened.

Consequences versus Justifications

Finally, in making the decision whether to admit or deny, suspects weigh the consequences of their actions and justifications. When suspects face extreme consequences (such as incarceration or the death penalty), they will often make a denial because they are emotionally unprepared to face the harshness of the consequences.

The suspect's realization process in an interrogation is comparable to the five stages of grief: denial, anger, bargaining, depression, and, finally, acceptance. By recognizing that an interrogation is a significant emotional crisis for suspects, the interrogator should expect that they will deny because they do not want to believe they have been detected. Many suspects then use anger as a release or defense to support their denial or in an attempt to dissuade the interrogator. Next comes bargaining — suspects look at alternatives and attempt to negotiate what they consider to be the best deal for themselves. Once that thought process has concluded, suspects go into submission, similar to the depression of grief, and, finally, to acceptance. The suspect cognitively recognizes and then accepts that he has been detected.

When judging the consequences, suspects must begin to justify to both themselves and the interrogator their reasons for participating in the incident. In many cases, suspects will have never verbalized these reasons to themselves, whereas in others they have clearly justified their behavior. Although they may believe that "everyone is doing it" and "it is not really harming anyone," they may have never clearly stated it to themselves.

When experiencing the emotional impact of being caught, suspects must now look for the justification for their involvement in the act. Often, it is the interrogator who helps the suspect find that justification that allows the suspect to overcome the denial process. Once the justification or rationalization is firmly set in the suspect's mind, the risk–benefit equation that the suspect has established begins to alter. At that point, the suspect will cease making denials and attempt to save face with the interrogator.

Involvement of Others

Generally, suspects are more likely to deny guilt if they acted alone than if with others. When interrogated, suspects who acted alone know the full circumstances of the case and if anyone else has been told of their involvement. They can clearly and accurately estimate their exposure in an investigation. Since they have such a clear picture of the likelihood of discovery, they often feel confident in their position and their ability to defend themselves.

When suspects have to evaluate what a co-conspirator might have said or done, it becomes more difficult to assess their own position accurately. Wondering who else might know what the other suspect might have said creates many decision-making problems for the suspects. Now they have to consider if accurate information presented by the interrogator might have come directly from the co-conspirator.

In other situations, denials might occur because one suspect attempts to protect the other. The peer pressure to not inform on each other can initially create denials. However, the primary weakness suspects is their uncertainty and distrust of the others involved. Interrogation of multiple suspects is usually an easier undertaking than attempting to gain an admission from a single perpetrator.

Truthful Denials

On occasion an interrogator can mistakenly confront a truthful suspect and this will clearly result in a denial. Typically, a truthful suspect's denials are direct and spontaneous. These denials can be specific, denying a particular detail of the incident, or broad, generalized denials of any involvement.

As a general rule, these types of denials become more dominant and numerous as the interrogation continues. They finally overcome an interrogator's ability to control the conversation. The persistence of these denials, including their spontaneity and intensity, is a clue for the interrogator in evaluating the suspect's truthfulness.

Part Two

Interviewing

Interviewing

7

The interviewer should understand that, although a meeting between a suspect and the interviewer may be nonaccusatory, for the purpose of simply eliciting alibis or explanations, it can turn into an interrogation at any time.

This chapter begins the discussion of different interviewing techniques by highlighting their differences from the process of interrogation. Generally, an interview is a fact-gathering process that attempts to answer the questions who, what, where, when, how, and why. The talking during the interview, unlike during interrogation, is dominated by the victim, witness, or suspect,[1] who responds to questions posed by the interviewer.

The interviewer might ask the suspect behavior-provoking questions to determine his truthfulness by asking for interpretable behavior consistent with that of a truthful or deceptive individual. In doing so, the interviewer might determine if the interviewee is a suspect in the crime, thereby significantly narrowing the focus of the investigation.

The interview's setting also tends to be much less formal than that of an interrogation. The interviewer often might pick a time and location convenient for the person being interviewed. In the earliest stages of an investigation, the interview is necessarily broad based, with the interviewer attempting to give direction to the investigation.

Since an interview is a noncustodial situation, *Miranda* warnings are usually not necessary. However, there might be situations in which a primary suspect is to be interviewed after the investigation has focused on him. This interview might not be intended to obtain a confession, but rather for the police to attempt to ascertain the suspect's alibi or explanations. In some

---

[1] People being interviewed might be victims, witnesses, or suspects whose true status is unknown — each can be considered a suspect. That status changes once the interviewer has evaluated their truthfulness and relationship to the incident.

cases, because the interview has narrowed its scope significantly and identified a particular suspect, a police interrogator might want to consider the wisdom of giving the suspect *Miranda* warning, in case the interview later changes into an interrogation and the suspect is taken into custody.

The interviewer should understand that, although a meeting between a suspect and the interviewer might be nonaccusatory for the purpose of simply eliciting alibis or explanations, it can turn into an interrogation at any time. The change from nonaccusatory to accusatory can be very direct or very subtle. In either case, the amount of talking done by the interviewer and suspect reverses dramatically. During the interview process, the majority of the investigator's questions are broad and open-ended to elicit a narrative response from the suspect. To clarify specific points, the investigator might use closed-ended questions. For example, an open-ended question might be "What happened next?" while a closed-ended question might be: "What color was the car?" or "Did she tell you that she had done it?"

However, once the interviewer has elected to confront the suspect, the interviewer does almost all the talking and offers face-saving rationalizations that, in the suspect's mind, minimize the seriousness of the suspect's involvement. The difficulty for police who go from an interview to an interrogation is that the suspect might refrain from further conversation with the officer. This change in tactics can also cause a suspect to invoke the rights of silence and counsel, which stop any further communications with the suspect. In the private sector, such a tactic is less significant because the employee does not generally have a right to counsel or silence (see Chapter 3, Legal Aspects, for additional discussion on the subject).

By contrast, an interrogation is designed to obtain information that might be incriminatory from a suspect who might be reluctant to give the information. The purpose of the interrogation is to overcome the suspect's initial resistance and open a dialogue that will encourage him to give information against his interests. An interrogator is still attempting to answer the six investigative questions (who, what, when, where, how, and why), but there are two basic differences between an interview and interrogation. In interrogation:

- The suspect generally talks only when confessing.
- The suspect resists telling the truth until convinced of the need to do otherwise.

While interviewers are talking with any suspect, victim, or witness, it is important that they look for personal agendas or reasons that can taint the information given during the interview. A sign of such a reason or agenda could simply be the suspect's reluctance to cooperate during an interview.

This lack of cooperation could have many reasons, for example, not wanting to be involved because the individual does not want to take time from work to testify in court. Certainly, this is not an unusual attitude because it requires the victim or witness to take the time to go to court and testify with little apparent benefit to them. Consider the arrival of a summons for jury duty. Although it is everyone's duty to assist in the criminal justice system, how many people are actually excited about the prospect of being selected for a jury and having to take time away from work, family, and/or home to be part of a trial? Therefore, is it any wonder that witnesses are often reluctant to supply information valuable to an investigation?

Victims or witnesses might also be reluctant to provide information because "to inform," "narc," or "rat on" is discouraged by friends, family, neighbors, and other peer groups. It also could be possible that giving information could result in the victims' being shunned by the people most important to them.

Another form of reluctance can come into play when the witness or victim is asked to give information against the interests of a family member or close friend. Here, long-term relationships might outweigh a significant criminal act. In a recent case, a man was alleged to have repeatedly molested his niece. These molestations took place over a number of years prior to the allegations. The niece finally came forward and told her mother about her uncle's activities. The case was turned over to the police and the uncle was arrested. The child's mother was put under significant family pressure not to testify and to drop the charges against the uncle. The family's reasoning was that the uncle had a good job, he was a wonderful member of the family, and this would ruin his life. The pressure from family members in this case could have damaged the prosecution; however, the mother continued to press for prosecution.

The interview of victims and witnesses is typically done at a time and place convenient to them. If interviewers believe that the individual might ultimately be the suspect and an interrogation could ensue, they should have the suspect come to their office or a location where a more formalized setting can be arranged. Regardless of whether the interviewer plans a nonaccusatory interview or an interrogation of a suspect, the behavior displayed by the interviewer should be one of reasonableness and fairness. There is never room for mistreatment of a witness or suspect by an interviewer. Yelling, screaming, and pounding fists on the table to obtain information from a reluctant witness are reminiscent of the days of the "third degree."

In the interview, the interviewer should open the lines of communication so the victim, witness, or suspect will begin to talk about the incident under investigation. Especially in the very earliest stages of an investigation when suspects do not yet feel that the investigation has focused on them, they might be inclined to talk at length with the police or investigator. It is during this time that the suspect might give incriminating statements that at first seem like nothing more than innocent remarks. Establishing the suspect's alibi or story in the earliest stages of the investigation can often be valuable in a later interrogation, once his stories have been disproved.

The value of this tactic in the police setting is significantly different from that in private settings. In general, the public law enforcement investigators have the manpower and resources to conduct in-depth investigations into the suspect's story. In most cases in the private sector, resources are much more limited; the company might not have the manpower or expertise to conduct an in-depth investigation. In addition, the lies told during the preliminary interview might have greater weight in a trial than in a presentation to a personnel manager or to company management.

In the private sector, a circumstantial case is rarely sufficient to obtain a termination. As a general rule, human resource departments require direct evidence in the form of an observation or a suspect's statement of involvement rather than circumstantial evidence. In the public sector, a suspect's statements or lies relating to an alibi might prove to be a valuable part of the prosecution's case in establishing the suspect's guilt.

The reliability of the eyewitnesses' or victims' testimony can also come into question because of their personal biases or perspectives. Often, investigators have found significant differences in witnesses' descriptions of an offender at the scene of a robbery. These differences could be based on the position of the witness making the observation, the age of the witness, the length of the observation, or any number of other factors. In many cases, investigators, the courts, and researchers have seriously questioned the reliability of eyewitness testimony.

A witness or victim might provide inaccurate information without intentionally doing so. On the other hand, witnesses or victims might also intentionally provide only a portion of the relevant information to the interviewer. This information could have been withheld so the victim did not have to disclose his negligent actions, such as not locking the safe that allowed the theft to take place.

Some witnesses and informants are motivated by revenge. They want to get even for a real or perceived insult from the suspect. In these cases, the interviewer needs to uncover the true motive to evaluate the information. In one case, a security officer stole $4,600 from a safe in the office of the president of a manufacturing facility. The guard discovered the combination to the safe in a secretary's phone list. The case was ultimately solved when the security officer's father-in-law called the company to tell them what his son-in-law had done. In this case, the father-in-law was motivated by an intense dislike of the man his daughter had chosen to marry. In another case, a man on parole for burglary was implicated in a break-in at a catalogue showroom from where thousands of dollars in precious stones were missing. The informant was the man's wife. While he was incarcerated, she discovered that she enjoyed living alone. To return to the single life, she effected his arrest, prosecution, and reincarceration.

Some individuals have a dislike for law enforcement, security, and loss prevention officials and will therefore fail to cooperate. In such situations, there may be little or no usable information to be gained. It might be necessary for the witness or suspect to believe there is some benefit in talking with the investigator, such as lower bond, reduced charges, or a station adjustment of the criminal activity without formal charges being brought against the suspect or friend of the witness. The reality of dealing with these resentful individuals is an everyday occurrence for the investigator. The desire to trade up for a more significant "catch" encourages an investigator to attempt this form of barter arrangement. Although it is common for investigators to "turn" a suspect because of their ability to prosecute him, care must be taken to assure that the information supplied by the informant is reliable.

Case Example

In an investigation of a series of burglaries from railroad boxcars in transit, three suspects were observed attempting to burglarize a boxcar in a railroad yard. The three suspects were apprehended and interviewed about their involvement in the rash of burglaries. During the interviews, one of the suspects offered to trade information for a reduced bond. The information implicated another gang member in the earlier burglaries at the yard. The suspect identified "Tommy Lee" as being involved in the earlier burglaries. The suspect provided information on the whereabouts of stolen merchandise as well as the location of Tommy Lee.

Subsequent investigation into the information provided by the arrested suspect revealed that Tommy Lee was currently wanted for armed robbery and had two other outstanding theft warrants pending. With the assistance of the local police, a photo lineup was arranged to verify that the suspect, in fact, knew and could identify Tommy Lee. The suspect picked Tommy Lee's picture out of the photo lineup and verified other personal information with an investigator who was familiar with Tommy Lee. Further investigation of the information provided by the informant resulted in the apprehension of Tommy Lee and two other suspects.

The interviewer also needs to be aware that a suspect or victim might omit or evade questions in an attempt to conceal information that he may not want to divulge. A victim, for example, might conceal the fact that a prostitute robbed him in a hotel room rather than face the embarrassment of his indiscretion. In other cases, the victim might conceal information because he himself was involved in something illegal or unethical. Consider the homeowner who falsifies the inventory of items stolen from his home. He includes furs, jewels, and other valuables that he never owned to inflate the claim. At other times, an officer might unwittingly interview the perpetrator of an incident before the investigation has focused on him. During the interview, the offender might attempt to mislead or misdirect the investigation by providing information that is false or that will take considerable time and effort to discredit.

Considering the impact that a well-organized and well-conducted interview can have on an investigation, it is worth the time and effort to plan and prepare for the optimum results. Chapter 2 outlines some of the elements necessary to prepare for the interview or interrogation, considering background information, case facts, location of the interview, and other factors that could create a supportive environment for the witness or suspect. Understanding the elements of the crime and what must be proven to obtain a conviction or a termination is critical in the interview process. Interviewers should think of themselves as a sponge soaking up a pool of water. In this metaphor, the interviewer rarely puts water into the pool that is being soaked up. By not giving information derived from other sources to the person being interviewed, the interviewer can test the truthfulness of the suspect's information. It is also necessary for interviewers to conceal what they know to prevent information known only to the suspect from leaking out. An interviewer's failure to do this might hamper or taint further inquiries. While interviewing victims or witnesses, investigators must also be careful regarding allegations made against particular individuals. Repeated indiscreet allegations of misconduct during interviews could result in later allegations of slander by the suspect. This should not deter an investigation — the employer and investigator have the right to investigate — but the investigator does not have the right to spread unsubstantiated rumors or allegations.

Prior to interviewing victims, witnesses, or suspects, the interviewer should consider which areas of the investigation they might be able to provide information on.

Case Example

An employee, we'll call her "Mary," embezzled $73,000 from a firm by using a weakness in the accounting system to have checks made out to her. She had one to three checks fraudulently issued to her each month for approximately 18 months. The company became concerned that the checks and balances within its system had been circumvented. In looking at the employees involved in the checks and balances, the company was particularly concerned that Mary might have been in collusion with others. Her older sister, a long-term and trusted employee, was in management at the company and was responsible for customer service issues. The sheer size of the loss indicated that the sister might have known of Mary's involvement in the theft. When the loss was discovered and Mary was identified as the individual responsible, an investigation was conducted to recover potential assets purchased with the funds. Mary was confronted and initially acknowledged her involvement in the theft of $3,000 from the company. Upon further investigation, the company found approximately $70,000 in other checks that were used to steal from the company.

Further interviews were planned to determine exactly how the system operated and who was responsible for the checks and balances. A list of people to be interviewed was drawn up, each person categorized by the types of information he or she would most likely be able to provide. This preplanning of the interview allowed the interviewer to focus specifically on employees who had information regarding the system in place and its checks and balances. Additionally, the list highlighted employees who knew the suspect, her background, and interests. The interviews were planned in such a way that the system and background information provided a picture of both Mary and her sister, "Barb." It had been planned that the final interview to be conducted was to be with Barb because of the potential for collusion between the two. It also was determined that Barb would be interviewed with two purposes in mind: (1) to determine whether she had direct knowledge of Mary's embezzlement prior to its discovery, and (2) to ascertain Mary's lifestyle and background. Barb was exonerated of any knowledge of her younger sister's embezzlement activities, and she supplied significant information relating to her sister's lifestyle and off-work activities, including insights into family relationships, social acquaintances, and interests.

Preplanning the Interview

In preplanning areas of inquiry, it is often worth the interviewer's time to make notes about specific areas of interest about which to ask during the interview. It might also be worthwhile to write specific questions to assure the accuracy of the way they were asked. Trial lawyers often use this tactic to ensure that the witness responds to a particular issue that might help prove a point or establish a response for later appeal. Lawyers planning for the questioning of the witness during trial use specifically selected words in the question so they can then evaluate the suspect's responses.

Although it can be in an interviewer's interest to have specific written questions, the interviewer should not go into an interview and read a list of questions. These should be included in the conversation in such a way that they do not seem out of the ordinary. Often, these particular questions form the key elements of, or are the reason for, the interview. To place any undue emphasis on these questions might alert a victim, witness, or suspect that the interviewer has particular interest in these areas of inquiry. Consequently, the key questions need to be camouflaged during the interview so the interviewer does not inadvertently reveal their importance. For example, when conducting a kickback investigation, an investigator might want to look at a buyer's phone records for investigative leads, but the request for phone numbers would not be for the buyer's phone alone. To conceal the target of the investigation, the entire buying department's phone records might be requested. Although investigators might not be able to conceal the fact that they are looking, they can at least conceal the identity of the object of their surveillance.

Supporting Tactics

The interviewer should also consider the use of face-saving rationalization, minimization, and justification tactics that will help witnesses feel more comfortable in giving information because they feel they are doing the right thing. In each interview, a person might not need this kind of "support" by the interviewer. However, in cases where a key interview is to be conducted, the interviewer should consider which type of support the witness might need. The witness's background, interests, and personality can offer clues to which support tactic the interviewer can provide support during the interview. These tactics are more fully explored in Chapter 10. With only slight modifications, these same tactics can be applied in both the interview and interrogation.

Rapport

One of the first needs to be addressed is establishing rapport with the victim, witness, or suspect. Almost any text on interviewing or interrogation encourages establishing rapport, but does not provide any direction on how this is done. The establishment of rapport is fundamental to the success of any interview, but this requires more than merely smiling. Individuals are more likely to confide in someone they feel is supportive and with whom they are comfortable. Even the most cooperative, agreeable witness can be turned off by an interviewer who fails to establish rapport.

Many times, officers use the authority of their badge and the power of subpoena or a search warrant to encourage a witness to cooperate. Although this process might be necessary under certain circumstances, it is not the optimum method for obtaining the desired information. For consumers, by comparison, the decision to buy is often positively influenced by a salesperson who makes them feel comfortable, not by a salesperson who is unlikable or seemingly uninterested.

In the private sector, the investigator does not generally have the ability to subpoena documents or records but must instead depend on the cooperation of the person to be interviewed. In many companies, this cooperation might be limited by the pressure that company management uses to conceal illegal acts or by company policies. Management often views an investigation in a different light than police, security, or loss prevention investigators do. Management's perspective is based on the need for profit and sales. From that view, taking an employee off the sales floor or away from duties can affect the bottom-line profit of the organization.

Often, company personnel policies restrict interviews without a specific allegation of misconduct against the employee. Thus, there are significant difficulties in conducting investigative or even fact-finding interviews within the private sector. The level of cooperation from line management can often be directly related to the backing of the company's senior management.

Establishing Management Rapport

The interviewer attempting to work within a corporate environment must first begin by "selling" upper level management on the need to conduct interviews. Because senior management tends to be oriented toward dollars and results, any discussion about conducting interviews needs to be a "sales presentation" focused on the benefits of interviewing. In planning for the interview and the presentation to management, the interviewer should have a clear purpose in mind for the interviews. The interviewer should plan to address management's objections, such as the potential for disrupting the sales function, potential morale problems, and the legal impact on the company as a result of interviewing or failing to interview.

One management consideration that typically comes up in the private sector is the impact of the interview on employee morale and the resulting job satisfaction. Often, management and the personnel department within the organization do not clearly understand the difference between interview and interrogation. Personnel is often hesitant to allow employees to be interviewed because of a fear of the interviewer's making unfounded or wholesale allegations against each person interviewed. Often, just taking the time to explain what is to be said and how it is planned can obtain management support for the process.

Ground rules for the interviews clearly established with management and human resources offices before any nonaccusatory interviews are conducted will increase the likelihood of gaining their support and the successful conclusion of the process. Although law enforcement officials can use their position to encourage management to cooperate, the in-house security or loss prevention representative generally does not have the same status within the organization. However, the failure of the law enforcement officer to take into consideration the business aspects of interviewing employees can create management resentment and make the process that much more difficult.

Complicating this issue further is the possibility that members of management might be involved in some illegal activity at the company. Such members of management might be reluctant to allow interviews with the associates because they are afraid that evidence of their wrongdoing might surface.

When management at a location is weak or suspected of wrongdoing, the investigator might wish to obtain the cooperation of senior management to overcome any reluctance to cooperate. For example, anticipating a manager's possible reluctance to cooperate because of a lack of floor coverage, the interviewer can arrange for additional staffing to help operate the facility during the time the interviews are taking place. Since police tend to be less familiar with the private sector, they need to be especially sensitive to the needs of the business before interviews are scheduled. This awareness is nothing more than establishing a rapport and a working relationship with senior management to make sure the lines of communication remain open and the needs of each are being met.

Establishing Rapport with the Victim, Witness, or Suspect

In establishing rapport, the interviewer can use several different tactics. Certainly, an authoritative, superior attitude on the part of the interviewer might cause some people to give information. However, it is more likely that this type of an attitude will increase the defensiveness of people being interviewed and make them reluctant to cooperate. Instead, the interviewer should assume a professional yet friendly approach to the person being interviewed. This can be done easily without attempting to be too familiar. Interviewers who are too blunt, who attempt to obtain information without establishing rapport, are often faced with a witness who is cold and uncooperative.

Common ground.   Initially, interviewers should attempt to establish rapport by finding some common ground or interest about which they can speak to the individual. People tend to like people who have similar interests and personalities. By reading the witnesses' or suspects' personalities, the interviewer can establish rapport by changing topics to discuss points of interest particular to them. Getting people to talk about themselves and their interests tends to make them feel comfortable and ease any apprehension. Interviewers must be able to read an individual's behavior to determine how long they should stay in the rapport-generating phase. With a senior executive who is a "get-to-the-point" type of individual, this phase may be extremely limited. Interviewers do not want to overstay their welcome, which might affect further cooperation.

As with the presentations to senior management, a sales presentation must be made to each victim, witness, or suspect to secure cooperation. This presentation highlights the benefits of providing information to the interviewer. The interviewer who knows of a previous complaint at the witness's residence might be able to use that as a benefit to encourage cooperation to assist in resolving this case. However, the witness might be reluctant to give information if that previous problem was never resolved. The witness might feel that, because nothing was done before, he or she should not go out on a limb to help.

In any case, the interviewer who can provide a benefit for cooperation in the interview will increase the likelihood of witnesses' cooperation. The benefit might be pride, case resolution, revenge, or anything else that returns something to the person interviewed. It might be as simple as showing respect for the individual.

Appearance and demeanor.   Often, the interviewer is judged by appearance and demeanor in his initial approach. During the first few seconds of the meeting, the victim, witness, or suspect makes a decision about the interviewer. The interviewer should take care to conceal handcuffs, weapons, or radios, the sight of which might seem to increase the seriousness of the incident and create a sense of unease at giving information.

Words such as *witness, victim, court,* and *testimony* or slang terms used by police and loss prevention can also create an unacceptable image. The interviewer should also avoid any words that trigger negative responses. This can be as simple as avoiding the term *witness.* Just as the interrogator avoids words that attach consequences, such as *steal, embezzle, fraud, kill,* and *rape,* the interviewer avoids using words that cause a witness to comprehend the consequences of giving information, such as lost time from work, attending court, or any number of other less-than-pleasant activities. The interviewer should also refrain from presenting any personal biases or expressing an outward disbelief of what the suspect has said.

Remember that a smile has opened many doors. In a recent study, participants were asked to determine people's trustworthiness and honesty based on the appearance of their faces. People who had a genuine smile were judged to be more honest and trustworthy than those who had scowling or expressionless faces. Is it any wonder that the harsh, cold interviewer might be less likely to produce desirable results than the interviewer who has a friendly demeanor?

Behavior.   How often have you met people and after only a short time felt as if you had known them forever? With such an individual, an instant rapport opened the lines of communication and made you feel extremely comfortable and trusting. To discover why these feelings exist, one need to only look as far as the similarities in thinking and interests. If we focus on the differences, rather than the similarities, between ourselves and our newly found friend, we begin to lose rapport with the individual.

Recognizing similarities between other people and ourselves is not as difficult as one might think. For example, common ground with any individual might be found in family, frustrations of work, bills, children, the need to own a car, or any of dozens of other similarities in our lives. Recognizing each of these similarities will assist us in forming a bond with the individual that we are addressing.

Thus, in looking at the victim, witness, or suspect, the interviewer must discover similar interests, dress, activities, friends, or beliefs as a means to assist in opening a dialogue with the person to be interviewed. Consider how often a common interest forms the beginning of a conversation or friendship.

Mirroring.   The interviewer who uses only words to build rapport has failed to use all the avenues of communication available. The words spoken between two people account for less than 10% of the communication between them. The vast majority of communication takes place using the tone of voice and emphasis on words. In addition, almost half of the communication between individuals is based on physical behavior, posture, and gestures. Understanding other levels of communication enables interviewers to incorporate them into their attempt to generate rapport.

By recognizing the fact that people like others who look, talk, and act similarly to themselves, the interviewer can consciously begin to model the speech patterns, speed of delivery, breathing, posture, and gestures of the individual with whom he is speaking. This tactic is called *mirroring*.

Interestingly, people who have established a high level of rapport with each other tend to mirror each other's behavior (see Figure 7.1). This mirroring shows up as similar body positioning, physiology, tone of voice, and even choice of words used between the two parties. Interviewers who have achieved rapport often find that the victim, witness, or suspect's body posture, position, and tone of voice are similar to their own.

When interviewers mirror an individual's posture, gestures, and physiology, they can create within themselves the same emotions that the suspect is feeling. The emotions that a person feels, whether fear, happiness, anger,

Figure 7.1 People with good rapport naturally tend to mirror or match each other's behavior.

or something else, are tied to behavioral and physiological clues. If one were to emulate the posturing of a Super Bowl player who had just lost the big game — shoulders slumped, head down, tension released from the body — one could begin to feel the depression and sense of loss that this person is feeling. The ability to change emotions can be as simple as changing the body posture. When a person cries, the head and eyes drop; when a person laughs, the head rises. Try to feel happy with your head down and note the emotional difference. When a child has fallen and hurt herself, the mother puts her hand to the child's chin and raises its head to look into her eyes, and very shortly the child stops crying. The change in head position does not match crying behavior, so it stops.

These learned physical actions that we have paired with our emotions are something that we unconsciously do when that emotion is dominant within us. Interviewers attempting to understand the emotional context of the individual with whom they are talking can develop within themselves the same emotion by mirroring the suspect's behavior. By doing this, the interviewer can also create a sense of rapport with the person.

To understand the elements of mirroring and how we interact with others around us, interviewers should begin to observe people in social settings. When three individuals are having a conversation, do their movements and gestures mirror each other or are they in contrast? If the three are all mirroring each other, there is complete communication going on. However, contrary posturing might mean that there are disagreements or that no rapport exists within the group.

The use of mirroring to establish rapport is merely one element of *neurolinguistics*, essentially the language of the mind. John Grinder, a linguist, and Richard Brandler, a therapist and mathematician, are primarily responsible for the development of neurolinguistics from their observations of noted psychiatrist Milton Erickson. It originally was developed when they taught people to model themselves after others who were successful, and thereby teach them to succeed also.

In certain instances, an interviewer will encounter a suspect or witness who is angry or suspicious of the interviewer's attempt to elicit information. In these cases, it is imperative that the interviewer establish rapport to alter this person's behavior. By beginning to mirror the voice, posturing, and behavior of the reluctant witness, the interviewer begins working on the subconscious level while the words spoken by the interviewer are having an impact on the individual's conscious mind. The individual hears the words, and, because of their similar tone, speed of delivery, and the interviewer's posture, begins to feel a responsiveness toward the interviewer.

Interviewers at this point can begin to modify their behavior and lead the individual to a more open, cooperative posture. The ability to successfully mirror another individual is based on the interviewer's observation of gestures and voice patterns and the interviewer's personal flexibility in modifying his own behavior to mirror that of the person being interviewed. This requires practice for the interviewer just beginning to use the technique. It is usually preferable to begin using the mirroring techniques in a social setting. While doing these mirroring exercises, interviewers should be consciously aware of how they feel toward the person they are mirroring. Once interviewers have attempted these techniques in the social setting, they will discover that they are able to recognize the emotional state of the person with whom they are speaking.

Verbal Neurolinguistics Techniques

In addition to mirroring posture, gestures, tone of voice, speed of delivery, and physiology of the individual, it is also necessary to understand that each one of us processes information and communicates on three verbal levels. While each person uses the three levels — visual, audio, and kinesic — to communicate thoughts and feelings to others, each person generally has one dominant channel that is used. Interviewers can modify their use of language to appeal to the channel that the person to whom they are speaking is comfortable using at the time of interview.

Visual mode.   An individual who generally communicates on a visual level would typically use conversation and word choices that are visual — they form a picture with the words. Such individuals use language as if they were watching a video and describing it. The interviewer might hear this type of individual say any of the following:

- When you see me say ...
- When I see something like this ...
- Come and look at this ...
- Picture this ...
- I'm not sure I see what you're saying ...
- Look at it this way ...

These individuals are using a visual mode to communicate and process information. Upon recognizing this mode of communication, interviewers should begin to use similar words that would "paint a picture" for the person to whom they are speaking. Interviewers who use the channel of communication similar to that of the interviewee considerably enhance the likelihood of rapport between themselves and the individual; this also results in clear communication between the two. Ask questions such as, "What did you see next?" "How did he appear to you?" "Try to look back and see if you can recall."

Auditory mode. Another individual might use the auditory mode as the dominant channel. Such an individual uses words that express hearing in their conversation. From these types of people, we will hear:

- Do you hear where I'm coming from?
- When I hear something like this ...
- This doesn't ring true to me ...
- I don't like the sound of this ...

All of these indicate that the dominant channel is auditory. The interviewer should ask questions such as

- What did you hear next?
- What did it sound like?
- Who talked next?
- What did he say?

Kinesic mode. The final method of processing information is kinesic. Examples of words or phrases that indicate this channel's use might be

- Get in touch with ...
- Get a handle on ...
- Let me get the feel of this ...
- I don't feel good about this ...
- Let me get a grasp on this situation ...

The interviewer might ask questions of this individual such as

- How did you feel when you saw this happen?
- How do you think they felt?
- Let's get a handle on how this happened.

Physiological Neurolinguistic Techniques

In addition to utilizing the mirroring and verbal clues to establish rapport and communication, interviewers can also use the body's physiology to discover the channel of most effective communication. The respiratory pattern of individuals can give an indication of the dominant channel. When people breathe high in the chest, they tend to be in a visual representation mode. If the breathing is relatively even and uses the entire chest and stomach area, they are typically in an auditory mode. Finally, individuals who are using their stomach when breathing are most likely in a kinesic state. To test this principle, note your own respiratory patterns when going to sleep or resting, listening to music, or watching a movie.

Chapter 5 noted that the suspect who has a labored respiratory pattern or continually hyperventilates during the discussion with the interviewer is under a tremendous amount of stress. The respiratory pattern referred to here simply denotes the neurolinguistic channel that the suspect is using.

The respiratory pattern is also reflected in the individual's voice. The person who is in a visual mode generally speaks quickly and has high-pitched tones. This type of speech pattern is often heard in witnesses who have just observed a crime or significant incident. Because of the emotional impact of the recent observation, the witness clearly visualizes the incident in his mind and processes the information on the visual channel. When an individual is in an auditory mode, the voice is rhythmic and very clear. In contrast, when an individual enters a kinesic pattern, the voice takes on a slow, deep quality. This is often expressed when an individual is extremely tired and the voice becomes slow, and low, as the individual feels the weariness of his body.

When interviewers use the elements of mirroring, physiology, and verbal neurolinguistic techniques to establish rapport, they have the ability to quickly achieve the rapport necessary to communicate with the victim, witness, or suspect. These techniques are clearly evident in the day-to-day interaction the interviewer has with family, friends, and business associates. Paying attention to the body language and words spoken by other individuals will allow the interviewer an opportunity to assess their modes of communication and utilize mirroring to establish rapport. By paying attention to your body positioning as you talk to other people, you will begin to identify similar gestures and posturing with the person to whom you are speaking. The next time you go out to lunch, look around at the postures and positions of the others in the restaurant. How many have their legs crossed at the ankle or knee or have the feet planted closely together. By examining the emotional state that you are in at this point, you can begin to make an assessment of the other's emotional state.

Case Example

As an example of the behavioral mirroring, the auditory and kinesic channels can be demonstrated though an earlier example of "Barb," the sister in the $73,000 loss who was asked to come to the personnel office for an interview. This interview was conducted 3 days following the discovery of her sister's involvement in the theft of the $73,000. As previously stated, Barb was a long-term, valued employee whose work record at the company was unblemished.

On her arrival for the interview, Barb was defensive and mildly uncooperative. Behaviorally, her body was closed and tense. When she was interviewed, the interviewer shook hands as she arrived and told her that he was sorry that he had to meet her under such a difficult set of circumstances.

At that point, Barb sat down and crossed her legs and arms. The interviewer modeled this same behavior and opened the conversation by discussing the positive work record that Barb had at the company. During this discussion, she used words that indicated the kinesic channel was dominant.

The interviewer began by discussing how Barb must feel about her sister's involvement, then asking how she felt when she first learned of her sister's problem. After about 5 minutes, the interviewer opened his arms and uncrossed his legs. Because the sister had now established a strong rapport with the interviewer, she behaviorally followed by dropping her arms to the side of her chair and uncrossing her legs.

At this point, the interviewer leaned forward and began to ask questions regarding Barb's sister. Barb sat forward and began to talk in animated terms about the shock to herself and the family. She went on to relate how she felt personally, and the embarrassment she felt. It was plain to see the relief she felt when she began to talk about the theft and her sister. The interviewer leaned to the side and put his hand to his chin and Barb followed suit, placing her hand to her cheek in the same manner. The interviewer was leading and Barb was behaviorally following because of the rapport between them. Her need to maintain rapport with the interviewer caused her to unconsciously follow his lead and move from a defensive posture into one of openness and cooperation.

The value of establishing rapport with the suspect, victim, or witness cannot be underrated. The preceding discussion showed that neurolinguistics, mirroring, and communication can be used to form a bond with the person being interviewed. The establishment of rapport results not merely from being pleasant, but rather from the establishment of both a verbal and physical communication that enhances the relationship and responsiveness of the person interviewed.

During the victim's, witness's or suspect's narrative, interviewers should begin evaluating the verbal and physical behavioral patterns of the person they are interviewing. The interviewer should attempt to establish a behavioral norm for the individual, considering the person's voice pattern, word choice, attitude, and physical behavior as well. By establishing this behavioral norm when the suspect is in the rapport-building phase, the interviewer will have access to clues to deception or informational areas with which the person is uncomfortable.

Selling the Interview

Once the interviewer has established rapport with the person to be interviewed, the next step is to sell that individual on the benefits of cooperation. Similar to the salesperson who presents the benefits of the product, the interviewer begins the interview by making a general benefit statement that contains two distinct parts. First, the interviewer must describe an assumed need of the person being interviewed. This could vary, depending on the individual's background or the circumstances of both the witness and the case. For example, when investigating a burglary, an interviewer might talk about the need to resolve the incident so that other homeowners in the neighborhood are not victimized in the same way. The need to avoid victimization of neighbors is thus established.

Another example might be the interviewing of witnesses who are reluctant because they had reported a crime that was never resolved because, they believe, of the inaction of the police. In this case, the interviewer could state the assumed need that everyone wants the person who caused the incident to be caught. The need to catch and punish the responsible person is thus established.

The second part of a general benefit statement is providing a benefit to witnesses that addresses their expressed or assumed need. In the example immediately above, the interviewer needs to state a benefit to address the perceived need that the person responsible for the present crime be caught and punished and that perhaps this investigation could also encompass the interviewee's previous complaint. To provide the benefit, the interviewer must explain the building of a case and the development of information. This will allow witnesses to understand that the quality of the information they might provide can help resolve the case with an arrest.

If a witness shows open skepticism regarding the interview, the interviewer might begin by restating the benefit, offering proof of past cases that were resolved by witness cooperation, and then expanding on that benefit to the case at hand. Obviously, if the person being interviewed is being cooperative and shows no signs of reluctance or skepticism, the interviewer can proceed without a lengthy sale of the reason for the interview. The difference between these two types of approaches can be illustrated using the analogy of a car salesman. If a customer comes in the door and expresses interest in a particular car and shows a willingness to buy immediately, the salesman immediately attempts to close the sale. However, when the customer is only beginning to shop, the salesman must handle customer concerns, identify customer needs, and establish in the customer's mind the benefits of purchasing the particular vehicle the dealership has for sale.

As with the salesman who discovers that the customer is reluctant to buy, the interviewer must determine the reasons for the witness's or victim's reluctance to cooperate in the interview. As mentioned earlier in this chapter, a witness might be reluctant to cooperate in an investigation for a number of reasons. It is the interviewer's job, in the earliest stages of the interview, to establish the victim's or witness's belief that cooperation in the interview is a correct action and benefits him. The benefit can take many forms: the apprehension of the individual responsible for the incident, recovery of the witness's or neighbor's property, or even simply doing civic duty and supporting the criminal justice system.

Investigators everywhere know that the likelihood of success in resolving any crime is based on the quality of the information provided by victims or witnesses. That information is directly related to the skill and intuitiveness of the interviewer.

Types of Lies

The subject of the interview might or might not be telling the truth to the interviewer. Answers given to questions might not be lies but mistaken perceptions due to poor memory, or biased for any number of reasons. Some answers might be based on assumptions or created information that matches the facts remembered from the incident. In other instances, the information provided is outright lies manufactured to escape detection. This section discusses types of lies that are intentionally meant to deceive the interviewer — not information that is merely incorrect.

There are five basic types of lies that a subject might use. Each has advantages and disadvantages for the subject and the interviewer. By recognizing the types of lies available to the subject, the interviewer might be better prepared to uncover the deception.

Direct Denial

The first form of deception is a direct denial of the act in question — "I didn't do it." While simple, this form of denial creates an emotional sense of disquiet called dissonance. The disturbance is a conflict between what is true and the attempted deception, which creates an internal battle in the mind. People will go to great lengths to avoid these types of feelings and might evade an answer that calls for a simple denial by talking off subject.

The evasive response allows the individual to avoid the internal conflict while seeming to answer the question. The response given to a question must be evaluated in terms of what was asked to determine if the reply was proper.

Former President Clinton became famous for the direct denial, "I didn't have sexual relations with that woman." This denial is an obvious lie based on what is known today of his affair with a White House intern. Clinton, at one point, defended his truthfulness using word definitions. Apparently, the oral copulation was not included in his definition of sexual relations. Definition is a common tactic for giving a truthful direct denial while concealing what really happened. The President was able to do this because he was never required to define the term "sexual relations"; he was able to create a definitional denial, hiding behind the latter interpretation of the term. This was really a lie of omission, which is the second common type of deception.

Lie of Omission

The lie of omission is the most common type of lie used by people. This lie is also simple to tell because the individual stays with the truth while omitting details that could create potential trouble. This lie also allows deceivers to make up information, if necessary, because they have not committed to a complete story as yet. The other benefit that subjects achieve is, if questioned about an omitted detail, they can say they "forgot" to mention it. Children regularly use this type of deception with their parents because it is not really lying in the children's minds. Everything they are saying is the truth, but they omit those details that would get them in trouble. This lie of omission also allows them to tell the same story as a group because the details are all true and the omissions are all the same.

In the example of President Clinton, he was able to carry on a deception because the interviewer failed to force him to define his terms. In most cases, there can be terms of "art" on which definitions must be agreed. For example, with sexual assault cases, it is important that the interviewer make the subject define terms. It does not matter whether the definition conforms to the interviewer's understanding of a term because the user will use whatever definition the subject wants to use. Defining terms creates a playing field with distinct boundaries so the subject will have a more difficult time playing word or definition games. The interviewer's asking questions and requiring definitions will generally force the deceptive subject into the third type of lie, fabrication.

Lie of Fabrication

The lie of fabrication is the most difficult lie a subject can attempt to use during an interview. To attempt a fabricated lie, suspects must be quick thinkers with good memories. They must be able to create information without contradicting themselves to make the deception confident and ring of truth. The lie of fabrication increases the subject's fear of detection, which will often trigger the autonomic nervous system response and its related physiological behaviors. This type of lie also requires an excellent memory so the story can be duplicated in later tellings. Many suspects attempting this type of lie are reluctant to tell the story more than once, fearing detection of contradictions.

Most fabricated stories are only preliminary outlines into which details are later added in response to the interviewer's questions. The weakness in this type of lie is in the details. The very first problem that a subject faces is whether the story can stand up to inspection during the investigation.

Case Example

In a recent case, the victim's home burned to the ground while he was allegedly out of the state, more than 100 miles away. Arson investigators found that the gas pipe to the furnace had been disconnected and the gas had ignited by the pilot light in the hot water heater. As insurance records were probed, it was discovered that this was the third suspicious fire for which the victim had filed a claim. It was also found that the victim, actually a renter, had forged the homeowner's signature on a bill of sale and reinsured the property claiming he, the renter, was the rightful owner. Since luck plays a large part in many investigations, it is only fitting that the insurance broker the suspect chose had also insured the home for the real owner. Things got worse for the suspect when his cell phone showed he was only a short distance away at the time of the fire, not out of state, as he claimed.

The problem with a fabricated story is its failure to stand up to the scrutiny of investigation. The story that is fabricated can be as damning as a confession when it contradicts the evidence in the case. In this example, the subject's own words led to a single conclusion about his involvement in the fire.

Whenever there is evidence pointing to the suspect, the interviewer or interrogator must first increase the power of it by allowing the subject to tell a lie covering or omitting the damning evidence. A common error is to ask subjects about the incriminating piece of evidence directly, allowing them to determine much of what the investigators might know and possibly even how they found out. Instead, allowing subjects to construct their story without knowing what the investigation has revealed can prove extremely helpful in several ways. First, it allows the interviewer a means to test the veracity of the subject's story, comparing what is known with what the subject says happened. Second, the interviewer conceals information about the crime that only the guilty would know. This method helps substantiate any resulting confession when the suspect reveals evidence that could be known only to the perpetrator. This concealment of evidence regarding the crime scene and suspect actions can prove useful during the polygraph testing of suspects. Polygraph examiners sometimes use a type of test called a Peak of Tension examination, which utilizes information withheld from the public. It uses a series of questions among which the truthful piece of evidence is included. An example might be "What was covering the victim's body?" Was the body covered with leaves, grass, tarp, sheet, box, etc? The guilty individual is the only person other than the police to have the information and should respond to that item during the examination. This strategy becomes useless if the interviewer or interrogator discloses the action or evidence.

Besides pinning themselves down to a specific story whose details can be checked for accuracy, with fabricated lies subjects must tell the same account each time or face discovery. This task is much more difficult than it first sounds. In a truthful story, each detail and event is linked to the ones before and after, making it easy to keep the flow of the story consistent. With a fabricated lie, the tale is linked in only two places, the beginning and the end. The details float between these two points changing order, appearing, and disappearing in the retelling. If subjects practiced the story, they did so in only one direction, from the beginning to its end. When asked by the interviewer to start at an arbitrary midpoint and tell the story forward or backward, the untruthful suspect has difficulty keeping the story in order. Details emerge, disappear, and change as the subject struggles to retell the story in an order not considered before.

Case Example

A 15-year-old boy was accused of forcing his girlfriend to perform oral sex on him in the basement of his parent's house. According to the girlfriend, she asked to stay at her boyfriend's house after a fight with her parents. While on the couch kissing, her boyfriend asked for her to perform oral sex on him, and she refused. As he became more insistent, she tried to leave by a basement door but was pulled back inside by her hair and forced into the basement bathroom. Her boyfriend pushed her to her knees and began to have her orally copulate him, finally masturbating himself to completion in the shower.

When questioned by police the following day, he said that his girlfriend slept over after a fight with her parents, leaving early the next day before his parents awoke. He denied that there was any sexual activity other than some kissing in the basement before they slept. About 3 days later, the boy was interviewed and he changed his story to match the girlfriend's, with the exception of denying that any force was used during the encounter. Astonishingly, the total change of story was a surprise to the detective and the boy's attorney. The young man evidently totally forgot what he had related to people several days before and had to resort to a story closer to the truth.

Another problem that the suspect encounters is the necessity to create unexpected details for the story he has offered. Most interviewers can tell countless stories of two separated suspects who reported the events of a situation, which made one wonder if they even attempted to concoct a story together. Interrogators having multiple suspects can usually find the weak link in the group and use the story variations to break down the suspects' resistance.

Structure of a Story

Another problem the suspect faces when attempting to use a fabricated story or alibi is to create a structure similar to a truthful recounting of events. In each story, there is what preceded the event, the event itself, and what followed the event. In a truthful story, these three parts are usually approximately equal in words and details. Students of statement analysis use word and line counts to make a preliminary judgment about the structure of the story being told. When the three pieces are about equal in words and content, there is a surface validity of the structure similar to a truthful story (see Figure 7.2). When suspects attempt to distort the structure by a lie of omission, they must necessarily leave out information about the event. The suspect's omission of details in the event portion of the story or alibi distorts the overall structure and the surface validity of it disappears (see Figure 7.3). In a similar fashion, when suspects attempt to anticipate questions they might be asked, adding details to avoid discovery, they also change the structure slightly (see Figure 7.4). This structure holds true for the first telling of the incident. As an individual is questioned and responds with details, he will naturally include these in later tellings, thus distorting the structure of subsequent stories.

When evaluating a story, individuals who provide short accounts, implausible answers, few references to themselves, and more indirect answers to questions are morelikely to be making a false statement than a true one. This makes sense because, at some point, the subject might be asked to repeat the story, and the simpler it is, the more likely that he will retain an accurate memory of the first telling. Furthermore, the more details provided to the interviewer, the more likely the story will withstand the scrutiny of an investigation. In general, it is more likely that an unstructured statement that skips around in the telling but is consistent in detail is the result of an upset subject, rather than an attempt at deception. It is much easier for a fabricated story to be told in a logical order because that is the way it was constructed and

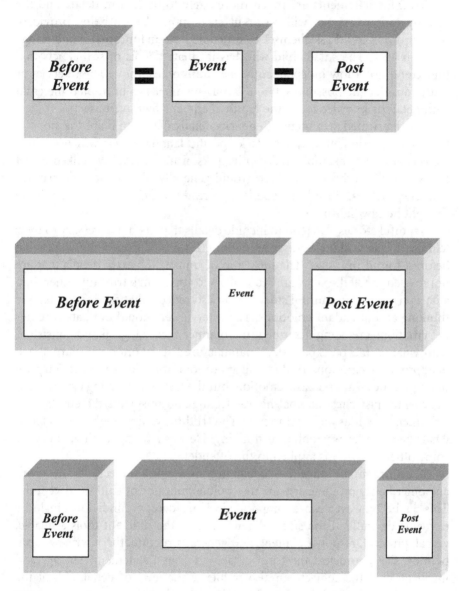

Figure 7.4   Often, a fabricated story contains excessive detail about the event, so the subject will face fewer questions about what happened, again distorting the structure.

because in an unstructured story there is a greater likelihood of a contradiction that might lead to the individual's detection. Once an emotional unstructured story has been told several times, during subsequent tellings it will follow a logical progression of the event.

Truthful statements are much more likely to be rich in detail, and the investigator's questions will result in even more detail's being provided. Investigators should ask themselves if people have inappropriate knowledge for their ages. The small child who has intimate details of sexual acts that they could not know independently is a common example. The interviewer must consider the possibility that a family member has prompted the child with detail or knowledge for the family member's own purpose.

The fabricated statement often lacks details that help place the story in time and location. It may also lack specific language that was used in a conversation. For example, a deceptive person might say, "We talked about the weather." Truthful individuals would generally offer a more descriptive dialogue, such as, "I said the clouds were really getting dark and he said he thought he saw lightning."

Truthful stories also tend to include details that are not necessary to their telling: "I was walking across the parking lot and dropped my wallet just before I found my keys." The inclusion of unusual or extra details that are not needed to tell the story are more likely to appear in a truthful rather than a deceptive story. A truthful story might also reflect what the individual was thinking and attendant emotions. The interviewer should evaluate whether the emotions are being described in a manner that is logical and consistent with what would be expected. A manufactured story often will have a lack of appropriate emotions, or they will appear out of the logical order. Surprise often precedes fear as a basic emotion, but the liar, never having experienced the event, must guess at what he was feeling and misplaces the emotion or only mentions it as an afterthought. The truthful victim might also refer to what the offender was doing or thinking, He was smiling, crying, angry, or some other emotion is applied to the offender.

These are simply guidelines to help in considering a subject's story. As with any other behavior, these are not an absolute indicator of truth or deception. This can become even more complicated when a deceptive individual includes elements of truth in the story. When using all the different tools available, verbal, physical, response content, and general structure, the interviewer can be more likely to detect the truth or deception in a statement. The age and intelligence of the subject can also influence the level of detail, as will the number of retellings of the event. Some details might be omitted in later stories just because the individual has tired of talking about the incident.

Lie of Minimization

The fourth type of lie a suspect might use is a lie of minimization. This form of lie generally admits that something has happened but downplays the significance. Police officers making a drunk-driving stop are often faced with this type of lie:

Officer: How much have you had to drink tonight?
Driver: Just two beers.

This lie might also be a lie of omission as the inebriated driver neglects to mention he has had a beer in each hand for most of the evening. While the driver admits to consuming alcohol, he minimizes the amount drunk. This kind of lie tends to remove some of the stress associated with the attempted deception, because the subject can rationalize that he is telling at least part of the truth, with the remainder relegated to the white-lie category.

The lie of minimization can be used whenever subjects want to stay close to the truth yet shade it in their favor:

- "I slapped her in the face." — The victim has a broken nose and fractured jaw.
- "I took only a couple of bucks." — The safe is missing $10,000.
- "I touched her only a couple of times." — The victim alleges a 4-year pattern of molestation.
- "I use grass only on the weekends." — Drug tests reveal that the subject has used a variety of drugs over the past month.

Suspects hope that "tossing a bone" to the interviewer will satisfy him, limiting further inquiries about the incident. The lie of minimization is like the first offer in a negotiation — one can expect that there is generally more to follow.

Lie of Exaggeration

The fifth common variety of lie is exaggeration. These lies are often found on résumés, where applicants exaggerate experience, knowledge, tenure, and salary. Informants are often guilty of using this type of deception in hope of obtaining some advantage. One of the most difficult tasks an investigator faces is evaluating the knowledge claims of an informant. Sometimes this knowledge involves no exaggeration, but an outright fabrication of information.

Many exaggerated claims can be tested by looking for inconsistencies in the subject's story. Is there a consistent pattern of facts? Con men and swindlers often make contradictory claims that escape detection because of their flamboyant personalities. These types of individuals are able to be convincing in their deceptions because they are creative and have extensive experience in deceiving others. With an air of confidence, they tell the most outlandish tales, clearly expecting that others will believe them. Many of these liars are psychopathic personalities who lack the guilt and emotions of a normal person, thus allowing them to carry the deception with little or no fear of detection.

Testing an informant's information must be carefully done, especially when it is being traded for some advantage. Jailhouse snitches are notorious for fabricating information to obtain a reduced sentence or other benefit. Some suspects will name others in an effort to cast suspicion onto another individual, exaggerating another's involvement while minimizing their own. There often is a desire to believe the first person to come forward, leaving the others to fend for themselves. Sometimes the only way to test the reliability of the information is to polygraph the individual before committing to any deal.

Structure of an Investigative Interview

Experienced interviewers, rather than using a rambling undirected approach, often create a plan when approaching a victim, witness, or suspect. One should strive for several objective goals in every interview:

1. Obtain an untainted narrative from the subject, detailing the incident or alibi in question.
2. Evaluate the veracity of the individual being interviewed.
3. Test the validity of the information being offered.

The following structured interview format is designed to achieve these goals by combining both behavioral and cognitive interviews. The interview begins, as always, by developing a rapport and establishing a behavioral norm for the person being interviewed.

1. Determine the subject's behavioral norm using questions the subject will probably answer truthfully.
2. Establish rapport with the subject using physical and conversational tactics.
3. Request the subject's untainted story. Give the subject a starting point in time and listen to the story without interruption. Just listen — no questions.
4. If you are unsure of the individual's guilt, include a behavioral interview to help determine the subject's truthfulness. This section of the interview can also help identify possible rationalizations, explanatory denials, and possible hurdles that might be used during an interrogation of the subject.

5. If the interviewer believes the subject is deceptive, he asks for the story or alibi to be retold, and listens for changes. Picking a starting point, the interviewer asks the subject to retell the story forward or backward from that point. The interviewer can now explore certain areas of the story or alibi with specific questions to force the subject into a fabricated lie. There might be significant changes in demeanor and behavior as the deceptive subject's stress level rises.

6. When the interviewer believes the subject is truthful, he might use the cognitive interview to assist the truthful subject with recall. The cognitive interview is discussed at length later in this chapter.

7. The interviewer closes the interview with the subject based on a plan either to interrogate or re-interview the subject later.

Allowing a Narrative

Once the interviewer has established rapport and sold the individual on the need to cooperate in the interview, the third step is to allow the individual to make a narrative response concerning the incident. The interviewer generally begins the interview by using open-ended questions that encourage a free-flow monologue from the victim, witness, or suspect. By allowing them to complete the stories they have to tell, the interviewer can develop an understanding of what they might know and what areas require further exploration. The first time the story or alibi is told, the suspect is at greatest risk for a deception to be discovered. This phase is like the opening night of a play, rather than the 200th performance when there are few, if any, errors. The first interviewer has the best opportunity to identify deception and to lock the subject into a story or alibi containing errors, which will not be substantiated by investigation.

During the preliminary narrative, the interviewer has an opportunity to begin to establish the circumstances surrounding the incident and ascertain what, if any, crime was committed and the elements necessary to prove the violation. In many instances, victims use incorrect terminology to describe a particular event. For example, people will say often that they have been *robbed*. By establishing the facts of the case, the interviewer might determine that it was in fact a robbery, either armed or unarmed. However, it might not have been a robbery in which a suspect, by the use of force, took an item of value from the victim, but rather a break-in, in which someone broke into a vehicle or residence and removed the item. A burglary, rather than robbery, was committed. A third possibility might be that the person left the item on a chair when they got up to get a drink of water and returned to find the item gone. In this case, a theft has been committed that might not be a burglary, depending on the location of the theft.

During the narrative, interviewers can encourage a continued monologue by nodding their heads in agreement at appropriate points in the
suspect's story. They can further encourage the individual's telling by using
noncommittal comments such as, "What happened next?" or, "I understand,
then what?" These types of noncommittal responses by interviewers show
that they are actively listening and interested in what the individual has to
say. During the narrative, interviewers might also find that the individual
gets off track into unrelated areas. During the untainted story, this is simply
noted and allowed. However, later, during the second telling, the interviewer
needs to keep the individual on track by returning to the point where he
began to divert. Simply saying something such as, "Going back to what
happened at the garage, what went on from that point?" can allow the
interviewer to reorient the victim or witness to the story line without interrupting the flow of information.

The victim's or witness's narrative allows the interviewer to continue to
establish the bond of rapport because the victim or witness feels that he has
valuable information that is appreciated by the interviewer.

Hearing the Untainted Story

In addition to allowing the victim, witness, or suspect to relate an overview,
the interviewer also has an opportunity to hear the story in an untainted
form. This first telling does not have the contamination of questions or
conversation and is the untested version offered by a deceptive subject. By
listening to and observing the story in its untainted form, the interviewer
might find a number of valuable clues to the mind-set of the person being
interviewed. For example, the interviewer might be able to ascertain percep-
tual or social biases on the part of the victim or witness that will taint the
credibility of information given. In addition, the interviewer has an opportunity to hear the story told by the witness or victim, who places his own
emphasis on the information. The interviewer can now begin to listen closely
and plan the direction of the follow-up questions. In many instances, it will
become evident that a victim or witness is manufacturing information based
on assumptions instead of observations. By listening closely, the interviewer
can plan for the follow-up questions and decide which areas to explore more
fully. Probably the biggest failure in interviewing is the failure to plan its
direction and the followup questions.

In some cases, as the interview progresses, individuals might become
uncooperative or reluctant to give further information. By having allowed
the individual to proceed with essentially an uninterrupted narrative, the

interviewer has had an opportunity to gain significantly more information than he would have by simply questioning the suspect.

The interviewer, who now has the narrative from beginning to end, can begin to test the truthfulness and consistency of the story. By evaluating the consistency of the story in both its direction and detail, the interviewer can evaluate its truthfulness. The interviewer will also have had an opportunity to observe the verbal and physical behavioral clues given during the interview. These behavioral clues will assist in identifying areas of sensitivity.

On occasion, when a victim or witness is extremely cooperative and credible, the interviewer might, prior to the scheduled appointment, ask the individual to make notes of the circumstances surrounding the incident for later discussion. By having had time to consider the information surrounding the incident, the individual will often be able to give a greater amount of detail regarding the circumstances. For those witnesses who might be reluctant or less than helpful, the location of the interview should be a more formalized setting, such as the police station or loss prevention office. In cases where several witnesses were present at the scene of the incident, it is beneficial to separate them so the more forceful observer does not dominate and taint the stories of the other witnesses.

The interviewer must also remember that information provided might be less than credible. While eyewitness testimony has been attacked for years by certain psychologists as unreliable due to the passage of time and stress associated with the incident, other psychologists have found that the memory was accurately and vividly recalled even after the passage of time. In assessing the individual's story, interviewers should not discount its validity simply because of incorrect details such as the color of a vehicle or inaccurate physical description. These discrepancies might be individualized perception problems on the part of the interviewee. This chapter later discusses a method of using behavior-provoking questions to elicit demeanor that is specifically related to truth telling or deception. However, this method is generally used in the latter stage of the nonaccusatory interview to determine the status of the subject — truthful or deceptive.

The first telling of the untainted story should be heard with very limited interruptions from the interviewer. To do otherwise contaminates the structure of the story and might limit the interviewer's ability to detect deception or truth. The interviewer might take notes but needs to pay attention to what is being said by the subject, looking for specific areas that need to be explored. These areas can be identified using some of the following observations:

- Watch the subject for large body shifts or changes in posture. Whenever a gross body shift is seen, note what was said that might have caused this behavioral change. Be prepared to return to that topic later to look for consistency of stress or other behavioral clues that the topic is of importance.

- Listen for information that was offered but unnecessary to the telling of the story. Why was that information provided at that time? If the information was given during later interviews with the subject, it might be that the information was added because of questions asked during earlier interviews.

- Listen for qualifiers during the recitation of the story or alibi such as, "Basically, that's it," "I think," "I believe," "Not really," "That's about all," "Probably," "All the time," "Just a few," as well as other similar phrases that might indicate assumptions, beliefs, bias, exaggerations, and minimization in the subject's story or alibi.

- Roughly judge the structure of the story or alibi to determine if there are lies of omission or fabrication at work. This can be done while taking notes by marking the notes at the beginning and end of the event and then comparing the space dedicated to the event to what preceded and followed it. Most people are internally consistent in their note-taking during an interview so the level of detail and overall structure of the subject's story can be roughly determined from the notes. This does not have the same validity as a written statement analysis but can give an interviewer a general indication of the story's structure.

- Note the relationships between people mentioned in the story or alibi. "He took me" versus "We went," which indicates an entirely different relationship between the parties. Different words indicate different relationships between people: friend, lover, wife, Annette, that woman. Are the words consistent in meaning or do they show a contradictory relation between people? For example, "I told them they were friends of ours and we felt just terrible about what happened, but that woman called all upset ..." Quite a difference exists between the descriptors "friends" and "that woman," giving the careful listener a clue about a possible deception or bias.

- Listen for changes in verb tense. There is a big difference in the meaning of "was" and "is" when talking about an individual. Tense changes tend to slip into the conversation naturally and are difficult for an individual to control totally. It is not unusual for a guilty suspect to talk about the deceased in the past tense before the body had been discovered. These tense changes can also indicate changes in relationships between people. "He was my father," is a statement regarding a relationship, but one that has changed over time. It could indicate any number of different changes and should be explored for biases in the subject.

Evaluating Neurolinguistic Eye Movement

This chapter earlier discussed the neurolinguistics of verbal communication. Visual, auditory and kinesic channels were typified by the style, speed, word usage, and even physiology changes in the individual. Similarly, the eyes are used by each of us as we begin to recall or create information from one of the previous channels. While observing the interviewee, the interviewer should recognize the value of eye movements and the information they can give the interviewer. By determining which representational system the victim, witness, or suspect is using, the interviewer can ascertain whether the information is being recalled or created. In the investigation business, created information is usually a lie; however, that is not always true.

Eye movement as an indicator for created and recalled information can be very useful in the earliest telling of an event. The first time a story or alibi is told, there is an incredible amount of information that must created for a successful fabricated lie. The suspect unable to anticipate all the details must create them in the context of telling the lie. The outline of the fabricated lie will not need any created information since the subject has already taken the time to do this. Even though the alibi is a lie, it is stored in the person's memory, making it unnecessary to do any creation of information. The suspect merely has to recite and remember carefully what was said previously. It is during the second telling, as the interviewer begins to ask questions, that the necessity to create information exists again.

For example, two suspects agree to an alibi that they were playing cards last night with a group of friends when the incident occurred. The danger of discovery lies in the detail, which was not prepared. The subject may reveal his deception in several ways: verbal pauses to construct details, eye movement to the creation side of the body (see Figure 7.5), and gross body shifts as a result of stress associated with the attempted deception among other things. The interviewer questions the subject about unanticipated details of the alibi.

- Who sat on your right?
- Who sat on your left?
- Who arrived first?
- Who left first?
- Who was the big winner or loser?

These or questions like them force the deceptive subject to create information; however, once the information has been created the subject simply has to retrieve it and correctly place it in the story or alibi. Thus, this tech-

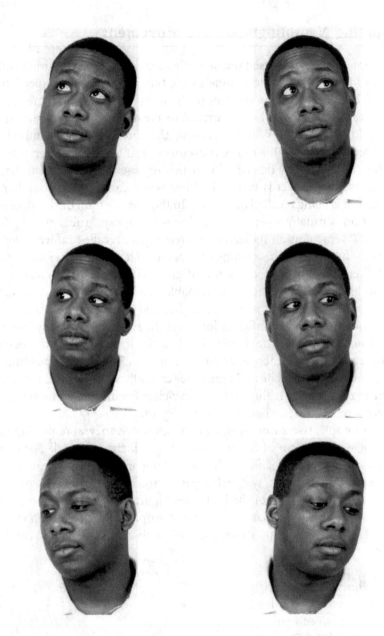

Figure 7.5 (Top left) Individual is creating visually. (Top right) Individual is recalling visually something he has experienced. (Middle left) Creating an auditory memory. (Middle right) Recalling sounds actually experienced. (Bottom right) Kinesic or touch. The subject is attempting to decide where he stands on a position. (Bottom left) Internal dialogues, getting in touch with one's feelings to make a decision.

nique is more likely to be of use the first few times the story or alibi is told than after multiple tellings of the story.

Creation can also take place with a truthful witness. As the witness recounts the words that were spoken, they are retrieved from the memory and often the eyes will either move to the left side or disfocus directly in front of the individual. Remember that this pattern applies to about 90% of the population and the interviewer has established the individual's pattern earlier in the encounter. If the interviewer were now to inquire about what the voice sounded like, the individual would first have to remember the words then move to the creative side to find words, which would describe the voice. This is not necessarily deception, even though it is creation, unless the individual is intentionally attempting to deceive the interviewer.

Part of the time when interviewers are observing the suspect during the narrative, they are establishing behavioral norms relating to the verbal and physical patterns of the individual. In addition, they are also observing the pattern of eye movements during the rapport building and the narrative portion of the interview.

To illustrate this neurolinguistic eye movement point, answer the following questions and note the positioning of your eyes:

- What was the color of the car you first learned to drive?
- What would the offspring of an elephant and zebra look like?
- Who is the first person who spoke to you this morning?
- What did that person say to you first this morning?
- How would it feel to sit in a tub of warm Jell-O?

The pattern of eye movements that you noted is related to the photos in Figure 7.5.

In response to the first question, you probably looked up to the left, recalling the color of that first car you were able to drive. This response is typical for all but approximately 10% of the population, who simply reverse the pattern of eye movements. In most instances, when we visually recall something that we have actually experienced, the eyes turn up and to the left. When we are recalling something that we have heard, the eyes turn to the left and straight across. When we are creating visually, the eyes will turn up and to the right. For example, in response to the question of how the offspring of an elephant and zebra would look, your eyes probably turned up and to the right as you visually created the image. If you were asked to imagine a siren that sounded like a bellowing elephant, your eyes would probably go to the right where most people turn their eyes when creating a sound. If you were asked to imagine what it would feel like to touch a piece of newly sanded wood, your eyes generally would move into a kinesic mode as you created this thought in your mind. Often, people's memory can be enhanced by having them position their eyes in the proper representational location, such as looking up and to the left to recover a visual memory.

Observation of eye movement takes considerable skill and concentration. Remember that, in approximately 90% of individuals, eyes turned to the left indicate the person is recalling something actually experienced or already created, and eyes turned to the right indicate creating. Also, remember that the eye movement might be very slight and incorporate a number of different positions in response to a particular question. Many of the 10% who do not respond typically are left-handed people who simply reverse the clues. However, neurolinguistic eye movement can be the same for both right- and left-handed people. Remember that the usefulness of this technique diminishes as the story is told repeatedly, and that, just because the information is created, it is not necessarily a lie.

The easiest was to begin to observe the neurolinguistic eye movement is to become cognizant of your own eye movement in response to questions and feelings you have during a conversation. In addition, use mock interviews to watch the pattern of eye movement to gain experience, understanding and confidence that the technique has validity.

Moving the eyes to the left and down generally indicates an internal dialogue within the suspect, victim, or witness. Often, this is the position of the eyes when a suspect is in submission during an interrogation and about ready to confess. At this point, the suspect is weighing the consequences of confessing and making a decision. This internal dialogue is represented by the head tilted forward and down with the eyes down to the left. In social situations, when we are being asked to respond to emotional situations, the eyes may go down and to the left as we debate what our response should be. Children being disciplined by a parent often turn their eyes in this way.

Case Example
The following example illustrates the value of observing neurolinguistic eye movements.

A jewelry company had $60,000 in loose diamonds shipped to its distribution center. Shortly after the diamonds were received, they were discovered to be missing. Because of the security controls at the facility, suspicions centered on two particular individuals, the receiving clerk and the clerk who would next have access to the diamonds.

In evaluating the background of the two individuals, it was learned that the receiving clerk, a male in his late 20s, had been with the company less than 6 months. His work record was unsatisfactory, he was disgruntled, and he was generally dissatisfied with the company. He had had some minor brushes with the law relating to disorderly conduct and traffic offenses. The second employee, a female in her early 20s, had been with the company just over 1 year. Her work record was also less than satisfactory and she had an attendance problem. Rumors among the employees claimed she was dating a man who was reputed to be the largest cocaine dealer in town. Further investigation revealed that she had been observed by other associates using drugs while on the company's property.

During the interview with the female clerk, it was determined she was not involved in the theft of the diamonds; however, based on her behavior, she probably was involved in using drugs during working hours at the company. Her neurolinguistic eye movements had been observed previously and helped elicit the confession to drug use. The interview questions were formulated in response to her eye movements.

Interviewer: Mary, let me ask you, what types of drugs have you ever just experimented with at any time in your life?

Suspect: Uh, well, I tried cocaine, marijuana, and PCP and some LSD back in high school.

Her eyes turned up and to the left as she visually recalled the different types of drugs that she had used.

Interviewer: Mary, let me ask you this … When was the very last time that you used any type of a drug during working hours here at the company?

Suspect: (Pausing, eyes up and to the right, she looks back at the interviewer) About 6 months ago.

Interviewer: And what kind of drug was that?

Suspect: (Eyes up and to the left) Marijuana.

From these questions, the interviewer was able to ascertain that the suspect was a drug user and had used marijuana on the job. However, the admission about the last time being 6 months ago was created and possibly a lie.

Interviewer: Mary, when was the very last time? You know, sometimes it's hard for a person to remember exactly the last time, because it's not like doing heroin or something.

Suspect: (Mary's eyes drift to the right and up, creating a response. She begins to speak.) Well …

Interviewer: No, Mary, that wouldn't be true. I mean the very last time, no matter how recently.

Suspect: (Eyes drop down to the left, move up and left.) This morning before the interview.

Interviewer: What did you use this morning?

Suspect: Marijuana.

The interviewer, during this sequence of events, was able to ascertain that the suspect had used marijuana on the job, but the time mentioned was most likely a lie. By watching the eye movements and recognizing that the suspect was again going to create a lie regarding the time of her drug use on the job, the interviewer could anticipate her response. By anticipating the lie and cutting it off, the interviewer was able to elicit an admission from the suspect of illegal drug use just before the interview.

The reader, being aware of his own eye movements and watching for the pattern of eye movements in social situations with others, will learn to assess the accuracy of information based upon these neurolinguistic movements.

A final word of caution relates to victims and witnesses. Many attempt to cooperate, giving as much information as possible. On occasion, subjects might not remember the information requested by the interviewer and will create details of which they have no active memory. This is not done to deceive the interviewer but rather to be as cooperative as possible. The information created by the victim or witness fits their memory of the event but might not be correct. Most often, when a subject's eyes turn from left to right, back and forth, it is because the individual is creating details and then testing them against the memory of the event. He then returns to creation when the detail does not seem correct and modifies the detail until it seems to fit his recollection of the situation. These types of manufactured details can create many problems for investigators, but they can be reduced if the victim and witness are given the preliminary instructions for the cognitive interview.

Leading the Interview

Once the victim, witness, or suspect has completed the narrative portion of the story, the interviewer returns to the beginning to lead the individual back to areas that need exploration. The interviewer will do this using closed-end questions that require specific answers such as details or a "yes" or "no" answer. The question, "Who was in the room with you at that time?" focuses the suspect's attention to a particular detail to which he must either lie or tell the truth.

In interviews and interrogations, interviewers must often conceal the areas in which they are particularly interested, especially when the witness is reluctant or hostile. Such witnesses are attempting to obtain as much information from the interviewer as the interviewer is from them. This information might be passed on to the perpetrator or used to protect themselves, should they later be identified as the individual responsible for the incident.

Interviewers conceal the areas of real interest by asking questions directly about other less important or irrelevant topics. Much the same thing is done during an investigation. Although the interviewers cannot avoid having it be known that they are investigating, they do not reveal the target of the investigation. The interviewer can do the same thing by focusing on less relevant areas of the story before bringing the suspect back to a point of particular interest.

At this point in the interview, interviewers might also ask the victim, witness, or suspect to produce evidence or documents that might help the case. In these situations, the interviewer might also ask specific questions regarding the evidence or documents that will establish the elements of the crime being investigated. In the event that the interviewer receives evidence or documents from a victim or witness, proper cataloging and chain-of-evidence procedures should be used to preserve the evidence's admissibility. Many departments give receipts for any documents or evidence received. In certain instances where the identification of a suspect is contemplated, the interviewer should have previously arranged a photo lineup that meets the legal criteria established by the courts.

Challenging the Untruthful Witness, Victim, or Suspect

The interviewer might also choose to explore discrepancies in the suspect's story, such as omissions, evasions, conflicts, or outright lies. The suspect's level of cooperation will determine whether the interviewer will challenge the suspect regarding truthfulness. The decision to confront an untruthful victim, witness, or suspect might be directly related to the pre-interview strategy the interviewer decided to follow. If the strategy was to keep the lines of communication open by not confronting the individual, a plan for re-interviewing should be prepared. The information provided by the individual should be thoroughly investigated prior to the next interview. In the event that the interviewee has lied, any subsequent interviews should take place in a less supportive and more controlled environment.

Case Example

In a recent kickback investigation, a vendor was identified as having been contacted by the buyer in an attempt to elicit a kickback. Credible evidence that this conversation had taken place was developed during interviews. The interviewer scheduled to meet with the vendor at a local restaurant. The interview was scheduled in this manner because all indications were that the vendor had been honest in his previous dealings with the company and had no outward reasons not to cooperate in the investigation.

During the interview, the vendor was evasive, omitting information that was previously known from the investigation. His physical behavior gave further indication he was withholding information. Because of the interview environment, the suspect was not challenged about these evident deceptions. In this case, a decision was made to re-interview the vendor when a more formal setting could be arranged. However, the second interview generated no incriminating admissions, primarily because the suspect was prepared and became increasingly uncooperative. In this instance, the location of the first interview directly related to its lack of success because the interviewer could not immediately confront the suspect about his falsehoods.

Using Rationalizations

With particularly weak suspects, an interviewer might be able to obtain additional information by indirectly probing the area that the victim, witness, or suspect is lying about. This indirect probing needs to be combined with rationalizations that allow victims, witnesses, or suspects to save face about their inability to tell the truth the first time. Like the suspect in an interrogation, witnesses who are withholding information need to have support and a face-saving rationalization that allow them to feel better about themselves. If the interviewer merely confronts the witness about a falsehood, the witness has to admit that he withheld information and that it was improper to do so. Utilizing the process of rationalization in the interview, a skilled interviewer removes the second stumbling block to the suspect's telling the truth. Now the individual has merely to acknowledge that he "forgot" to tell something. The rationalization process also allows witnesses to save face with the interviewer because they think the interviewer does not believe they "intentionally lied."

Shifting to Interrogation

The second possibility an interviewer must consider is whether a direct accusation of untruthfulness should be made and an interrogation be conducted. In this method, suspects are confronted with their lies and the interviewer begins to dominate the conversation using rationalization to minimize the seriousness of the lies or involvement. The ultimate goal is to elicit the truth from the reluctant victim, witness, or suspect.

With that change, the interview has moved into an interrogative phase where the interviewer begins to offer reasons and excuses that the individual did what he did and thus encourages the suspect to confess by allowing him to save face. Further discussion of the tactics utilized in an interrogation are discussed in detail in Chapters 9 through 15 of this text. The decision by an interviewer to confront the suspect should be soundly based on several factors:

1. Pre-interview strategy.
2. Completeness of the overall investigation.
3. Location and timing are conducive to an interrogation—that is, it is private and nonsupportive for the suspect.
4. The interviewer's reasonable certainty that he can elicit the information from the suspect and that this confrontation will not affect future cooperation.

In a situation where the interviewer has ascertained that the individual being interviewed is being deceptive, the interviewer should consider postponing a confrontation until the completion of the investigation, which may uncover the reasons for the individual's deception. The ability to re-interview should not be underestimated. The time and effort expended by the interviewer to establish rapport with the person in the initial interview can be used as a springboard for any follow-up interviews. In these, after additional investigation has been conducted and relationships in the investigation are more clearly defined, it might become evident why the suspect lied about a particular portion of his story.

At any rate, the ability of the interviewer to ascertain a suspect's deception can often lead to new investigative leads, even though the suspect lied. For this reason, it is often preferable to keep a suspect talking in an interview format rather than to switch to an interrogation. If an interrogation is unsuccessful, it can close all lines of communication between the interrogator and the suspect.

Using Cognitive Interview Techniques

The study of police interviewing techniques illuminated a number of problematic areas that prevented witnesses from developing the most details from their memory. Often it was the way in which the interviewer probed for information that actually prevented the witness from recalling details. The most significant observation was the frequent interruptions of the witness by the interviewer. These interruptions cause two distinct problems for the witness. The most obvious is that it breaks the concentration on the memory by having to switch back and forth to answer the interviewer's questions. The second problem is that it shortens responses to questions because the witness expects to have only a short time to answer before being interrupted again.

Another difficulty observed in the study of traditional police interviews was the order of questions, which can cause witnesses to have to shift attention to different parts of their memory. Questions that caused difficulty in retrieval were questions of visual observation followed by questions for auditory memories. The lack of logical sequencing of the questions reduced the level of information retrieved from the witnesses' memory. The interviewers who were studied also used more closed-end questions to interrupt the recollection of events, such as, "What was the color of the car?" These interruptions generally produce less concentration and free recall of the event. Although less of a problem, some officers were noted to use negatives, "You don't remember ..." when beginning questions or offering judgmental opinions like, "You shouldn't have been in that area, but ..." Questions like these tend to inhibit a person's cooperation.

To overcome these problems, an interviewer might decide to use cognitive interviewing techniques. These techniques were systematized to enhance the recall of information by victims or witnesses under a grant by the National Institute of Justice, United States Department of Justice. The techniques used in the cognitive interview have been used in whole or in part by investigators for many years. However, this is the first time that the technique has been quantified in a study to show that it is an effective method for obtaining information from eyewitnesses. Studies have shown that the information elicited from a witness through the cognitive interview technique can be more correct than information from someone who is interviewed under hypnosis and far exceeds the information developed during standard interviews. Thus far, the cognitive interview has successfully avoided the pitfalls hypnosis has faced in the courts. Additional research studies have shown that the cognitive interview technique reduces the impact that leading questions have on feeding information to witnesses. Finally, it was also shown that using all the parts of the cognitive interview together, as explained below, enhances the eyewitness's ability to recall information more significantly than when they are used separately.

The following techniques incorporated in the cognitive interview are utilized to enhance the recollection of the victim and witness:

1. **Establish rapport:** The interviewer starts the process by establishing rapport with the witness or victim.
2. **Reconstruct the circumstances of the event:** The interviewer asks the witness to reconstruct how the incident began and the circumstances preceding it, which provides a context for the memory and allows the witness to "warm up" before actually attempting to retrieve the memory of the event. The interviewer instructs the witness to think about what the environment looked like, considering weather, lighting, or cleanliness of the room. In addition, the subjects are also asked to recall their emotional mind-set at the time of the incident. Asking the witness to use imagery helps in retrieving details of the event.
3. **Instruct the eyewitness to report everything:** The victim or witness is informed not to omit any details, no matter how small. The interviewer explains that even very minor pieces of information might be important to the investigation. This point is important, because no witness is really trained in what is relevant to report. Another part of the instructions is to let the subject know that the interviewer might ask the same question several times during the interview. Many people perceive these redundant questions as an expression of disbelief by the interviewer and they then stop cooperating. Letting the witness know at the onset that topics will be addressed more than once lessens the likelihood of this misunderstanding. The interviewer should limit interruptions of the witness's account and use closed-end questions — but only after the full account has been given.
4. **Recall the events in different order:** The interviewer might instruct the eyewitness to start from the middle or end and move either forward or backward through the story at a number of different points.
5. **Change perspectives:** The interviewer might ask the witness to change roles or positions with another person in the incident and to consider what he or she might have seen.

The cognitive interview's basic value is that it reconstructs the circumstances in a number of different ways in the witness's mind. A person not in law enforcement rarely has an idea of what might be of value to the investigator, and the small details obtained by this method often lead to the recollection of other details.

The cognitive interview also includes five techniques to develop specific items of information:

1. **Physical appearance:** The witness is asked if the suspect reminded him of anybody and why. Was there anything unusual about the suspect's appearance or clothing?
2. **Names:** If the suspect spoke a name during the incident, how many syllables did it have or what was the first letter of the name?
3. **Numbers:** If a number was involved, was it a low number or high number, how many digits were in it, and were there any letters that were in sequence? This is especially valuable in attempting to remember license plate numbers.
4. **Speech Characteristics:** Ask the witness if the voice reminded him of anyone and why. Were there any unusual accents, words, or tone of voice used by the suspect?
5. **Conversation:** The eyewitness should be asked if there were any reactions to what was said, if any of the reactions were unusual, and if there were any unusual words or phrases included in the conversation.

Using the Selective Interview Technique

The selective interview technique can also be incorporated as part of a fact-gathering interview to determine the truthfulness of the individual being interviewed. In the selective interview, a series of behavior-provoking questions are asked in a nonaccusatory manner. These questions are designed to solicit interpretable behavior that is typical of either a truthful or untruthful person. This interview is especially beneficial when questioning several suspects regarding a specific incident such as arson or theft at a warehouse.

It is important to remember that, for these interview questions to be effective in soliciting interpretable behavior, the interviewer needs to ask the questions in a sincere, non-accusatory manner. Each question should refer to the specific issue or incident under investigation. This constant reference to the incident minimizes the possibility that an outside issue will cause concern or behavioral changes in the suspect. For example, if a suspect were asked, "What do you think should happen to someone who would take something from the company?" the interviewer would not know if a typically guilty response was the result of the specific incident or some other theft from the organization. By changing the wording of the question, the interviewer can reduce the level of concern of an individual who is responsible only for a side issue, such as the unrelated theft of a small amount of merchandise. Therefore, the question should be asked nonspecifically: "What do you think should happen to the person who stole the missing $2,000 deposit taken from the safe?"

The subject answering the "what should happen to" question does so based on his perception. The truthful individual answers it based on what should happen to the person who committed the theft and usually will offer strong punishment as the solution. The guilty individual evaluates the question as what should happen to him or her specifically and responds with a weak punishment such as, "Pay the money back." Each question in the behavioral interview distinguishes between the truthful and guilty in three ways: (1) the physical behavior of the subject, (2) the verbal behaviors of the subject, and (3) the content of the individual's answer to the question.

Questions Asked

A sample of the types of questions asked during the selective interview follows:

- Who do you think started that fire in the warehouse?
- Is there anyone you suspect?
- Is there anyone you know well enough to vouch for? In other words, in your opinion is there anyone above suspicion and who wouldn't do anything like steal that $2,000 deposit?
- Before we go any further, let me ask you, did you start that fire in the warehouse?
- Do you think that $2,000 deposit was stolen?
- Do you think the fire was intentionally started?
- Who do you think would have had the best opportunity to start that fire if they wanted to? I'm not saying that person did, but if someone wanted to?
- Is there any reason that you can think of that someone would say they saw you take that $2,000 deposit out of the safe?
- What do you think should happen to the person that started that fire in the warehouse?
- Did you ever just think of doing anything like stealing that $2,000 deposit?
- How do you feel about our conducting this investigation into this fire?

In addition to these questions, investigators might elect to ask additional investigative questions that they feel are appropriate.

In interpreting the verbal and physical responses to each of these questions, it is important to apply the rules and principles discussed in Chapter 5, "Interpretation of Verbal and Physical Behavior."

Remember that people who are telling the truth about the issue under investigation are likely to give direct answers during the interview. In addition, they are often helpful and cooperative in their responses. On the other hand, people who are not telling the truth are not as specific, direct, or helpful. In many cases, their responses are vague, too elaborate, short, or evasive.

Control Questions

To test the validity of truthful behavior observed during the interview, the interviewer asks a control question, one that is similar but not directly related to the issue under investigation. For example, while investigating the theft of a deposit from a company, the investigator might ask the suspect, "Did you steal that missing $2,000 deposit from the safe?" The suspect denies involvement and the interviewer responds with the control question: "Did you ever do anything that could be considered a violation of company policy?" The theory is that if a suspect is displaying truthful behavior during the interview, he should show some concern or behavioral change to the control question. If the suspect does not show any concern or behavioral change to the control question, it should alert the interviewer that the suspect might be attempting to control his deceptive behavior. If the suspect shows more concern to the control than the issue question, it reassures the interviewer that the suspect is probably telling the truth regarding the issue under investigation (see Figure 7.6).

Case Example

An investigation was conducted with a bank that had a $3,500 deposit missing. During one of the interviews, a male employee displayed behavior that was typical of truthful people. However, when asked the control question, "Did you violate any bank policies that you would not want your supervisor to find out about?" he did not show any concern. This made the interviewers cautious because they knew the suspect had violated bank policy by writing two checks when he had insufficient funds in his checking account. The interview went as follows:

Interviewer: Before we go any further, let me ask you, did you steal the missing $3,500 deposit?

Suspect: No. (Calm, direct)

Interviewer: Have you ever taken any money from the bank?

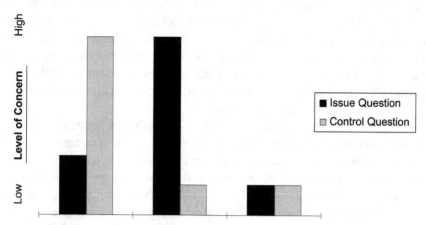

Figure 7.6 Generally, suspects who respond behaviorally more significantly to the control than to the issue question are telling the truth. However, suspects who react to neither the issue nor the control question might be attempting to control their behavior and should be eliminated as potential suspects.

Suspect: No.

Interviewer: Did you violate any bank policies that you would not want your supervisor to find out about?

Suspect: No. (Calm, direct)

There was no significant change in this suspect's demeanor. Therefore, the interviewer believed that this suspect was capable of displaying truthful behavior even when he was not telling the truth. An interviewer confronted with a "good liar" should never eliminate him as a suspect on the basis of behavioral responses alone. Individuals capable of controlling their behavior are more difficult to identify, and the control question allows the interviewer to test the credibility of the suspect's behavior.

As noted in Chapter 10, "Reducing Resistance—Rationalizations," it is important to identify an individual's motive for committing the crime and the resulting fears of a confession. If interviewers believe that the suspect might be involved in the issue under investigation they might decide to ask questions that can evoke the motive of the crime or the suspect's fears to confess them. One question asked might be, "Why do you think someone would have started that fire in the warehouse?" If the suspect responds that perhaps the individual was mad at the company, the interviewer can assume that the fire might have been started for revenge or because the perpetrator was not treated fairly at the company. A question that might identify an individual's fear would be, "Let me ask you a hypothetical question, Bob. If you had taken the missing $2,000 deposit, what would be the biggest reason you would not want to tell the truth?" If the suspect responds by saying that he would be concerned about his parents' finding out, the interviewer can hypothesize that embarrassment might be the suspect's hurdle. During the interrogation, the interrogator can attempt to overcome the suspect's primary hurdle.

In conclusion, the selective interview is a good investigative tool that can be used while investigating an incident that could have been committed by any of several people. Using structured questions and evaluating the suspect's verbal and physical responses will allow the interviewer to eliminate truthful individuals from the investigation while focusing on those responsible. However, remember that these interviews, like any other investigative tool, are not infallible. The purpose of these interviews is to enhance the interviewer's ability to identify the innocent and focus the investigation on the guilty suspect.

Using Questions of Enticement

An enticement question is a behavior-provoking, nonaccusatory question that entices a suspect to change or consider changing his original story. This question can be used during either an interview or an interrogation.

Purpose

The interrogator uses the enticement question in an attempt to identify the true status of the suspect. The guilty person is more likely than a truthful individual to be accurately identified with an enticement question. The enticement question can be used during an interview to offer suspects an opportunity to change their story. Regardless of whether the suspect actually changes or merely considers changing the story, the interviewer can observe the delay as the guilty person weighs his options. This delay is highly indicative of a deceptive individual. During the interrogation, an enticement question can also be used to overcome weak denials or to enhance the interrogator's ability to develop the admission of the suspect.

The origin of the enticement question is uncertain. However, the presentation of fictitious evidence certainly has been used by investigators for hundreds of years. One of the first actual references to this type of a question can be found in the book *Police Interrogation* by Captain Kidd[2] of the Berkeley, California, Police Department. Published in 1940, this is one of the earlier comprehensive texts on interrogation.

---

[2] Kidd W.R., New York: R.V. Baguino, 1940.

Presentation of the Question

Before an enticement question can be used effectively, suspects should be locked into the details of their alibi. Once they have committed themselves to the details, the enticement question can be presented in an attempt to shake their story. It must be presented to suspects so that they must consider that there is evidence of their guilt. The interviewer should preplan the type of enticement question that will be most effective. It can be used when referring to real evidence developed during the investigation or to fictitious evidence that could logically have been uncovered. This real evidence might be the observation of the crime by a witness, fingerprints, tire tracks, or other physical evidence found at the scene of the crime.

Regardless of whether the evidence is real or fictitious, the interviewer only implies the evidence's existence. This is preferable to a flat statement that the evidence exists because it allows the interviewer a way out if the suspect demands proof of its existence. In cases where real evidence of the suspect's guilt exists, it might not be in the interviewer's best interests to present it as an enticement question. Merely implying the existence of evidence frees the interviewer from having to reveal it.

The enticement question is usually worded as, "Is there any reason why…[your fingerprints, your tire tracks, your picture] were found at the scene of the burglary?" If an interviewer uses an enticement question such as, "Is there any reason that a witness would say that they saw you at the drug store just before the clerk was killed?" and the suspect immediately denies his presence, and, furthermore, demands to face this accuser, the denial might or might not be deception. Regardless, the interviewer has no current interest in presenting a witness but has left himself a way out. The interrogator can reply that the investigation is continuing, with numerous individuals being interviewed, but if there was a reason that the suspect was present in that store sometime during the day, the interviewer would prefer to talk about it now so the subject need not be inconvenienced again later.

Prior to the interviewer's using an enticement question, suspects should be locked into their story or sequence of events. The enticement question should also take into account the method used to commit the crime. For example, an enticement question such as "Is there any reason that your fingerprints would be present at the scene of the burglary?" might not be effective. This question's effectiveness is dependent on whether suspects wore gloves during the perpetration of the crime. Guilty suspects, because of their intimate knowledge of the circumstances surrounding the burglary, can immediately discount the evidence presented by the interviewer because they wore gloves. Because of the suspect's certainty that this evidence could not exist, he can quickly make a denial. However, if the interviewer had presented an enticement question such as, "Is there any reason that you can think of that a witness to the burglary would have identified you as being responsible?" then the suspect has to consider the possibility that he was observed at some point during the burglary. The suspect must also consider whether he was implicated by an informant, should admit being in the area but not being responsible for the burglary, or should stick to the original story. If the suspect changes the story; the interviewer recognizes his probable guilt. In other instances, the guilty suspect must consider whether the evidence alleged by the enticement exists, and what options exist. These considerations result in a delay in the suspect's response, which the interviewer in turn recognizes as deceptive behavior and indicative of probable guilt.

The interviewer must make sure, however, that there is no legitimate reason for the suspect to agree to the possibility of some alleged evidence linking him to the crime. For example, if the suspect does go into the safe at certain times to perform his duties, it would serve no purpose to ask if there is any reason his fingerprints would be found in the safe.

Interviewers are limited in an enticement question only by their inventiveness. For example, a rape suspect was apprehended approximately three blocks from the scene of the rape. The victim was almost positive in her identification of the suspect as the person who raped her. During a subsequent interview with the suspect, the interviewer asked, "Is there any reason that you could think of that the arresting officer would say your zipper was open when he arrested you?" The suspect paused and considered this statement before responding. Then snapping his fingers, he said, "Oh yeah, earlier in the day I did break my zipper while I was running so maybe that's what he saw." The guilty person's frequent attempts to explain away damaging evidence led him to invent alibis or admit to fictitious evidence.

The following are examples of some commonly used enticement questions.

- *Implying an eyewitness* — Katherine, as you know, we will be talking to everyone here today regarding that missing $600. Is there any reason that you can think of that any of the people we will be talking to would say that you took that missing $600?
- *Implying handwriting evidence* — Pat, as you know, anytime we do an investigation, we will use the services of outside experts. For example, if a situation involves handwriting, we retain the services of a handwriting expert. What we do is send the handwriting expert samples of the individual's writing so he can compare that person's handwriting with that of the handwriting found on the ___ [check, contract, etc.]. Pat, is there any reason you can think of that the handwriting expert would say that your handwriting matches the handwriting found on that ___ [check, contract, etc.]?

- *Implying physical evidence such as fingerprints, footprints, tire tracks* — Jennifer, in many situations like this, we will take the fingerprints of the individuals to see if their fingerprints match any fingerprints that were found at the scene. Is there any reason that you can think of that your fingerprints would have been found [inside of the safe, at the house, on the gun, etc.]? If you had to go into the safe for some reason, that is important to know in case they find your fingerprints.
- *Implying closed circuit camera evidence* — Kelly, as I mentioned to you before, we use closed circuit video cameras quite extensively throughout the store to watch what both customers and employees do. When we review that videotape, is there any reason you can think of that we would see you taking money out of Carolyn's cash register?
- *Asking the suspect to remember* — Jonathan, do you think it is possible you could have been on Forest Avenue at the dock at the time of the burglary, even though you don't remember? The reason I ask that is we will be talking to residents and I don't want them to say they thought that you might have been involved because they saw you nearby at that time, especially if you had a reason for being there.

Obtaining the Subject's Biographical Information

At the conclusion of the interview, interviewers should obtain additional biographical information of the person they interviewed. Attempting to obtain this information at the beginning of the interview can contribute to the witness's becoming reluctant to give information simply because he does not want to be involved in a prosecution or termination. The correct spelling of names, dates of birth, social security numbers, and residence addresses are important to the overall investigation. Many interviewers fail to ask for additional phone numbers for work or other family members in case it should be difficult to locate a critical witness. The interviewer should also obtain the correct spelling and addresses of all the companies referred to during the interview.

Obtaining a Written Statement

In some cases, it might be useful for the interviewer to obtain a written or permanent statement from the witness. This statement could be in a narrative form, question and answer format, or video or audiocassette tape with permission (check local and state statutes). An alternative to the written statement might be to have the witness initial the field notes of the interviewer to confirm their accuracy. (For additional discussion of this topic, see Chapter 14, The Statement.) If the interviewer intends to use statement analysis techniques to evaluate the subject's story, the written statement should reflect the untainted version of the story or alibi prior to any questioning. Statement analysis can often give insights into the subject's truthfulness, motives, and concealment, leading to more valuable follow-up questions.

Closing Professionally

Before leaving, the interviewer should restate what was said by the subject so that it is clear to both what was said. The interviewer should ask if what he just repeated was accurate or if there was anything else the subject recalled. If any other information is given, it should be explored before the interview is terminated.

Regardless of the outcome of the interview, the interviewer should remain friendly and supportive. This way, the lines of communication will remain open in the event a re-interview is necessary. This will more likely occur under pleasant terms because the rapport remains unbroken. In almost any case, it is in the best interest of the interviewer to thank the suspect and remind him that he might need to ask additional questions later. By doing this, the interviewer gains the individual's agreement to cooperation in another interview.

How the question requesting another interview is phrased is critical to obtaining an affirmative response. Since the interviewer wants the person to agree, the use of an assumptive question that directs the proper answer is often used. The interviewer might say, "I'm sure you wouldn't have a problem talking with me again if it were necessary, would you?" By having the question asked this way, the individual is encouraged to say he would have no problem with a later interview. This agreement is essential because, once an individual has agreed, it increases the likelihood that he will submit to another interview.

Finally, it is in the best interest of the interviewer to leave a business card or phone number where he can be reached should the witness recall any other information. It is not unusual for a victim or witness to recall additional details of the incident after having had time to reflect.

Often, a statement of expectation can encourage a subject to call with additional information. Saying, "If you recall anything let me know," indicates to subjects they might not remember additional facts and the interviewer does not expect to hear from them. Using a statement of expectation can increase the possibility of follow-up contact by the subject. The statement of expectation could be similar to the following: "Many times people remember other details as they think about an event they observed. I am sure you will too. What I would like you to do is call me with the additional information that you remember. Here is my card and number where I can be reached. That wouldn't be a problem would it?"

Inviting people to call when they remember anything allows them to feel that they should continue attempting to remember other details and that a call is expected. By leaving a number, the interviewer has made it easy for the victim or witness to contact him. If a subject has any difficulty in identifying and contacting him, it often results in the information's not being relayed.

Why People Confess 8

A secret is a most difficult tale to keep.

Fundamental to a discussion of interrogation is an understanding of why people choose to confess. We have chosen to limit our comments on confession to simple understandable reasons, rather than to use complex psychological terminology. The decision to confess may be a simple or complex decision for suspects, depending on their emotional and psychological makeup. Undoubtedly, some might not even be able to give a reason that they chose to confess. However, there seem to be some common reasons that people have confessed.

Believed Involvement Could Be Proven

The most common reason for confession is that suspects believed their guilt was known. This belief removes a significant barrier to confession. Once they believe that their guilt can be proved, their resistance is greatly reduced. When one considers how often people talk about their crime when they are caught in the act, it confirms this reduction in resistance to a confession. Even the most hardened criminals will often discuss the incident once they are convinced their guilt is known. Many investigators, recognizing this reduction in resistance, close the case at an opportune moment when they have the suspect "with his hand in the cookie jar."

Interrogators can make their job much more difficult by failing to act in a manner that conveys confidence in the suspect's guilt. The lack of confidence can be the manner in which the interrogator approached the suspect and tone of the interrogator's speech. Once suspects sense their guilt might be uncertain, there will be a corresponding increase in their resistance to confessing.

Suspects Put Their Own "Spin" on the Crime

"As long as they know I did it, I might as well justify why and put my own spin on the situation." This is the underlying conclusion suspects derive when they believe they are caught. Criminals are masters at rationalization. They have to be to commit their unlawful acts: "I have no money — you have a car — I am taking your car." This logic makes sense to them and confirms their right to commit the crime. Of course, this is an obvious oversimplification of the process. Many criminals are very rational in their actions, plan, and selection of a victim. They clearly weigh the likelihood of detection against the rewards of the act.

However, once caught, the pattern of rationalization resurfaces to justify and twist the circumstances in their favor: "He shot at me last week. Over at my crib, you guys were out there. Backing out, he fired off two rounds at me. And I threw a 40-oz. bottle through his windshield. I saw him in there tonight, went and got my bat, and busted him upside the head."

This could be a real or contrived story that explains his action in a more understandable fashion. It is intended to soften the feelings another might have for the suspect and helps him deal with the psychological issues of his involvement.

Guilt

The third most commonly given reason for a confession is that the individual felt guilt for committing the crime. This reason is found less often with the career criminal than the first-time offender. Genuinely sorry for what they have done, these individuals seek forgiveness and sometimes punishment from the victim and society for their transgressions.

These subjects seek relief from inner turmoil and anxiety by making a confession. In doing so, it seems as if the weight of the world has been lifted from their backs. They are making an emotional decision to confess, momentarily ignoring the realities of the punishments they are facing. These individuals, when genuine, often learn from their mistakes. However, many individuals who express guilt do so only in an effort to sway punishment and preserve their image.

Reputation

Career criminals and gang members might confess to enhance their reputation with their cohorts. These confessions might not be real and their legitimac should be viewed with a critical eye. With the influx of gangs and the resulting peer pressure for status within the gang came more confessions to build reputations of the gang members. This kind of confession might be found with the "wannabes," or fringe members, of the gang. These youths, attempting to gain acceptance from the group, confess in an attempt to gain status. It is like a rite of passage for the gang member as he does his first crime.

Reputation in a group is often enhanced with certain types of crimes, such as murder, burglary, or cleverness. Less likely admissions would be to child abuse, wife beating, or sexual abuse of children. People in general will posture to appear a particular way during innocent conversations, and criminals are no different in their personal needs. While unbelievable to the layman, seasoned investigators have all seen criminals who could not stop bragging about what they had done, which, in turn, led to their capture.

Adrenaline

A man and his fiancée approached the trailer of a drug dealer. Knocking, they waited for the door to open. When the door was opened by the dealer, they shot him in the head, killing him instantly. Entering the trailer, the two encountered the dealer's girlfriend, who they likewise killed. A quick search of the trailer revealed drugs and money, which they quickly pocketed and then fled from the scene.

Within hours of the double homicide, the man and his fiancée attended a party where they both told of their evening's exploits. Without their bragging it might have taken days to solve the murders, if at all. Why confess? Reputation, daring and "loose" lips.

After committing a crime, a person has a rush of adrenaline, which acts like a runner's high to buoy the spirits of the criminal. This physiological rush gives a sense of well-being and security that can overcome the fear of detection. Euphoria mixed with drugs and alcohol is a prescription for opening the mouth and talking.

Sometimes, the adrenaline rush mixed with guilt and other factors causes a spontaneous admission. There is no thought of the consequences, just a blurting admission from which the suspect cannot turn back. These types of confessions are often made to the first person to arrive at the scene of the crime. Once the first admission has been made, there is no reason for the suspect to later deny guilt.

Loose Lips Sink Ships

We have all heard the World War II slogan, "Loose lips sink ships." It exhorted citizens not to talk about things related to the military because it might cost lives of our boys in the service. If criminals would pay attention to this motto, our jobs would be much more difficult.

A secret is a most difficult tale to keep. Every word must be censored to prevent the secret's escape. It is only the most watchful of censors who can control the urge to talk. This becomes even more difficult when speaking to people who are trusted. These people, friends or even the interrogator, are judged to be able to deal with the truth and deal with it in a way favorable to the suspect. Jailhouse confessions or the interrogation room confession often have similar dynamics. Trust, bravado, or a simple need to tell a secret combine to bring an admission.

Protect Another

Some confessions occur in part to protect another from complicity in the crime. The first suspect believes his guilt is known and he has no other option than to confess to the crime. This suspect sacrifices himself, taking full blame for the incident, believing it is unlikely that the co-conspirators have been identified. This failure to implicate others is viewed as a pillar of the suspect's reputation and might gain him an advantage in the future.

However, others might falsely confess to protect a family member for whom they feel responsible or have a debt of honor to repay. This confession might be totally false or just an omission of facts that protects another and links the confessor to the crime.

Less frequently, a suspect might offer a false confession for an economic gain to protect the real offender. Drug abusers or others who have run up tabs to dealers or bookies might confess falsely to pay their debt in a barter fashion — time in prison versus a much less acceptable option offered by the dealer or bookie.

Tossing a Bone

Some confessions are offered by guilty suspects to keep interrogators from probing for an even darker secret. The suspect "tosses a bone" to the interrogator in an attempt to evade questioning on an even more serious incident.

For example, a cashier confesses to taking change from her register to keep from admitting the theft of a missing deposit. Likewise, a burglar admits a vandalism to divert attention away from the commercial burglary. These admissions relieve some internal tension and offer a plausible reason for the suspect's deceptive behavior or actions.

The unwary interrogator can become diverted from the original goal by this insignificant admission. By accepting and focusing questioning on the secondary issue, the interrogator indirectly tells the subject that his guilt is uncertain, which might increase the subject's resistance to confessing to the original issue. This is just the first ploy in the negotiation for the suspect's confession. The toss-the-bone admission is on the table and can be ignored until the central issue has been resolved. Once that has been clarified, the interrogator returns to explore the secondary admission.

Quid Pro Quo

Quid pro quo has become famous in sexual harassment claims where a supervisor offers some form of advantage to an employee in exchange for sexual favors. Confessions also might occur in situations where an individual seeks an exchange of confession or information for an advantage: *one hand washes the other.* Informants are often cultivated in this manner when they have been caught and attempt to gain favor by giving information on criminal activity or by cooperating with authorities.

Confessions and guilty pleas are often a game of what the charges and sentence will end up being. Career criminals often refuse to confess because of their experience in the criminal justice system and an understanding of how the game is played. These people play the cards that are dealt, going through each hand — probable cause and evidence suppression hearings, motions and jury demands to get the best deal from the prosecutor before they plead and make a confession. Some confessions are made to secure a lesser criminal charge; however, the interrogator must be careful never to make promises or offers of leniency that might invalidate a confession. The courts have suppressed confessions that were obtained in this manner.

Get It Over With

Another reason some people confess is just to be done with the problem and move on with their lives. They are at a loss to see any other way out and confess as a result of the futility of continued denial. This decision to confess is often an emotional one, made because of a seeming absence of other options.

Suspects in this situation stand in the shambles of their lives and just do not care anymore. They see their reputation, career, and family disappear as they knew them. The weight of this realization creates an internal emotional state, which subjects escape by putting the incident behind them and moving on with their lives. This confession creates hope for a new beginning and a light at the end of the tunnel.

Did No Wrong

Some suspects freely discuss their involvement because they do not believe that what they have done is wrong. This belief might be a moral, ethical or legal position. Some cultures accept the right of revenge for another's actions, so the suspect could have acted in a way that is culturally acceptable, but illegal.

For example, a suspect might admit to the bombing of an abortion clinic or animal research facility to further a political agenda. This confession gives the suspect a forum to express his moral outrage of a perceived wrong to a larger audience. Dr. Kevorkian confessed to assisted suicides in violation of Michigan law for just this reason — a political agenda regarding the right to die.

Other confessions result from a misunderstanding of the legal implications of the suspect's actions. For example, a property owner sets a trap for a burglar that causes the burglar's death when he enters the premises. The property owner might genuinely feel that he could use deadly force to protect his "castle." The property owner's confession is based on his misunderstanding of the law and the use of deadly force. The failure to recognize the seriousness of the situation reduced his resistance to making a confession.

Trusts the Interrogator

Interrogators, like salesmen, sell themselves as much as their products, in this case, a confession. If there is no trust in the salesman, customers are reluctant to buy. It is the same with the suspect. Once the suspect and the interrogator have developed a relationship of trust, making a confession is like talking with a supportive friend.

With the development of trust in the interrogator, the suspect must also contend with a fear of disappointing him. This is similar to the fear one might experience in disappointing any person important in one's life. Disapproval is a strong influence in anyone's decision-making and becomes more so as the relationship deepens.

Wanting Help

Certain suspects confess because they recognize that they are out of control and need help to get back on track. These types of people might genuinely be remorseful of the criminal behavior in which they were involved. As an attempt to end the behavior and make a clean start, they begin by confessing.

The motivation for the crimes could vary from financial to sexual, but the suspect's compulsion to re-offend is an inner need and not a rational decision to commit a crime. In this situation, suspects understand what they are doing is wrong but need help to control their behavior. The confession is the first attempt to regain control of their lives.

Cannot Say "No"

Some suspects just have a difficult time resisting the interrogator and are so compliant that they confess. Compliance varies in people and significantly affects whether they will conform to another's ideas or will. The more compliant an individual is, the more likely that he will confess. Compliance and suggestibility are also strongly associated with individuals who have given false confessions. However, merely being suggestible and compliant does not necessarily equate to an automatic false confession. For a further detailed discussion, refer to Chapter 4, Memory and False Confessions.

Some people have difficulty saying no when asked something in a persuasive manner. A good interrogator is nothing if not persuasive.

Physical and Emotional Abuse and Threats

Physical and emotional abuse are prohibited by the U.S. courts, but are used in other countries around the globe. While we would like to believe that the "third degree" tactics are long gone from the United States, we are reminded periodically that this is not so. A District Commander was recently fired from a large metropolitan police department for abusing prisoners to obtain confessions.

Any confession obtained by the use of physical force or extended psychological coercion is inherently unreliable. Prisoners subjected to brainwashing during the Korean War were confined at length while being pressured psychologically to condemn the United States. Similar treatment of American prisoners by the North Vietnamese during the Vietnam conflict attempted to break the will of captured pilots. Under these types of pressures, people will say almost anything to stop the torture and mistreatment.

Threats made by the interrogator can also cause a suspect to confess. Threats to cause physical harm or to take away a suspect's children could cause both an innocent and a guilty suspect to confess. Thus, any resulting confession obtained through this type of coercion should be rightly suppressed as unreliable.

Remember, it is always best to treat a suspect the way you would like to be treated yourself: with dignity and respect.

Why Do Suspects Confess?

The preceding outlined just some of the more common reasons for confession, but was certainly not an exhaustive list of all the possibilities. There are probably combinations of these and other reasons for some people, while other suspects might have a single identifiable reason for confessing. The wise interrogator uses the time after the confession to discuss the suspect's decision-making process with him to hopefully better understand the next individual.

Part Three

Establishing Credibility

The Accusation

9

Many of the problems faced by interrogators during an interrogation have their origin during the opening moments of the accusation.

The accusation is the last step in the investigative process. The investigator has conducted an investigation that developed the necessary evidence to believe the suspect is involved in the issue under investigation. The interrogator has prepared a plan and considered the room setting as part of the overall plan for the interrogation. Interrogators should also consider the different accusations available and the different ways they can establish the credibility of the investigation. In doing so, interrogators must establish the suspect's belief that his guilt is known for certain. Failure to convey this belief to the suspect will result in a more difficult interrogation and probable denials.

This chapter discusses the different ways to begin an interrogation. Interrogators should realize that each method of beginning has benefits and pitfalls. It is often the opening moments of the interrogation that dictate its success or failure, and many of the problems faced by interrogators during an interrogation have their origin during the opening moments of the accusation. Suspect denials or a difficulty in developing an admission are often problems created by interrogators themselves because of their choice of accusation. Interrogators should consider the impact of the accusation they intend to use in light of later potential problems.

Positioning

The interviewer should have selected the witness and arranged the chairs prior to the suspect's entering the room. This procedure will minimize distractions to the suspect. The chairs should be spaced 3 to 4 feet apart, with no desk or table to separate the participants. This separation is a comfortable distance for both the suspect and interrogator. However, interrogators more comfortable using a desk during the interrogation should position the chairs so that only the corner of the desk separates them from the suspect.

Attitude

The interrogator's attitude should be that of a mediator seeking the truth rather than that of a dominant, authoritative figure. Taking the role of a mediator instead of an opponent allows the interrogator to reduce some of the suspect's fears. Interrogators should also exude confidence, in both their approach and word choice. This show of confidence will often help conceal any mistakes the interrogator might make during the interrogation. In addition, interrogators should display professionalism, not superiority.

Introduction

Interrogators should consider how they want to present the accusation. As discussed earlier, they can sit behind a desk to give them additional authority, stand if they want to come across as even more authoritative, or sit directly across from the suspect. Each of these positions will give the suspect a different feeling toward the interrogator. Ideally, since interrogators want to reduce the suspect's level of defensiveness, positioning the chairs directly across from each other or slightly off to one side will lessen the confrontational feel of the meeting (see Figure 9.1). Unless there are clear reasons not to do so, the best positioning is chairs across from each other without any barriers between the suspect and interrogator.

Impressions Given by the Interrogator

Interrogator must consider the role they are to play. To a certain extent, they are actors in a play, and the roles they choose serve to satisfy the needs of the suspect. Interrogator should consider their dress, language, and professionalism and the impact that each of these might have on the suspect. A professional impression will enhance interrogators' ability to handle the cas successfully and increase their own stature with co-workers. Meanwhile, by matching their dress and stature to the subject's, interrogators can often establish rapport more rapidly than if they dressed otherwise.

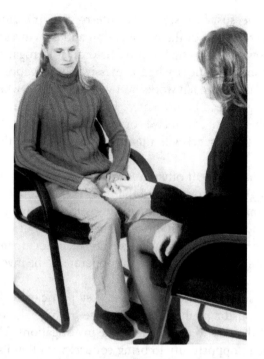

Figure 9.1 Remove any barriers between the suspect and interviewer or interrogator.

Selection of the Accusation

Once the interrogators have considered their image, positioning, and attitude, they should consider the different methods of beginning the interrogation. The choice of a particular accusation is dependent on many factors — the type of case and the suspect's personality and criminal history should be considered. The case facts and the certainty of the suspect's guilt also play a role in determining which approach will be successful in obtaining the suspect's admission.

Factual Approach

One common method of accusation is the factual approach. The suspect is locked into his story or alibi in great detail by the interrogator. Once a suspect has committed to the details of the case, the interrogator uses the evidence developed during the investigation to disprove the story. Initially, the interrogator gives the appearance of believing the story, which encourages the suspect to tell more and more lies. As suspects become overconfident, they begin to embellish the tales. This will prove to be their undoing.

Following the suspect's story, the interrogator presents evidence that establishes the credibility of the investigation and convinces the suspect that his guilt is known. The factual approach to an interrogation can be quite successful in those instances when a massive investigation has been conducted. The factual approach works best when clear, overwhelming evidence of the suspect's guilt can be presented. However, when the evidence is only suggestive, rather than conclusive, of the suspect's guilt, the interrogator might find that the suspect will attempt to explain away the incriminating evidence.

Public law enforcement often uses the factual approach to convince suspects that their guilt is provable and that they should cooperate in the investigation. Sting operations and homicide investigations are good examples of when to use a factual approach. Inviting suspects in to discuss their involvement and being able to present wiretap or video documentation of it can often result in a suspect's willingness to cooperate in the investigation or give testimony.

In major case investigations, once the key participants have been identified, the interrogator might approach those individuals with a peripheral involvement in the case to cooperate in the investigations. These individuals are often given an opportunity to bring counsel with them so that they will be more likely to make a rational rather than emotional decision when confronted. However, counsel for the suspect should be invited to meetings only when the evidence of guilt is so overwhelming that it will immediately convince counsel of the benefits of cooperation. A meeting of this type is generally conducted in conjunction with the prosecutor, who will usually ask for the suspect's testimony to support other portions of the case in return for a plea arrangement.

Interrogators presenting evidence in this type of case need not be aggressive or condescending but instead simply can be mediators who are working from a position of power. During this approach, the case is built systematically and overwhelmingly to convince suspects that it is in their best interest to cooperate with the investigators. Imagine the suspect who has repeatedly denied knowing another individual and suddenly must face photos of them together or recordings of their conversations. Overwhelmed by this evidence, the suspect often offers cooperation in the investigation.

The factual attack, however, is clearly less effective in cases without overwhelming evidence of the suspect's guilt. In many investigations, the evidence developed is circumstantial and open to interpretation. When the evidence is circumstantial, it often encourages suspects to deny simply because they are under the mistaken belief that circumstantial evidence is not conclusive or cannot convict. In many cases, circumstantial evidence, when presented alone or piece by piece to the suspect, does not have the emotional impact of direct evidence such as wiretap or fingerprint evidence.

In the majority of instances, the factual approach only creates problems for the interrogator who now must convince the suspect that the total picture of the evidence does indicate the suspect's guilt. The suspect, however, might offer other plausible explanations for the incriminating evidence and is less likely to accept the interrogator's belief in the suspect's guilt because of the evidence's circumstantial nature.

Often, the factual evidence of a suspect's guilt might be merely one specific observation, for example, a cashier's taking $20 out of the register and putting it in a pocket, or the suspect in the area of the robbery. Although each of these observations might have value in the presentation of the overall case, it might not be sufficient in and of itself to convince suspects that their guilt is known for certain. The cashier who has placed the money in a pocket might counter that he merely placed it there until he could get change and that he had intended to put it back later. The suspect who has been observed on a street near the robbery might manufacture a story that explains away this observation. Lying about the alibi, however, might later prove to be the suspect's downfall.

Therefore, only when significant, irrefutable evidence of a suspect's guilt is available can a factual attack be easily used to overwhelm suspects and convince them that they should confess. Interrogators who attempt to use a factual approach without sufficient facts run the risk that suspects will recognize the case weaknesses and not confess because they believe their lies cannot be disproved. Also, using a factual approach on a specific issue might reduce the likelihood of the interrogator's being able to expand the suspect's admissions into other areas of involvement.

There exists one additional problem with the factual approach. When there will be a circumstantial presentation of facts in an attempt to convince suspects they have been caught, the interrogator runs the risk of an innocent subject's recounting the details and making a convincing false confession using information supplied by the interrogator.

Direct Accusation

An accusation commonly used by interrogators is the direct accusation. The direct accusation is generally used in a single-issue case where the incident is clearly defined. The directness of the accusation allows the interrogator to tell suspects of what exactly they are being accused. The interrogator is interested in obtaining an admission on a specific incident and must focus the suspect's attention on that single issue. To focus the suspect, the interrogator must use the very direct accusation.

This direct accusation is more suited for public law enforcement than for the private sector. The public law enforcement community is usually more likely to be focused on a specific incident, whereas the private sector often interrogates on a pattern of merchandise or money theft. The private sector also has to be concerned about employee morale and the company image. This concern generally precludes the use of the direct accusation on a regular basis.

In public law enforcement cases, the suspects might invoke their rights under *Miranda*. If they do so, the interrogation must stop immediately or any resulting confession could be rendered inadmissible. The police interrogator should avoid tactics that will cause a suspect to invoke these rights.

On the positive side, the direct accusation can also elicit additional behavioral clues from the suspect. These additional behavioral clues can help the interrogator to eliminate an innocent suspect from the investigation. For example, a direct accusation might be helpful when the investigation has focused on two suspects who might be involved in the incident, but further investigation is unlikely to develop conclusive proof of either's guilt. An interrogator's use of a direct accusation can often identify the person responsible for the incident.

Interviews with the two suspects might only give the interviewer behaviors indicative of deception but not identify which of the two suspects was actually involved. One of the suspects may have behaved deceptively because he was involved in the incident, but the other suspect's behavior might be a result of a related side issue or knowledge of who is really responsible. The suspect's denials resulting from the direct accusation can be evaluated by the interrogator. These denials can give interrogators direction as they probe for the truth.

Another use of a direct accusation is to refute denials voiced by the suspect during the interrogation. Whenever a denial is used by the suspect, the interrogator must reaccuse with an equal directness. This directness may be as strong as the following:

Suspect: I didn't do it.

Interrogator: Bob, just a minute. From the investigation, there is no question that you are responsible for the break-in.

However, the interrogator's reaccusation might be much weaker if the suspect's denial is weaker.

Suspect: But ... I ... I didn't do it (spoken weakly).

Interrogator: Bob, that's just not true.

The problem with the direct accusation is that it invariably elicits an emphatic denial from the suspect. This is especially true in the earliest stages of the interrogation when the suspect is strongest. Interrogators, because of their directness, have then forced the suspects to defend their contention that they were not involved in the incident under investigation. Because of the directness of the interrogator's accusation, the suspect generally takes the path of least resistance and thought. He lies, using a denial.

The interrogator must now overcome two problems to enable suspects to confess: first, the suspects' unwillingness to admit their involvement and, second, the fact that they have now lied to the interrogator and must tell additional lies to defend that position.

With all the accusations, there is some preliminary conversation that takes place with the suspect prior to the actual beginning of the interrogation. The interrogation begins establishing a behavioral norm for the suspect by asking biographical questions to which the individual will likely respond truthfully. The interrogator observes the suspect's verbal and physical behavior that is the person's norm for this encounter.

The interrogator then attempts to develop rapport with the suspect. One favored method is asking suspects to tell a little about themselves. The interrogator is expressing interest in the suspects' favorite person, themselves. The interrogator listens for information that might be used to establish rapport or to use as a possible rationalization.

The preferred sequence to use during a direct accusation is as follows:

- *Relate the Issue.* The first part of the direct accusation is an introduction. The interrogator introduces himself and the witness, if one is used. The interrogator then tells the suspect that an investigation has been conducted and reveals the issue they will discuss in the interview/interrogation. At the beginning of the direct accusation, it is important to focus the suspect's behavioral responses specifically on the issue under investigation. The interrogator makes sure that the suspect understands that the discussion is about a single incident and is not a general inquiry. This can be done by gesturing to an investigative file representing the work done on the case. This file is the embodiment of the investigation and is something tangible for the suspect to see.

By identifying the reason for the interrogation, the interrogator focuses the suspect's attention directly on the issue and away from any side issues. For example, consider the mind-set of the suspect who has been burglarizing vehicles in and around the town over the last six months. The interrogator mistakenly believes the suspect is involved in a residential burglary. The suspect, although innocent of the residential burglary, might show deceptive behavior when questioned about the residential burglary because of the thefts from vehicles. This deceptive behavior is related to the side issue of the vehicular burglaries rather than the residential burglary.

The following is an example of the opening statement: "Bob, my name is Detective Wayne Hoover, with the City Police. As you might be aware, we have been questioning individuals regarding a burglary to a residence at 1237 Holly Court in the city. During the break-in, some jewelry and electronic equipment were stolen."

The interrogator has clearly stated the reason for the meeting and what was stolen. The suspect's behavioral responses should now be reflective of his role (if any) in the residential burglary rather than of any side issues.

- *Make Clear, Simple Accusations.* The interrogator must make a clear simple accusation to the suspect. This accusation must have only one meaning and must be direct enough so the suspect is not confused by what the interrogator means. The purpose of this statement is to throw the suspect off balance by its directness and to demand a denial from the suspect — a denial that can be interpreted by the interrogator as being truthful or deceptive.

The following is an example of a direct accusation: "Bob, it is clear from our investigation that you are responsible for the break-in at 1237 Holly Court in the city last night."

- *Pause.* Once the interrogator has made the direct accusation, the suspect should be allowed an opportunity to respond. In almost all instances, the suspect will make an emphatic denial to the direct accusation. The interrogator can then evaluate the strength and spontaneity of the denial and its content. This evaluation will help the interrogator to eliminate the suspect from the investigation or focus on him as the primary suspect.

The following is an example of denials from truthful and deceptive individuals:

Truthful suspect: "You're crazy, I didn't break into any house last night!" (The suspect's denial is direct, spontaneous, and he might physically lean forward.)

- **Untruthful suspect:** (clears throat) … I'm sorry, you've got the wrong guy. It wasn't me. (Weak voice, no eye contact, slumped in the chair).

- *Repeat the Accusation.* Once the suspect has made an emphatic denial in response to the direct accusation, the interrogator should cut off further denials and repeat the direct accusation. Even during this early stage of repeating the accusation, the interrogator should begin to minimize the seriousness of the issue under investigation.

The following is an example of the interrogator re-accusing the suspect: "Rob, just a minute. There is no question about the fact that you went into the house on Holly Court, but my concern is ..."

The interrogator must confidently reaccuse the suspect to let him know that the investigation indicates that the suspect is involved in the incident. The interrogator attempts to stop any other denials and moves on to the rationalizations.

- *Lead into Rationalizations.* Following the reaccusation, the interrogator begins to use the rationalizations which he believes will minimize the seriousness of the incident in the suspect's perception and allow the suspect to save face. These rationalizations will be based on the suspect's background, motive of the crime, or other issues that will be discussed in the section on rationalizations.

A Problem with Direct Accusation — The primary problem with the direct accusation is that, because of its directness, it encourages the suspect to lie using a denial and then forces him to defend that position with additional denials. Although interrogators can overcome his denials and obtain a statement of guilt, it generally results in a more difficult interrogation than was necessary. In certain circumstances, the direct accusation, even though it results in denials, is effective in identifying the individual not responsible for the particular incident, which allows the interrogator to eliminate an innocent suspect from suspicion.

The interrogator should never unnecessarily use this form of interrogation to eliminate suspects from an investigation. It is generally used only when an investigation is stalled and is unlikely to clear or convict a suspect of involvement. The choice is to interrogate each of the two suspects in the hope of clearing one through the interrogation and then focusing on the second suspect, or to let the investigation wither and die. In some cases, this might be the only method to resolve the case.

The interrogator assesses the strength of the initial denial from the suspect and continues to offer rationalizations. As the interrogation continues, the interrogator attempts to determine whether the denials are increasing in strength, which would be typical of the truthful, or decreasing in strength and frequency, which would be typical of the deceptive (see Figure 9.2). The initial difficulty for the interrogator is that even the guilty might respond strongly at first, but, as the rationalizations have their effect, the guilty suspect will deny less frequently and become more docile. The opposite is true of the truthful individual. The truthful suspect increases the strength of the denials and takes control of the interrogation.

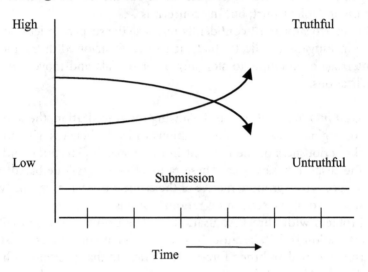

Figure 9.2 This chart illustrates the relative resistance of truthful and untruthful suspects. The truthful suspect's resistance to a confession increases as time passes in the interview, whereas guilty suspects' resistance lessens until they are ready to confess.

Introductory Statement Approach

Another approach to beginning the interrogation is the introductory statement, which uses a factual component and an emotional appeal that allows the suspect to save face. The interrogator builds the credibility of the investigative process in the early stages of the interrogation and uses a process of rationalization to minimize the seriousness of the suspect's involvement in the issue.

This particular accusation has a tremendous flexibility. It can be used with or without a nonaccusatory interview. It can also be used when there is direct evidence of an individual's involvement in the incident or when the suspect has been implicated but is not linked by direct evidence to the crime.

The interrogator has the best of both worlds, factual and emotional, by using an introductory statement. It allows the suspect to make a rational decision to confess rather than an emotional one. In the direct accusation, the directness of the interrogator's statement encourages most individuals to deny quickly. However, the introductory statement makes no accusations initially, which allows the suspect to listen to what the interrogator has to say.

Although an emotional approach can be used for a large percentage of suspects, it generally has little impact on the street-sharp, experienced individual. Using both a factual and an emotional component allows the introductory statement to be more effective with any type of suspect. The introductory statement allows the interrogator to discuss the process of investigation and establishes the credibility of the investigation, which instills the belief in the suspect's mind that he is caught. Establishing that belief can help obtain a confession even in the experienced, street-hardened suspect. About 95% of those who would ever confess are susceptible to a combined factual-emotional approach. The remaining 5% will not confess unless the interrogator presents proof of guilt. While not directly accusing the suspect of anything, the interrogator utilizes his own behavior to tell an underlying story to suspects. This underlying story conveys a separate message to the suspect, telling them about the real reason they are present.

Prior to beginning the introductory statement, the interrogator might find it beneficial to review some biographical information with the suspect. The review of the biographical information allows the interrogator to establish rapport with the suspect and calm his own nervous feelings. In addition, it also allows the interrogator an opportunity to evaluate and develop a set of baseline behaviors for the suspect. Utilizing these behavioral norms, the interrogator can assess changes in the suspect's behavior as he begins to discuss the case at hand. Furthermore, it begins to let the suspect know an investigation has been conducted. It might also be helpful to ask the suspect to tell a little about himself, which may identify possible rationalizations.

Interrogator's Behavior — Interrogators are telling two stories during the course of the introductory statement. On the surface, they are telling the police or loss prevention story. The introductory statement is spoken in nonaccusatory tones and in an offhand manner. Interrogators will use subtle variations in voice and eye contact to tell the secondary story.

The underlying secondary story is how the suspect actually was involved in the incident and the methods that he used to commit the crime. By being indirect, interrogators can avoid having the suspect make any form of a denial that would make the interrogative process more difficult.

If the introductory statement is presented to both a truthful individual and an untruthful individual, their reactions are markedly different. The truthful suspect listens closely and enjoys being told about the police or loss prevention story. The guilty suspect reacts to the same words differently: "I've been caught!"

Suspect's Behavior — The suspect's behavior during the introductory statement can be interpreted as either truthful or deceptive. The truthful individual has a relaxed, open posture and a face that remains relaxed and interested.

Guilty suspects often have a stiffness to the body and move in a jerky, abrupt manner. The face takes on a fearful, hunted look as they realize that their involvement in the incident has been discovered. The guilty's nodding of the head is often abrupt and mistimed.

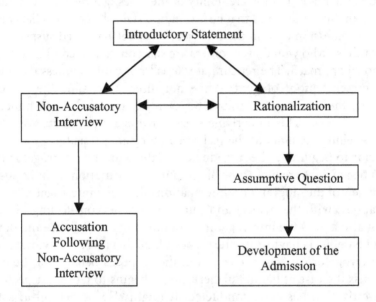

Figure 9.3 The introductory statement establishes the credibility of the investigation in the suspect's mind, while allowing the interrogator to change strategies in response to his actions.

Introductory Statement Options — The interrogator has a number of options when using the introductory statement (see Figure 9.3). The introductory statement can join with rationalizations and lead to the assumptive question. If the interrogator is uncertain of the suspect's guilt after using the introductory statement, he can use a nonaccusatory interview to elicit additional behavior typical of innocence or guilt. If the interviewer begins the encounter with a nonaccusatory interview, he can slide into the interrogation by following the interview with the introductory statement. The introductory statement then leads to offers of rationalizations and the assumptive question.

Construction of the Introductory Statement for Loss Prevention — Private Sector

The basic construction of an introductory statement does not differ between the public and private sectors, although modification of terminology and subtle changes of technique might be required. The first example below is a standard introductory statement used in a theft case in the private sector.

Explanation of the Interrogator's Role — In the first part of the introductory statement, the interrogators identify themselves as members of the loss prevention staff and define their role in the company. It is in this first part of the statement that interrogators let the employee know that employees are the most important asset the company possesses. Interviewers also describe the three factors that relate to shortage within the company (1) paperwork errors, (2) shoplifting, and (3) employee's taking things.

The interrogator also relates to the suspect that the loss prevention department's primary concern must be with those employees who would be causing tens of thousands of dollars in cash or merchandise losses rather than something of a minor nature. This statement is the interrogator's first attempt to begin minimizing the seriousness of the suspect's involvement in a theft.

As interrogators talk to the suspect, they consciously attempt to avoid causing the suspect to deny. For example, if the suspected employee was stealing cash, the employee would be more likely to make a denial if the interrogator worded the opening statement this way: "Bob, my name is _____. I'm a member of the loss prevention staff here at the company and it's my job to protect the assets. Assets of the company are money, merchandise, building, fixtures, and our most important asset is our employee."

In this example, the interrogator put the word *money* first in the list of the company's assets. Guilty individuals might make a denial to protect themselves, and it would not sound unusual if the denial came immediately after the word money. However, when interrogators attempt to avoid denials, they position the word money at the end, so the suspect is unlikely to make a denial because he failed to deny taking any of the other assets. For example: "Bob, my name is _____. I'm a member of the loss prevention staff here at the company and it's my job to protect the company's assets. The assets of the company are its building, fixtures, merchandise, and money, but our most important asset is our employees."

The suspect is less likely to deny taking the money because he did not deny stealing any of the other assets, the building, fixtures, or merchandise. When money is finally said, it would appear out of place for the suspect to deny only money, so he remains quiet.

Explanation of How Losses Occur — During the second part of the introductory statement, interrogators detail how losses occur via internal theft. The purpose of this second point of the introductory statement is to tell the suspect indirectly how he is stealing without interrogators' being so direct that the employee can make a denial. This is generally done by mentioning the theft about midway in the explanation. The same strategy of placement, as previously discussed, is used to avoid denials. A denial to the properly positioned known theft method would seem out of place, even to the guilty. The method of theft thought to have been used is placed in the middle rather than at the end of the second part of the statement, so that the suspect cannot be sure what his exposure is in the case. Placing the suspect's method of theft at the end of part two would help the suspect to identify how much the interrogator knows about the theft. For example, if the suspect were stealing money by failing to ring sales, the explanation of how losses might occur would be as follows: "Employees might cause losses by taking money right out of the register. They might write up fraudulent credits or voids. They might fail to ring up sales. They might pass merchandise off to friends or carry merchandise out themselves."

Eye contact in the early portions of the introductory statement can be effectively used to emphasize the points an interrogator wishes to make. For example, after saying "failing to ring up sales," the interviewer should subtly pause and make eye contact with the suspect. This short pause and eye contact sets "failing to ring up sales" apart from the other examples of theft. The pause and eye contact, however, should not be so long that the suspect has an opportunity to make a denial.

The second purpose of the explanation of how losses occur is to elicit behavior from guilty suspects regarding their involvement in other thefts. Often, an investigation will identify only one of several methods an employee is using to steal from the company. This section allows interrogators to observe deceptive behavior from the guilty suspect when they mention a particular type of theft activity in which the suspect is engaged. The resulting stress as suspects mentally recreate in their mind another method of theft they used often results in a noticeable behavioral change. These behavioral changes might be as subtle as an on-time blink of the eye or as obvious as a large shift in the trunk of the body.

Regardless of the behavior, interrogators should recognize there was a reason that the suspect showed more stress when he or she heard "passing merchandise off to friends" than when "writing fraudulent credits" was mentioned. The interrogator should mentally file this information for use during development of the admission. Interestingly, asking a guilty suspect how a theft might be committed by an employee will result in the suspect's offering the method actually used in the theft under investigation.

Explanation of How Investigations Are Conducted —The third part of the introductory statement is an explanation of how investigations are conducted. This section describes investigative techniques that might have been used in the investigation. The explanation of how the investigation was conducted must be in sufficient detail to convince even the street-sharp individual that an in-depth investigation has been conducted.

Although many types of evidence could be developed during an investigation, it is generally most effective for the interrogator to discuss techniques that would develop direct evidence of a suspect's involvement (i.e., surveillance, shopping service, undercover agent, or videotape recording) versus circumstantial evidence of guilt (i.e., register audits, computer reports, or charting of register shortages).

The interrogator speaks in general terms regarding the investigation and never gives any details or evidence. It is inappropriate for the interrogator to give the suspect any specific information at this time. In any of the three sections discussed thus far, the comments made by the interrogator should never be focused directly on the suspect, but rather be of a general nature discussing overall employee theft activity.

The interrogator should avoid words that are threatening to the suspect or too descriptive. For example, an interrogator might say "customers' taking things without paying for them" rather than "shoplifting." The word shoplifting re-creates the seriousness of the activity and attaches connotations of punishment. The other phrase describes the same activity in a much less threatening way.

By now, the interrogator has conveyed the underlying message that the suspect is present because of "employees' taking things." The suspect is also probably aware that the theft might be the result of "failing to ring up a sale" and that an in-depth investigation into losses has been conducted. If this message has been successfully conveyed to the guilty suspect, he realizes that there is a strong likelihood he has been caught; however, the interrogator was never direct enough to allow the suspect to initiate a denial.

Discussions of Why Employees Make Mistakes: Rationalizations —During the fourth part of the introductory statement, the interrogator begins to rationalize the suspect's actions. These rationalizations focus the suspect's attention on resolving the incident rather than on the consequences of actions. The next chapter discusses the structure and methods to reduce a suspect's resistance to confessing.

The rationalizations used in the fourth part of the introductory statement are presented using third-person pronouns. The interrogator constantly refers to others — they, them, people, individuals — and never uses words that would refer specifically to the suspect, such as "you" or the suspect's first name. By talking about others and the reasons *they* became involved in an illicit activity, the interrogator can offer rationalizations for the suspect's behavior without inviting him to deny involvement.

Most suspects will not make a denial at this point because the interrogator has not been direct enough to make them to feel threatened. As suspects listen to the rationalizations, their behavior will begin to change as the rationalizations reduce their resistance. The interrogator will note behavioral changes: suspects will begin to open their closed body posture and relax some of their muscle tension. Once the suspect's resistance has been reduced sufficiently, the interrogator can make a transition statement.

Test for Submission — Once interrogators believe that the suspect is behaviorally close to confessing, they offer him a transition statement to verify that he is, in fact, ready to give an admission. The transition statement makes it evident that the rationalizations the interrogator had previously been using directly applied to the suspect. The interrogator makes this evident by using the suspect's first name and the second-person pronouns, "you" or "your." The following is a basic transition statement made by the interrogator: "Mark, the problem is that we don't know the problems you face outside of work."

Soft Accusation or Assumptive Question — Once interrogators have observed the behavioral clues indicating the suspect's susceptibility to confessing, they use a soft accusation or an assumptive question. The assumptive question bypasses asking if the suspect did something and requests information about some aspect of the crime, such as how many times the suspect did something or when was the first or last time he did it. The following are some examples of assumptive questions:

- What would be the most amount of money that you took from the company in any one day?
- What would be the most amount of merchandise that you took from the company in any one day?
- When was the very first time that you took money from the company?
- What was the most expensive piece of merchandise that you ever took from the company in a single day?

Follow-up Question — Whenever suspects react in a way that indicates they are going to make an admission, the interrogator immediately uses a follow-up question, a question directly related to the soft accusation. The follow-up question is an exaggeration of what the suspect could have actually done. The purpose of the exaggeration is to continue to minimize, from the suspect's perspective, what he or she has done, and to thereby encourage an admission.

Interrogator: Bob, let me ask you this. What is the most amount of money that you took from the company in any single day?

Suspect: (Pause, looks away)

Interrogator: Was it a whole day's receipts in any single day?

Suspect: Geez, no.

Interrogator: Great. I didn't think it was that much. Would you say that it was more or less than $1,000.00 in one day?

Suspect: Less.

Interrogator: Okay. How much was it?

Suspect: $20.00.

The interrogator immediately supports the denial as an admission letting the suspect know that he has confessed. The suspect now realizes that he has made an admission and is drawn into a dialogue, which develops the admission.

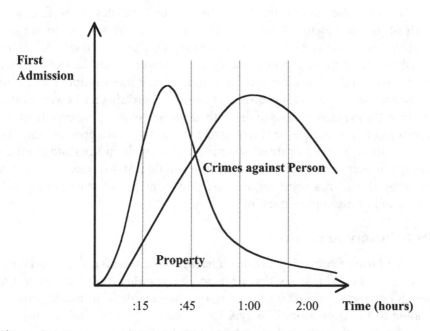

Figure 9.4 For property crimes, a first admission is most likely to occur between 15 and 45 minutes. With crimes against people, most admissions occur between 45 minutes and two hours.

Length of the Introductory Statement

In almost all interrogations, it will take some time for a suspect to feel comfortable in confessing. With the introductory statement, the interrogator should not anticipate receiving an admission of guilt before approximately 15 minutes (see Figure 9.4). The graph in Figure 9.4 illustrates the frequency with which individuals made first admissions versus the amount of time they were interrogated. This graph resembles a bell curve.

What this means is that very few individuals will give an admission in the opening moments of the interrogation; however, as the interrogation continues, the number of suspects giving an admission increases until approximately 45 minutes, after which the number will diminish very rapidly. There exists approximately a half-hour window during the interrogation when using an introductory statement during which most individuals will confess if they are susceptible. This half-hour window occurs between 15 and 45 minutes into the interrogation. Although some suspects will confess in the first 15 minutes of interrogation, the interrogator should time the presentation of the soft accusation or assumptive question based on the half hour of high probability and the suspect's behavior.

Generally, the interrogator should spend 5 to 7 minutes on the first three parts of the introductory statement: (1) who we are and how we do our job; (2) how losses occur; and (3) how we investigate. This section establishes the credibility of the investigation and forces suspects to consider the fact that they have been caught. The most common mistake new interrogators make is to expand these areas by talking too long. Instead of increasing the power of these sections, the expansion tends to dilute their impact, making subjects think the interrogator is trying too hard to convince them they have been caught. The fourth part of the interrogation, why mistakes are made, justifies and rationalizes the suspect's behavior. The interrogator should plan to spend a minimum of 10 to 15 minutes justifying a suspect's actions before attempting a soft accusation or assumptive question.

Participatory Accusation

Another form of accusation that the interrogator can use is called a participatory accusation. This accusation tends to be somewhat more difficult to use simply because the suspect is invited to participate in a decision-making process leading to the confession. This type of accusation generally takes longer to complete than the introductory statement or the direct accusation because the interrogator allows the suspect to talk while leading him in the proper direction. However, it does provide the interrogator with some positive benefits. In many ways, the participatory accusation begins as more of an interview than an interrogation because of the amount of talking the suspect does. In addition, it allows suspects an opportunity to define the boundaries of their jobs and actions, or to present an alibi before any actual accusation is made by the interrogator. In this way, the participatory accusation limits the ability of a suspect to explain away any incriminating evidence.

In a police case, the alibi a suspect might attempt to use should be obtained before an interrogation. This might increase the likelihood that suspects will lie about their alibi, and even if they do not confess, these lies can become key evidence in their prosecution. Because this interrogation is nonaccusatory in its earliest stages, the suspect typically cooperates by giving the required information and details. Once the details have been established, the interrogator can begin the process of moving into an accusatory format.

In the private sector, the interviewer or interrogator is often interested in whether suspects knew they violated a particular policy. For example, in some companies, employees are offered a discount on merchandise they purchase for themselves and immediate family members. Employees who violate this policy often will claim that they did not know or understand the policy. For an employee to be terminated for the violation, the interrogator must prove two elements. First, that the employee acted outside the specific guidelines of the policy, such as receiving money for the purchase of a piece of merchandise by someone who was not an immediate family member, and second, that the suspect understood and knowingly violated the policy.

The participatory accusation affords the interrogator an opportunity to have suspects define their understanding of the policy before the interrogator ever gets into an interrogation of the actual violation. By approaching the interrogation in this manner, the interrogator has eliminated an often-used explanation for the suspect's action.

The participatory accusation works extremely well in police cases, when a suspect's alibi might be the key to breaking the case. In addition, this type of accusation is extremely effective against upper-level management or in complex fraud cases. This accusation forces suspects to define the boundaries of their decision-making process. By defining them and disclosing that they make decisions based on certain criteria, they can no longer hide in gray policy areas. Before suspects recognize what the interrogator is interested in, he has led them to commit to a specific sequence of events. If they offer any exceptions to the way they do things, the interviewer or interrogator follows up by determining the frequency and circumstances surrounding the exceptions. This effectively commits the suspect into an alibi, story, or decision-making process with which he must live.

Construction of the Participatory Accusation

The construction of the participatory accusation is a multi-step process.

Introduction. Interrogators identify themselves to the suspect and make some preliminary rapport-building remarks. They begin by developing a behavioral norm utilizing the suspect's responses to questions about his background. Once interrogators feel comfortable with the suspect's behavioral norm, they can move on to the next portion of the accusation. Again, there can be significant benefits to letting suspects talk about themselves for a short period of time.

Establishing the Suspect's Alibi and Actions on the Job — Here, interrogators ask the suspect to define the boundaries of the interrogation. The suspect's alibi is developed in detail, including times, places, and names. It is critical to lock the suspect into the alibi moment by moment so that in the future he is unlikely — or unable — to change the story. If he does change the original story, the original alibi can be used to refute his truthfulness in subsequent alibis.

When the interrogator is reviewing the suspect's decision-making process or training, a detailed description of how the suspect does his job is developed. By developing this detailed description of activities in handling transactions, purchasing, or other tasks, the interrogator locks the suspect into a sequence of events. Now, even weak circumstantial evidence can become damning evidence. Up to this point, because the employee had not committed to a sequence of events, he could explain away any deviation from the norm simply by saying, "Well, sometimes we do it that way."

Case Example

In a case where a company's director of transportation was suspected of receiving kickbacks from a vendor, the only evidence was his having an excessive amount of expendable income, far exceeding the director's salary.

He was questioned about how he handled his day-to-day activities. He then discussed how he handled financial matters within his department. Once these details had been defined, the director was asked to describe why he gave so much business to a particular company, when it seemed to violate the parameters he had described. Had the interrogator approached this differently, the suspect could have given any number of reasons that he chose to do what he did However, because the interrogator did not let the suspect know what he was investigating, the suspect defined the actual boundaries of his activity. The circumstantial evidence showing he violated his own policies became even more damning in the suspect's eyes.

Promoting Cooperation through a Story — During this section of the accusation, the suspect joins the interrogator in developing a story that promotes the cooperation of the guilty. They develop a story in which certain decisions must be made regarding losses to an imaginary company owned jointly by the suspect and the interrogator. The interrogator and the suspect have, in this story, become partners in a business, one that has suffered significant losses at the end of the first year. The interrogator asks the suspect how they might resolve the large shortage in their business.

The interrogator points out to the suspect that certain employees in their business have violated policy and procedure by taking money and merchandise. In the story, the interrogator asks the suspect to decide how he would feel toward an employee who cooperated and talked about the reasons the employee made the errors as opposed to an employee who did not cooperate in the investigation.

The conclusion reached by the suspect is that you would feel better about an individual who cooperates than one who lies or stonewalls an investigation.

Discussing How Investigations Are Conducted — Once the suspect has come to the conclusion that it is good to talk about a problem and the reasons it occurred, the interrogator begins to draw the suspect into a discussion of how investigations are conducted. This may be done in one of two ways. If the suspect is particularly responsive, the interrogator may ask how he would investigate a particular incident. As the suspect offers investigative avenues, the interrogator expands upon them, describing the types of information that can be obtained using that method.

In some instances, a suspect will not be responsive and the interrogator will simply describe different investigative methods and the types of information that could be obtained from them.

It is particularly important for the suspect's alibi to be known before discussing the investigation in this interrogation. For example, in a residential burglary, several young males were identified as being responsible. In discussing how the investigation could be conducted, the interrogator discussed latent fingerprints. One of the youths replied that he had been in the house visiting recently and had probably left his fingerprints on or around the stove. Although this admission put the youth in the home, the interrogator had not yet established an alibi and the suspect explained away any physical evidence that would have indicated his involvement.

The investigation section, like the investigation section in the introductory statement, is designed to establish the credibility of the investigation in the suspect's mind. It is here that suspects are forced to recognize that their guilt is known. This is even more evident to suspects who offer methods of investigations because they soon realize that if they could think of these methods, certainly law enforcement professionals had thought of them.

Creating Rationalizations — Rather than offering reasons and excuses for the suspect's behavior, the interrogator questions the suspect about why someone might become involved in the incident. The interrogator allows the suspect to offer excuses and then expands on them. In the event that the suspect does not offer reasons or excuses, the interrogator must take a more active role in offering justifications to the suspect.

As in the introductory statement method, the early stages of rationalization are done in the third person to avoid placing suspects in a defensive position where they might offer denials. By having suspects offer their own rationalizations for an action, the interrogator is more likely to hit upon the justification most favored by the suspect. Once again, the interrogator must watch the suspect for behavioral clues to tell how long the process of rationalization should continue. At some point, the interrogator must make the decision to personalize the rationalization through the use of a *transition statement* that applies everything that has been discussed to the suspect directly.

Offering the Soft Accusation or Assumptive Question — Once the interrogator believes that the suspect is behaviorally receptive to making an admission, he prepares to offer the soft accusation. The soft accusation is an assumptive question that addresses some detail of the suspect's involvement. The assumptive question makes it clear that the suspect is involved and avoids the last defensive barrier the suspect might have.

Transcript of a Tape

The following is a transcript of how this interrogation could be developed. Although this particular example deals with the private setting, only minor changes are necessary to make it applicable to public law enforcement officers.

Fred: Good morning, Doug. I'm _____ from the corporate office. I just wanted to cover a few areas with you regarding the store. What do you think of the training you received here? Do you think the training is good?

Doug: Not really. The only training I've ever had is when Mr. Thompson, the District Supervisor, brought in a little VCR and played it when the store was slow, but it's better than what I've had before.

Fred: Do you think you pick things up pretty quick?

Doug: Yes.

Fred: How do you handle a check sale?

Doug: A customer comes in to make a purchase. They ask if I'll ring up the sale and sometimes I will ask beforehand if it is cash or a check. If they say it is a check, I will say fine. I will tell them the amount, they would write out the check and give it to me, and I then say I need to see your driver's license.

Fred: Yes.

Doug: Then I write down the driver's license number and the state that it is from.

Fred: Where do you do that? On the face of the check, back of the check?

Doug: Oh, it should be on the back of the check.

Fred: Oh, is there a stamp or something you should use?

Doug: Yes.

Fred: *Do you* always do it that way — I mean, do you do the same thing the same way all the time? You're consistent when you do the job and you always do it the same way when you take a check?

Doug: Yes.

Fred: So you always do it that way?

Doug: Yes.

The suspect has now committed to doing a certain job the same way all the time.

The interviewer might also cover charge sale or other types of transactions.

Fred: How about like another sale. A cash sale, how do you ring up a cash sale?

Doug: Customer comes in and they give me the item. I then ring in my sales number, then I ring in the number on the ticket, and then the amount.

Fred: OK — and then the customer gives you a $20 bill and then what do you do?

Doug: Then I give him change for it.

Fred: Do you ring that $20 bill into the register?

Doug: No, I ring up the sale.

Fred: *As* the amount tendered — $20 amount tendered?

Doug: Oh, yes.

Fred: And then when you count the money back, do you count it once, double count it, do you count it as it is coming out of the till and then count it again when you're giving it to them or what?

Doug: Well, if they give me a $20 bill, I put the $20 bill right on top of the register.

Fred: Yes.

Doug: And let's say it's a $5.50 item and the register obviously shows that there's $14.50 in change. Then, I'll take out the bills and the 50 cents, and then I'll count out their change to them again.

Fred: OK, and you always do it that way? I mean you do the same job. You sound like a guy that does the same thing the same way all the time.

Doug: Yes.

Fred: OK, let me do this another way. Say you and I own a store, OK, Doug and Fred's Shoe Store. We have this store and we open it up and after a year we really watch the overhead, we watch the rent, we watch how much we're paying for the merchandise, we watch our advertising costs, we watch everything, I mean, you and I really busted our bottoms to really go and do a good job here and make a lot of money. At the end of the year, what happened was instead of making money, we lost money. We take the inventory and all that stuff, and it turns out we lost $30,000. What would you do?

Doug: Probably have a heart attack, I mean ...

Fred: Try and find it?

Doug: Yes, I mean I'd...

Fred: Hire a bookkeeper or something, maybe hire an auditor to try and find it or...

Doug: Well, I don't know if I'd do that. I'd go back and I'd review my sales, and I'd review the paperwork and a ...

Fred: Are you an accountant?

Doug: No.

Fred: Neither am I. If I were a partner in the business, we'd hire auditors. OK — so say we had the auditors and they came and looked at all the books and all the records. They then said, you know, there's a couple of things where you're receiving the merchandise here and you're not counting it right. There are some markdowns here and they're not taken care of, all of them, the proper way. Therefore, there is a little more of this shortage. There are also a couple of other things that I saw that really bothered me. I mean, I'm an independent auditor talking to you and I have to tell you, Doug, I saw you take a couple of bucks out of the cash register and buy milk on the way home when I rode home with you that day. It's your store and you had a right to, but it sets a bad example for your employees. And Doug, you know, you got these guys that keep coming in and you keep giving them discounts all the time. It's your store; you have a right to do it, but it causes shortages and it sets a bad example for your other employees. Furthermore, I've got to tell you that I think your employees are probably responsible for most of your loss. And we say there's no way. He said yes, I'm pretty sure that it is. I can't prove it, but I think it is. What would you do?

Doug: Well, if I'm paying the auditor for his advice, obviously I have to change my procedures, so I'm not setting that bad example. Hopefully, I can turn the profit picture around.

Fred: But he brought up something else. I mean we ask him what to do? You're telling us we got this problem and what we do about it. He says here's what you do, hire some consultants. These consultants come in and they put a video recorder over the front cash register and record everything for 3 months. They also put a video recorder in the back with time and date generator over the back door. They have a couple of investigators that do surveillance and look at everybody who comes in and what they're bringing when they come in and what they're leaving with when they take it out. They then pull the documentation and go through the detail tape and make sure that everything was rung up and paid for. They gather all of this documentation and after 3 months, they come in to you and give it to you and they say, yes, we found that your niece is taking cash and my nephew is taking merchandise, what would you do then?

Doug: Boy, I don't know. If you could prove it, I would probably have to sit down and talk to him about it.

Fred: They've got it. They have the documentation. That's the case. You can do anything with the case that you want to do. You can take it to criminal court, you can take it to civil court, you can do anything in the world that you want with this case. The case is cast in concrete. There's not a question of whether they did it or not; you know they did it. You've got the tape. You have the tapes and you watch them take the money, all right?

Doug: OK.

Fred: And not record the sale and put the money in their pocket. You have the detail tape to show that they didn't record the sale and you have the videotape to show the shoes went out and you have the videotape that shows the guy handing the money to the salesperson, who puts it in his pocket. I mean it's not whether they did it or not. They did. You have it on tape. You have the detail tape. You have the whole thing.

Doug: OK.

Fred: So that isn't the issue. The issue is what do you do about it?

Doug: Well, I'd still want to find out why they did it.

Fred: Why, is that important?

Doug: Well, yes. I mean, if there was reason.

Fred: Sure. I can understand that because there are a lot of reasons that people do things. So you sit down and talk to them?

Doug: Yes.

Fred: OK, you talk to the niece and you say, "Niece, I understand that you've been taking some cash out of the cash registers," and she says, "Sure. Nothing wrong with that, I saw you do it. You took $2 out of the register and bought milk on the way home; and Doug, he's been giving discounts to friends. I didn't think there was anything wrong with it." What would you do?

Doug: I guess it probably depends on how much she's done or I don't know ... I don't know what I would do.

Fred: Well, at least she was honest, right?

Doug: Yes.

Fred: I mean, that means something.

Doug: Sure.

Fred: I mean, do you suppose that if you and I changed our ways, and if we set some black-and-white examples and we followed those examples ourselves, she might make a good employee in the future?

Doug: Yes, she could — I would hope so.

Fred: Well, let's go the other way, we talk to my nephew and say nephew, you've been taking merchandise out the back door and he says "No, I haven't." I say, listen, you know I'm as embarrassed by the situation as you are, but you've been taking merchandise out the back door and he says screw you — OK, what would you do with him?

Doug: I'd probably say "screw you" back to him, and I'd probably have to get rid of him.

Fred: I'm the director of loss prevention for the company and my responsibility is protecting the company assets. Now the niece is somebody who wants to work for herself. She's being honest and straightforward, and you can deal with her and the nephew you can't. You see what I mean?

Doug: Yes.

Fred: Which brings us down to the reason that we're here today. We had to conduct an investigation in the store, and I am aware of the fact that you know that you're responsible for some of the inventory shortage here. What I'd like to do is clear up the amount and see whether you want to work with me on the thing or not.

Doug: What are you talking about?

Fred: What I'm talking about is I'd like to ask you when's the last time that you failed to record a sale and kept the money?

Doug: I never have.

Fred: Doug, let me explain the way we do an investigation. What we do is... I'll talk about the last one. It's one that I just finished up yesterday. We had a case where I got a call from the store manager and she says, "Listen, I have something that happened." This happened a couple of months ago. She called me up saying this happened and "I just can't believe it. I've been working with this assistant manager, we're good friends; we've been working together for a year. The other day, I worked from 8 until 5 and she worked from 1 until closing. That afternoon, we got in some merchandise. There was this pair of sandals, a hot seller on the market. I ordered a case, and I only got one pair in each size. I know that because when I got them, I marked them myself. I put them out. I was just fuming that I only got one in each size. I left at 5 o'clock, and then I came back that night because this store was in the mall and there was a theater in the mall and I went in the store. This gal and I have been trading each other's makeup all along. She's got permission to go into mine and I have permission to go into hers. Anyway, there's this bathroom in the back of the store that we use, and I noticed I didn't have my makeup, so I went into her purse to look at the makeup. The bottom line is there's a brand new pair of these sandals that were still ticketed, that I ticketed, in her purse." The manager says to me, "I couldn't believe it." I went up to the registers to look at whether they had been rung up. They hadn't been rung up, so I went back into the stock and a pair was missing from the stock and they were a pair that I had just received, so I stayed until we closed that night to see whether she took them out or paid for them or anything. She didn't; I could still see them bulging through the purse. What would you do if you were me and you got that call?

Doug: I'd have to go and investigate it.

Fred: What would you do?

Doug: Talk to her.

Fred: You'd go talk — so you talk to her and you say "Listen, you know, you took that pair of sandals last night that you didn't pay for" and she denies it. Then finally you convince her that you knew and could prove the truth and so she finally said "OK, I took the pair of sandals." Now you ask, have you ever done it before? And she says no. Is she telling the truth?

Doug: I don't know.

Fred: You don't know — so you know what we did was put a video camera and recorder in the back stockroom and we saw her take three pairs of pumps, two pairs of sandals, fourteen different cans of shoe polish, and the last thing that she took was with her boyfriend. She put a case of shoes out in the trash and picked it up later in a '57 Chevy and drove it over to the garage. So when I talked to her, I talked to her about that case of shoes. I didn't even let her know how the thing started, OK. I just talked to her about the last thing and I explained to her about the case of shoes and she said that she didn't take it. She finally understood that we had it sealed up tight and she said, "Yeah, OK I did it." And I asked her if she'd ever done anything before and she said no and then you know after a little conversation I convinced her, and she said OK, this is what I've done. She told me about this, this, this, this, and this. Then she told me more than I knew about. I'll tell you that right up front, she told me more than I knew about. She told me about every single thing that I knew about over that 3-month period of time without me having to coach her. Is she telling me the truth?

Doug: Yeah.

Fred: She probably is, right?

Doug: Right.

Fred: That's the way we do it here. This isn't something where anybody flies out 2,000 miles to talk to somebody if only one little iffy deal happened. It's not a question of whether something is or isn't probable or whether it is or isn't just one time. You and I both know the extent of this and the only question is whether you want to resolve it here or not. I think that you do. You know it's like when I go home and I find cookie crumbs around my son's mouth, and I say, "Mark, you been in the cookie jar" and he says, no I haven't — I mean I got a problem there. It's my own son, I can't work with him. I can't believe what he's telling me because I know the truth — I got the proof. With him, it's the cookie crumbs —with this, it's something else. I go home and say you been in the cookie jar and he says, "Yes Dad, I'm sorry I didn't get lunch and I couldn't wait till supper and I was hungry." That's a whole different ball game. I'm able to deal with that one. I really would like to resolve this one with you today.

Now, Doug, when was the last time you took money from the store? No matter how recently?

Interrogation Time Limit

Although confessions have occurred after 1 hour of confrontation, the odds of obtaining a confession drop rather dramatically that late in the interrogation. However, in especially emotional cases, such as a homicide, it might require more time to reduce the suspect's resistance. There is no absolute time limit to an interrogation, but the interrogator should use good judgment in deciding when to stop. Unless the incident is a particularly heinous crime, most interrogators conclude interrogations at a maximum of $1\frac{1}{2}$ to 2 hours without gaining a first admission. It is the "totality of circumstances" surrounding the interrogation that determines if the time length is excessive. In complex cases, in which development of the admission is difficult, a number of hours following the first admission might be required to document the admission. That extra time would not be considered unusual.

In the private sector, most interrogators begin to back out of an interrogation when no admission has been gained by about 1 hour and 15 minutes. An interrogator's good judgment and assessment of the likelihood of an admission from the suspect should identify the point at which the interrogation should be concluded.

Countering Suspect Interruptions

The guilty suspect might attempt the tactic of trying to rush interrogators into playing their hand early. They should avoid taking this bait. By allowing the suspect to control the interrogation, the impact of the introductory or participatory statements is lost and the interrogator's ability to obtain an admission will be hampered.

Suspects who tell the interrogator to "Get to the point!" or ask, "Are you saying I stole?" are attempting to draw the interrogator into a premature direct accusation. The interrogator who immediately gets to the point and makes a direct accusation plays into the suspect's hand. The direct statement allows the suspect to make a denial.

Some suspects will repeatedly ask the interrogator to get to the point. When it is obvious that the introductory statement is not having the desired impact, the interrogator might simply use a direct accusation and move to rationalizations handling the suspect's denials as they are made.

The interrogator should attempt to put the suspect off without directly answering his question. This might be done by simply saying, "Just a minute, let me finish what I'm telling you, and I think you'll see exactly what my point is."

Most interrogators are inclined to directly accuse a suspect who interrupts with these questions, but by doing so they can create a more difficult interrogation. Interrogators should recognize that a suspect who attempts these types of tactics is giving additional evidence of guilt. It is unusual for a truthful suspect to interrupt an interrogator telling the police or loss prevention story.

Learning the Introductory Statement

The following examples of the introductory statement provide a structure for those first using the technique. Interrogators will ultimately individualize the introduction to their own style; however, the purpose of the examples is to offer each interrogator a firm foundation upon which to build.

The best way to learn the technique is to follow the building process outlined below:

1. Read the following pages aloud several times.
2. Read the following pages aloud into a tape recorder several times.
3. Review the tape and listen to your voice and word emphasis.
4. Use an outline of the introductory statement, using headings for the key parts and important phrases.
5. Repeat the introductory statement, using only the outline, into the tape recorder several times and review it.
6. Practice using the outline in role-playing with a friend or co-worker.
7. Discuss the content and flow with your friend or co-worker.
8. Practice the soft accusation with a friend or co-worker to develop proper timing for the follow-up question and to support the admission.
9. Try the introductory statement in a "field" interrogation when the subject's guilt is certain.

Sample Introductory Statements

The following are examples of introductory statements. Note that the difference between the public- and private-sector versions is minimal, while the structure remains the same. In the private sector, the interrogator uses the terms *employee* and *company* while, in the public example, the interrogator uses *neighbors* and *community*. There also is a slight difference when talking about types of losses or crimes. The public-sector statement talks about crimes against property and persons, while the private sector typically compares the theft of money and property.

Summary Construction of the Introductory Statement

1. Verify the suspect's personal background to establish behavioral norm: "Are you still living at …?"
2. Develop rapport. I'm going to be telling you a lot about who I am and what I do, but, before I do, tell me a little about yourself.
3. Who we are and what we do.
4. Types of losses or crimes.
5. How investigations are conducted.
6. Summary of possible rationalizations — short discussion of why mistakes are made — impulse, accidents, peer pressure, financial: "You know, people make mistakes for a lot of reasons. Sometimes …"
7. **First Rationalization.**
   a. Choose the first rationalization based either on the background of the suspect or behavior observed during the summary.
   b. State rationalization (e.g., peer pressure). "We've all had times in our lives when peer pressure has influenced us, and we did things we didn't really want to do."
   c. Create a story or illustration that helps the suspect understand peer pressure: "I remember one time that I …"
   d. State moral of story: "So everyone can be influenced by friends. That's a lot different from someone who takes a job with the intention of taking things."
   e. Link back to the investigation: "That's why we sit down to talk to someone after an investigation, to find out the reasons."
8. Change the subject's perspective: "Let's say you owned your own company and you had two employees …"
9. **Second Rationalization:**
   a. Choose the second rationalization based on the suspect's background or behavior observed during the summary. If personal information is known about the suspect that might relate to the reason for the theft, a rationalization that mirrors that personal situation should be used. This rationalization might be the same topic as the one just used.
   b. State rationalization (e.g., financial): "We've all had times in our lives where our money doesn't go as far as we would like it to go."

    c. Create a story or illustration that helps the suspect to understand financial pressure.

    d. State moral of story: "If someone takes money to pay for bills or to take care of their family, that's a lot different from someone who is taking it to go out and buy drugs."

    e. Link to investigation. "The investigation is very clear as to what happened, we just need to understand why things happened."

10. Address the suspect's hope or mental state: "Sometimes a person thinks that by saying nothing, the problem will go away and nothing will happen. That's why we do the investigation up front — so the company can still resolve the situation even if the individual decides to say nothing. That's why it's important that people understand that they have the ability to influence the company's decision-making process. That's why we need to get this resolved today!"

11. Protect evidence: "Many people wonder why an investigator doesn't just lay out on the table exactly what he knows that indicates an individual was responsible for a series of issues. The reason that is not done is not to try to trick a person, but rather to answer the most difficult question in any investigation. That question is not who did it, that was resolved through the investigative process. The real question is, 'Is he shooting straight with us when he tells us these things?' When the interviewer responds, 'Yes,' the absolutely most difficult question is, 'How do you know?' If the investigator had given up all the evidence surrounding the incident, he would have to say, 'I don't know,' but because he held back things that were then told him by the subject, he could respond, 'I know the person is telling me the truth because he told me things that I already knew.' Thus, when people say that they are sorry or attempt to explain what difficulties they were facing in their life, the interviewer can believe those things."

12. Test for submission: "The difficulty is, we don't know what problems *you* might be facing outside work."

13. Assumptive question — used only if the interrogator believes the subject is ready to make an admission. "Bob, what's the most amount of money you took in any single day?"

14. Follow-up question — used when the subject gives admission behavior before answering the assumptive question. "It wasn't $10,000 was it?"

15. Support admission — lets the subject know he has confessed and supports the admission. "That's great, from the investigation I didn't think it was quite that much. What's the most you took in any day? Could it have been as much as $9,000?"

16. Develop admission, answering the investigative questions of who, what, when, where, how, and why.

17. Written statement, letter of explanation.

Introductory Statement — Private Sector

Part 1 — Establish Behavioral Norm

"Hello, Bob. My name is _____. I just need to go over a few things with you. What is the correct spelling of your last name? What is your current address? Your Social Security number is 555-22-4444? What is your date of hire? Your date of birth is 3/21/75 and your position with the company is P. M. Manager?"

Verify the subject's background to establish a behavioral norm and let them know you have done a thorough investigation.

Part 2 — Develop Rapport

"Bob, I'm going to be telling you a lot about who I am and what I do, but, before I do, why don't you tell me a little about yourself."

This will allow the interviewer to develop rapport with subjects. Offering subjects a chance to talk about themselves allows the interviewer to obtain information about which rationalizations might be effective.

Part 3 — Who We Are And What We Do

"As I said, my name is _____. I'm with the Loss Prevention Department here at the company. My job is to protect the company's assets. These assets include the building, fixtures, merchandise, money and, the most important asset, the employees who work here.

"Like all companies, we have losses and we know these losses come in a variety of different forms. Sometimes it's employee error, where someone in Receiving writes down that they received five boxes but really only got three. Two boxes are missing but nobody took them; it's just a paperwork error. Sometimes, a customer will come in and take something and leave without paying for it. It's also employees taking things (*pause*). The major concern of the company is those employees who would be taking trailer loads of merchandise or tens of thousands of dollars, rather than something of a minor nature."

Part 4 — How Losses Occur

"To repeat, employees sometimes take things. There are many ways an employee could take money and merchandise from the company. They could take money by just taking it out of the register or from another employee's register. They could make up a phony void, (*pause and eye contact*) or a phony refund. They could take money from a customer, short-changing them, or from another employee. They could take money from Lost and Found or take it out of the safe."

The interviewer should pause and make direct eye contact after the explanation that he believes is most likely the method the subject is using to steal. The manner of theft the subject is involved in should be positioned in the middle of the examples given.

"Employees could take merchandise in many ways. They could conceal it on their person and leave without paying for it. They could place it in another box and pay a lower price for it. An employee could pass merchandise off to a friend or relative, not charging them for it. They could under-ring the merchandise, not charging the correct amount. They could also ring all the merchandise up, then void some things out, allowing a customer to leave with everything, They could take merchandise out the back door and hide it and come back later that night to get it. They could even take merchandise and later refund it at another store, not claiming themselves as an employee."

The interviewer should carefully observe the suspect's behavior for indications of other ways he has been involved in dishonesty at the company.

Part 5 — How Investigations Are Conducted

"When we have losses, we initiate an investigation. I don't know how familiar you are in the ways in which investigations are conducted, but here are some of the things we do during an investigation:

- We use a shopping service that will send people in to make controlled purchases from an individual. They will evaluate if correct cash handling procedures are being followed, if the register is being rung properly, if paperwork is filled out, or they might even leave a receipt behind to see what happens to it. Is it used later to void a sale or make up a phony refund? They also look at customer service issues and the general demeanor and courtesy with which the employee is treating the customer.
- Sometimes we use undercover employees who are members of the loss prevention department. They work beside other employees to see exactly what's happening and what's being said, and then they report back to us daily. Sometimes we conduct surveillance by concealing

ourselves in the area to see what is happening, or we might sit outside and see if someone takes merchandise out the back door. We also see who comes out the front door, what they come out with, if it was rung up, who they come out with or if someone comes back after closing and re-enters the store.

- During investigations, we might also use video cameras. Now, you might have seen cameras in some stores that are in plain view or in a dome. Those are there primarily as a deterrent. I don't know many employees who would stand right under a camera, wave at it, and do something wrong. When we conduct an investigation, we use cameras that cannot be detected by employees. We use cameras that have a pinhole lens the size of the end of this pen. You can put these cameras in a false ceiling or put them in a box in the stock room. If you wanted to you, you could video tape any area of the store. Sometimes when we are video taping a register, we will also use a register interface, which will overlay the transaction as it is being rung up on the video. Now we can see the customer, the cashier, the merchandise that is being rung up, the price it is rung up at and if items are voided out and the customer is allowed to leave with everything.
- There are many other ways in which we get our information and conduct an investigation. These include receiving help from other employees, audits, salting registers, sending out credit and refund letters to determine if the customer actually made the return, to name just a few. The problem with an investigation is, although it will tell you exactly *what* is happening and exactly *who* is responsible, it doesn't tell you the most important thing, and that is *why.*"

This area usually has greater impact on the subject if the interrogator uses examples of investigative techniques that could develop direct, rather than circumstantial evidence, e.g., observation or video tape of theft versus a pattern that showed the employee present during all the incidents.

Part 6 — Summary of Rationalizations

"You know, people make mistakes for a lot of reasons. It could be peer pressure, when someone has influenced us into doing something we wouldn't have normally done or when we are trying to help out a friend or relative. Sometimes it's financial pressures. Our money doesn't go as far it needs to for us to pay all the bills or we may have unexpected bills we didn't count on. Sometimes, we just act impulsively and do something without thinking about it."

As you give a summary of the different reasons people make mistakes, evaluate the subject's behavior. Often he will give you behavioral clues as to which rationalization is acceptable to him.

Part 7 — First Rationalization

State rationalization:

> "You know, Bob, I think almost everybody has heard the term 'peer pressure' and understands what it means. We're put into a lot of situations in our lives because of our friends and how they think. We do things that maybe under ordinary circumstances we wouldn't do. But, because we have our friends, or we have other people who think in a particular way, they tend to force our thinking in a direction that we might not consider appropriate.

Create story that helps the suspect's rationalization:

> "I can give you a perfect example. When I was a kid back in high school, I never smoked, and my friends said, "We're smoking cigarettes, come on and have one." I really didn't want one, but finally I said, "Okay" and I tried one. Today I don't smoke cigarettes and my parents don't smoke cigarettes. I was put in a position where everybody was doing it, and it became very difficult for me not to go along with the group.
>
> "I think what's really happening here is just that. When we're dealing with a situation like this — it's not the person's idea, but rather a group idea. You hear, "We need to keep up with the Joneses," or, "You gotta wear the right clothes," (certain types of jeans or jackets or sweaters). They're popular, and if a person doesn't wear them, then he's not a good person.
>
> "Well, that's crazy, letting the clothes decide. However, that's the way people are, especially people who feel that wearing the right clothes or keeping up with the Joneses is important. If they do that, and if they feel that's important, then it tends to put pressure on their friends.
>
> "There is a big difference between someone who goes out and solicits, rather than having situations brought to them. I think that's very important to know. In a lot of cases, people or friends of associates will come into the store and say, "Listen, give me this at a discount," or, "I'm not going to pay for this," or, you know, "Don't say anything. I'm going to carry this out."
>
> "They really put an individual in an awkward position. They put that person into a position where they either force him not to charge the right amount, or they force him to let them walk, or do something else that

under normal circumstances he wouldn't let anybody do. The key here, I think, is not so much that it's happened, but rather it's did he go out and say to people, "It's okay, come on in, you can take as much as you want" or did they come to him and say, "This is what I'm going to do," and put an individual on the spot? Because, if that's what happened, I think it's important that we understand that. If I thought for a second that he was going out and telling friends, "Hey, just come on down. You can take anything when I'm working," I don't think I could deal with that, but I don't believe that's the case. In most situations that I deal with, it's not an associate, but rather those friends coming in and putting them on the spot that causes the biggest problems.

Moral of story:

"I think what's really happening here is just that. When we're dealing with a situation like this — it's not the person's idea, but rather a group idea.

Link back to the investigation:

"That's why we sit down with an associate at the conclusion of an investigation — so they can get something on their side."

Part 8 — Changing the Subject's Perspective

"Let's say you owned your own company and you came in on your day off and saw two of your employees doing something wrong — no ifs, ands, or buts about it. You saw it with your own eyes. Both of them have been really good employees and have done a great job for you. Before you make any decisions as to what you are going to do about it, you decide to sit down with them to find out why it happened. You sit down with the first person, and he says, 'You're crazy — it never happened. I don't care what you think you saw; it never happened.' How do you feel about that person when he sat there and looked you in the eye and lied? Let's say you sit down with the second person and he says, 'I'm really sorry. I know it was wrong.' Then he walks you through his thought process and the difficulties he was facing at the time that caused him to make the error in judgment. Of the two, who would you rather work with?"

Part 9 — Second Rationalization

State rationalization:

"Bob, I think that we set people up for problems simply because of how much they get paid. Probably one of the most difficult things to do is to work around beautiful items that are really expensive and yet not be paid enough to afford them. Most people make pretty close to minimum wage, I would imagine. The thing is, once a person is around nice things, it's only natural to want them for himself."

Create story or illustration that helps suspect understand the rationalization:

"This also happens with friends. I mean, if friends have some money and they're suddenly wearing fancy jeans that cost $40–50 a pair, or they're wearing skirts that may cost $100, you can rest assured they can afford these things. While another person is working hard for the money that he earns, maybe he doesn't have as much as they do at home. All of a sudden, they're treating him differently, simply because he doesn't have the same things they have.

"A person wouldn't be human if he didn't want them, too. But yet, he's not making enough to pay for it even though he's diligently working, doing a good job; he can't buy those things.

"We also expect our employees to look good. I mean, that is the image of the company — the person that the customer sees. Our employee is our representative, and we don't want him coming in here looking like a slob. We want him to dress nice, look sharp. The company would like the employees to look nice, but do we turn around and say, 'Here's money for clothes,' or, 'Here's a raise.' No, we don't! So we have to recognize that part of the situation is a result of how the company views itself and what it considers important."

"What I don't want to see is somebody put into a position of doing something because of peer pressure, frustration, financial problems, or making an error in judgment that causes them to do something that under normal circumstances they wouldn't do. I think that's the key here.

"Many times people do things because they need the money. I think that's important, because, if there was a need, a legitimate need, that's something that every one of us can relate to.

"We all have bills, whether they're phones, heating, rent car payment or insurance. We all have things that we have to pay. There are times when we have extra money and there are times when we run short. Sometimes, we're put in a position where we don't have an alternative. "

Moral of story:

""We do something that maybe we wouldn't have been raised to do, or we wouldn't do under normal circumstances at all, however, we're put into a position where we have a need.

"We're not going out and blowing the money on drugs or booze or good times. We're using it for the necessities of life, to keep our head above water, and I think that's important."

Link back to the investigation:

"That's why we sit down with an associate at the conclusion of an investigation — so they can get something on their side."

Part 10 — Address the Suspect's Hope and Create Urgency

Sometimes a person thinks that by saying nothing, the problem will go away and nothing will happen. That's why we do the investigation up front so the company can still resolve the situation even if the individual decides to say nothing. That's why it's important that a person understand that they have the ability to influence the company's decision-making process. That's why we need to get this resolved today.

Part 11 — Protect Evidence

"Many people wonder why an investigator doesn't just lay out on the table exactly what he knows that indicates an individual was responsible for a series of incidents. The reason that is not done is not to try to trick a person, but rather to answer the most difficult question in any investigation. That question is not who did it; that was resolved through the investigative process. The real question is, "Is he shooting straight with us when he tells us these things?' When the interviewer responds "yes," the absolutely most difficult question is, 'How do you know?' If the investigator had given up all the evidence surrounding the incident, he would have to say, 'I don't know,' but, because he held back things that were then told him by the subject, he could respond, 'I know the person is telling me the truth because he told me things that I already knew but didn't tell.' Thus, when the individual says he is sorry or attempts to explain what difficulties he was facing in his life, the interviewer can believe those things."

Part 12 — Test For Submission

"Bob, the difficulty is that we don't know what difficulties *you* might be facing outside work."

The interviewer should evaluate the subject's behavior for signs of acceptance while being prepared to handle a possible denial.

"During any investigation, many things are uncovered and known absolutely. But often, it's the reason mistakes are made that doesn't come out. These things are important to the company to show why things happen and to show also that the employee cares. This is why at the conclusion of every investigation, we sit down with the employee and discuss the results and assess the attitude of that employee toward the company."

Part 13 — Assumptive Question

"Bob, let me ask you this, what's the most amount of money you took in any single day?"

If the subject delays or gives admissible behavior, immediately ask a follow-up question. If he attempts to deny, stop the denial and return to Part 9.

Part 14 — Follow-up Question

Interviewer: It wasn't $1000.00, was it?

Bob: Oh, no!

Part 15 — Support the Admission

Interviewer: That's great, from the investigation I didn't think it was quite that much! What's the most you took in any day? Was it more or less than $900?

Bob: Less!

Interviewer: What would be the most amount of money you took in any one day?

Bob: Five dollars.

Part 16 — Develop the Admission

Ask the investigative questions of who, what, when, where, how and why:

- What did you need the money for?
- When did you take it?
- Where did you take it from?
- How did you take it?
- Who else is taking money?

Part 17 — Written Statement

Letter of explanation:

"What we need to do now is get a letter of explanation in your own words, so you have an opportunity to say that you are sorry that this happened. I am sure that you would be willing to do that, wouldn't you?"

Introductory Statement — Law Enforcement

The following is a sample introductory statement that could be used in the investigation of a burglary. The suspect was to be questioned because his vehicle was observed parked several blocks from the scene of a burglary to a gas station at approximately 2:00 a.m. The suspect's vehicle was observed by a patrol officer, who noted it in his log. There is no other direct evidence that links the suspect to the incident.

Part 1 — Establish Behavioral Norm

Hello, Steve. My name is _____. I just need to go over a few things with you. What is the correct spelling of your last name? What is your current address? Your Social Security number is 555-22-4444? What is your date of hire? Your date of birth is 3/21/75 and your position with the company is P. M. Manager?

Verify the subject's background to establish a behavioral norm and let him know you have done a thorough investigation.

Part 2 — Develop Rapport

"Steve, I'm going to be telling you a lot about who I am and what I do, but, before I do, why don't you tell me a little about yourself.

Part 3 – Who We Are and What We Do

"Steve, as I said, my name is _____ and I'm a detective with the City Police. I appreciate your taking the time to come in and talk to me today."

If the suspect is to be taken into custody at the conclusion of the interrogation, it might be necessary for the law enforcement officer to give the suspect his *Miranda* rights prior to any interrogation. If the suspect will be free to leave following the interrogation, even if he admits his involvement, the *Miranda* rights may be omitted. Officers should consider any special departmental guidelines or requests from the prosecutor's office when deciding whether to give the *Miranda* warning.

"Steve, I'm sure you're aware of what a police department does for a community. Really, our job is to protect the community, its homes, businesses, and citizens from any type of criminal activity. To do that, we get involved with a number of different complaints.

"For example, some might be traffic problems or safety problems that we have to deal with on a daily basis. Other times, we have to deal with businesses or homeowners who are filing false reports in an attempt to obtain a fraudulent insurance settlement. Then we have those instances when someone is genuinely a victim. The department's primary concern obviously has to be with the most serious type of incidences: homicides, rapes, rather than something of a minor nature, like a small item being taken or someone driving over someone's grass."

Part 4 – Different Types of Crimes

"As investigators, we're asked to look into any number of different types of crimes. I am sure you are aware that our community, like any other community, has its share of problems. Those problems range from homicide, to rape and arsons, to people breaking into buildings (*pause, eye contact*), taking things out of cars, or even out of homes."

Part 5 – How We Investigate

"When we discover or receive a problem or a complaint from a citizen, the case is assigned for investigation. When it's assigned for investigation, we'll use any number of different techniques to attempt to establish who was responsible for the incident under investigation. For example, if the case calls for it, we might utilize latent fingerprinting. Now, I'm not sure how familiar you are with latent fingerprinting, but what we do is go to the scene of a crime and begin by dusting those areas that will hold a fingerprint. In using these types of techniques, we're able to develop latent prints and can often determine who was responsible as a result.

"In some areas, an individual will be careful not to touch any type of a smooth surface but might touch a piece of paper, and the oils and perspiration from the fingers are actually absorbed into the fibers of the paper and can be held there for years. By using special techniques, such as lasers, the crime lab is able to develop prints that can be used for comparison purposes.

"In other instances, we'll locate a particular tool that might have been used as a weapon, or as a means to gain entry to a building. This is particularly important to us, because, by using scientific techniques, we can establish the unique marks a tool makes and compare those with the pry marks at the building. This establishes that a particular tool was used to gain entrance or as a weapon.

"We also recover physical evidence, like hair samples. With these hair samples, the lab can do a DNA analysis. Like a fingerprint, it is unique and can identify a person.

"As investigators, we'll also attempt to talk to people or other officers who are constantly patrolling the streets, asking them if they saw anybody or observed anything unusual in or around the area of a particular incident. In this way, we can often initially focus our investigative efforts in a particular direction.

"Like any department, we have informants who supply us with information that helps us resolve any number of crimes during a year. Some of these informants are paid for their services. Others do it to obtain a reward or simply to stop what they think is an improper activity.

"These, as well as many other different types of investigative techniques, help us to identify the individual responsible and begin to develop the case. It may supply us with the information necessary to obtain a search warrant so that we can search a home, vehicle, or garage, wherever we believe we might recover additional evidence of the individual's guilt."

Interrogators should watch for a behavioral reaction as they mention places where evidence or missing property could be concealed. This will assist them during development of the admission or might give additional investigative leads should the suspect fail to confess. Interrogators should modify the investigative methods described to those which, if they had been used, could have developed information pointing to the suspect's guilt. They do not say that they have fingerprints or other evidence directly but rather imply that evidence might have been available because of the investigative efforts used. For example, if this were a forgery case, the interrogator would describe how a document examiner might be used.

Part 6 – Summary of Rationalization

"There could be any number of reasons that people make errors in judgment. It might be because of their friends. We've all heard at one time or another about peer pressure and the power it exerts over people. In other situations, it might have simply been an impulsive decision. People don't think through the consequences of their actions. Financial difficulties, an unexpected bill, or a personal emergency can all cause people to do something that they wouldn't ordinarily do. Or it might be …"

The interrogator offers a variety of one- or two-sentence reasons that an individual might become involved in an error in judgment. This is done for two reasons. First, it allows the interviewer to open the subject's mind to the vast number of possibilities as to why an individual might have done something wrong. Second, it allows interrogators to test possible rationalizations they might use later in the interrogation. If they observe particular interest in one of the summary rationalizations, they will then use it as the first rationalization. If they do not observe a particular interest in any of the rationalizations, they will select the first rationalization based on the background information available on the suspect.

Part 7 – First Rationalization

The interrogator selects a rationalization that he feels might justify the suspect's actions. This rationalization initially is based on background information or possible motives for the crime. The interrogator should expand this example using the outline above to structure the rationalization. Further explanation and details about the structure can be found in the chapter on Showing Understanding.

> "The investigation, while it can identify a suspect and show that he was involved, rarely shows the reason that he did it. For example, when an individual is under financial pressure, perhaps having just lost a job, he sometimes does things to take care of his family that he wouldn't do under ordinary circumstances. These outside pressures and influences cause people to make decisions that if they had plenty of money, they would never even consider.
>
> "In other situations, individuals are influenced by their friends, their peers, who have an idea, and they press and press and press that idea until they get their way. Even if it's a bad idea, eventually this constant pressure can cause the other people to do what they never would have done on their own. Many times, the person who is put in this position is forced to judge between a friendship that they value and what they know is right and wrong. But, because of the environment their friend puts them in, they make a decision on the spur of the moment to do something just so that they can keep him happy. This impulse decision is not always in their best interest, but still they make the decision to go ahead to appease their friend. If they had taken the time to think things through, they probably would never have done anything. But, because of their friends, they made a decision on impulse — perhaps a decision that they later regret."

The interrogator continues to rationalize until the suspect appears behaviorally ready to confess. The structure of the latter part of the interrogation remains essentially the same, regardless of whether the interrogator is in the public or private sector. After the initial rationalization, the interrogator uses a change of perspective and then returns to rationalization. Once the subject's resistance has been significantly reduced, the interrogator moves on to handling the suspect's hope, creating urgency, protecting evidence, and then using a test for submission before finally moving to the assumptive question to obtain the initial admission.

Part 8 — Changing the Subject Perspective

Let's say you owned your own company and you came in on your day off and saw two of your employees doing something wrong, no ifs, ands, or buts about it. You saw it with your own eyes. Both of them have been really good employees and have done a great job for you. Before you make any decisions as to what you are going to do about it, you decide to sit down with them to find out why it happened. You sit down with the first person, and he says, "You're crazy, it never happened. I don't care what you think you saw; it never happened." How do you feel about that person when he sat there, looked you in the eye, and lied? Let's say you sit down with the second person and he says "I'm really sorry. I know it was wrong." Then he walks you through his thought process and the difficulties he was facing at the time that caused him to make the error in judgment. Of the two, which one would you rather work with?

Part 9 — Second Rationalization

State rationalization:

"Bob, I think that we set people up for problems simply because of how much they get paid. Probably one of the most difficult things to do is to work around beautiful items that are really expensive and yet not be paid enough to afford them. Most people make pretty close to minimum wage, I would imagine. The thing is, once a person is around nice things, it's only natural to want them for himself."

Create illustration that helps the suspect understand the rationalization:

"This also happens with friends. I mean, if friends have some money and they're suddenly wearing fancy jeans that cost $40–50 a pair, or they're wearing skirts that may cost $100, you can rest assured they can afford these things. While another person is working hard for the money that he earns, maybe he doesn't have as much as they do at home. All of a sudden, they're treating him differently, simply because he doesn't have the same things they have.

"A person wouldn't be human if he didn't want them, too. But yet, he's not making enough to pay for it even though he's diligently working, doing a good job, yet he can't buy those things.

"The company also expects its employees to look good. I mean, that is the image of the company — the person that the customer sees. The employee is its representative, and they don't want him going in to work looking like a slob. They want him to dress nice, look sharp. The company would like the employees to look nice but do they turn around and say, 'Here's money for clothes,' or 'Here's a raise.' No, they don't! So we have to recognize that part of the situation is a result of how the company views itself and what it considers important."

"The thing that I don't want to see is somebody put into a position of doing something because of peer pressure, frustration, financial problems, or making an error in judgment that causes them to do something that under normal circumstances they wouldn't do. I think that's the key here. A lot of times people do things because they need the money. I think that's important because, if there was a need, a legitimate need, that's something that every one of us can relate to.

State rationalization:

"We all have bills, whether they're phones, heating, rent, car payment, or insurance. We all have things that we have to pay. There are times when we have extra money, and there are times when we run short. Sometimes, we're put in a position where we don't have an alternative. We do something that maybe we wouldn't have been raised to do, or we wouldn't do under normal circumstances at all; however, we're put into a position where we have a need.

Link back to the investigation:

"We're not going out and blowing the money on drugs or booze or good times. We're using it for the necessities of life, to keep our head above water, and I think that's important."

Part 10 — Address the Suspect's Hope and Create Urgency

"Sometimes a person thinks that, by saying nothing, the problem will go away and nothing will happen. That's why we do the investigation up front so the company can still resolve the situation even if the individual decides to say nothing. That's why it's important that a person understand that he has the ability to influence the company's decision-making process. That's why we need to get this resolved today."

Part 11 – Protect Evidence

"Many people wonder why an investigator doesn't just lay out on the table exactly what he knows that indicates an individual was responsible for a series of issues. The reason that is not done is not to try to trick a person, but rather to answer the most difficult question in any investigation. That question is not who did it; that was resolved through the investigative process. The real question is, 'Is he shooting straight with us when he tells us these things?' When the interviewer responds, 'Yes,' the absolutely most difficult question is, 'How do you know?' If the investigator had given up all the evidence surrounding the incident, he would have to say, 'I don't know,' but, because he held back things that were then told him by the subject, he could respond, 'I know the person is telling me the truth because he told me things that I already knew but hadn't mentioned.' Thus, when the individual says that he is sorry or attempts to explain what difficulties he was facing in his life, the interviewer can believe those things."

Part 12 — Test For Submission

Test for submission

"The difficulty (as I mentioned earlier) is that an investigation doesn't always reveal the reasons that something happens. Bob, the problem is, we don't know what type of outside pressures you faced."

The interrogator should assess the suspect's behavior after presentation of the test for submission. If the suspect tightens physically or begins to make a denial, the interrogator should control the denial and return to rationalizations in an effort to continue to reduce the suspect's resistance to a confession. If the suspect shows no outward signs of concern at this statement, the interrogator should proceed to the soft accusation. The interrogator should evaluate the subject's behavior for signs of acceptance, while being prepared to handle a possible denial.

"During any investigation, many things are uncovered and known absolutely. But often, it's the reason mistakes are made that doesn't come out. These things are important to the community to show why things happen and to show also that the individual cares. This is why, at the conclusion of every investigation, we sit down with the individual and discuss the results and really assess his attitude toward the community."

Part 13 – Soft Accusation – Assumptive Question

Interrogator: Bob, let me ask you this, what was the greatest number of buildings you broke into in the last 6 months?

Suspect: (Delays, looks away.)

Immediately ask the follow-up question.

Interrogator: Was it as many as 50?

Suspect: Oh, no!

Interrogator: That's great. From the investigation, I didn't think it was anywhere near that many. Forty?

Suspect: Less.

Interrogator: What do you think would be the most accurate number?

Suspect: Five or six.

The interrogator enters the development phase of the interrogation.

Introductory Statement for Fugitive Apprehension

The following example can be used during the search for fugitives. The primary difference in this third example is the duration, which is condensed because this is a field situation often in a friend's or relative's home or place of employment.

Part 1 — Who We Are and What We Do

"Hello Mary. I am _____ with the U.S. Marshals. I appreciate your taking time to talk with me today. I'm not sure if you're aware of what the U.S. Marshals do. The marshals are responsible for federal court protection, prisoner movement and security, and recovering individuals who have failed to show up for their court appearances (*make eye contact*).

"Basically, we have three areas of responsibility, court security, prisoner movement, and investigation. The investigation area focuses on the recovery of individuals who have missed their court appearances. The people who have missed their court dates often contact friends and relatives to ask for help or simply find out family news.

"Our major concern is when a relative or family member has offered help to a person who has failed to appear for court, rather than someone who was merely contacted by the family member who missed court."

Part 2 — Types of Crimes We Investigate

"We are responsible for investigating a variety of different incidents relating to people who have been charged with a crime. For example, we might investigate attempted escapes from courts, assaults or other attacks on prisoners being held in the federal system, illegal substances being brought into the jail, family members or friends who assist an individual who has missed a court appearance (*make eye contact*), or we might look into people who provide money or places of concealment to the fugitive. In other instances, we might investigate who helped a prisoner escape from custody or the backgrounds of other people who might have helped the person avoid recapture."

Part 3 — How We Investigate

"When we are attempting to find people who have missed their court dates we conduct an investigation to discover as much as possible about the individuals and their friends and family. We use a variety of different techniques to determine whether the fugitive has contacted friends or family members. These methods could consist of any techniques that would establish whether contact and assistance had been rendered. For example, we might use handwriting to determine if certain letters were written by the fugitive and delivered to a particular residence. To assist in this, we might have the mail to a particular location observed to locate any letters or notes from the person we are seeking.

"In addition, we might also monitor phones that we believe the fugitive might use to contact friends or relatives. We can also monitor e-mail or instant messaging used with computers for people to talk with one another. Another investigative technique that we might use is undercover agents in the community where the individual has friends and family. In this way, we are often able to discover whether there has been communication between the friends and family and the individual we're looking for. In other situations, we might purchase information from people who know the friends and family of the person we're seeking. Other times, we might use surveillance in an attempt to learn whether contact is being made. We might also use many other techniques if the situation called for them. These might include DNA analysis, fingerprint analysis, or tracing credit card numbers, money orders, or checks made out to the person we're seeking.

"Once we've completed our investigation and have an understanding of who the person has contacted or obtained help from, we conduct interviews with those people to determine whether they initiated the help or were simply responding to a request from the fugitive. We understand that, in any situation when a friend or family member has asked for assistance, it is extremely difficult to turn that person down. However, it becomes a question of whether that family member or friend is truthful in regard to what the investigation has already revealed.

Part 4 — Protect Evidence

"People often wonder why we just don't tell them immediately what the investigation has revealed. Unfortunately, while an investigation often answers many parts of the story, the one question it does not answer is whether the friend or family member is being truthful. The only way we can establish that is to hold back the results of the investigation and have that friend or family member confirm what is already known. When this happens, we can then believe whether it was the individual we're seeking who contacted them or whether the friend or relative offered to help."

Part 5 — Change Perspective

"I think that people often feel differently about people who told the truth. For example, have you ever been a boss or supervisor? (*Or use the story of a parent with two children or other change-of-perspective story.*) Let's imagine you are a supervisor, and we walk out the door and observe two of your employees doing something absolutely wrong. We've got to talk to them. The first employee comes in and says, 'I don't know what you are talking about. I didn't do anything.' How would you feel about that individual?

"The second employee comes in and says, 'I'm sorry. I screwed up. Let me tell you what was going on in my life and in my mind when I made that error in judgment.' Of those two people who would you feel better about? I think almost everybody would feel better about the second person."

Part 6 — Rationalization

If it seems necessary, you might want to add rationalizations to overcome the resistance.

Part 7 — Soft Accusation

"Let me ask you this — when was the very last time _____ contacted you?"
"Let me ask you this, what was the most amount of money you lent him since he missed his court dates? Did he approach you for help, or did you approach him and offer to help?"

If the friend or relative denies having contact or knowledge of the fugitive's whereabouts, the interviewer might want to consider using an enticement question to challenge the denial of the friend or relative. Additional discussion of the enticement question can be found in the chapter on interviewing.

"Is there any reason you can think of that there would be records of a phone contact between you and _____?"

"Is there any reason you can think of that a neighbor would say that _____ has been in your home recently?"

"Is there any reason you can think of that a friend of yours would have said you were contacted by _____?"

If the individual hesitates or changes the story, the interrogater should press the interrogation, returning to showing understanding and offering reasons and excuses that the individual did not tell about the contact when first asked.

The introductory statement can be mixed with portions of the participatory accusation to offer even more flexibility to the interrogator. With the knowledge of the different beginnings to the interrogation, an interrogator has a multitude of options in confronting a suspect.

Part Four

Reducing Resistance

Rationalizations 10

Rationalization is the engine that drives an emotional interrogation.

The driving force behind an emotional approach to interrogation is the process of rationalization. Rationalization is usually a one-sided discussion presented to the suspect by the interrogator, who offers excuses or reasons that minimize the seriousness of the crime and make it easier for the suspect to confess by allowing him to save face without sacrificing the elements of the crime. The rationalization is an integral part of the introductory statement method and the participatory accusation method. In each of these openings to an emotional interrogation, they allow the interrogator to offer excuses or reasons that minimize the seriousness of the crime and make it easier for the suspect to confess.

Contrary to the practice of many interrogators, the emotional appeal requires that the interrogator do almost all the talking until the suspect gives an initial acknowledgment of guilt. The suspect is never questioned about why he did something, but rather the interrogator offers reasons or excuses for why he did. This one-sided discussion by the interrogator allows him to control the direction of the interrogation much more easily than using questions directed at a suspect. An interrogator who attempts to use direct questions is often led astray by a suspect who is attempting to stall, sidetrack, or deceive him. Asking questions also provides the suspect with information about the interrogator's target and what he may already know.

The interrogator who offers rationalizations to a suspect is not asking about investigative facts to further the interrogation. Instead, the interrogator discusses the reasons that the suspect became involved. If the interrogator chooses to discuss the factual elements of the case, the suspect could take issue with the interpretation of the evidence and attempt to explain it away. However, in the emotional interrogation, the interrogator simply says, "You did it," ignoring the circumstances surrounding the how and concentrating on the why. By concentrating on the reasons the suspect became involved, the interrogator can offer any number of them for the suspect's actions, either real or fictitious.

Rationalization is an integral part of each of our lives. In almost everything we do, we justify or rationalize reasons for why we do what we do — consider the driver who goes 64 miles per hour in a 55-mile-per-hour speed zone because he believes that police officers do not write tickets until the driver is going 10 miles over the speed limit. There are also the office workers who take pencils home and justify their actions by the fact that they do some office work at home, or because the company has plenty and the items do not cost much. Another employee can justify taking merchandise but not cartons of merchandise or money, and yet another employee can justify taking cartons of merchandise and money as long as he does not go into the safe and touch the deposit. In the progression of rationalizations, still other individuals can justify taking anything as long as they do not physically harm another person. Others can justify taking anything so long as they do not kill anyone, and so on. Each person, through parents, church, and society, has developed moral guidelines that justify actions. These guidelines form the basis of our day-to-day decision making. When we violate one, we use the process of rationalization to bring ourselves back into equilibrium with our moral guidelines.

Concept of Rationalization

The process of rationalization allows the interrogator an opportunity to develop a relationship with the suspect. This relationship is one of an understanding mediator rather than an adversary. It allows the suspect to view the interrogator as an understanding individual who faces problems and turmoil in his everyday life, just as the suspect does. Clearly, when suspects distrust the interrogator, they are less likely to confess. The process of rationalization creates a nonjudgmental relationship between the suspect and the interrogator, fostering trust between the two.

The process of rationalization also allows the interrogator to create the perception of transferring guilt to someone or something other than the suspect. This guilt transference assists the interrogator in psychologically minimizing the seriousness of the suspect's offense. It makes the suspect a victim of circumstances instead of the initiator of the incident.

Rationalizations also allow the interrogator to focus the suspect's attention on the resolution of the incident rather than on the consequences. This refocusing of the suspect's attention is fundamental to allowing a suspect to believe that it is in his interest to confess involvement in the incident. Suspects who continually focus on the consequences of their actions and the impact these consequences will have on their lives are less likely to confess than are suspects who focus on the future and put the incident behind them.

Finally, the process of rationalization allows the interrogator to overcome the hurdles or fears suspects have in confessing. Typically, suspects must reconcile their fears of the consequences before they will make an admission. Generally, most suspects fear one or more of the following, which stand in the way of a confession:

- Arrest and prosecution
- Embarrassment
- Termination
- Restitution
- Bodily harm to himself or family

Interrogators are like salesmen. They must understand and answer the objections the potential customer has before the customer will buy the product. Once salesmen understand the customer's objections, they offer benefits of their product that overcome the customer's reluctance to buy. If the product's benefits outweigh the customer's objections, the customer will make a purchase. Salesmen handle their customers' skepticism by stating and restating benefits, offering proofs, and expanding on the benefits. For a customer who is potentially indifferent, the salesman uses closed probes to uncover needs and offers benefits to handle those needs.

The needs of the customer can be complex. There can be personal as well as corporate needs salesmen must fulfill before the customer will purchase. In the same way, interrogators must recognize that suspects have a complex group of needs. Image, financial, and family needs all come together to form the basis of the final hurdle that the interrogator must overcome for the suspect to confess.

The interrogator should understand the concept of hope as it applies to interrogation. Hope is really the cornerstone of an interrogator's understanding of the suspect. Suspects hope that if they do not say anything, the interrogator and investigation will not have developed information sufficient to terminate or arrest them. If the investigation has not developed sufficient evidence, then the suspect will not have to be embarrassed or pay restitution. Interrogators must, through establishing credibility of the investigation, remove the suspects' hope that they have not been caught. The process of rationalization returns the hope that his life will not be completely devastated as a result of confessing. The suspect who says, "Well, I don't care, just lock me up" has given up hope. The interrogator must first renew hope through rationalization before they will be susceptible to an admission of guilt.

Determining Which Rationalization to Use

Interrogators should consider a number of factors prior to selecting the rationalization to use during the interrogation. They must consider motive, the suspect's background, and receptivity to any rationalizations presented. In most interrogations, the initial rationalizations selected by the interrogator are educated guesses based on the case facts, possible motive, and background of the suspect. Suspects themselves, during the interrogation, will decide on the selection of the most successful rationalization. The interrogator offers the rationalizations and observes the suspect's behavior to determine which rationalization seems to have the greatest effect in reducing the suspect's resistance.

Motive of the Crime

The motive behind the incident will often lead the interrogator to the proper rationalization. In many cases, the motive can be accurately guessed based on the investigation and the background of the suspect. In the early stages of an investigation, a suspect's motive might not be evident from the limited facts available. The most common motives are theft, revenge, sex, and curiosity.

The **theft** motive could be the result of a true or only perceived financial need of the suspect or his family. This need might be a result of bankruptcy or being over the limit on credit cards. In many cases, simply having an opportunity to steal might have been a sufficient temptation for the suspect. In some corporate environments where theft is common, even the most honest individuals might steal because it is the norm of the group. Some studies indicate that as much as 30% of the population would steal if given the opportunity; however, only 10% of the population would still steal if they had to look for a way to do it. This base 10% are often motivated by greed and are typically the more hardened and experienced criminal element.

A second motive, **revenge**, can play a part in a number of different crimes. It might be the cause of theft of a deposit to make a supervisor look bad. Sabotage might be justified to get even for a real or perceived insult. It might even justify the killing of another individual. The need to get even can burn like a fire inside an individual, weakening the moral fiber until it breaks.

The third motive is **sexual**. This motive can justify anything from theft to rape or the killing of another. Many people become involved in theft to steal for lovers when their salaries will not support the gifts they want to give.

Sexual deviance can also account for the torture and killing of victims. Sexually motivated killings often tend to be vicious, brutal acts by sexually deviant suspects.

Finally, **curiosity** or **thrill seeking** can also be a motive for crime. These might start an innocent adventure, but the temptation overcomes suspects' good sense and they do something that they should not. Youngsters often shoplift out of curiosity to see if they can get away with it or simply for the adventure. Once they see how easy it is to shoplift from the store, this motive is generally replaced with the theft motive. Now, the youths take expensive items they could not otherwise afford.

The previous motives were discussed as individual reasons for committing the crime, but a suspect's actual reasons are often more complex. A crime might have begun as a theft because the suspect needed cash, but it culminated in rape because the suspect had an opportunity and inclination to do so. This sexual urge, however, can be complex in and of itself. The sexual act is often secondary to the need to denigrate the female because of some past experience.

Interrogators need to recognize that the motivation for any incident can range from simple to complex. Often, it is only after evaluating the case facts and background of the suspect that a true motive becomes apparent.

Background of the Offender

The background of the offender can give the interviewer or interrogator direction in selecting the proper rationalization. A suspect's educational, financial, and social situations all can help to indicate the proper rationalizations to use.

Interrogators should consider what might cause them to confess were they in the suspect's position. Often, such role reversal gives interrogators an insight into the suspect's mind-set that will indicate a proper rationalization. However, interrogators should not place too much emphasis on this role reversal because of the different moral and ethical values a suspect may have. Consider an example in which the background investigation of a suspect indicates that his financial problems might be the reason for committing the crime. These financial problems include having his car repossessed, wage assignments, and eviction from his apartment. Although most people would consider that they are having financial difficulties, the suspect views the situation only as a momentary cash flow problem. He has $20 and a date for Saturday night, and he sees the situation in an entirely different light from most people. Remember, each person individually justifies how he spends his money. Some individuals will not own a credit card or will pay the balance on the card at the end of each month, whereas others carry a small balance and pay it off as soon as possible. Still others run it up to the limit and then obtain another credit card. Each of these individuals has a considerably different financial perspective.

The interrogator, reviewing the background of the suspect, is looking for his value system. By understanding how he thinks and what is important to him, the interrogator can present rationalizations that coincide with the suspect's thinking. Consider the rationalization used on a teenager who was the second child in the family. The suspect's older brother was a straight-A student, letterman on several school teams, and one of the most popular boys in his class. The suspect was an average student, with average performance in scholastics, sports, and social relationships. The interrogator used the rationalization that the suspect became involved in the incident because he was trying to be noticed by his parents. Although this approach might seem clichéd, the effect on the suspect was significant. The rationalization was developed along the following lines:

> You know, Bob, I think the reason that this happened was not because you're a bad person, but rather to call out to your parents and say, "Notice me, too." For years you have had to walk in the shadow of your brother who is lucky enough to be a straight-A student and the most popular kid in class. It's got to be awfully hard to follow someone like that. You know, moms and dads often begin to focus their attention on the child who does the best. It does not mean they don't love you, but sometimes, it does not seem like they do. I think what has happened here is not so much for money or anything like that, but I think it was a call to your parents to say, "Notice me; I'm a person, too."

By considering the motive of the crime along with the suspect's background, an interrogator can often make an educated guess as to why a suspect became involved in the incident. Consider the case of a nurse who administered lethal doses of medication to her patients. Why might this woman have killed these individuals? These types of cases are seen in hospitals and nursing homes. The interrogator must consider the background of the suspect in relation to the possible motives. Some motives in this situation could be that the nurse

- Was simply lazy and trying to reduce her workload.
- Had a mental apparition.
- Saw this as a way of reducing the suffering of the patient.
- Saw this as a way of reducing the hardship and suffering of the family.
- Was influenced by another individual to do this.

Considering these and other potential motives to commit the crime, the interrogator should begin to look at the suspect's background and decision-making process. Although the background alone might not indicate which motive directed the suspect's action, the interrogator can often make an educated guess at what the most likely motive for the crime was. Once interrogators have considered the most likely motive, they begin to consider what they might say that would justify the suspect's actions, recalling that their primary goal is to transfer guilt and overcome the hurdles of the suspect.

Behavior of the Suspect

While presenting the rationalization, interrogators must study the suspect's behavior to determine whether the rationalization is having the desired impact and whether the rationalization should be continued or other rationalizations tried. Receptive and nonreceptive behavior by the suspect are discussed below.

Receptive Behavior. If suspects accept the rationalization presented by the interrogator, they will display receptive behavior, including warm, accepting eyes. The muscles around the corners of the eyes might relax and the eyes will begin to moisten. Suspects are then allowing the interrogator to look below the surface and into their eyes as the rapport deepens.

Suspects might occasionally nod in agreement and their bodies' overall physical tension will begin to relax as they accept the interrogator's rationalization for their actions. The closed defensive barriers of the arms and legs will begin to open, and the shoulders will lose their tension and begin to slump. The suspects' denials will become less frequent and finally will cease altogether as they move toward a submissive posture.

Nonreceptive Behavior. Nonreceptive behavior by the suspect can consist of cold, hard, unaccepting eyes that take on a flat look that does not allow the interrogator's gaze to penetrate below the surface. The muscles around the eyes tighten into an unaccepting frown. Suspects might roll the eyes to amplify their disbelief of the interrogator's statements.

The suspect's body will maintain its tension and closed defensive posture. Denials will continue unabated during the rationalizations that do not meet the suspect's needs. The frequency of the suspect's denials will increase as he reacts negatively to the unacceptable rationalizations.

Interrogators who recognize the behavioral clues of acceptance and non-acceptance will modify the rationalization to meet the suspect's needs. Interrogators can be eloquent while relating rationalizations, but if the rationalizations do not meet the suspect's needs, they will fall on deaf ears. Consider the following case example and the suspect's comments following the interrogation.

Case Example

The director of training for a convenience store operation was interrogated regarding the theft of cash from franchise owners. Approximately a year prior to the interrogation, the suspect had surgery for a brain tumor and had recently been diagnosed with another tumor. The suspect was under a severe financial strain because of the expense of his operation and the medication. He was well liked by co-workers. The most likely motive for the suspect's stealing was financial problems; investigators suspected that the stolen money was used to pay medical bills and for his medication.

The interrogator used an introductory statement to establish the credibility of the investigation and followed it with rationalizations that placed blame on financial problems. During the rationalization, the suspect showed receptive behavior and began to open his body posture. The suspect had uncrossed his legs and positioned his feet flat on the floor, opening his arms to the sides of the chair, indicating that he was near submission. The interrogator, in the final stage of the rationalization, attempted to focus the suspect's attention toward the future rather than the present by saying, "When a problem occurs we have to put it behind us and look down the road where we'll be at 5 or 10 years from now. While right now it might seem like the most important thing in the world, as the years pass, it becomes less and less significant."

The suspect immediately crossed his legs and arms, indicating that he did not like what he was hearing. The interrogator dropped this line of rationalization and returned to the financial problems as a reason that people make errors in judgment. After a short period of time, the suspect uncrossed and opened his legs, once again nearing submission.

The interrogator now attempted to minimize the seriousness of the incident by talking about the size of the company and the amount of sales it had. Then the interrogator said, "The company is looking for some common ground to begin a discussion so they can understand the reasons this happened." As this was said, the suspect once again crossed his legs and folded his arms across his chest. The interrogator, recognizing the suspect's disagreement, immediately returned to a discussion of the financial reasons for the crime. Shortly thereafter, the suspect went into submission and confessed.

During a discussion with the suspect following the interrogation, he related that there were two things that the interrogator said that just did not ring true. The first statement the suspect said he disagreed with was looking down the road to the future. The suspect said, "I have no future. The doctors have discovered another tumor, and I'll be lucky to be alive a year from now." The second area of disagreement was in establishing common ground. The suspect related, "When you talked about common ground, there is no common ground. Two weeks ago, another director was caught stealing and I'll be lucky if I'm not arrested like he was."

The post-interrogation interview with the suspect revealed the reasons for the change to a nonreceptive body posture. Although the interrogator was not sure specifically what the suspect's objections to these rationalizations were, it was evident from the change in his physical behavior that he did not like what he was hearing. When interrogators observe nonreceptive behavior, they should immediately change rationalizations and attempt to use other face-saving justifications.

The important thing for interrogators to realize is that the rationalization offered to the suspect does not have to be the real reason or motivation behind the suspect's activity. What interrogators are attempting to do is look for excuses that the suspect can accept. That reason might be the real justification the suspect made to himself, or it might simply be a reason that he thinks others might accept to justify the behavior.

Transactional Analysis

Transactional analysis attempts to explain the role people take during conversations and general contacts between people. This area was founded by an American psychologist, Eric Byrne, and made famous in the book *I'm OK — You're OK: A Practical Guide to Transactional Analysis*, by Thomas A. Harris. The theory is that people take one of three roles during human contact, which are called transactions. These three roles are parent, adult, and child. When a role is forced on another person, conflict will generally arise. In an interrogation, the interrogator will often be perceived as the parent talking with a child. If the other individual accepts this role, it will be a complementary discourse and the resulting interaction will proceed without conflict. An interrogation using the direct accusation positions the interrogator as the parent talking with the subject, who is assigned the role of a child. This quickly forces denials to occur and often encourages the suspect to react in an emotional fashion, not unlike a child: well, go ahead and send me to my room; see if I care! This is not what the child really wants, but with the loss of perceived power the child uses only emotion to make a response, one that cuts the lines of communication. Figure 10.1 illustrates the dynamics involved in an adult–child transaction.

This type of interaction can still result in the interrogator's obtaining an admission; however, several probable results can be anticipated from this type of transaction. First, because of the role and general directness of a

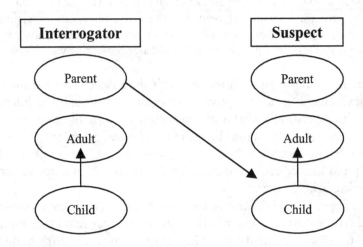

Figure 10.1 Parent–child communication.

parent's accusation, the child will be placed in a position where the first instinct is to deny. The suspect must now use continued denials to protect the initial decision to lie. Second, the role of the child is one where the lines of communication have become strained, and active listening by the suspect is diminished. The role of the parent is often viewed as judgmental, and even rationalizations might not be as effective as they could be because of the roles chosen. Finally, the signs of submission will be pronounced. Like a child who finally submits to a parent, there might be crying, exaggerated body slump, and loss of eye contact.

The most successful encounter is the adult-to-adult transaction that is encouraged by an interrogator using a modified emotional approach (see Figure 10.2). The introductory statement and rationalization combine to create this transaction.

The adult-to-adult transaction succeeds because the suspect and the interrogator are not positioned in the encounter as adversaries, but rather as equals attempting to solve a problem. The interrogator might also offer opinions, as an older, wiser parent might to adult children, but it is done as a means of discussion, not command. This approach creates several likely outcomes. First, there is a dramatic reduction in denials by the suspect. This situation allows the rationalizations to be more effective because the interrogator's presentation is not being interrupted and the suspect is listening for information. Second is the muting of the behavioral clues of submission. In a classic interrogation in which suspects use denials to protect themselves, submission is very pronounced. In the modified emotional approach, denials are rare, but the clues to submission are more difficult to see. The rationalizations are used to test the suspect's resistance to a confession by using quotes

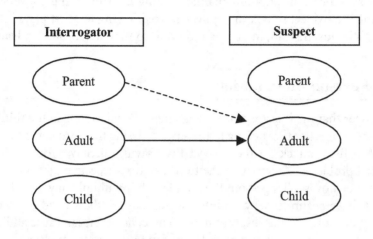

Figure 10.2 Adult–adult transaction.

and changes in person, beginning with the third person (he, she, they, them, others) and later to the collective "we," and then finally to "you".

When a suspect attempts to take control, it will be a reversal of the parent–child, with the suspect taking the role of the parent attempting to dominate the child (interrogator) in the conversation.

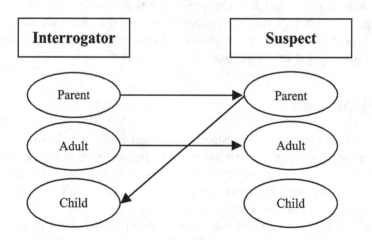

Figure 10.3 The suspect takes the role of parent and the interrogator responds as an adult or parent.

In this type of interaction, suspects are attempting to control the conversation. They might be trying to force the interrogator into a childlike anger that will bring the encounter to a close, or just to dominate the exchange. Generally, the proper response is to avoid childlike replies and deal with the parent statements in an adult manner, taking control of the conversation, allowing the suspect to take an equivalent role. Trying to resist plays into the suspect's hands. Instead, interrupt and use it to the interrogator's advantage.

Third Person Presentation

Remember that the interrogator presents the rationalizations in the third person because it is less threatening to the suspect. Using the third person is much less of a direct attack on the suspect than saying directly, "You are having financial problems." Often, with the third person, suspects might not be sure the interrogator is talking about them and so they withhold any denials. Once suspects have begun to deny, an interrogator can use the second person pronouns (you, your) or the suspect's name. These, however, can cause additional denials by suspects because they feel the need to defend themselves.

Interrogators might offer several different rationalizations to the suspect. As they present each of these rationalizations for the suspect's actions, they observe his behavior to see which one he most readily accepts. When they discover a rationalization that the suspect accepts, they should begin to talk more about it and limit the other rationalizations. This will enhance the rapport the suspect feels with the interrogator and will further reduce the suspect's resistance to confession.

Interrogators might use the same rationalization a number of times during the interrogation. The appropriateness of the rationalization and its effectiveness in overcoming the emotional resistance of the suspect depends on the suspect, the interview, and the interrogator.

Using Quotes

Interrogators use stories and statements from other people or the media because they do not attribute a statement or belief directly to them. They are merely recounting the situation or event without necessarily taking a position with which the suspect could disagree. This situation gives interrogators several distinct advantages in the conversation.

First of all, interrogators can distance themselves from statements that appear judgmental or critical, while still getting the benefit of making the point of the story. A statement such as, "My neighbor said that people like that are just worthless," might be a point the interrogator wants to make but cannot say it him- or herself, so attributes it to another. This use of another person's words does nothing to disrupt the rapport that has been built with the suspect and might even enhance the attitude of the suspect toward the interrogator.

The use of quotations also allows interrogators to test the boundaries of the suspect's beliefs and resistance without committing to a position. If they use a personal story without testing a suspect's belief system, they might damage their credibility in the suspect's mind. Once the suspect disagrees with the interrogator, the suspect might begin to look for other areas of disagreement, and distrust begins to build. Once interrogators have a sense of whether the suspect agrees or disagrees with the statement or story, they can choose whether to personalize it to themselves or their own belief system.

Minimizing the Seriousness of the Offense

During the interrogation, the interrogator also minimizes the seriousness of the crime from the suspect's perspective, playing down the seriousness or the scope of the suspect's involvement. Interrogators might assist the suspect in minimizing the seriousness by saying, "And sometimes it's really nothing more than an error in judgment, a mistake," or, "What is important here is that a person doesn't get blamed for things he wasn't been involved in, just because people often think the worst about others," or "Everyone can make a mistake in judgment."

Minimizing the seriousness of the suspect's involvement is a twofold process. First, the rationalizations begin to justify the reasons behind a suspect's actions, and, second, the interrogator begins to contrast the incident with more serious crimes. The interrogator discusses a robbery but compares it with a robbery in which the victim was shot or killed so as to minimize the seriousness of the present incident. For example, the interrogator might say, "All we're talking about here is taking some money. I mean, nobody was shot, nobody was hurt, and I think that's important here. I'm glad that this thing didn't get out of hand."

Focusing the Suspect's Attention on the Future or Past

Interrogators can also attempt to focus the suspect's attention on the future or the past. Using positive statements about the suspect's past performance or future draws the suspect's attention away from the present situation. The interrogator who focuses the suspect's attention on the past might highlight the good that a suspect has done. This good might be raising a family, job performance, or any other skill that the suspect has. The suspect needs to feel that the incident being investigated is only a small portion of his life. When dealing with a young individual, the interrogator focuses the subject into the future because the suspect has had only limited experience. The older the person, the more likely that leading them into the past will make sense.

As most people grow older, they begin to tell stories about the past; the interrogator merely uses this preference of perspective to illustrate the rationalizations.

Often, however, an interrogator will focus a suspect's attention to the future. Whenever anyone makes a mistake, that mistake, because of its immediacy, seems to be the most serious error that was ever made. However, by focusing the suspect's attention on the future, the interrogator can minimize the seriousness of this error. Interrogators might say something like

> "I remember when we were kids and we didn't study for a test. It seemed like the most important thing in our life at that moment because we knew we weren't going to do well. But, you know, looking back on that test now, it really wasn't that important. A single test means very little, but to us then, it was the future, where we would succeed or fail. What was really important was what we learned from that mistake. We went on and studied for other tests and did better as a result of learning from that mistake. While the single event itself was not important, the overall positive impact it had 10 or 20 years in the future was enormous."

With individuals who have been extremely responsible or have significant job responsibilities, it is often to the benefit of the interrogator to point out past successes and the good things that happened before the incident. The interrogator highlights the fact that all the good things that the suspect has done should not be forgotten and that the suspect just made an error, an error that should not outweigh all the positives accomplished thus far in life.

Offering a Positive Outlook

The interrogator might also offer the suspect a positive outlook during the interrogation. This positive outlook makes the suspect aware that there might be benefits to making an admission. The interrogator does not tell the suspect that things are going to turn out well, nor does he offer to help the suspect. In the short term, the interrogator is there neither to help nor to have things turn out well for the guilty suspect. That does not mean, however, that the cooperation a suspect shows in making an admission does not have benefits. It might be the benefit of feeling better because he talked through a problem that had seemed unresolvable. The lifting of an emotional weight is a wonderful feeling. It could also be the perceived benefit of being understood by family, co-workers, or others by explaining the reasons he became involved in the incident.

This positive outlook shows suspects that others are capable of understanding their problems. It also allows them to consider what potential benefits they might derive from confessing. Many suspects focus only on the negatives of confessing without ever considering what positive benefits they might derive from making an admission.

These methods of showing understanding are crucial to the interrogator's success in reducing a suspect's resistance. The interrogator's warm, conversational tone of voice is important in developing rapport and trust with the suspect. Interrogators should present their rationalizations or other methods of showing understanding to the suspect in a sincere, positive manner. They sell the belief that it is good to talk through problems and to resolve them. A persuasive argument can help the suspect develop these same feelings. Creating a level of trust with the suspect allows interrogators to sell themselves and the wisdom of a confession.

Relating Personal Stories

Interrogators might use personal stories from their own lives to illustrate the rationalizations. As mentioned above, it is wise to test the suspect's beliefs and boundaries before personalizing a story. It is a rare individual who has not at one point or another in life been short of money and under some financial pressure. This might have occurred only when you were a child and wanted to buy that very special toy but did not quite have the money to do it. How did it feel? What impact did this have on how you dealt with others during this time? Personal stories by the interrogator illustrate the rationalizations and their impact on everyday life. They help portray the interrogator as a human being who has faced adversity in life. Interrogators should never let themselves appear dishonest to the suspect. Saying something like, "When I was 16, I was a burglar and look at me today," only detracts from the professionalism and trust the interrogator is attempting to achieve. Simple stories about children and life, but ones that do not necessarily relate to dishonesty, are most effective in showing understanding.

An interrogator could discuss his feelings when his friends wanted him to start smoking. The interrogator did not have any desire to smoke but ultimately took a cigarette. Now today, the interrogator is a nonsmoker, but at that point in life, his friends' influence caused him to do something that he would never have done on his own.

Children make wonderful stories for illustrating the rationalizations:

> "My son, Jonathan, when he was 3 years old, cut up our bedroom blanket with his scissors. Now I knew my wife didn't do it and I didn't do it. He is the only 3-year old running around the house with a pair of scissors. I couldn't change the fact that the blanket had been cut up and ruined, but what was important was that he

learned from his mistake. As a parent, I had to make him understand that what he did was wrong and that he couldn't just go around cutting up things around the house anytime he wanted. It was important that he learned that there was a right way to use the scissors and a right time to use them. Now, this does not mean that he wasn't punished, but the important thing is that he learned from his mistake so he never made that same error again."

Illustrating with Current Events and Publications

Rationalizations can also be illustrated by newspaper and magazine articles. Current events or topical news items often make excellent illustrations for the rationalizations. The interrogator might ask the suspect to consider famous people and the reasons they might have made the mistakes they made. Showing the suspect that even the rich and famous can make an error often helps in minimizing the seriousness of the suspect's actions. The error does not make them bad people, just people who made a mistake. Transposing a suspect's feelings onto others who have problems helps the suspect feel less isolated and fearful about how he will be viewed.

Avoiding Threats or Promises

The interrogator should never threaten or promise anything to a suspect during the interrogation. Promises made to a suspect should not be made unless they can be carried out and the promise is one that would not be likely to make an innocent person confess. To tell suspects that if they confess, they will maintain their job or not go to jail might, under certain circumstances, make an innocent person confess just to get out of the situation. Threatening physical harm to a suspect might also cause an innocent person to confess.

Interrogators should also be cautious about any promise they make during an interrogation. Promising a suspect to "tell his side of the story" to others is acceptable, but promising that a suspect will not be prosecuted when the interrogator knows that a prosecution will occur is not acceptable. Interrogators need to maintain an ethical outlook on the process of interrogation. Those who believe that it is okay to "lie to a liar" or that "he [the suspect] is just getting what he deserves" soon becomes no better than the criminals with whom they are dealing.

It certainly is acceptable to make promises to suspects to obtain their cooperation. The state's attorney who offers the suspect immunity or a lesser sentence for cooperation does so only with strong evidence of the suspect's guilt. The making of a promise or agreement of a lesser charge should be made by the prosecutor only after careful review of the evidence and subject's background. The courts have clearly held that a promise of leniency by the investigator will taint the suspect's confession.

Structure of Showing Understanding

One of the most difficult areas for a new interrogator to master is the process of rationalizing with a suspect. Many new interrogators are just told to tell stories and keep talking to the suspect with no framework or direction to the conversation. The interrogator knows that the hoped-for result is to obtain a confession from the suspect, but the challenge is how to get there. Observation of the suspect's behavior is one way to monitor how close the interrogator is to getting a confession; however, it does little to structure the approach for the interrogator, leaving it instead to trial and error.

Instead of looking at the goal of the confession, the following structure allows the interrogator to have a series of intermediate steps that move the suspect intellectually and emotionally toward telling the truth. First of all, an interrogator has to make a decision whether he wants the suspect to make an emotional or rational decision to confess. Using certain accusations encourages an emotional decision to confess, while others lead the suspect to decide rationally to confess. If the suspect makes an emotional decision to confess, there will, in all likelihood, be denials interrupting the flow of the conversation.

The following structure formats the interrogator's approach to showing understanding.

1. **Accusation** —The interrogator chooses one of several ways to begin the interrogation. The selection can often predict whether the suspect will react emotionally or rationally. Regardless, the suspect is told either directly or indirectly that he is involved in the incident.
2. **Transition Statement** —The interrogator moves from the accusation to showing understanding of the suspect's situation using a statement similar to: "An investigation shows what happened and who is involved, but it doesn't necessarily tell the reason something happened." This statement opens the way for the following rationalizations and tells the suspect that the reason behind the incident might be important.
3. **Summary of Possible Rationalizations** — Next, the interrogator offers a series of possible rationalizations to the suspect. These are not long stories, but instead just a sentence or two designed to open the suspect's mind to the wide array of possible excuses that would allow him to save face. The second purpose is for the interrogator to present

the rationalizations and see if the suspect reacts favorably to any of them. Commonly, the interrogator would list six or seven possible excuses ,each being a sentence or so in length. The interrogator does not use the word "you," which would personalize the statement to the suspect and likely cause a denial. Instead, the sentences are delivered in the third person: "people," "they," or "them." For example, "**People** make errors in judgment for a lot of different reasons. Sometimes, it might be financial difficulties that are overwhelming **them**. In other instances, it might be an impulsive decision that wasn't thought through carefully. Still others might have been influenced by **their** friends to do something that was totally unlike **them**. Other times it might be the result of ..." The interrogator observes the suspect to determine if any of these offered rationalizations struck a responsive cord. If the suspect's behavior indicates an interest in any of the topics, then that will be developed as the first rationalization. If, as is often the case, the suspect does not react significantly to any of the summary rationalizations, the interrogator then chooses one based on the suspect's background information.

4. **Rationalization 1** — Individual rationalizations also have an internal structure that is repeated each time a new rationalization is offered. The interrogator merely has to plug in the pieces and an easily built rationalization is available.
   1. State the rationalization topic.
   2. Offer two universal examples that everyone might have experienced.
   3. Give an example of the rationalization in story form using the third person.
   4. State the moral of the story.
   5. Link back to the investigation.

The structure begins with a stated topic or rationalization. In this example, the first rationalization will be financial pressures, but it could be any other rationalization that made sense to the suspect based on his background: "Probably one of the greatest difficulties in people's lives is when they run into financial problems, sometimes through no fault of their own." The interrogator clearly mentions the topic and its broad application to people and their problems.

The interrogator next offers two universal examples of financial problems to which most people will have been exposed. The purpose of this universal example is to allow the suspect to better internalize the example to his own life: "Everyone has gotten an unexpected bill or had something like a car or furnace break down at the worst possible time." The interrogator chooses these two examples that most people would have experienced or would know someone who has had this type of problem.

The interrogator expands this into a story that illustrates the point being made, preferably drawing on real examples occurring in everyone's lives instead of making up a story. If the interrogator were to make up a story, the suspect might observe deceptive behavior in the interrogator. He could use a story from the news that is relevant, or one from his or someone else's life. Referring to someone else's difficulty might allow the interrogator more latitude in telling the story than if it is personalized it to the interrogator. Regardless, the interrogator should refrain from telling stories about himself that reflect poor ethics, dishonesty, or criminal behavior. The transition to the story is done by saying, "You know, I remember when something happened for that very reason..." The story is related in the third person and the suspect is never placed in a position of having to deny because the interrogator said anything that was too direct about his being involved.

The interrogator finishes the story with a moral that offers a clear reason for telling the anecdote: "That is why people, even good people, can find themselves in a position where there seems no other way out." The interrogator then finishes the rationalization by linking it back to the investigation, saying "That's why, in an investigation, we try to sit down with people and understand the problems that caused them to make that error in judgment."

To this point, the suspect has been told that the reason things happen is important to understand. His awareness of possible excuses has been broadened by the summary of rationalizations and then its application was internalized to the suspect with the first rationalization example. The suspect by now has a sense that there may be a benefit to a confession but has not yet come to that conclusion on his own. Until the suspect decides there is a benefit to a confession, he will remain skeptical of what is being told.

5. **Change the Suspect's Perspective** — The next section of showing understanding allows suspects to reach their own conclusion about the benefit of confession and cooperation. As with most decisions, once suspects have reached a conclusion by themselves, they internalize it as part of their belief system. At the conclusion of the story, suspects are comfortable with the idea that confessing is the right thing to do.

The story is told ambiguously, not relating what trouble the individuals are involved in. Essentially, the story puts the suspect into the position of having to judge someone else's mistake. One of the two people in the story denies any involvement, even though he was observed, while the second says he is sorry and explains why he became involved in the incident. Suspects are then asked which of the two they feel more comfortable with, to which they will probably respond, "the second one." The interrogator supports this selection and alleges most people feel the same way. The story can be changed based on the individual's background and experiences, to a parent seeing his children doing something wrong, two friends doing or saying something inappropriate, and a judge dealing with two people charged with a crime, or other similar story lines. In each, the central theme remains the same: one person cooperates and explains why, and the second individual stonewalls. The following example might be commonly used when an individual has work experience:

Interiewer: Mike, have you ever been a boss?

Subject: No, never.

Interiewer: Well, let's make you a boss for a minute. You are responsible for supervising a group of people. We walk outside and see two of your employees doing something absolutely wrong. (Note: The interrogator lets the suspect decide what the word "**wrong**" means, resulting in perfect communication of the story because it fits the exact mental image the suspect is constructing.) There is no question about it being wrong. We stood right there and watched it happen. We have to talk with them. Let's say we bring in the first person, and they say "I didn't do anything. You didn't see anything. And do what you have to do." (The word they is grammatically incorrect, but is used so that the gender of the person being described is ambiguous matching the internal story the suspect has created for himself.) How would you feel about that person?

Subject: I wouldn't like it; he was lying to me.

Interiewer: Exactly. Let's say we bring in the second person and **they** say, "I screwed up. I was wrong. Let me tell you what was going on in my life and mind when I made that error in judgment." Out of those two people who do you feel better about?

Subject: The second one.

Interiewer: I agree, and I think most people would feel the same way. One told us to jump in the lake and the other worked to help us understand why the error happened. You know, I think another reason people commonly have problems is …

The suspect has now internalized the idea that there is a positive benefit to cooperation. He has observed a problem from a different perspective and seen that he would feel different about the individual who cooperated with him. The process was also important from the interrogator's perspective because it was the suspect who came to the conclusion, without being told, thus creating a powerful self-imposed belief. The interrogator now returns to the second rationalization, which may not be the same as the first. The actions of an individual committing a crime often need several different rationalizations to justify his actions. For example, the physical abuse of a child might need two or more rationalizations to allow the suspect to save face. First, the interrogator might use frustration at being unable to control the child's crying, but this does not account for the severity of the injuries inflicted. So, a second rationalization might be used: the strength of an adult and the fragility of a small child. Combining both rationalizations allows the suspect to save face. Remember that there might be a pattern of abuse requiring the interrogator to correct the reasons for the suspect's actions. Some people will say that it was an accident, thus removing the intent to commit the crime; however, the interrogator continues the interrogation, obtaining the details known only to the offender. These details often clearly show that the incident could not have occurred by accident. The interrogator then returns to rationalization to again allow the suspect to save face.

6. **Rationalization 2** — The interrogator returns to the rationalization looking to justify why the suspect became involved in the incident. As mentioned in the previous paragraph, the rationalization might be different or a variation of the first one used. The construction of the second rationalization is the same as the first one: state the rationalization, offer two universal examples, expand the story, state the moral, and, finally, link back to the investigation. The interrogator makes some small changes in the second rationalization because the suspect has moved mentally and emotionally into a more receptive position. The expanded story in this second rationalization is customized to have a main character who is similar in circumstances to the suspect. For example, if the suspect is unemployed and divorced with two children, then the story being told will have a person of similar but not exact biographical background. The suspect sees that there are others like him facing similar challenges. Interrogators in these later rationalizations can begin to use the term "we" as they begin to understand the suspect's boundaries and beliefs. This further deepens the rapport between the two.

7. **Rationalizations 3, 4, etc.** — The suspect might need several rationalizations to feel comfortable contemplating a confession. The rationalizations that are being accepted by the suspect should result in an

observable behavioral change in the suspect. The frequency and intensity of denials begin to decrease. The interrogator might notice the suspect's body begin to lose tension and slowly appear more open. The suspect moves to a more upright position in the chair as the resistance diminishes and the arms move away from the body. The suspect's eyes moisten. There is a depth to the eyes, and the muscles around the eyes soften. These behaviors might be easily seen or subtle, depending on the individual and the interrogator's strategy.

The interrogator must now deal with the final internal conflicts and doubts the suspect may feel. These are presented in a way that does not threaten the suspect emotionally, but instead keeps the lines of communication open with the individual. Anytime the interrogator needs to convey information to the suspect that might prove disconcerting, it can be done using quotes from others. For example, if the interrogator wants to point out the suspect's inappropriate behavior or statements, he could do it in one of three ways:

1. *You are acting like a child making those kinds of statements.* With a statement such as this, the interrogator has challenged the suspect's self image and will likely receive a less than kind reply from him.

2. *I know several people who might think that statements like that would be childish. Letting people believe that someone is acting like a child never helps anyone feel good about them.* The interrogator is able to make the point without directly challenging the suspect, thus maintaining the level or rapport.

3. *I heard someone say ...* The interrogator can test a suspect's resistance to ideas and statements by quoting another person. The interrogator can see the suspect's response to these without becoming personally involved in making or believing the statement or idea. Recognizing the suspect's behavioral reply to these, the interrogator either discards them or expands on the idea presented. This is very much like a trial balloon used by politicians to gauge public support without taking a particular position on the issue.

8. **Addressing the Suspect's Hope or Hurdle** — Suspects at this point in the interrogation are struggling with fear of the future. They have a glimmer of hope remaining, "I hope if I say nothing I won't get arrested," or, "I won't be embarrassed," or, "I won't lose my job" or something similar. The interrogator speaks this hope aloud for the suspect and moves to address it. The interrogator, by voicing the suspect's unspoken concern, is able to address it and then both the interrogator and the suspect can push it out of the way. The interrogator, using the third person, handles this again so the suspect must

neither confirm nor deny its accuracy: "I know that many people think to themselves, 'If I don't say anything then I won't be embarrassed.'" The interrogator selects what he believes is the hurdle or fear that the suspect is struggling with and puts it on the table to be specifically handled. The hurdle might have been identified during an interview or from something said previously by the suspect. If the interrogator has no idea what the hurdle might be, he can ask the suspect, using the third person: "If someone were involved in an incident, what do you think would be their biggest concern that would keep them from telling the truth?" What the suspect says next is usually what they are concerned about.

Suspect: I guess not wanting everyone to know what happened.

Interrogator: Sure, and I think that is a valid concern, but what people don't realize is that investigators are looking to discover not only who did something, but also why it happened as well. When the investigation has identified the "who," it can be easy to understand the "why" if the person who did it chooses to say. However, if they do not want to talk about the reasons, the investigation does not just stop. The reasons have to be discovered from others who would never have been contacted otherwise. So what really happens is that more people become involved instead of just the few who had a need to know.

In the above example, the interrogator has now addressed the suspect's hope of no one finding out. The next step is to create an urgency to talk about the problem.

9. **Creating Urgency** — This step deals with the suspect's feeling of loss of control. Many people at this point in the interrogation feel like a victim. They perceive themselves as being powerless to control their destiny or influence the decision-making. This is again presented to the suspect in the third person so there is no loss of face with the interrogator. The interrogator again talks about the way most people feel at this point in the process. This statement almost always parallels the feelings of the suspect and the helplessness they feel. The purpose of using this statement at this time is to empower suspects and give them some hope for the future. Salesmen do this same thing with customers to create an urgency to decide to buy: "The rebates are over tomorrow," or "I can't guarantee this price after today." Each of these comments indirectly urges the buyer to make a decision now rather than waiting. The following is an example for the interrogator:
   • "Many people don't understand that they have a power to influence people and their feelings. If someone chooses to wait and then tries to explain what happened, people wonder how sincere that expla-

nation really is: is it really true? It's like having a series of keys to doors; behind each door are options, and the keys to make those options more or less likely to be used. The trouble with the keys is that they have to be given back soon, and then it is beyond the power of that person to influence the outcome. Think back to those two employees we talked about earlier. Which of the two used those keys? It would be easy to make up your mind about one, but the other really required soul searching because of his positive attitude. Once a person leaves, those keys have to come back."

The interrogator has told the suspect indirectly that the time has come to decide what he is going to do. Many people need a deadline to make a decision; otherwise they will procrastinate, never making up their mind. An interrogator might suggest withdrawing from the conversation with the suspect, which also creates urgency. The interrogator could also have someone knock on the door and say it is time for another project. The purpose of these tactics is the same: to create a sense of urgency to decide.

10. **Protecting the Evidence** — The time has now come for the interrogator to protect his evidence or lack thereof. This section might be used earlier in the interrogation if the suspect challenges the interrogator to produce evidence. If the interrogator were to refuse to produce the evidence, the suspect would assume that it does not exist. If interrogators were to provide the evidence, they would have told the suspect exactly what is known. Since neither avenue benefits interrogators' purpose, they must take another path that offers a benefit to the suspect for withholding the evidence from him or her. This puts the suspect in the awkward position of having to argue that the interrogator should do something that would harm him, a request the interrogator would rightly refuse. If the suspect has not brought up the presentation of evidence, then the interrogator will do so using again what most people think.

   • "Most people think, why don't they just tell me what they have to be done with it? The reason we don't tell people is not to try and trick them, but rather because we have a very difficult question to answer. That question is not, "Did this person do something?" That is why we do an investigation. Instead, it is to answer the most difficult question we are posed, "Is he shooting straight with me?" If we gave up the evidence, we would never know and couldn't be fair to the person. The reason we hold back information is so when we are asked, "Did he shoot straight with you?" we can say, "Yes." Then the question becomes, "How do you know?" We know because he told us what we already knew, so we can believe him when he said he was sorry and gave the explanation.

11. **Test for Submission** — The interrogator next tests to determine if the suspect is ready to confess. This test consists of a statement making it plain that everything talked about to this point applied to the suspect. The statement is personalized using the word "you" and the interrogator evaluates the individual's resulting behavior, either stopping a denial and returning to rationalization or proceeding to obtaining the admission using an assumptive question: "The problem is, we don't know what difficulties you faced in your life."

The statement is made slowly, giving the interrogator time to anticipate whether a denial or admission is going to be made by the suspect. Most often, if the suspect's behavior has been properly observed, the timing is right for an admission. The behavior associated with an admission could be a nod or dropping of the head, causing the interrogator to use an assumptive question along with a follow-up question to obtain the first admission of involvement.

Transition Phrases Between Rationalizations

Any number of phrases can be used to move between rationalizations and other components of showing understanding. The following are some common transitional phrases:

- Isn't it interesting …
- It is just like when …
- Most people think …
- There is another interesting thing …
- There are three things important to consider …
- Have you ever been …

Each of these can be used to link the rationalizations and examples together, making moving from one to the next a seamless logical progression.

Examples of Rationalizations

The following are examples of rationalizations, minimization, focusing on the future, and positive outlook. The interrogator must remember that the process of showing understanding to reduce the suspect's resistance might take some time. It might require that the interrogator talk for 15 to 30 minutes or longer, using rationalizations, personal stories, and other justification tools to reduce the suspect's resistance sufficiently to allow him to make an admission of guilt.

The use of rationalization can be difficult because it does not have a script and might require the interrogator to conduct a monologue for a few minutes to more than an hour. Once understood, a rationalization can be constructed out of any situation or object. To a large extent, rationalizations can be constructed as a contrast between two things. By using a contrast, it makes the rationalization easier for the suspect to follow the interrogator's point.

To begin to develop rationalizations, interrogators pick a topic and ask themselves what is interesting about the topic and how does it happen? What is interesting about a cup? List the positives about a cup, such as it holds liquid; the cup has a handle; the cup has a top; the cup keeps things hot and cold. Next, contrast the positives against a negative as in the following:

Positives versus Negatives

"The great thing about a cup is that it holds a liquid and has a top to keep the liquid hot or cold. We can tell there is liquid in the cup, but is it any good? That is the real question. The cup is made of plastic so we can't just look and tell, so we open it. We investigate to try to determine whether the liquid is good to drink. When we do an investigation, we do the same thing in a way. We know there is a liquid, but we are not sure if it is good or bad. The only way we can tell is to investigate and talk with the person and try to understand if he is a good person who made an error in judgment or someone who just doesn't care."

The interrogator in the above example used liquid in a cup to illustrate why there is a need to talk with people, contrasting the liquid and discovering its quality represented understanding someone who had made an error.

Job Pressures

"People do things they wouldn't ordinarily do for many reasons. Sometimes they might feel under tremendous pressure because of their jobs or because they have ambition and want to get ahead. They might want to look good at work and make a good impression. Sometimes things like this happen because of that.

Financial Pressure

"Sometimes people do things because of financial pressures. You know, it's awfully easy to get credit these days. Almost every day I get an offer for a credit card in the mail with a $5,000 line of credit to spend just like that. The next thing people know, their monthly payment on the credit card is way more than they can afford. It sure seems simple at first, but paying it back can be really difficult.

Minimization

"I think we all have made a mistake or an error in judgment at one time or another. Nobody is perfect. A lot of times, our mistakes seem a lot bigger than they probably are. Maybe a person had a time in high school when he asked this girl out for a date and she turned him down. It seemed like your whole life was ruined, but you got up the next day. It still hurt, but as time went on you put it behind you and went on with your life. There were other girls that you asked out, girls who accepted, fun times that you had, and your life went on. That was one small moment in your life. Years later it doesn't seem very significant."

Focusing on the Future

"You know, Bob, I think it's important that we all learn from the mistakes that we have made in our lives. It would be a terrible shame if we didn't. We would be doing the same things over again at 50, making the same mistakes we made in our teens. It's an important part of growing up, making mistakes. We should do it while we are young so we can learn from them so that later on we're not making those same errors. Look at the auto insurance industry. The rates are really high when we're young, and after we turn 25, they go down. Why? Because we are better drivers and we don't make the same errors we did when we were young. "

Positive Outlook

"Think about two kids playing baseball in the living room. One of them throws a ball and breaks a lamp. Now, you're the parent who is responsible and you ask them if they were playing baseball in the living room and broke the lamp. One of the kids says, 'Hey, we didn't do anything, it wasn't us.' You go to the other child and he says, 'I'm sorry. We were playing ball in here. I threw it. It bounced off the wall and broke the lamp.' He explained exactly how it happened and why. Which one are you going to feel better about? The one who said he was sorry and talked to you about it? Or the one who said he didn't do anything wrong when you know that he did. Doing something wrong doesn't make us a bad person, but when we do make a mistake, it's important to get it cleared up and go on with life."

Examples of Rationalizations with Choice Questions

The following are examples of rationalizations along with choice questions that logically work well with them. Interrogators often review at least the broad topics they will discuss before they meet the suspect. This section 8 helpful during the preinterrogation review.

Remember that the rationalizations presented to suspects do not have to be the real reasons they committed the crime, but rather an acceptable alternative that merely allows them to save face when they confess.

General

"Bill, frequently we find that the people we talk to are basically honest people who at some point in their lives find that events beyond their control caused them to do something that is out of character. Medical bills, family problems, and financial pressures are things that can push a person into doing something he never dreamed he could do. We all have our breaking points. Decisions have to be made about what to do with the evidence gathered during this investigation. It is very important to know as much about the person as possible before making any final decisions. Certainly, someone who has been under severe pressures and was forced into doing something is a much different person from someone who had ill intentions from the very beginning. It's very important that we understand your side of what happened, especially if a personal crisis was the motivation behind these mistakes. We know much of *what* happened from the investigation, but what we now must learn is equally important — *why* it happened."

Suggest Impulse

"I can see, if this was an impulsive decision and you didn't intend to ..."

This rationalization can also be effectively used in some homicides, batteries, or incidents where the injury or damage inflicted could be explained as an impulse. One difficulty in using this rationalization is that it removes the element of intent from the suspect's actions. If the rationalization is used, the interrogator must often confront the suspect again to establish the element of intent. In other circumstances, the facts of the case establish the intent. For example, the suspect agrees that he started the fire impulsively, not intentionally. The physical evidence indicates five points of origin and use of an accelerant to spread the fire. The suspect's intent can be inferred from the physical evidence developed by the investigation.

Choice Questions

"Did you plan on this happening or was it just an impulse?"

"Was it for no reason at all, or was it to show them where they went wrong?"

"Did you mean for this to happen, or did it just get out of hand?"

"If this just happened on the spur of the moment without your thinking about it …"

This rationalization can be used for theft or damage to property cases. It is also effective in cases where the suspect might reasonably have made an impulsive decision without thinking through the consequences. Even if a homicide was planned out by the suspect, an interrogator might use an "impulse" rationalization to reduce the seriousness of the crime. Most people view mistakes made under pressure very differently from a planned event. The suspect who impulsively decides to rob a store because of pressure is viewed differently from the individual who coldly calculates a robbery.

Choice Questions

"Did you plan this out, or did it happen on the spur of the moment?"

"Did you take the job here with the intention of doing this, or did it happen on the spur of the moment?"

"Had you planned on doing this all along or did you just suddenly decide without thinking it through?"

Blame Victim (Company or Supervisor)

"Bob, if this happened out of frustration because of the way your boss picked on you …"

This rationalization can be used for theft or damage to property. The victim can be blamed in almost any crime from a homicide to a sex crime to theft. The guilt is transferred to the victim by the interrogator, who portrays the suspect as a victim of circumstances. The suspect became involved because the victim dressed or acted a certain way, flaunted wealth, or made advances to the suspect. The interrogator can even blame a child victim of sexual abuse for appearing older and tempting the suspect. In the private sector, the company or supervisor can be blamed for lack of security or poor working conditions. However, the interrogator should be careful about placing blame on the company or supervisor because of personnel considerations and employee morale. In some cases, management might not understand the interrogator's efforts to shift blame from the suspect and be concerned that the interrogator was focusing on real inadequacies of the company or supervisor. On occasion, this shifting of blame can create problems with a management team who fails to understand the process.

Choice Questions

"Was this planned out or just done out of frustration?"

"Did you want to hurt the company or was it just to bring attention to the problems?"

"Did she come on to you or did you start this whole thing?"

Blame Poor Pay

"Cindy, I don't know how you can make it on just $7.00 per hour ..."

This rationalization can be used for theft, robbery, burglary, or embezzlement cases. The interrogator blames an insufficient income for causing the suspect to steal. Generally, the interrogator uses examples that show the high cost of living in today's economy. Discussing the price of eating out or just clothing children illustrates the impact of low pay. Personnel managers often dislike this rationalization because they consider that the pay rate is fair for the skill level and responsibility of the position.

Choice Questions

"Were you going to sell it for a profit, or was it just for yourself?"

"Did you use the money for a bad purpose like booze and drugs, or was it to pay bills?"

"Did you need the money for bills or was it just to party?"

Blame Fellow Worker or Friends

"I don't think this would have ever happened if everyone else wasn't doing it too ..."

This rationalization can be used in cases where someone else other than the suspect is involved in the same issue or when other people have done the same thing before. The idea for becoming involved in the incident is transferred to another person and the suspect was just following the pack. People usually view the one who had the idea as being more guilty than those who just followed along. An interrogator who transfers the idea to another helps minimize the seriousness of the suspect's participation in the crime.

Choice Questions

"Was this your idea, or someone else's?"

"Was this your idea or did you get involved only because others were doing it too?"

"Did he come to you or did you approach him to do this?"

Blame Poor Security

"I think the company's the one to blame since they didn't have good security in the first place ..."

This rationalization can be used in most types of cases. The interrogator expands on the idea that the victim, person, or company was tempting the suspect because they did not take the necessary precautions to safeguard their property. The victim's failure to safeguard his property was like asking to be ripped off.

This rationalization works well with the "blame victim" rationalization: "If they had lights and a decent set of locks, this certainly wouldn't have happened. What do they expect when it's so dark around the building?" Effectively, the suspect was put into a tempting situation that left him almost no choice in the matter. If the victim had been security conscious, the suspect would never have been tempted to get involved. A personal story could be about a mother who bakes a cake and leaves it on the counter only to have the family eat it while she is out. The cake was for a bake sale, but she didn't leave a note or hide it to protect it. She just left it on the counter to tempt her hungry family.

Choice Questions

"Did you go looking for the [item] or was it just lying around?"

"Did you think of doing this all along or was it only because security was so bad?"

"Was the door locked or did they leave it open?"

Blame the Economy (Politicians, Creditors)

"All you have to do is look at how the cost of everything keeps going up ..."

This rationalization can be used during any type of theft or economic gain case. This rationalization works well with the rationalization of low pay. The interrogator blames rising costs for the suspect's money not going as far as it used to. The economy can be blamed for the suspect's losing a job or being unable to find a job that pays wages decent enough to have kept him out of trouble. Consider articles about the rising costs of business and plant closings, which make wonderful examples for the interrogator to use. Relating the rate of inflation to pay raises the suspect has received shows the suspect in a very personal way how these changes affect his daily life.

Choice Questions

"Did you take the money for a bad reason or a good reason such as paying bills ...?"

"Were you paying for your family's needs or were you just going to party?"

"Did this happen because you were looking for trouble or because you couldn't find a job?"

Blame Peer Pressure

"If what happened is that your friends kept pressuring you to do this ..."

This rationalization can be used when others might also be involved. The interrogator shifts the blame for the idea to friends or family members who pushed the suspect into becoming involved. The interrogator can also refer to indirect pressure the suspect has felt, wanting to dress like friends and go to the same places they go. The pressure the suspect feels because of the need to belong to a group is often an acceptable rationalization for a suspect. This is especially true of younger suspects or individuals belonging to gangs. This rationalization works well on suspects from broken homes who have replaced family with their peers. The difficulty in using peers is the loyalty shown toward friends. This can often be overcome by not attempting to identify the friends until after the suspect has confessed. To attempt to have the suspect implicate others too early might result in an increased resistance to confessing.

Choice Questions

"Did you want to do this all along or was it because the others pushed you into it?"

"Did you go out and offer to do this, or did they just ask you?"

"Did you make money selling this, or was it just doing them a favor?" (*Private sector: very useful in cases involving discount abuse.*)

"Does this happen all the time, or just a few times?"

Exaggerate Loss, Frequency, or Seriousness

It appears the loss could be a lot more now.

This rationalization can be used for cash register shortages or inventory shrinkage. It is also a useful method to minimize the seriousness of the incident by exaggerating the frequency or size of the loss. This can be used effectively during the development phase to make the suspect's involvement less significant.

While interrogating a burglary suspect who had stolen loose gems and jewelry, the interrogator exaggerated the loss and blamed the homeowner for trying to get more out of the insurance company. The suspect denied the large loss, claiming to have stolen only a smaller amount during the burglary. This rationalization was used along with peer pressure to shift the blame to the accomplice and the homeowner.

Choice Questions

"Are you responsible for all the things [money or merchandise] missing or only a small part of it?"

"Are we talking dozens of times or just a few?"

"Could it have been $30,000 or $40,000 or a lot less?"

Propose Loss of Control

"I don't think you had any intention of this getting to the extent it did."

This rationalization can be used for thefts over a long period of time. It can also be used for crimes of violence, sexual harassment, or damage to property. The suspect "saves face" by admitting having something go too far even though he did not intend it to happen.

The interrogator portrays an innocent situation that gets out of hand and goes further than anticipated. In a beating, it could have started out as a simple fight that escalated into a homicide when the suspect struck the victim's head against the curb repeatedly. The use of this rationalization might require the interrogator to reinterrogate to establish the element of intent. Intent might make a significant difference in how a person is charged criminally. The suspect's lack of intent might even make it difficult to terminate the employee in the private sector.

Choice Questions

"Did you mean to cause those injuries or just didn't know your own strength?"

"Did you think it was going to be this much, or did it just get out of hand?" (*Theft or damage*)

"Did you know it had gotten this bad or did it just get out of hand?"

"Did you mean for it to go this far or did it just happen too fast?"

Blame the Use of Alcohol/Drugs

"I think it was the drugs that caused you to do things that you normally wouldn't do."

"All you have to do is look around and see that most people try."

These rationalizations can be used for thefts, accidents, damage to property, rape, child abuse, and homicide when it is known that the suspect has a problem with drugs or alcohol. Other crimes can also be attributed to the use of drugs or alcohol. The interrogator can discuss how addictive even cigarettes can become, and how people are almost driven to fulfill this need. This rationalization might create some difficulties in the private sector, where management might wrestle with the issue of rehabilitating the employee through drug- or alcohol-treatment programs. This issue might also raise questions in the private sector about termination, because drugs and alcohol in some cases fall under state or federal disability acts that preclude discriminations because of a disability like drug or alcohol dependency.

Choice Questions

"Can I tell them that you will stop taking the drugs or alcohol?"

"Did you realize what you were doing or was it only after it happened?

"Did you use the drug during working hours, or was it only on breaks?"

"Was it to get high, or just to relax?

"Were the pills for yourself, or were you going to sell them at work?"

Emphasize Borrowing

"If you planned on paying the money back all along ..."

This rationalization can be used for theft of money or some types of property. The interrogator minimizes the loss by focusing the suspect's attention on "loan" rather than on theft. Although the loan was unauthorized, suspects are allowed to save face by agreeing that they had intended to return the money or property. The intent to deprive permanently can be established by the frequency of the "unauthorized loans" and the failure of the suspect to have repaid them. Intent can also be established by the amount of time elapsed between the taking of the money and the confrontation with the suspect. It is difficult for suspects to convince anyone they intended to repay the money when they concealed the "loan" and a significant period of time elapsed before its discovery. However, suspects often take comfort in the rationalization that they intended to repay the money. Many embezzlers start with borrowing and actually repay some of the money at first, but gradually these repayments fall further and further behind, then cease all together.

Choice Questions

"Were you going to keep the money all along, or were you going to pay it back?"

"Were you going to keep that item or did you just want to borrow it so you could have some time to see if you wanted to buy it?"

Play One Against the Other

"I would rather see you get your side of the story in first, before …"

This strategy and rationalization can be used when it is known or believed that two or more suspects are involved in the issue under investigation. The interrogation is often easier when multiple suspects are involved. When only one is involved, the suspect is totally aware of his position and can accurately assess exposure. When multiple suspects are involved, a suspect can only guess what the others have said that might incriminate him. Generally, these types of cases are easier for interrogators to resolve because they can drive a wedge between the suspect and co-conspirators, obtaining a confession from one, with others falling like dominos.

In one interrogation, two cousins were confronted about the theft of merchandise from a jewelry store. Finally, one of the women admitted stealing two Timex watches worth about $60. The second suspect continued to deny any involvement. The interrogator of the first woman entered the second interrogation room and told the second suspect that her cousin was getting the matter cleared up and that she needed to cooperate. He also told her that her cousin had told him about the watches. She responded, "That bitch, I can't believe she told you about the Rolexes!" What followed was an admission to the theft of two diamond Presidential Rolex watches with a combined value of over $25,000.

It is not uncommon for a suspect to reach an incorrect conclusion and think the worst has happened. In presenting the evidence to the suspect, the interrogator should be specific enough to have the desired impact, but, as in the previous case, vague enough to let the suspect make the mistake.

Choice Questions

"Was it your idea or someone else's?"

"Did you realize he was going to do this all along or did you think he was kidding?"

Identify the Hurdle

On occasion, during the latter stages of the interrogation, a suspect might become submissive but still be reluctant to confess. There seems to be a stumbling block holding the suspect back from a confession. The interrogator should ask the suspect what he is afraid of or concerned about. The interrogator could also say, "Let me ask you a hypothetical question. If you did do something like this, what would be your biggest concerns?" The suspect will not answer and will simply sit silently. The interrogator should present a hypothetical situation to the suspect, then ask the suspect to speculate on what great fear might be keeping the individual in the story from telling the truth about the incident.

Once the suspect has pointed at a particular hurdle, the interrogator should restate the hurdle and announce that he believes that is the suspect's greatest fear as well. The interrogator then begins to overcome the hurdle by again showing understanding and refocusing the suspect on the future or past.

> *Interrogator:* Let's say another person was in the same situation you are. What do you think would be his biggest concern about telling the truth? Don't tell me you did anything, but just your best guess why this person wouldn't want to talk about what he did.
>
> *Suspect:* He'd be afraid of friends finding out.
>
> *Interrogator:* Afraid of people finding out; I'm sure that's what you're concerned about too. These are the kinds of things that we want to handle as quietly as possible. No one is here to embarrass anyone unnecessarily.

By specifically confronting the suspect's fear, the interrogator works to reduce the hurdle in his mind. A suspect who fears termination can often be convinced to confess by discussing if the company could terminate him even without a confession. Once the suspect realizes that his hope of maintaining his job is gone, even if he continues to deny involvement, he will often confess it.

Correcting the Rationalizations

Interrogators should consider what problems their choice of rationalization might cause the case. As pointed out earlier, certain rationalizations might remove the intent necessary to prove a violation of the law or a policy. If an interrogator elects to use the rationalization, it might be necessary to correct it after the first admission. After the first admission, when the suspect is much less resistant to a confession, he usually will go the next step to correct the intent.

Sometimes, the introduction of a second interrogator, who expands the admission and corrects the intent issue, is helpful. This second interrogator is not bound by the previous rationalizations, nor is the suspect embarrassed to change his story because he has not lied to the new interrogator. A factual presentation of evidence that establishes the suspect's intent is often all that is necessary to obtain his additional admission. Factual evidence becomes even stronger as the suspect's resistance to a confession weakens. Even circumstantial evidence can become more damaging in the suspect's mind as he weakens emotionally.

An interrogator's failure to correct a rationalization that removes intent can result in difficulty terminating an employee or establishing probable cause for the suspect's arrest. Knowing what is necessary to prove the crime enables interrogators to recognize deficiencies in an admission before they obtain the written statement.

Denials

11

No matter to what extent the interrogator attempts to avoid denials, he will on occasion still have to face them.

Chapter 6 discussed the causes of denials and strategies to avoid offering a suspect the opportunity to deny. Unfortunately, no matter how much the interrogator attempts to avoid causing denials, they cannot always be avoided. The more difficult suspects especially will attempt to deny so that they can defend their position of noninvolvement. Very strong-willed suspects will, on occasion, simply make a blanket denial, telling the interrogator they have never done anything. Typically, such suspects are not going to allow the interrogator an opportunity to use an introductory statement or participatory accusation, but rather make a blanket denial as their opening gambit.

Most suspects will be polite and wait for an opportunity to enter the conversation and make a denial. Since the interrogator is doing all the talking, this should limit the suspect's ability to enter into the conversation. Avoiding long pauses or silences can also assist in deterring denials. Silence during rationalizations invites the suspect to enter the conversation and make a denial.

Types of Denials

There are two unique styles of denials. Although in both denials suspects refuse to acknowledge involvement, the denials occur in different places. The methods used to handle them are dramatically different.

Emphatic Denial — Any response from a suspect that refuses to acknowledge the truthfulness of the accusation is an emphatic denial.

"I didn't do it."
"You're wrong. It wasn't me."

Explanatory Denials — Any response from a suspect that offers an excuse or a reason why he could not or would not be involved in the incident is an explanatory denial.

"My mom and dad didn't raise me that way."

"My father's a policeman."

When Denials Occur

Denials occur at a number of points during an interrogation. The primary difference between the handling of denials in an interview and in an interrogation is that, during the interview, the interviewer allows the suspect, victim, or witness to voice the denial. During an interrogation, the interrogator will attempt to control the conversation to avoid the suspect's making a denial.

In an interrogation, the first place interrogators are likely to encounter a denial is after the accusation. In rare instances, interrogators might encounter denials by a dominant suspect even before they make any formalized accusation. In general, the suspect who is going to deny involvement will do so in response to the direct accusation of an interrogator. Those suspects who are offered an accusation before their resistance has been reduced to a level permitting an admission will also make a denial.

The second place that interrogators can expect denials is during rationalizations. Typically, interrogators find that suspects will attempt to interrupt the rationalizations with denials and protestations of their innocence. In general, denials tend to diminish the longer interrogators rationalize the guilty suspect's involvement. In the early stages of rationalizations, while suspects are physically and emotionally strong, they will offer more and more denials to protect their position. If interrogators are offering rationalizations that do not meet the needs of the suspect, they expect that denials will surface more and more frequently. As suspects weaken and have less resistance to making an admission, the number of denials tends to decrease.

The third place at which denials can surface is at the presentation of the choice question. The interrogator offers an acceptable versus unacceptable choice such as, "Did you use the money for bills or for drugs?" The suspect's response is, "I didn't use it for either," is a denial. The denial surfaces because the suspect's resistance to a confession was still too high. The presentation of the choice question was asked before the suspect was in a submissive frame of mind and all his denials had stopped. The interrogator who elects to use the choice question to test the suspect's susceptibility to making an admission should expect that it will encourage an emphatic denial if the suspect is not ready to confess.

Finally, denials occur during development of the admission. Denials that occur then might be truthful or untruthful. For example, a suspect admits to the theft of merchandise from his employer, but denies the theft of money because he did not do that. The copycat killer might make an admission to some crimes but deny others because he had no involvement in them. During the development of the admission phase of the interrogation, the interrogator needs to be especially conscious of evaluating denials for their truthfulness.

Emphatic Denials

Emphatic denials by a suspect are essentially a defensive posture with which he hopes to hold the interrogator at bay. In the early stages of interrogations, suspects will typically use the emphatic denial to defend themselves. To use the metaphor of a gladiator fighting another gladiator, the emphatic denials are the shield and the explanatory denial is the gladiator's sword. At first, the suspect merely uses his shield to deflect the rationalizations offered by the interrogator, only later resorting to the sword.

Suspect's Behavior

The suspect makes emphatic denials in two ways, physically and verbally. Interrogators can anticipate a denial by recognizing the verbal and physical behavior associated with it. By anticipating the emphatic denial, an interrogator can often control it or even stop it from even being verbalized.

Physical Behavior. The suspect about to make an emphatic denial will physically manifest a number of behaviors that will be observable to the interrogator. The most prominent behavior observed will be the suspect's shaking the head "no." This indication or "emblem" of the word "no" is learned behavior and almost always precedes a denial. The suspect might not make a full movement of the head from side to side, but rather make only a partial movement. This partial emblem will be an abrupt quick shake of the head to one side before the head moves slightly towards the interrogator as the suspect speaks the denial. Shaking the head "no," shows the suspect's disagreement with what is being alleged by the interrogator.

Other facial characteristics can also be noted in conjunction with shaking the head "no." Because the suspect is disagreeing with the interrogator, typically the brows will pinch down and together in a frown. The muscles around the mouth will begin to tighten to form the initial words the suspect will speak. As the mouth tightens, the interrogator can often hear an intake of breath that prepares the suspect to speak as soon as an opening in the interrogator's monologue occurs. Finally, although eye contact might break momentarily while the suspect makes the denial, generally his eyes will make contact with the interrogator's eyes as the denial is spoken. In the later stages of the interrogation, the eye contact might not be present as the suspect's resistance to confessing weakens. Just before suspects enter submission, they might not make any eye contact with the interrogator.

Five identifiable behaviors allow the interrogator to anticipate an emphatic denial:

- Shaking the head "no," either a full or partial movement
- Tightening the mouth
- Taking a breath
- Frowning the brows
- Making eye contact

The first three behaviors will be present every time a subject attempts a denial. Watching from just below the nose to the top of the chest will allow the interrogator to see the shake of the head, tightening of the mouth, and taking a breath. When asking an assumptive question when a denial is possible, interrogators should focus their eyes between the suspect's nose to upper chest looking for denial behavior.

Verbal Behavior. Suspects might also give a verbal clue that they are about to make an emphatic denial, which is generally spontaneously delivered in response to a statement with which the suspect does not agree, or to a pause in the conversation. To make an emphatic denial, the suspect might also attempt to interrupt the interrogator while he is offering rationalizations . These interruptions to deny are often preceded with permission-asking phrases. A suspect who attempts to interrupt by saying, "but," "can I," "may I," "please, sir," will generally conclude these phrases with, "I didn't do it." An interrogator who hears this type of verbal clue should anticipate an emphatic denial and react accordingly.

Handling Emphatic Denials

The primary concern of an interrogator handling the emphatic denials of the guilty is to avoid a "did too–did not" exchange with the suspect. This is the kind of argument we had as children that was generally never resolved. Unfortunately for the interrogator, an interrogation that deteriorates into a "did too–did not" exchange is a stalemate. In interrogation, stalemates are won by the guilty.

The second important consideration in handling emphatic denials is to recognize that an emphatic denial is significantly different from the explanatory denial. The interrogator not only handles each differently, but recognizes that an explanatory denial means he is making progress with the suspect.

The interrogator can use a number of conversational techniques to control a suspect's emphatic denials.

Use the Suspect's First Name

The use of the suspect's first name is an effective means of stopping an emphatic denial. When people hear their names, they immediately stop what they were about to do or say and pay attention to the speaker. As we grew, when people called our name, we realized that we were doing something inappropriate or that somebody needed us. This learned behavior causes most people at least to pause in their attempt to join the conversation. Interrogators can use a suspect's first name at several points during the interrogation to gain the suspect's attention or momentarily cause him to stop what he is doing.

Discuss Important Areas

In any interrogation, the suspect is torn by a desire to leave and a desire to stay and resolve the issue. On the one hand, the suspect is denying involvement, but on the other hand, the suspect stays because he is curious to see what information the investigation has revealed about him.

The suspect's desire to know the amount of information that has been developed can be used by an interrogator to get the suspect to be quiet and listen. The interrogator tells the suspect that the information he is going to present is important because the suspect is going to have to make an important decision. The suspect generally interprets this statement to mean that the interrogator will be discussing specific evidence that proves the suspect's involvement. The interrogator, however, has no intention whatsoever of discussing specifics but rather returns to providing rationalizations. The suspect, however, pauses to hear the expected evidence so he can make up a story to explain it away. As the suspect waits for the evidence to be presented, the rationalizations begin to reduce resistance to confessing.

Tell the Suspect that He Will Have a Chance to Talk

Especially in the early stages of the interrogation, a suspect might continually interrupt the interrogator with denials. Telling suspects that they will have a chance to talk as soon as the interrogator is finished often appeases them so that they will do the socially acceptable thing and maintain silence while the interrogator talks. That silence allows the rationalizations to chip away the suspect's resistance. Even momentary silence by the suspect allows the interrogator to show understanding and establish a rapport that moves a suspect closer to submission. More dominant suspects will continually interrupt, attempting to talk over the interrogator.

If the interrogator is unable to get suspects to wait, it is sometimes effective to offer them an opportunity to speak. The interrogator tells them to go ahead and say what they have to say. The suspect usually says, "Well, I didn't do it." The interrogator then asks if there is anything else he would like to say. The suspect generally will respond, "Just that I didn't do it." The interrogator should acknowledge the suspect's position and immediately take control of the conversation and begin rationalizations again.

Suspects who continually want an opportunity to speak rarely have much to say beyond an emphatic denial. "I didn't do it." They have no prepared presentation other than to discuss specific evidence. Since the interrogator has avoided presenting specific information, the suspect is at a loss for words and the interrogator can again take control of the conversation. However, if the interrogator has presented evidence too early, suspects will have much to say on the subject as they begin to make explanations and excuses for the incriminating evidence.

Advise the Suspect that it is Better to Say Nothing than to Lie

One of the more effective techniques in stopping emphatic denials of the guilty is to tell them that it is better to say nothing at all than to lie about the incident. The interrogator relates that, "To have the investigation be able to show that they lied only makes things look worse for them." The interrogator should tell suspects that it enhances their position to say nothing rather than to make unnecessary denials. Denials that do not match the investigative results will make people question their sincerity. Surprisingly, many suspects will discontinue all denials in response to this interrogation tactic.

Interrupt the Suspect and State the Denial for Him

Another effective method of handling the denial is to cut off the suspect's verbal denial, and then state it for him. The interrogator might say, "Bob, just a minute. You're probably thinking 'I should say I didn't do it.' That is often the first reaction we have in a situation like this. The problem is that saying 'I didn't do it,' doesn't mesh with the investigation and only makes people wonder." The interrogator has kept control of the dialogue and expressed understanding about the suspect's motivation to deny. This establishes rapport but does not cause suspects to feel they have to protect a position because they did not actually say, "I didn't do it."

Create Curiosity

The interrogator can also sometimes control denials by creating curiosity. Once the suspect attempts to break into the conversation with a denial, the interrogator interrupts as he would to control any denial but instead offers a statement designed to create curiosity: "Bob, just a minute, I think there are three things that you need to consider. The first is ..." This type of statement causes a suspect to delay and listen to the interrogator. Many times he will not interrupt for a number of minutes, waiting to get all the information promised by the interrogator.

Turn an Emphatic into an Explanatory Denial

When an individual continues to offer emphatic denials, one possible cause is that the rationalizations presented to him are incorrect; they are not effective in letting him save face and minimize the seriousness of the incident. One way to manage the continuing denials is to identify the correct rationalization by turning the emphatic denial into an explanatory denial and letting the suspect identify a face saving rationalization.

Suspect: I didn't do it.

Interrogator: Well, Bob why wouldn't you do it?

Suspect: Well ... I ... wasn't raised that way.

Interrogator: Exactly, that's what I thought all along!

The interrogator now has encouraged the suspect to give a reason that he could not or would not have been involved in the incident. The interrogator handles this just like an explanatory denial, agreeing with the statement and turning it into another reason to confess.

Use Behavior to Control the Interrogation

Interrogators can also, to a certain extent, control the suspect's emphatic denials through their own verbal and physical behavior. They can use gestures, commonly observed emblems, and conversational reactions to tell the suspect that they do not want the suspect to speak. For example, upon observing the suspect's attempt to deny, the interrogator uses the emblem "stop," (raising the hand, palm out), to tell the suspect he is not permitted to speak. In conjunction with this, the interrogator turns his head and breaks eye contact, looking away and telling the suspect indirectly, "I don't want to hear this" (see Figure 11.1). However, these two gestures in the early stages of the interrogation are insufficient by themselves to stop the denial. The interrogator must use his behavior in

Figure 11.1 To stop a denial, the interrogator turns his head and uses the stop gesture or "emblem."

conjunction with the preceding tactics to help stop the suspect's denial. For example,

> *Suspect*: But … (shaking head) … no.
>
> *Interrogator*: Bob, just a minute. There are some important things that we need to discuss. (Hands up in "stop" gesture turning head away.) The important thing here that I think you need to understand is that… (returns to rationalization)

As the suspect's resistance to a confession lessens, he becomes less aggressive and the interrogator can control any emphatic denials simply with the emblem of "stop" and turning the head (see Figure 11.1).

The interrogator should also use the conversational tactic of talking faster and increasing volume slightly. This tactic is the same one individuals use during conversations when they are interrupted. They tend to speak just a little bit faster and a little bit louder to talk over the person attempting to interrupt. In the same way, the interrogator talks over the suspect who attempts to interrupt with an emphatic denial.

Change the Psychology of the Room

With especially difficult suspects, as the interrogation approaches 45 minutes and there still has been no significant headway, it might be necessary to change the psychology of the room. This is done by the interrogator's physically changing positions. Up to now, the interrogator has been seated across from the suspect with several feet of space separating them. The interrogator, recognizing that the suspect has significant resistance to confessing, might want to challenge his resolve.

Several means can be used to change the psychology of the room. The first is for the interrogator to stand, as if he is going to leave. As the interrogator stands, he expresses exasperation with the suspect's inability to cooperate and tell the truth. The interrogator might say something like, "Bob, I just can't believe that we can't get this straightened out. You act like you don't care and I just don't believe that." The movement by the interrogator is not meant in any way to be physically intimidating to the suspect. Rather, it is designed to challenge suspects who believe they can outlast a persistent interrogator. The movement of the interrogator often will result in a change of posture by the suspect. The interrogator, while rising, continues to talk to the suspect, but does not raise his voice, while allowing exasperation to creep into his tone. The interrogator should challenge the suspect by saying,

> "You know, Bob, I'm not here to aggravate you, I'm just here to get this thing straightened out. If you don't care, then that's fine. The investigation has already resolved the issue. The only reason for talking to you is to get your input and your side of the story. If you don't care, then that's fine. The investigation can be handled without your participation."

The interrogator then expresses his belief that this is not what the suspect really wants. The interrogator tells the suspect that he is sure the suspect does want it to get straightened out. Then the interrogator returns to his seat across from the suspect and continues the process of rationalization. When the interrogator initially stands and then reseats himself, the suspect often changes positions in the chair. This shift of position is the result of the interrogator's movement in the behavioral zones of the suspect. Often this postural shift by the suspect will move him into a less defensive position that makes the rationalizations more effective. The interrogation should be conducted while seated.

Unnecessary standing or movements during the interrogation can disrupt its smooth flow.

In certain instances, the more difficult suspect might not change posture and continue to defy the interrogator. The interrogator, who is now standing, tells the suspect that the meeting is over and that they are going to leave. As the interrogator does so, he continues to express disbelief in the suspect's lack of cooperation. Once the interrogator has gotten the suspect to stand, the interrogator returns to the process of rationalizations. After a moment or two, the interrogator suggests that the suspect sit down because there are "a couple of other things" to discuss with him. Once seated, the interrogator immediately returns to rationalizations.

The benefit of getting the suspect up and moving around is that he may return to his chair in a different posture, one in whichhe is more receptive to the interrogator's rationalizations. This tactic is used only in those circumstances when the suspect is not responding to the emotional appeal after 45 or more minutes. Having the interrogator or suspect move around when the emotional appeal is reducing the suspect's resistance often has the effect of increasing the suspect's resistance.

The final way to change the psychology of the room is to exchange roles with the suspect. An interrogator who is making little or no headway with a suspect might change roles and give him the opportunity to interrogate the interrogator. For example, the interrogator places a pen in his pocket and asks the suspect to ask if he (the interrogater) has a pen in his pocket. When the suspect does so, the interrogator denies that the pen is there. Most suspects will challenge the interrogator, saying that the pen is, indeed, there. The interrogator again denies the pen's existence.

This exchange goes on for a moment or two until the interrogator removes the pen from the pocket. The interrogator then asks the suspect if he believed that the pen was not in the pocket just because the interrogator said it was not there. The suspect will respond that he did not believe the interrogator. The interrogator should then say,

> "Exactly — you and I both knew the pen was there. We could see it. It's the same with this investigation. The investigation is very clear. Simply saying that you didn't do something is not sufficient to convince anyone. The problem that we face with the investigation is that it doesn't tell the *reason* ..."

The interrogator can then immediately return to the process of rationalization.

Use an Enticement Question to Stop a Suspect's Denial

Under certain circumstances, an interrogator might use an enticement question to break the cycle of denials. The enticement question, discussed in Chapter 7, is a question that presents either real or fictitious evidence that causes the suspect to change, or consider changing, his story. In Chapter 6, the question was used during an interview and the suspect was allowed to respond, either by changing the alibi or by pausing to consider changing his story. The question is used differently, however, when an interrogator is attempting to handle a suspect's emphatic denial.

The interrogator still implies that he has evidence by using the introductory phrase, "Is there any reason..." but does not pause for the suspect to respond at the end of the question. Instead, the interrogator immediately stops any response from the suspect:

> *Suspect*: But, I didn't take it (*weakly said*).
>
> *Interrogator*: Pat, is there any reason that you can think of that ... [interrogator selects one enticement that best fits the case facts: (1) there is a videotape of you taking the money? (2) that your fingerprints were found in the safe? (3) that you were observed taking the deposit?] Wait a minute before you answer that. That wasn't fair and I shouldn't have said anything. But you know its better to say nothing than to deny and have the investigation show the opposite. I think the greatest concern is not that this happened, but why ... [interrogator returns to rationalization].

Using an enticement to stop a denial generally works best when the suspect is only weakly denying involvement. Sometimes, an interrogator who uses an introductory statement will find that the suspect will make a tentative, weak denial to the soft accusation. A partial enticement question can often stop the denials from continuing past the first one. This type of question can be used only once to stop a suspect's denials. Its repeated use dilutes the enticement impact and might even cause a suspect to question whether the information exists. The interrogator, in stopping the suspect's response and immediately returning to rationalizations, does not allow the suspect time to evaluate the question fully. This can make the suspect believe the evidence actually exists.

Regardless of which method interrogators use to control the suspect's denial, it is imperative that they immediately return to the process of rationalization. The rationalization is the driving force that reduces the suspect's resistance to confessing and the interrogator returns to it as soon as he has regained control of the conversation. Especially in the early stages of the interrogation, the interrogator must be prepared to handle the emphatic denials of the guilty. The interrogator's hands are generally out in front so that all he has to do upon seeing any of the behavioral clues of a denial is to raise them to a stop position (see Figure 11.2).

Figure 11.2 The interrogator (facing) uses her hands to gesture and also to control the suspect's attempt to deny.

Truthful Emphatic Denials

The interrogator should always be alert for truthful suspects who have been identified inadvertently as guilty by the investigation. This generally occurs in investigations that develop only circumstantial evidence.

Truthful denials are spontaneous and direct. The suspect has good eye contact and gets progressively stronger as time goes on. The truthful suspect continually interrupts the rationalizations with protestations of innocence, and denials sound spontaneous and genuine. As a general rule, truthful suspects stay to convince the interrogator of their innocence and do not walk out. The guilty might deny, but they often leave before they have convinced the interrogator of their innocence. By contrast, their eye contact is tentative and gestures are overdone and dramatic. Finally, the positioning of the suspect's body when making a denial can be an indicator of his truthfulness. The truthful suspect sits straight in he chair, leaning forward aggressively, defending his position. The guilty suspect who is making a denial slumps, with the trunk of the body back in the chair, using the legs as a barrier to keep the interrogator away.

Once interrogators recognize that the suspect might be truthful, they should change the direction of the interrogation. They might discuss specific evidence against the suspect or interrogate him on a secondary issue. For example, if a suspect were to be suspected of stealing money from a register, the interrogator might begin an interrogation about the theft of merchandise from the company. Similarly, if the suspect were to be suspected of a robbery and the denials appeared to be truthful, the interrogator might go to a secondary issue of involvement in thefts or burglaries in the same area as the robbery occurred.

The interrogator should remember that the suspect's behavior during the interview initially was indicative of deception. Although this is not always a guarantee of the suspect's involvement, there generally is a reason that the suspect appeared deceptive. It is possible that the suspect is not guilty of the main incident but of involvement in a secondary issue, and that involvement created the deceptive behavior. Generally, when suspects are confronted on a secondary issue of which they are guilty, the denials will be less emphatic and delivered from a more reserved, submissive posture. An interrogator, comparing the denials to the main issue and secondary issues, often sees and hears a dramatic contrast. This contrast in the strength of denials leads the interrogator in the correct direction and can be helpful in convincing the interrogator of the suspect's truthfulness in the main issue.

Explanatory Denials

An explanatory denial is the first offensive stroke by the suspect. It is the gladiator's sword, as the emphatic denial was the shield. In general, the explanatory denial is most likely to be a truthful statement that is made by the guilty suspect. The suspect is attempting to sidetrack the interrogator by having the interrogator challenge what is often a true statement. The explanatory denial, "I wouldn't do that because my father is a policeman," when challenged by the interrogator might bring a response such as, "Well, go ahead and call the Barrington Police Department and ask them. You'll find my father is working right now."

Although the suspect's statement is supposed to sidetrack the interrogator and show his truthfulness, it is also telling the interrogator a direction to proceed with his rationalizations. The suspect, on the one hand, has been repeatedly denying involvement, while, on the other, attempting to think of reasons or excuses that would show the interrogator why he would not be involved. The interrogator, recognizing that the introductory phase for the explanatory denial is different from the emphatic denial, asks for an explanation.

The explanatory denial is often preceded by introductory phrases that cry out for the interrogator to ask for an explanation. For example, if the suspect were to say, "I wouldn't do that. It's impossible. It couldn't have been me," the interrogator could respond, "Well, why is that Bob?" The suspect might then make any of a number of explanatory denials:

- The security is too good here.
- I wouldn't want to jeopardize my job.
- I don't want to go to jail.
- I don't need the money.
- I'm a born-again Christian.
- I love my wife.
- I'd never hurt a fly.

The interrogator accepts the explanatory denial as a true statement and turns it around as another reason for the suspect to confess. The interrogator expresses excitement that the suspect has joined him in resolving the problem and responds with something similar to one of the following statements:

- I hope that is true.
- I was hoping that you'd say that!
- I'm glad you mentioned that!
- Exactly, that's great!
- Good, that's one more reason to get this cleared up!

The interrogator delivers the preceding statements with excitement. This excitement and the statement itself have a number of functions. First, they allow the interrogator once again to dominate the conversation; the interrogator has invited the suspect to give an explanatory denial in a sentence or two but does not want the suspect to continue talking. By being excited, the interrogator can talk over the suspect's statement and, again, take control of the conversation. Second, by being excited about what the suspect has said, the interrogator discourages the suspect from bringing it up again. The suspect is reluctant to return to this statement because it was received so positively by the interrogator. Instead of being the knockout blow the suspect had intended, it was turned against him. Finally, the statements of excitement by the interrogator afford him an opportunity to think about what to say next in response to the suspect's explanatory denial.

The following is an example of how to handle the explanatory denial:

> *Interrogator*: Sometimes these things happen because we feel that we are not being treated fairly. We do the best we can, but it is recognized instead...
>
> *Suspect*: I wouldn't do that.
>
> *Interrogator*: Why is that, Bob?
>
> *Suspect*: I don't need the money. I've got plenty of money in the bank.
>
> *Interrogator*: I'm sure that's true. I don't doubt for a second that you've got money in the bank. That tells me a lot about you as an individual. It says that this wasn't something that was plotted out over a long time but rather was probably done on the spur of the moment. A response to a pressure that I'm not even aware of. You know, I think there are several things that we should consider...

The interrogator begins a new rationalization, playing off the fact that the suspect has money in the bank. The suspect has told the interrogator that the reason he did it was not economic. The interrogator now uses rationalizations that would justify the suspect's behavior on the basis of something other than an economic reason.

Although an explanatory denial is generally a true statement, and typically interrogators accept it and turn it to their benefit, such a turn is not done if the suspect attacks the interrogator racially or sexually. A suspect who says, "You're only saying this to me because I'm [Black, Puerto Rican, Oriental, Native American, etc.] ..." should be confronted immediately by the interrogator. The interrogator should handle these types of statements by saying,

> "I can understand how you might think that, but that is the reason we do an investigation. An investigation doesn't have anything to do with whether a person is black or white. It deals only with the facts, and the facts of this case are irrefutable. An investigation doesn't care about the race or the sex of an individual; it deals only with facts. In the past, I'm sure there have been abuses at one time or another, but that's the reason that we're required to conduct an investigation that is both thorough and extensive, to develop these facts so there can't

be any abuses of power. You know, I think that the one thing that is important that you understand here is this ..." (interrogator returns to rationalizations)."

If the interrogator fails to handle an explanatory denial, the suspect will immediately believe that the interrogator could not refute the statement. Suspects who recognize that the interrogator could not refute their statement will immediately press their advantage by repeating the explanatory denial again. If the interrogator still does not handle the explanatory denial, suspects will become more forceful in stating their position: "But I've already told you, I've got plenty of money in the bank. I don't need it." If the interrogator still doesn't refute or address the explanatory denial, suspects will recognize that the interrogator cannot overcome this statement and will focus their defense in this area to counter any claims made by the interrogator.

If the interrogator attempts to take exception to the suspect's explanatory denial, the suspect can prove the position or at least sidetrack the interrogator:

> *Suspect*: But I love my wife.
>
> *Interrogator*: That's not true. You didn't love your wife.
>
> *Suspect*: Of course I did. Just the other day I bought her flowers. You don't buy flowers for somebody you don't love.

The suspect has now sidetracked the interrogator into a position where the interrogator can be defeated because the suspect can now talk about degrees of love and the instances where he showed it.

In handling the denials, interrogators should recognize the differences between an emphatic and explanatory denial. They should also recognize the differences in handling these two types of denials. On the one hand, the emphatic denial is stopped, preferably before it is ever spoken by the suspect. However, to handle the explanatory denial, the interrogator asks for an explanation and turns the explanation around after accepting it as another reason for the suspect to confess.

Part Five

Obtaining the Admission

Obtaining the Admission 12

If the interrogator has sufficiently reduced the immediacy of the consequences in the suspect's mind, the suspect will be prepared to make an admission of guilt.

During any interrogation, the most difficult point for the interrogator to ascertain is when the suspect is ready to confess. The behavior of suspects can often give subtle clues to their susceptibility to making an admission. However, the interrogator observing these clues still might not know exactly when to ask for the admission.

It is at this point that interrogators will attempt to bring the suspect into the conversation with an admission of guilt. The suspect has emotionally accepted the fact that he has been caught and has worked through the risk–benefits scale, realizing that he must face the consequences. The interrogator has offered rationalizations that allow him to save face and has focused his attention on the future, rather than on the consequences at hand.

Mind-set of the Suspect in Submission

As the rationalizations begin to have their effect and the suspect begins to accept his fate, he begins to withdraw emotionally, becoming quiet and withdrawn. All denials stop. As suspects enter the submissive phase of the interrogation, they reach the lowest ebb psychologically that they will reach during the course of the interrogation. In this phase of the interrogation, their eyes might begin to tear up or they might even cry as they wrestle with the realization that they have been caught and must face the consequences. They still, however, are searching for a way out that will allow them to save face or reduce the consequences.

In this phase of the interrogation, suspects are unable to give narrative responses to questions. An interrogator who asks the suspect to answer open-ended questions such as "Why did you do it?" will be answered with only silence as the suspect grapples with a response. On the other hand, the suspect might clearly have in mind the actual reason he did become involved but is also weighing accepting the face-saving devices of the rationalizations offered by the interrogator. At this phase, the interrogator's questions should require only one-word responses.

Behavior of the Suspect in Submission

The behavioral keys of submission in a suspect are recognizable. As the suspect withdraws emotionally, eye contact reduces to almost zero. For most suspects, the head drops down, they look toward the left knee, and begin to have an internal conversation with themselves, discussing the pros and cons of confessing. As they do this, the trunk of the body often tilts forward and the shoulders slump as the tension drains out of the muscles. The interrogator might notice the suspect's eyes begin to moisten and tear. A few suspects might cry at this point. The suspect looks much like an athlete who has just lost the biggest game of his life, slumped over, head down, teary eyed, and defeated (see Figure 12.1).

Shortening and Repeating Rationalizations

When interrogators recognize the submissive behavior of the suspect, they should begin to shorten the rationalizations and repeat them more often. When suspects withdraw emotionally, they listen to less of what the interrogator is saying, so repetition of the rationalizations is important to continue the process of acceptance by the suspect.

The interrogator selects the rationalization that seems to have been most effective in allowing the suspect to save face. If the interrogator has been using rationalizations that focus on peer pressure and financial problems to allow the suspect to save face, he now selects the one that seemed to have had the greatest emotional impact. As the interrogator focuses on that rationalization, he becomes repetitive, to be able to continue to communicate with the withdrawn suspect.

Closing Physically with the Suspect

As the suspect begins to withdraw emotionally and breaks eye contact with the interrogator, the interrogator can begin to close physically. In the early stages of the interrogation, interrogators slowly close the gap between themselves and the suspect. This movement toward the suspect was slow and

Figure 12.1 A suspect in submission is slumped over, withdrawn, and defeated. All verbal and physical denials have stopped as the suspect begins an internal conversation to decide if he should confess.

deliberate, covered by the movement of the hands as they begin to occupy the space closer to the suspect. As the suspect becomes used to the hands' being positioned closer to him, the interrogator can lean slightly forward and occupy that space with the trunk of the body. As the interrogator does this, he slowly inches forward on the chair, using the hands to gesture and occupy the suspect. When the interrogator reaches the edge of the seat, he merely pulls the chair up under him and begins the inching process again.

In the early stages of the interrogation, this movement typically is slow because suspects are neither physically nor emotionally ready to allow the interrogator into their space. However, as the suspect withdraws into submission, the interrogator can accelerate this closure with the suspect. The suspect is no longer watching the interrogator and has emotionally withdrawn, which makes this closure more acceptable. The interrogator moves closer physically to increase the intimacy of the conversation with the suspect. Suspects, as they reach the final decision to confess, will in most cases place both feet on the floor and open the arms, reducing any barriers to the interrogator. The interrogator continues to move closer until his chair is right next to the suspect. Sometimes, female suspects will not uncross the legs as they enter submission. Women, because of their instruction as children, are often more comfortable with the legs crossed than uncrossed.

Controlling the Suspect

The interrogator has recognized the emotional susceptibility of the suspect to confess and has observed the suspect's barriers dropping (the suspect's legs uncross and the arms unfold and go to the sides of the chair). The suspect's head drops as he begins the internal conversation with himself. The interrogator shortens the rationalizations, repeating them over and over. The interrogator is now sitting close to the suspect and attempts to develop eye contact. If suspects are left too long in this submissive pose, they will get stronger and might elect to deny again. The interrogator must now make direct eye contact with the withdrawn suspect and ask for an admission.

One way to gain the suspect's attention is to achieve eye contact. This can be achieved by having him look up at the interrogator. Using the suspect's first name will often cause him to look up. When he looks up, the interrogator holds his eyes with his own, giving the rationalizations greater impact and preparing the suspect for the first admission. In some cases, when the suspect has withdrawn significantly and begun to cry, it might be necessary for the interrogator to lean over and look up at the suspect to make eye contact (see Figure 12.2).

Avoiding Physical Contact

The suspect who has reached the lowest level psychologically is defeated and at an emotional low. Physically touching the suspect could form a bond between the interrogator and the suspect. This touching is similar to placing one's hand on the shoulder of the grieving widow to console her at a funeral. But, although this is an effective technique for a suspect in submission, the current legal climate makes this an unwise choice for the interrogator. An interrogator who touches the suspect might later be accused of battery, which is defined as touching another in an offensive manner. Although the suspect at this point in the interrogation might not find the interrogator's touch offensive, the interrogator could later be accused of touching the suspect offensively, or, in the case of a woman, of touching her sexually.

Although physical contact is legally an unacceptable method to support the suspect, it can be an effective means of consoling a suspect in submission. The answer lies in the partial gesture. The interrogator reaches out to place a hand on the shoulder but never completes the touch. The hand is left approximately an inch above the arm and never makes physical contact. This nonthreatening supportive gesture is recognized by the suspect, and it cements the bond the suspect feels with the interrogator. The interrogator, however, is not exposed to a potential liability caused by the physical touch.

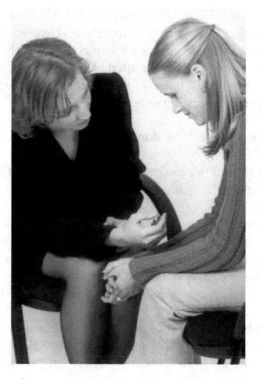

Figure 12.2 Once the suspect is in submission, the interrogator moves closer, shortens the rationalizations, and attempts to develop eye contact with the suspect.

Interrogators should anticipate that any movements or gestures they make in the interrogation might later be questioned in criminal or civil court. Consequently, they should be conservative in any movements or gestures that could be interpreted as threatening to the suspect. The partial gesture by the interrogator solves this problem and still allows for the benefits that physical contact can achieve, without the liabilities.

Testing for Submission

When a suspect shows only minimal behavioral cues relating to submission, the interrogator might need to evaluate his level of resistance by testing for submission. The test for submission is almost always used when an interrogator begins the interrogation with an introductory statement. The use of the introductory statement generally avoids the suspect's need to deny but makes determining the individual's resistance to a confession more difficult.

The test for submission is a personalization of the rationalization or a statement that makes it clear that the conversation has been about the suspect. Insertion of the word "you" creates a statement that a suspect recognizes as a challenge. The suspect will either attempt a denial or offer behavior consistent with the submissive phase of the interrogation. The following statements might be used to test for submission:

> "Bob, the problem is we don't know what difficulties you have faced in your life."
> "The purpose of this conversation is to try to understand the problems in your life."

Both of these statements make it clear that the discussion up to this point was meant for the suspect. The interrogator reads behavior consistent with submission and moves to the assumptive question to obtain an admission. If the suspect shows signs of resistance and attempts to deny, the interrogator stops the denial and returns to rationalization to further reduce the subject's resistance.

A test for submission is used whenever the modified emotional approach is being used because the signs of submission are muted. The muting of the behavioral signs results from the change in decision-making from emotional to rational.

Using the Assumptive Question

The assumptive question used by the interrogator is based on the rationalizations he has offered during the interrogation. The questions always assume that the suspect was involved in the incident but avoids questions such as, "Did you do it?"

The interrogator also avoids incorporating any harsh language into the question. The interrogator, through the use of rationalization, minimizes the seriousness of the suspect's involvement and focuses his attention on the future. By using harshly realistic words, such as *steal, embezzle, fraud, kill*, or *rape*, the interrogator can undo all the work done up to this point. These words recreate in the suspect's mind the incident's seriousness and bring to the forefront the inherent consequences. Using these types of words during the interrogation can rekindle a suspect's need to deny and set the interrogation back significantly.

Testing the Waters

When to use the question to obtain the first admission is difficult for the interrogator to decide. If he asks the question before the suspect is ready, the suspect will make a denial. If the interrogator waits too long, and the suspect emotionally recovers from submission, the interrogator is likely to get a denial. Before the interrogator asks a question designed to elicit the first admission, he should first have a sense that the suspect is ready to confess. For this reason, the interrogator tests the waters with the suspect to determine susceptibility to confess. Testing the waters can be done in several ways.

Transition Statement

During the early stages of rationalization, the interrogator spoke in the third person when discussing why people make mistakes. This strategy allowed the suspect to internalize the rationalizations without having to face the reality that the interrogator was talking about him. The transition statement tests the waters when the interrogator recognizes behavioral clues that the suspect is in submission. These behavioral clues include breaking of eye contact, open body posture, feet flat on the floor, and shoulders in slumped position. The interrogator now uses the suspect's name and directly applies all the rationalizations to the suspect. The interrogator might use a statement such as "Mark, the problem is that the investigation doesn't show what type of problems you're facing."

This statement focuses all the previous rationalizations directly on the suspect. While making the transition statement, the interrogator watches the suspect's reaction. If the suspect makes eye contact, tightens, and leans slightly back, it means that he was not quite ready for an admission. If interrogators observe such behavior, they control any denials that the suspect makes and immediately go back to rationalizing in the third person.

However, if the suspect does not make eye contact, or slowly nods yes, the suspect is susceptible to a confession and the interrogator uses a choice question or soft accusation to obtain the suspect's first admission.

Choice Question or Soft Accusation

Another way to test the suspect's susceptibility to an admission is to ask the choice question or make the soft accusation. Generally, when asked prematurely, they elicit a denial from the suspect. However, the interrogator can present these questions to the suspect periodically to determine his resistance to answering with an admission.

In the very earliest stages of the interrogation, presentation to the suspect of a choice or assumptive question will result in an immediate denial. The interrogator, expecting the denial, is ready to stop it and return to the ratio-nalization or justification process. As suspects become less resistant to giving an admission, they respond less emphatically and spontaneously to these pre-sentations. Asking these questions of the suspect is like periodically putting your finger under a faucet to determine the water's temperature. Only when you feel the temperature is just right do you put your hands in.

The difficulty with this use of the choice question or soft accusation lies in the possibility that the time is inappropriate, renewing a cycle of denials by the suspect. This can create a more difficult interrogation because the suspect has now denied involvement.

Suspect's Behavioral Shift

When suspects are in submission, with no eye contact, and all denials have stopped, they are having an internal dialogue with themselves. Often, as this internal dialogue concludes, the interrogator can observe a behavioral shift in the suspect. This behavioral shift can occur at the point where the suspect has decided to confess. As a general rule, this shift occurs in the trunk of the body, or the hand might lightly slap the thighs, as though to say, "What the heck, go for it." The interrogator, observing these behavioral clues, should immediately respond with a choice question or soft accusation to obtain the admission.

The interrogator should remember that submission by a suspect can vary from the most withdrawn and defeated look to a more emotionally calm appearance. The variability of the behavior associated with submis-sion is due primarily to the emotional state of the suspect. In the most dramatic form, evidenced by the suspect's beginning to cry, communication between the interrogator and the suspect is like that between parent and child. The suspect responds as a child by emotionally withdrawing and finally acquiescing to the parents' wishes. The communication between two adults is less emotionally submissive, with the suspect reaching the decision rationally after weighing the options. If the interrogator has successfully used the introductory statement to establish the credibility of the investi-gation and provided rationalizations that justified the suspect's actions, the suspect will often come to the conclusion that it is best to cooperate. When the interrogator has to overcome the suspect's denials during the classic emotional interrogation, the behavior associated with the submission tends to be more pronounced.

Asking Assumptive Questions

An interrogator's use of assumptive questions leapfrogs the final defensive barrier that a suspect has erected to oppose the confession. The suspect is often prepared to answer the question, "Did you do it?" with a denial. This final defense barrier can be breached by using the assumptive question. An assumptive question assumes that the suspect did, in fact, do it and asks for an admission regarding some aspect of the crime. Two general types of assumptive questions are effective at this point in the interrogation.

The Soft Accusation

The soft accusation is generally used at the conclusion of the introductory statement or participatory accusation. It generally asks for an admission about some aspect of the crime and is a one-sided question broad enough to cover a number of issues.

One of the difficulties that an interrogator faces is not knowing exactly what the suspect is thinking. For example, during the introductory statement, the suspect might be thinking he has been caught taking money out of the register, although the interrogation is really about use of fraudulent documents to steal. Consequently, the interrogator could lose an admission from the suspect if he were to ask a narrowly focused soft accusation, such as, "What was the most amount of money you took using fraudulent credits since you started at the company?" or "When did you plan to take his car?"

Suspects might make a denial because the introductory statement led them to believe that they had been caught taking money directly from the register. Recognizing the error in their thought process, they might quickly deny because they never considered it a possibility that they were caught using the fraudulent documents. If the interrogator had asked the question more broadly, the problem would been have avoided; for example:

> *Interrogator*: Bob, let me ask you, what was the most amount of money that you took from the company in any single day?
> *Suspect*: $20.
> *Interrogator*: And how did you do that?
> *Suspect*: By just taking it out of the register.

The interrogator can now take advantage of a miscalculation by the suspect. In fact, this admission might be a complete surprise to the interrogator, who did not know about the missing $20 from the register. Approaching this question broadly allows the suspect to make the mistakes and the interrogator to profit from them.

Construction of the Soft Accusation. The suspect has been listening only partially, so it is necessary to alert him that something different is about to happen. To do this, the interrogator uses the suspect's first name to gain his attention. Then, the interrogator tells the suspect that he is about to be asked a question to which a response is necessary: "Bob, let me ask you…" Alerting the suspect that he will be required to respond enhances the likelihood of an admission from the suspect because he is listening closely.

Wording of the Soft Accusation. The interrogator makes the soft accusation in a slow, deliberate voice, to address some aspect of the crime. Some examples of soft accusations are listed below:

- What would be the greatest amount of money that you took from the company in any one day?
- When was the first time you considered buying the gun?
- What would be the largest amount of merchandise that you took from the company in any one day?
- When did you begin to plan this out?
- When was the first time you used an illegal drug?

The interrogator makes direct eye contact with the suspect toward the end of the soft accusation. The suspect will begin to respond as soon as the question's meaning becomes evident to him. In the first soft accusation example, the question's meaning becomes clear only after the interrogator says the word "took": "What would be the most amount of money that you took from the company in any one day?" The suspect who is going to deny will often begin shaking his head at this word. The behavioral differences between an admission and a denial are very marked (see Figure 12.3).

Suspect's Response to Soft Accusation. If the suspect uses any form of behavioral denial, the interrogator immediately attempts to stop the denial and returns to the techniques for reducing resistance. If the suspect shows behavioral signs relating to an admission, the interrogator immediately uses a follow-up question to get the suspect to confess.

The suspect will respond to the interrogator's question in one of three ways: deny, make an admission, or pause to consider his options.

Interrogators must be prepared to handle a suspect's denial whenever they ask a question that attempts to elicit an admission of guilt. Recognizing the behavioral clues of a denial as differing from the behavioral clues of an admission is critical in anticipating the suspect's response.

Follow-Up Question. A suspect might also pause to consider an answer signaling that the suspect is susceptible to making an admission. The interrogator immediately fills the pause with a follow-up question that exaggerates

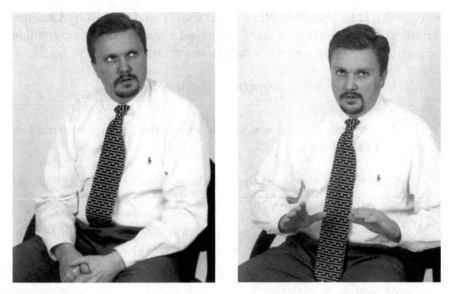

Figure 12.3 (A) The suspect is about to make an admission. The head drifts to the side, the brows arch, the eyes are averted, and the lips are pursed or go slack. (B) The suspect is about to make a denial. There is an intake of breath, tightening of the mouth, and shaking of the head "no." The hands may also be used in a stop gesture.

the seriousness of the suspect's involvement. Examples of the follow-up question are listed below:

- What would be the greatest amount of money that you took from the company in any one day? Was it a $1,000 in one day?
- When was the first time you considered buying the gun? Was it the first day that you met him?
- What would be the largest amount of merchandise that you took from the company in any one day? Was it more than $5,000 in merchandise in one day?
- When did you begin to plan this out? Did you begin to plan this a year ago?
- When was the first time you used an illegal drug? Was it five years ago?

Generally, when the suspect is presented with these exaggerated questions, the immediate response will be a denial. The exaggerated followup question used by the interrogator shocks the suspect before he can make a decision about what to say. When suspects pause to consider a response, they are thinking about two things: how much did they steal in any single day, and should they confess. The interrogator, recognizing that the suspect is considering an answer, immediately asks an exaggerated question about an amount that is far above what the suspect could have been involved in. Since the suspect has not had time as yet to consider the wisdom of responding, he immediately makes a denial which is, in fact, an admission of guilt.

> *Interrogator*: Was it as much as $1,000 in one day?
>
> *Suspect*: No way!
>
> *Interrogator*: Great. I was sure it wasn't that much. How much do you think it was?

The interrogator recognizes that this denial is an admission of guilt and supports the suspect, letting him know that he has confessed.

> *Interrogator*: That's great, Bob. From the investigation, I didn't think it was anything like $5,000. How much was it? Would you say it was more or less than $2,500?
>
> *Suspect*: Less!
>
> *Interrogator*: Good! Well then how much do you think it was?
>
> *Suspect*: $20.

The first admission of guilt from suspects is most likely a lie that minimizes the seriousness of their involvement. However, the suspect is now over the most difficult part of the interrogation — the first admission. The first admission, be it for $10,000 or 10¢, is the most difficult one to achieve because it is the first time the suspect has acknowledged any dishonesty. It is no longer *whether* the suspect is an honest or dishonest individual, but rather *how* dishonest. The interrogator will attempt to discover this during the next phase of the interrogation, development of the admission.

The Choice Question

The choice question, like the soft accusation, is assumptive and asks about some aspect of the incident. It differs by offering the suspect two incriminating choices from which to choose and is an extension of the rationalization previously offered to the suspect. The choice question generally incorporates a good (acceptable) and a bad (unacceptable) choice. Selection of either the acceptable or the unacceptable choice is by the suspect's first admission of involvement.

Some examples of choice questions are

- Did you use the money for bills or was it for drugs?

- Did you plan this thing out or did you do it on the spur of the moment without thinking?
- Did you mean to do this or was it an accident?

The choice question should be presented only when the suspect has shown the behavioral signs of submission and all denials have stopped. The only exception to this rule is when the interrogator elects to use the choice question as a method of testing the suspect's susceptibility to making an admission. The choice question increases in effectiveness when the interrogator is able to close physically with the suspect, thereby increasing the bond between interrogator and suspect.

Interrogators should reach a peak of sincerity when presenting the choice question. As with the soft accusation, they use the suspect's name to draw his attention to the question. They also become repetitive as they attempt to encourage the suspect to make a decision and select one of the two choices presented. The repetition is important, because of the suspect's withdrawal. In addition, interrogators encourage the suspect to select one of the choices by emphasizing the good over the bad choice, for example:

- **Good Choice:** I'm sure it was to pay bills, wasn't it, Bob? If it was, that proves we're talking about something anybody could have done...It was for bills wasn't it? It was, wasn't it Bob. It was for bills, right?
- **Bad Choice:** If the money was used to buy something like drugs, then we're wasting my time. That's a whole different story..., but that doesn't seem right, I can't believe it was for drugs, Bob. It wasn't, was it? I'm sure it wasn't...

By encouraging the suspect to take the more acceptable of the two choices, the interrogator continues the process of face-saving. The interrogator should understand that the suspect's selection of the more acceptable choice does not necessarily correspond with the real reason the suspect became involved. However, in most cases, the reason the person did it is less important than the fact that he did do it. In general, it does not make a difference to the case whether the suspect used the money for bills or drugs. Merely intending to permanently deprive the owner of property is sufficient to prove theft. However, in certain cases such as arson, the use of a choice question such as, "Did you start the fire by accident or was it on purpose?" might create problems in a prosecution. This choice of "by accident" lacks the intent that is a necessary element of the crime of arson. However, the acknowledgment that the suspect started the fire might be sufficient to obtain a conviction when combined with the physical evidence of an accelerant's being used and multiple points of origin. It should be noted, however, that the easiest way to encourage a suspect to admit starting a fire is by saying it was an accident. After the initial admission, the interrogator can then go back and reconstruct the facts with the suspect and get an admission showing the intent. Remember, the hardest part of any interrogation is getting the first admission. Following that, the suspect is more likely to give a complete confession.

Acknowledging Acceptance of the Assumptive Question

Once the suspect has acknowledged involvement, the interrogator must support the suspect's decision. The suspect might have admitted to the choice question by either nodding his head in agreement or using a one-word answer, "Yes" or "No." Rarely is a suspect able to respond with a full narrative at this point. Once the suspect acknowledges involvement, the interrogator must let him know that he has confessed. Often, suspects do not even realize that they have made an admission of guilt.

Case Example

A gang member was being interrogated regarding the theft of a handgun from under the register at a liquor store where he worked. The interrogator utilized rationalizations that the suspect had taken the gun to protect himself and family members against threats from other gangs.

During the rationalization the suspect went into a head-and-shoulder slump and his eyes began to tear up. The interrogator narrowed the rationalizations to the choice question, "I'm sure you didn't take the gun to do anything bad; it was just to protect your family. It was, wasn't it?" The interrogator observed the suspect nod to the choice slightly, but neglected to support the admission by letting him know that he had confessed. Instead, the interrogator attempted to go back and rationalize for a moment longer. At this point, the suspect realized what he had done and immediately recrossed his arms, sat up, and a mask of coldness dropped across his face.

The admission was lost because the interrogator failed to let the suspect know he had confessed by supporting his admission. Any delay on the part of an interrogator in supporting the suspect's admission of involvement can lead to a retraction.

Observing Behavioral Clues of an Admission

The behavioral clues that an interrogator can observe when a suspect is about to make an admission are significantly different from those observed when a denial will be forthcoming.

During an admission, the suspect's face tends to be relaxed. The eyes break contact and lose focus, drifting away. The suspect's lips either purse tightly or go slack. The eyebrows arch as she considers a response to the question. Since the suspect is not intending to speak, she does not take a breath. The positioning of the head is also significantly different in an admission from that in a denial. When making an admission, the head might slightly drop toward the chest or drift toward the left side of the body. In general, the eyes become unfocused as the suspect considers the response to the choice or soft accusation (see Figure 12.4).

Figure 12.4 Individual recalling visually as she considers a response. This behavior often occurs during the making of an admission.

In contrast, suspects who are going to deny tend to make eye contact with the interrogator and shake their head no, a response that almost always precedes a spoken denial by the suspect. Because they are not accepting what the interrogator is saying, suspects' eyebrows frown as they prepare to make a spontaneous denial. As soon as the interrogator finishes the sentence, the spoken denial will start. To prepare to speak, suspects begin to tighten their lips and take a breath so they will be able to speak as soon as there is a break in the dialogue. Figure 12.5 illustrates the behavioral clues an interrogator

ADMISSION   DENIAL

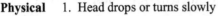

Physical Behavior

ADMISSION	DENIAL
1. Head drops or turns slowly	1. Shake head no
2. No eye contact, drifts, or unfocused	2. Eye contact
3. Arches brows	3. Frowning brows
4. Pursed of slack lips	4. Tightened lips
5. No breath taken	5. Takes breath to speak

Verbal   PAUSES   SPONTANEOUS RESPONSE

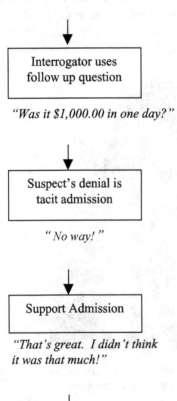

Interrogator uses follow up question

"Was it $1,000.00 in one day?"

Suspect's denial is tacit admission

"No way!"

Support Admission

"That's great. I didn't think it was that much!"

DEVELOPMENT OF ADMISSION

"Was it more or less than, say..."

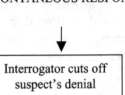

Interrogator cuts off suspect's denial

"Just a minute, Steve..."

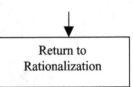

Return to Rationalization

"You know sometimes these things happen because..."

Figure 12.5 This chart illustrates the behavioral differences between a suspect making a admission and one making a denial.

should look for, to tell whether a suspect is going to make an admission or denial with the proper follow-up procedure for either.

The interrogator should recognize the behavioral clues of submission and their importance to the susceptibility of an admission by the suspect. The use of an assumptive question, either the soft accusation or choice question, affords suspects an opportunity to begin their dialogue with the interrogator. The interrogator recognizes that the suspect is emotionally unable to answer open-end questions but is capable of responding to closed-end probes such as the soft accusation or choice question. Acceptance of either one of these questions by the suspect is not the confession but merely a first acknowledgment of guilt. Once the suspect has acknowledged involvement, the interrogator moves into the next phase of the interrogation, development of the admission.

The following are sample introductory statements for both loss-prevention and law-enforcement personnel are provided below.

Sample Introductory Statements

Loss Prevention

Part 1 — What We Do and How We Do It

"Hello, Cindy? I'm _____ with the loss prevention department here at the company. It is my job to protect the assets of the company. These assets are the building, fixtures, merchandise, cash, and the employees who work for us. The employees are certainly the most important asset in the company.

"As you might know, there has been a fairly high shrinkage in the department here. We know that at one time or another everyone makes mistakes. That's just human nature. We also know that shortage, or shrinkage as we call it, consists of a number of things. This shrinkage figure consists of customers who take merchandise by carrying it out without paying for it, and it certainly consists of the errors in paperwork that are part of our everyday jobs. It's also employees taking things [*pause, eye contact*]. The major concern that the company has is those employees who would be taking trailer loads or cases of merchandise or $10,000 out of a safe. Things that would add up to thousands and thousands of dollars' worth of property or money. Because every employee is a valuable asset here at the company, we feel it is important to sit down and discuss the results of an investigation that we have conducted."

Part 2 — How Losses Occur

"As I mentioned, besides customers taking things and paperwork errors, employees sometimes take things. There are many ways that an employee could take money and merchandise from the company. For example, an employee could use fraudulent credits to take money. They could use phony voids, void out sales, and then keep the money. They might work directly out of an open register and not be ringing up sales. It is also possible that some employees might just take money right out of the register and cause a shortage in that manner." [*The interviewer should pause and make direct eye contact after the explanation that he believes is most likely how the suspect is stealing. The manner of theft that the suspect is involved in should be positioned in the middle of the examples given.*]

"Of course, there are many other ways that an employee could cause losses to the company besides just taking money. For example, they could wear merchandise out of the store, they could give a customer more merchandise than that customer paid for, and possible that the employee could just pass merchandise off to a friend or conceal it on their person and carry it out after they're done working for the evening." [*The interviewer should watch for behavioral changes during the examples offered the suspect. The changes may be the result of stress that might indicate involvement in that method of theft.*]

Part 3 — How Investigations Are Conducted

"You're probably not familiar with the manner in which security investigations are conducted at the company. We use any number of avenues to generate information that will bring the investigation to a satisfactory conclusion. It is only at the very end of that investigation when we have evaluated all the evidence that we have accumulated that we'll sit down and talk with any of the employees. Since you might not be familiar with how these investigations occur, let me just discuss some of the ways that we gather information. Many times in evaluating a high-shrinkage department, we'll place an undercover employee in the department. This undercover employee is looking for a number of things, such as errors in paperwork, errors in procedure that may occur, employee dishonesty [*pause — eye contact*]. These undercover employees will then file reports concerning their findings here in the department. Another way in which we will continue the investigation is actual surveillance by members of the loss prevention department. This surveillance might be conducted by the investigators' concealing themselves in the area or simply walking through the department.

"Additionally, we use a shopping service in which we have people come in to make controlled purchases from various registers and store personnel. It is during these purchases that the shopper is determining if correct cash-handling procedures are being followed, if the register is being rung properly, and if paperwork is being filled out. The shopper is looking as well at the general demeanor and courtesy with which the employee is treating the customer. We will also, on occasion, stop customers as they are leaving the department and question them as to how they were treated and, at the same time, check to determine if the merchandise they purchased matches up with the sales receipt.

"On many occasions, we will also use video cameras that use pinhole lenses to conduct a surveillance of a particular area or register in an attempt to determine exactly what procedures and perhaps problems are occurring at that register. We might also, at the same time, monitor that register to determine exactly what is being rung and in what departments.

"There are many other ways in which we get our information and conduct an investigation. These include receiving help from other employees, audits, salting registers, and sending out credit and refund letters to determine if they actually were received, to name but a few. [*This area usually has greater impact on the suspect if the interrogator uses examples of investigative techniques that could develop direct rather than circumstantial evidence, e.g., videotape of theft rather than patterns showing an employee's being present at all incidents.*]

Part 4 — Discussion of Why Mistakes Are Made

"There are many reasons that employees might make a mistake in judgment and take something from the company. [*Expand on several rationalizations for an employee's being involved in theft at the company, e.g., peer pressure, financial pressures, or impulse. Part 4 might account for up to two thirds of the time spent on the introductory statement. The rationalizations should be at least ten minutes in length or longer, depending on the suspect's behavior.*]

Rationalization: Impulse.
"Cindy, you know, I think this whole thing really just boils down to advertising. When we're talking about doing something on impulse, that's really one of the big things that advertisers try to play on. We do the same thing here in the store when we try to display merchandise

or when we try to put it together in such a way that it's pleasing to the eye — so pleasing that it becomes a fad to wear that particular item.

"In a lot of cases, with the prices that stores are charging, and with the pressures we put the store associates under, it becomes difficult for them to fight off that temptation to do something they know isn't right. But yet, we are in a situation that people at school are wearing particular items or we're held in better regard because we wear a particular garment, and, all of a sudden, we do something that we probably shouldn't do because we do it on impulse without thinking the consequences through.

"I think that's important when we're talking about a situation such as we're dealing with here. The worst thing in the world in this business is having to deal with that person who's really premeditated things, who's thought things through, who came to the company with the idea that they were going to get as much as they could, for as long as they could, and they don't care about anything.

"That's entirely different from the associate who comes here, who works around the items day in and day out, and finally temptation takes over. I think that's totally different.

"You know, when I was a kid, I can remember that my dad told me, "Don't touch the candy on the table," and he put a big bowl of candy there, my favorite kind of M&Ms. I love M&Ms. He said, "Don't touch them — you're not to have any," and then he walked out of the room.

"Well, I sat there and looked at those M&Ms and thought about how good they were. When I got up that morning I didn't think to myself, I'm going to run out and I'm going to get as many M&Ms out of the kitchen as soon as my dad turns his back.

"But, what happened to me was that the temptation overcame me and I took just a few. Who was really at fault? Was it me, or was it my dad? Obviously, I disobeyed him, but, on the other side of the coin, he put me in a position where I couldn't win. If he had stayed in the room and enforced that rule, or if he had taken the bowl of candy and put it away so it was out of view, I would have been able to deal with that a lot better, but the problem is that I was put into a situation where I couldn't win.

"A lot of times, especially when we're young, we make errors in judgment. We do things without really thinking them through, either because we don't have the experience that an older person might have, or we've never been exposed to it, or whatever. Look at, for example, insurance rates. When are the insurance rates on your car the highest? It is up until the time you're 25. Why is that? That's because the younger age is when most people have accidents — they make mistakes

— they're reckless because they're driving too fast because they haven't seen the consequences of driving fast yet.

"These things can happen over and over again and I think that's what happened here. I think this is a situation where it was done on impulse."

Rationale: Peer Pressure.

"You know, Cindy, I think almost everybody has heard the term *peer pressure* and understands what it means. We're put into a lot of situations in our lives because of our peers, our friends, and how they think. We do things that maybe under ordinary circumstances we wouldn't do. But, because we have our friends, or we have other people who think in a particular way, they tend to force our thinking in a direction that we may not consider appropriate.

"I can give you a perfect example. When I was a kid back in high school, I never smoked, and my friends said, "We're smoking cigarettes; come on and have one." I really didn't want one, but finally I said "OK" and I tried one. Today, I don't smoke cigarettes; my parents don't smoke cigarettes. I was put in a position where everybody was doing it, and it became very, very difficult for me not to go along with the group.

"I think what's really happening here is just that. When we're dealing with a situation like this, it's not your idea, but rather a group idea. You hear, 'We need to keep up with the Joneses.' or 'You gotta wear the right clothes, certain types of jeans or jackets or sweaters.' You know they're popular and if you don't wear them, you're not a good person.

"Well, that's crazy, letting the clothes decide. However, that's the way people are, especially people who feel that wearing the right clothes or keeping up with the Joneses is important. If they do that, and if they feel that's important, then it tends to go over, putting pressure on their friends.

"If what has happened here is that this situation was brought to you, rather than you going out and soliciting, I think that's very important to know. In a lot of cases, people or friends of associates will come into the store and say, "Listen, give me this at a discount," or, "I'm not going to pay for this," or, you know, "Don't say anything, I'm going to carry this out."

"They might have really put you in an awkward position. They put you into a position where they either force you not to charge the right amount, or they force you to let them walk, or do something that under normal circumstances you wouldn't let anybody do.

"The key here, I think, is not so much that it's happened, but rather it's, did you go out and say to people, 'It's OK, come on in, you can take as much as you want,' or did they come to you and say, 'This is what I'm going to do,' and put you on the spot? Because, if that's what happened, I think its important that we understand that. If I thought for a second that you were going out and telling your friends, 'Hey, just come on down, you can take anything when I'm working,' I don't think I could deal with that, but I don't believe that's the case. In most situations that I deal with, it's not an associate but rather those friends coming in and putting them on the spot that causes them the biggest problems."

Rationale: Financial Problems.

"Cindy, I think that we set people up for problems simply because of how much we pay them. Probably one of the most difficult things to do is to work around beautiful items that are really expensive and yet you're not being paid $30 to $40 an hour. You're making pretty close to minimum wage, I would imagine. The thing is, once you start being around nice things, it's only natural to want them for yourself.

"This also happens with friends, I mean, if you've got friends who perhaps have some money and they're suddenly wearing fancy jeans that cost $40 to $50 a pair, they're wearing skirts that may cost $100, you can rest assured they can afford these things. You're working hard for the money that you earn, but maybe you don't have as much as they do at home. All of a sudden, they're treating you differently, simply because you don't have the same things they have. You want them, too.

"You wouldn't be human if you didn't. But yet, you're not making enough to pay for it even though you're diligently working, you're taking very few days off, and you're doing a good job, but yet, you can't buy those things.

"And, you know, we also expect you to look good. I mean, you're the image of the company. You're the person that the customer sees. You're our representative, and we don't want you coming in here looking like a slob. We want you to dress nice, look sharp. We'd like you to wear our clothes because you're a walking mannequin. You're a walking advertisement for how good our clothes can look on a person. If you look good people think, 'Boy, I'd like to look like that,' or, 'I would like my wife or my girlfriend to look like that.' Then they go ahead and buy it.

"We'd like you to look nice, but do we turn around and say, 'Here's money for clothes,' or, 'Here's a raise.' No, we don't! So we have to recognize that part of the situation is a result of how the company views itself and what it considers important. The thing that I don't want to see is somebody put into a position of doing something because of peer pressure, frustration, low pay, or making an error in judgment that's causing them to do something that under normal circumstances they wouldn't do. I think that's the key here. A lot of times people do things because they need the money. I think that's important because, if there was a need, a legitimate need, that's something that every one of us can relate to.

"We all have bills, whether they're phone, heating, rent, car payment, or insurance. We all have things that we have to pay. There are times where we have extra money and times when we run short. Sometimes, when we're put in a position where we don't have an alternative, we need to do something that maybe we weren't raised to do, or we wouldn't do under normal circumstances; however, we're put into a position where we have a need.

"We're not going out and blowing the money on drugs or booze or good times. We're using it for the necessities of life, to keep our head above water, and I think that's important. If that's the case, then I think this all can be settled and done.

"During any investigation, many things are uncovered and known absolutely. But often, it's the reason mistakes are made that don't come out. These things are important to the company to show why things happen and to show also that the employee cares. This is why at the conclusion of every investigation, we sit down with the employee and discuss the results to assess the attitude of that employee toward the company."

Part 5 — The Soft Accusation or Assumptive Question

Interrogator: Cindy, what was the most amount of money that you took at any one time from the company?

[If the suspect delays and looks away, immediately ask] Cindy, did you ever take something like $1,000 in a single day?

Cindy: Oh no!

Interrogator: That's great, I knew from the investigation that it wouldn't be that much! Would it be more or less than $900 in one day?

Cindy: Less!

Interrogator: What would be the most amount of money that you took in any one day?

Cindy: $5.00.

The interviewer then enters the development of admission phase.

Law Enforcement

The following is a sample introductory statement that could be used in the investigation of a burglary. The suspect was to be questioned because his vehicle was observed parked several blocks from the scene of a gas station burglary at approximately 2:00 A.M. The vehicle was observed by a patrol officer, who noted it in his log. There is no other direct evidence that links the suspect to the incident.

Part 1 — Who We Are and What We Do
    "Hi, Jack, my name is _____ and I'm a detective with the City Police. I appreciate your taking the time to come in and talk to me today. [*If the suspect is to be taken into custody at the conclusion of the interrogation, it might be necessary for the law enforcement officer to give the suspect his Miranda rights prior to any interrogation. If the suspect will be free to leave following the interrogation, even if he admits his involvement, the Miranda rights may be omitted. Officers should consider any special departmental guidelines or requests from the prosecutor's office before omitting Miranda warnings.*]

    "Jack, I'm sure you're aware of what a police department does for a community. Really, our job is to protect the community, its homes, businesses, and citizens from any type of criminal activity. To do that, we get involved with a number of different complaints.

    "For example, some might be traffic problems or safety problems that we have to deal with on a daily basis. Other times, we have to deal with business- or homeowners who are filing false reports in an attempt to obtain a fraudulent insurance settlement. Then we have those instances where someone is genuinely a victim. The department's primary concern obviously has to be with the most serious type of incidents — homicides, rapes — rather than something of a minor nature like a small item being taken or someone driving over someone's grass."

Part 2 — Different Types of Crimes

    "As investigators, we're asked to look into any number of different types of crimes. I am sure you are aware that our community, like any other community, has its share of problems. Those problems range from homicide to rape and arson to people breaking into buildings [*pause, eye contact*], taking things out of cars, or even out of homes."

Part 3 — How We Investigate

"When we discover or we receive a problem or a complaint from a citizen, the case is assigned for investigation. Now, when it's assigned for investigation, we'll use any number of different techniques to attempt to establish who was responsible for the incident under investigation. For example, if the case calls for it, we might use latent fingerprinting. I'm not sure how familiar you are with latent fingerprinting, but what we do is go to the scene of a crime and begin dusting those areas that will hold a fingerprint. In using these types of techniques, we're able to develop latent prints and can often determine who was responsible as a result.

"In some areas, an individual will be careful not to touch any type of a smooth surface but might touch a piece of paper, and the oils and perspiration from the fingers are actually absorbed into the fibers of the paper and can be held there for years. By using special techniques, such as lasers, the crime lab is able to develop prints that can be used for comparison purposes.

"In other instances, we'll locate a particular tool that might have been used as a weapon, or as a means to gain entry to a building. This is particularly important to us, because by using scientific techniques, we can establish the unique marks a tool makes and compare those to the pry marks at the building. This establishes that a particular tool was used to gain entrance or as a weapon.

"We also recover physical evidence, like hair samples. With these hair samples the lab can do a DNA analysis. Like a fingerprint, it is unique and can identify a person.

"As investigators, we'll also attempt to talk to people or other officers who are constantly patrolling the streets, asking them if they saw anybody or observed anything unusual in or around the area of a particular incident. In this way, we can often initially focus our investigative efforts in a particular direction.

"As does any police department, we have informants who supply us with information that helps us resolve any number of crimes during a year. Some of these informants are paid for their services. Others do it to obtain a reward or simply to stop what they think is an improper activity.

"These, as well as many other different types of investigative techniques, help us to identify the individual responsible and begin to develop the case. It may supply us with the information necessary to obtain a search warrant so that we can search a home, vehicle, or garage — wherever we believe we may recover additional evidence of the individual's guilt." [*Interrogator should watch for a behavioral reaction as they mention places where evidence or missing property could be concealed. This will assist during development of the admission or might give them additional investigative leads should the suspect fail to confess. The interrogator should modify the investigative methods described to those that, if they had been used, could have developed information pointing to the suspect's guilt. For example, instead of saying that they have fingerprints or other evidence directly, they infer that evidence might have been available because of the investigative efforts used. For example, if this were a forgery case, the interrogator could describe how a document examiner might be used.*

Part 4 — Discussion of Why Mistakes Are Made

[*The interrogator should expand on several rationalizations that he feels might justify the suspect's actions. These rationalizations initially are based on background information or possible motives for the crime.*]

"The investigation, although it can identify a suspect and show that he was involved, rarely shows the reason that he did it. For example, when people are under financial pressure, perhaps having just lost a job, they sometimes do things to take care of their family that they wouldn't do under ordinary circumstances. These outside pressures and influences cause people to make decisions that, if they had plenty of money, they'd never even consider having to make.

"In other situations, individuals are influenced by their friends, their peers, who have an idea and they press and press and press that idea until they get their way. Even if it's a bad idea, eventually this constant pressure on others around them can cause the other people to do what they never would have done on their own. Many times, the person who is put in this position is forced to judge between the friendship that they value and what they know is right and wrong. But, because of the environment that their friend puts them in, they make a decision on the spur of the moment to do something just so that they can keep the friend happy. This impulse decision is not always in their best interest, but still they make the decision to go ahead to appease the friend. If they had taken the time to think things through, they probably would have never done anything. But because of their friends, they made a decision on impulse, perhaps a decision that they later regret.

[*The interrogator continues to rationalize until the suspect appears behaviorally ready to confess. Once the suspect has shown signs of submission, the interrogator should use a transition statement to focus the interrogation on the specific incident.*]

"Jack, as you know, we've been investigating the break-in at the [*name of the business*] and the circumstances surrounding it. The difficulty, as I mentioned earlier, is that an investigation doesn't always reveal the reasons why something happens. Jack, the problem is we don't know what type of outside pressures you faced."

[*The interrogator should assess the suspect's behavior after presenting the transition statement. If the suspect tightens physically or begins to make a denial, the interrogator should control the denial and return to rationalizations in an effort to continue to reduce the suspect's resistance to a confession. If the suspect shows no outward signs of concern at this statement, the interrogator should proceed to the soft accusation.*]

Part 5 — The Soft Accusation or Assumptive Question

Interrogator: Jack, let me ask you this, what was the amount of merchandise that you took from the gas station last night?

Suspect: (Delays, looks away)

Interrogator: [*Immediately ask the followup question.*] Did you take $10,000 in merchandise?

Suspect: Oh, no!

Interrogator: That's great. From the investigation, I didn't think it was anywhere near that much. Would you say that it would be more or less than $5,000?

Suspect: Less.

Interrogator: What would be the amount of merchandise that you took from the station?

Suspect: Just some cigarettes and oil.

Interrogator enters the development phase of the interrogation.

Part Six

Development of the Admission

Development of the Admission

13

Development of an admission requires patience and persistence by the interrogator.

The suspect has just acknowledged involvement in the issue under investigation by accepting one of the interrogator's assumptive questions. However, this acceptance is not a confession, but merely the first admission in the development process. The interrogator takes the first admission that the suspect makes and develops it into a legally acceptable confession by having the suspect provide details of the crime. The interrogator then expands the initial admission into other areas of dishonesty or criminal activity within the community or company.

The scope of the development might be merely the details of the specific incident under investigation — answering the questions who, what, where, when, how, and why — or it might be much more. In the public sector, the interrogator will attempt to expand details of the suspect's involvement to other areas of criminal activity. In addition, the interrogator might attempt to develop information that will assist other investigations or he will attempt to turn the suspect into an informant to assist in other investigations.

In the private sector, expansion of the initial admission is used to make investigative decisions to recover assets, or to recover evidence that will allow prosecution. The expansion in the private sector might cover the theft of money and merchandise, and knowledge of others involved in dishonesty at the company, as well as secondary issues such as consumption of company goods, unauthorized discounts, and drug usage.

As part of the initial preparation for the interrogation, interrogators should consider in what other incident the suspect might have been involved.

They should have taken into consideration the suspect, background, patterns of activity, and intelligence or informant information.

Interrogators should be aware that, often, what is revealed during an investigation is merely the tip of the iceberg. Suspects are generally not apprehended until they grow bolder and become sloppy, not taking adequate precautions. As a development strategy, interrogators should work under the premise that the suspect might have been involved in a number of incidents. They should consider that the suspect's other illegal activities might not have come to the attention of police or loss prevention. This conclusion seems obvious when one considers the case clearance statistics of police departments. Theft, burglary, and other nonpersonal crimes traditionally have a low clearance rate because often there are no witnesses to the criminal's activities. Personal crimes, such as rape, battery, robbery, or murder, generally have a higher clearance rate because there are witnesses and a focused investigation by the authorities.

In the private sector, interrogators should consider that certain types of theft might not show up as a cash loss but appear later as an inventory shortage. For example, a series of register shortages totaling $150 might indicate that the suspect has stolen $150 directly from the register. If the interviewer were to stop the development of the admission at this point, he might miss the fact that the suspect had also engaged in the theft of cash through voids and fraudulent credits. Additional losses might be later reflected as a merchandise shortage at inventory if the suspect was failing to ring sales and simply pocketing the money. The interrogator should remember that there are usually more questions than answers in an investigation. If you know one thing from an investigation, it is that you do not have all the answers.

Acceptance of the Soft Accusation or Choice Question by the Suspect

Once the suspect has made an admission by accepting the choice question or soft accusation, the interrogator must immediately do two things. First, the interrogator must give the suspect a statement of support. The suspect has made one of the most difficult decisions of his life, to admit wrongdoing, and the interrogator must support his decisions. The suspect is teetering and needs to be assured that he has made the correct decision by confessing. This can be done by the interviewer's simply saying, "That's great. I was sure from the investigation that we weren't talking about doing this because of drugs." Second, the interrogator must present the statement of support immediately when the suspect makes an acknowledgment of involvement. This lets the suspect know that he has confessed and made the right decision in doing so.

The suspect is emotionally withdrawn at this point in the interrogation and incapable of answering broad, open-ended questions, such as, "Tell me how this happened." Because of the suspect's emotional mind-set, the interrogator attempts to draw out the substantiation of the admission using brief questions that can be answered with single words or nods. These initial brief questions form the foundation of the substantiation and begin to draw the suspect into conversation.

Up to this point the interrogator has spent much time attempting to minimize the seriousness of the crime and break down the suspect's resistance to confessing. After suspects make an initial admission, they are wavering at a point where they could back off and recant the admission. The interrogator, after supporting the suspect, must be sure not to use any harsh words or phrases that connote punishment. Using harsh terms such as rob, rape, or steal re-create the seriousness of what the suspect has done and he might back away from the admission.

The initial questions used by the interrogators are closed-end questions that begin to extract the details of the incident or the circumstances surrounding it. These questions are questions of commitment that build the credibility of the statement. Their purpose and that of the development process are to substantiate the suspect's involvement. The substantiation assures others who were not present during the interrogation that it was the suspect's confession and not the interrogator's creation. These questions of commitment supply the details and background of the incident that can be known only to the person responsible.

For example, these questions might elicit the time that the actual theft occurred, where the money was deposited, how the money was used, or how it was paid or transferred. These questions might also identify the location of additional evidence that could be recovered by an investigator — for example, the location of a murder weapon or the location of stolen property.

In most cases, the next step in an investigation is to recover the additional substantiating evidence or documents. This evidence, for example, might be bank records, canceled checks, or sales receipts, any of which could help substantiate the confession. The loss prevention investigator very often does not take this next step to recover additional evidence. It is often sufficient in the private sector simply to utilize the suspect's written statement to establish involvement in the crime and allow for termination and perhaps prosecution. It is more likely that a police investigator will attempt to recover additional evidence of the suspect's involvement to prepare a much more solid case for prosecution.

Although the suspect has made an initial admission, it is unlikely that the interrogator has yet established the elements necessary to prove the crime. During the development phase, the interrogator develops information and statements that establish the elements of the crime, the suspect's mental state, and proof of the suspect's intent. Sometimes, even innocuous statements made by a suspect during development can prove critical in the prosecution or termination of the suspect. The interrogator should note any statements that will help prove the case.

The interrogator has not taken any notes since the accusation was made; however, once the development of the admission is sufficiently under way, the interrogator should begin to make notes of the suspect's admission. The note taking generally begins after the suspect has made a number of admissions and appears to be comfortable talking about his involvement. Once interrogators see the suspect becoming comfortable, they can make an off-hand comment that they want "just to jot a couple of notes" so that they don't keep going over the same topics or forget anything. This allows the interrogator to make notations that will be used as the foundation for a later written statement.

In a specific-issue case, the interrogator answers the six investigative questions (who, what, where, when, how, and why) focusing specifically on the incident in question. It is likely that the suspect will not tell the interrogator the complete truth even at this point in an interrogation. Suspects often withhold key elements that they feel will jeopardize their current story or create more serious problems. Their deception, even in the developmental phase, might form the basis for impeaching their testimony at a later hearing or trial. The interrogator should consistently probe for the truth while recognizing that suspects might not be entirely candid.

During the development phase of a specific crime, the interrogator is looking for additional investigative leads that can be followed. These leads might allow the acquisition of additional information that will corroborate the suspect's confession and enhance the likelihood of a successful prosecution.

An interrogator should recognize that, with the exception of homicide, many people involved in one type of criminal activity have often been involved in other types of incidents. The interrogator, while the suspect is in a state of reduced resistance, should attempt to identify other areas of the suspect's criminal activity. Although investigation into these other areas might not result in a prosecution, it might allow investigators to clear files by closing the case as solved but not prosecuted. In some cases, the suspect will make an admission that will enable the interrogator to link him to other crimes that may be provable, possibly resulting in other prosecutions' being brought against the suspect.

Techniques to Expand the First Admission

In almost all instances, the interrogator should attempt to expand suspects' initial admission of guilt into the full scope of their involvement. Although there might be some exceptions in certain cases, this will generally be the goal of the interrogator. The following techniques can easily be utilized to expand that initial admission.

The Worksheet

Interrogators should prepare a worksheet for note taking during the development phase of the interrogation. On the worksheet they should specifically note the elements of the crime under investigation that will be necessary to prove the suspect's guilt. In addition, they should have considered other types of criminal activity in which the suspect might have been involved. This evaluation may be based on a pattern of similar *modi operandi* (MOs), activities taking place in a similar geographic area, or other similar crimes. The interrogator might also note any behavioral clues observed during the introductory statement that might indicate involvement in other types of crimes.

The worksheet allows interrogators to make sure they have consistently covered each area of inquiry. It allows them an opportunity to take notes in a portion of the worksheet set aside for that particular type of crime. In addition, the worksheet can also contain background information on the suspect, suspicions, or implications that the interrogator might want to remember to ask about.

Resistance-Reducing Techniques

During development, interrogators should return to the techniques that reduced the suspect's resistance to a confession. These techniques showed understanding through focusing the suspect's attention on the future instead of the current situation. They also minimized the seriousness of the suspect's involvement through the use of rationalizations, offering the suspect a positive outlook that gave hope for the future after he resolved the incident in question. The interrogator might also use a change of perspective to have the suspect look at the situation from another point of view. This is especially helpful during the development process, when the interrogator is attempting to get the suspect to detail his entire involvement.

Development of the admission requires patience and persistence from the interrogator. Although the suspect has acknowledged involvement, he might not yet be willing to talk about all the details of the crime. Development of an admission is like tilling a garden; it requires the gardener to go through a plot of land in different directions a number of times, constantly turning over the old ground looking for new clumps of dirt, before the soil is properly prepared. In the same way, the interrogator constantly reviews previous topics in an effort to uncover new information. An interrogator's decision to change topics does not mean he is no longer interested in that topic but merely has ceased making headway and so begins to probe a new area.

The interrogator should also make supportive comments that minimize the suspect's admissions. Being supportive during the development of an admission is critical to the expansion process. The interrogator who scolds the suspect by saying, "Why didn't you tell me that before? Come on, let's just get this whole thing cleared up. What's wrong with you?" is less likely to develop full admissions than the interrogator who is supportive. The supportive comments remind the suspect what a difficult time this is, and how hard it will be for him to remember certain details of the incident. This statement by the interrogator has a second purpose, which is to justify the interrogator's persistence during the development process. The interrogator tells the suspect he is not returning to the topic simply to annoy the suspect, but to help him remember during a very difficult time.

The interrogator might re-accuse the suspect during the development phase of the interrogation and return to rationalization to correct the initial admission. It would not be unusual for a suspect to claim that a fire started by accident when, in fact, it was deliberately set. The claim of accident is then addressed, using the crime scene where there were multiple points of origin and a return to rationalization to justify why the subject did not admit that in the first place. Regardless of the initial admission, the suspect will, most of the time, minimize the incident's seriousness by giving only a face-saving explanation that must be overcome to get to the real truth. The reaccusal of the subject thus might correct the selection of the alternative first chosen by the suspect and lead to additional admission.

The Assumptive Question

The use of assumptive questions by the interrogator during the development of an admission can enhance the ability to obtain additional information from the suspect. As discussed in previous chapters, the assumptive question skips over the issue of whether the suspect did something and addresses how often or when he did it. Asking a question such as, "Did you do it?" invites a denial from the suspect; however, the assumptive question with its follow-up question often leads to additional admissions. The delay of a suspect in responding to an assumptive question is a good clue that information is being withheld. The interrogator then utilizes an exaggerated follow-up question that results in a denial, which is actually an admission of guilt by the suspect. This very quickly leads to a specific admission and additional development paths, as the following dialogue illustrates.

> *Interrogator*: Steve, what would have been the most number of radios that you took from the company?
>
> *Suspect*: [*Pauses, looks up and to the left.*]
>
> *Interrogator*: Are we talking like 100 or more?
>
> *Suspect*: Geez, no!
>
> *Interrogator*: Great! From the investigation I didn't think it was anything like that. How many do you think, more or less than 50?
>
> *Suspect*: Less, maybe three.
>
> *Interrogator*: All right, great, but you know ...

The assumptive question can also be used when the interrogator has made an educated guess regarding other incidents in which the suspect might be involved. The interrogator uses the neurolinguistic eye movements and the pauses in the suspect's responses to lead to additional information. This also allows the interrogator to test the veracity of the tale by determining if the suspect is creating information or actually recalling from memory. Remember that these eye movements are only indicators and along with the suspect's language can help lead the interrogator to the truth.

Use of Exaggeration to Encourage Admission

Interrogators should always exaggerate what they are saying to the suspect. Start with a high amount or with the more serious issue to allow the suspect to minimize what he has done. For example, if a suspect who stole $20 from a register were asked, "Did you ever take a whole day's receipts?" the theft of $20 seems insignificant by comparison. This encourages the suspect to get closer to the truth because it does not seem so bad. This same tactic can be utilized in a number of ways during the development phase.

A second example might be attempting to expand the items taken during a burglary:

> *Interrogator*: Did you take as many as four TVs from the house?
>
> *Suspect*: No way!
>
> *Interrogator*: Good. I didn't think it was that many. How many TVs did you take? Was it three?
>
> *Suspect*: No, it was only two.

While the exaggeration is not necessarily true, the suspect should be told that the interrogator understands how difficult it is to remember everything immediately because of the length of time since the incident occurred. The interrogator might illustrate this point by relating the difference between somebody who would go into a safe and take $10,000 at one time and someone who took just a few little things over a long time that just added up. The interrogator should offer that it would be easier to remember something larger or serious than something of a minor nature. The interrogator then substantiates the admission of the suspect, detailing locations, times and amounts. This tactic allows the subject to save face and covers his conscience's reluctance to withhold information.

Use of the Investigation as a Wedge

The interrogator should avoid any show of impatience with the suspect. Showing impatience plays into suspects' hands and shortens the development process. Rather, the interrogator should empathize with suspects, reminding them that it is difficult to remember, but that there are still things that they have not recalled yet about the incident. During development, the interrogator should repeatedly assert that it is important that the suspect tell the interrogator what the investigation has already discovered. By the suspect's confirming what is already actually known in the investigation, the subject will show cooperation. Thus, the use of the investigation as a wedge can encourage the suspect to give additional admissions, hoping to substantiate what he believes the investigation has already uncovered. As interrogators encourage the suspect to make additional admissions, they might use other techniques, such as focusing on the future or changing perspective to illustrate their points.

In response to an interrogator's use of the investigation as a wedge, many suspects will respond, "Well, just tell me what the investigation has and I'll tell you whether it's correct or not." The interrogator should not reveal any evidence at this point in the interrogation. To do so will only compromise the interrogator's ability to develop additional admissions. The interrogator should counter the suspect's move by expressing understanding that the suspect does want to know what the investigation has revealed. The interrogator might say something like the following:

> "Bob, I understand what you're asking. I'd like to be able to just sit here and tell you everything that the investigation has revealed. But I can't do that. The reason that I can't do that is not to be a hard guy or to cause you any difficulty, but because I have to make some important decisions about how truthful you are being with me. I need to know whether you're cooperating in the investigation. One of the ways that I can assess your cooperation is by holding back what I already know, so when you tell me the things that I already know, I can feel comfortable that you are being straight with me."

The interrogator can explain that others who make the final decision, such as personnel, store management, or a prosecutor, will be asking a very difficult question. That question is, "How do you know the suspect has cooperated?" The interrogator then explains to the suspect that this question is the most difficult question to be answered. The question of whether something happened has already been answered by the investigation, but the only outstanding question is the level of the suspect's cooperation and truthfulness.

Substantiation of Amounts

The Length of Involvement. The interrogator must establish the length of involvement in criminal activity during the process of substantiation. The time that a suspect has been involved in the criminal acts will give the interrogator a sense of the scope of the problem. The length of involvement can be expanded closer to the true time frame through the use of exaggeration as discussed earlier in this chapter. It is also beneficial for the interrogator to attempt to arrive at the true time frame for purposes of averaging amounts and estimating the total number of incidents.

An interrogator must recognize that suspects will often attempt to minimize the length of their involvement in criminal activity. A standard response from suspects is, "This is my first time." Only rarely do investigators apprehend someone the first time they do something. The interrogator, however, recognizing that the suspect will attempt to minimize his involvement, utilizes exaggeration to reduce the level of seriousness. For example, an interrogator might ask an 18-year-old suspected of breaking into cars, "How long has this been going on? I mean have you been doing this since, like, you were 11?" This will generally result in a denial from the suspect and allow the interrogator to expand the length of activity. Some suspects might have been involved at age 11, so the interrogator should reduce the age further if the suspect's background is particularly bad.

The Most Taken at Any One Time. Often it is worthwhile to have the suspect identify the most amount of money or merchandise that he stole at any one time. This is particularly important in the private sector when attempting to develop the total amount of money or merchandise stolen from a company. This will also assist the interrogator in estimating the scope of the suspect's involvement. For example, if a suspect acknowledges stealing merchandise valued over $300 on a single occasion, the interrogator should anticipate that the suspect's total involvement is significant. Although this is not necessarily a true gauge of the suspect's overall theft activity, it can give the interviewer a sense of the upper limits of the dollar loss the suspect has caused.

The Average Amount Taken Each Time. When theft activity covers months or even years, the interrogator might have to resort to averaging to determine the extent of the suspect's theft activity. Few suspects keep track of the items or cash they have stolen. It is necessary for the interrogator to have the suspect give a best estimate. Generally, it is better to do the averaging after the interrogator has developed the length of involvement and the largest single theft activity. To do otherwise will encourage the suspect to limit the length of involvement and reduce the overall admission.

Suspects should be encouraged to give a total dollar figure that is both fair to them and as close to the truth as possible. One of the major difficulties faced by suspects who have been involved in ongoing theft activity is estimating a total dollar figure stolen. Suspects typically underestimate the value of the money and merchandise that they have stolen because they are only taking small amounts over a long period. An interrogator can illustrate how small amounts add up by having the suspect think about the cost of cigarettes, newspapers, or eating out over a year's time. Any of these calculations will assist the suspect in understanding how small amounts add up over a long period of time. Once again, suspects need to be supported by the interrogator during this calculation. They must understand that the interrogator sees them as an entirely different person, as someone taking only small amounts that added up over time, instead of seeing them as someone who would go into a safe and take a large amount at one time.

The interrogator, in presenting the newspaper example, simply calculates the cost of a newspaper purchased each day and on Sunday. This amounts to perhaps $4 per week, or over $150 per year. If interrogators attempt to develop an admission this way, they will overestimate the suspect's theft activity because they are not taking into account that the employee does not work every day or week of the year. The correction for this error can be made using averaging.

By having the suspect establish an average amount stolen and an average frequency of his activity, an interrogator should be able to arrive at estimates close to the suspect's actual involvement without being over. Averaging takes into account the days or weeks the suspect did not steal by locating the average between zero theft activity and the largest amount the suspect stole.

This averaging can take one of several forms, but it is most often used in general cash and merchandise thefts from companies. In this type of averaging, the suspect is encouraged to give a daily or weekly average amount stolen that can be calculated into a total monthly average and finally an estimated total theft figure.

By starting the average on a daily or weekly basis, the suspect is encouraged to arrive at a figure closer to his actual involvement. An interrogator starting out on a daily or weekly development strategy is giving the impression that the suspect's frequency is typical of the theft activity of other employees. Furthermore, this strategy tends to use smaller numbers that minimize the suspect's involvement until a grand total is calculated. These smaller unit numbers make this kind of totaling more palatable to the suspect.

The List of Items. In many cases, suspects will remember specific items that they took. It is beneficial for the interrogator to simply ask suspects to recall all the different types of items they have stolen from residences, businesses, vehicles, or companies. The interviewer should continue to list these items without regard to the quantity or value. Once the suspect can no longer recall any additional items, the interrogator should return to the number, value, and origin of the items.

When returning to the quantity of the items stolen, the interrogator should use the working assumption that more than one item was taken by the suspect. This is especially true in internal theft cases. The use of exaggeration once again will help the suspect to minimize his actual theft activity.

An example of exaggeration might be asking a suspect, "What would be the greatest number of shirts you have taken? Are we talking about 50 or 60?" The suspect responds, "Oh no, just three or four." By exaggerating the total theft activity, the interrogator has minimized the seriousness in the suspect's mind and encouraged him to make an admission closer to the truth. Once the quantity has been established, the interviewer should have the suspect identify the particular items by value, style, or description. Once this has been done for all the items listed, the interrogator can calculate a total dollar figure for the suspect's theft activity.

In public law enforcement, the location of theft is the next most important area to cover. The interrogator attempts to establish the origins of all items so that they can be compared with robbery, burglary, or theft reports on file.

The Total Dollar Figure. The interrogator should have been taking notes during the later part of the substantiation process. It is preferable for the interrogator rather than the suspect to do the note taking. If suspects are allowed to make a list, they might recall what they had said previously with greater ease because of the notes of admission. Also, allowing the suspect to list the items stolen reduces the interrogator's ability to test the suspect's truthfulness. By having the suspect go back and repeat the items from memory, the interrogator might find that the suspect unwittingly makes additional admissions. Finally, allowing suspects to write the list of the items shows the suspect the magnitude of the theft and might actually reduce the admission because they realize the large dollar value of the merchandise. This can be quite a shock because the interrogator has been minimizing the seriousness each step of the way.

When the suspect can list no additional items of stolen merchandise, the interrogator totals their value. Without telling the suspect the total, the interrogator should then ask the suspect what he believes is the total. Regardless of how the suspect responds, it is to the interrogator's benefit. If the suspect responds with a number higher than the calculated figure, the interrogator returns to the substantiation of that amount to determine how the suspect arrived at that figure. Often the suspect will make new admissions or increase the number of items to account for the difference.

If the suspect gives a figure substantially lower than the amount already substantiated, the interrogator must rationalize and support the suspect. The interrogator should tell the suspect that merchandise and money have a way of adding up over time. To illustrate this point, the interrogator might refer to the mock calculations of money spent on newspapers, meals, or cigarettes over a year's time. Then the interrogator should tell the suspect that the person who would take $1,000 at one time out of a safe is entirely different from one who takes small amounts over a long period of time that add up to the same figure.

The interrogator should again ask the suspect what would be the most merchandise he could possibly have stolen. If the suspect again gives a figure over and above the total calculated, the interrogator should return to the substantiation-of-amounts technique.

Sometimes, a suspect will set the amount of the theft activity at the approximate figure calculated from the items listed. The interrogator should then say, "That's approximately right based on what we have here, but there are some things that you have not remembered at this point based on the investigation." Here the interrogator continues the development by using the investigation as a wedge to get additional admissions. The interrogator also might support the suspect by reminding him what a difficult time this is for the suspect, having to remember small things over a long time.

The Repetition of Topics. Patience and persistence are the interrogator's assets during development. The interrogator should return to each area previously discussed and attempt to gather additional admissions from the suspects. It can be frustrating for the interrogator to be spoon fed small admissions by the suspect, who all the while is lying about his involvement. However, it is imperative that the interrogator not berate the suspect for failing to remember or for lack of cooperation during development. The interrogator should empathize with the suspect by recounting that it is a difficult time and hard to remember things that were done over a long time. The suspect should be repeatedly told that the interrogator believes he is cooperating and that he will remember additional items he took.

Upon returning to the previous topics to continue development, the interrogator should use an assumptive question, such as "What else did you think of in this area?" When returning to the previous topics, it is often helpful for the suspect to relist items stolen and reestimate the frequency and length of involvement and other information already substantiated. By asking a suspect to repeat previously developed information, an interrogator will be able to determine whether the figures and information vary significantly from what was previously said.

To lie requires a good memory. Suspects who are making up information during the development phase of the interrogation will rarely be able to recall consistently what they have previously admitted. An interrogator who discovers that the suspect is unable to recall what was previously admitted should anticipate that the suspect has not been entirely candid. This is generally a good indication that the suspect has not made a full statement of his activities as yet.

The Mental Review of Places. In an attempt to jog suspects' memory regarding specific items stolen, the interrogator should have the suspect mentally review his house, bedroom, and vehicle. Often, suspects who mentally walk through their residence will recall particular items or incidents that need to be discussed. This technique is also effective for loss prevention representatives, who can have suspects mentally walk through the store or warehouse, department by department, in an attempt to identify items that they stole. As the suspect *mentally* walks through these areas, the interrogator should use educated guesses to expand the admission. The interrogator suggests items frequently stolen from the company or residences and observes the suspect's behavior. If the suspect pauses after a suggested item, the interrogator should use a follow-up assumptive question, "How many of those did you take?"

Interrogators often find it beneficial to suggest items that the suspect could have used personally. Individuals often begin their theft activity taking things they need or want and only later expand to stealing for profit or friends. It might also be helpful to ask the suspect to consider gifts he has given to friends or family. These gifts could have been merchandise or property "liberated" at no cost to the suspect. In internal theft cases, a company catalog of merchandise might also be used to refresh a suspect's memory. This strategy can also assist the interrogator, by determining specific descriptions and the prices of the merchandise stolen.

Finally, it is always to the interrogator's benefit to ask suspects what else they should discuss. If the suspect's resistance to a confession has been reduced significantly, he might give additional information against his own interests. Occasionally, the suspect mistakenly believes the interrogator has additional information and is merely testing him, so he makes another admission. Others just want the slate wiped clean so they have no ghosts in their closet. But, for whatever reason suspects provide the information, the interrogator can derive additional admissions just by asking.

Broad to Specific Issue

One area of strategy that interrogators might consider in the development process is whether to go from nonspecific incidents offered by the suspect to the specific criminal act or go from the specific crime to other areas of involvement. This decision must be made early in the interrogation, sometimes as early as the opening accusation. Selection of the direct accusation identifies the issue and might limit development to other crimes because the suspect sees that issue as his only exposure. The assumptive question might also allow the interrogator to broaden the attack by asking for the total number of times a crime was committed, without identifying the specific incident. The admission from the suspect might not include the crime that is known, thus gaining additional confessions of wrongdoing.

Some organizations with collective bargaining agreements are prohibited by their contract from approaching the interrogation with this broad-to-specific strategy. Under the contract, the union requires that the specific incident be addressed before "going fishing" into other areas where the suspect's criminal activity is only speculated.

Behavioral Peak of Tension

One of the difficulties in any interrogation is to establish an end point or direction for the interrogator. It is especially difficult when interrogating a pattern of theft activity or frequency of activity, some of which might not be identified. The behavioral peak of tension is a method for the interrogator to determine, through the suspect's behavioral responses, the extent of the suspect's involvement in terms of total dollar value or frequency. The interrogator asks:

- "Do you think the amount of money you have taken could be as much as___?"
- "Do you think this happened as many as ___ times?"

The blank space is filled in with varying amounts, beginning with what is believed to be a known truthful figure. The interrogator uses an amount that far exceeds any involvement the suspect could have. Asking a question with an amount that significantly exaggerates the suspect's involvement will compel the suspect to make an immediate emphatic denial. The interrogator has now established a behavioral picture of how the suspect looks when making a truthful denial. This also further minimizes the seriousness of what the suspect has actually done. The key behaviors for the interrogator are the spontaneity of the denial and its strength, along with the suspect's eye contact. When the suspect is truthful, the denial will be spontaneous and firm, with no hint of hesitation. The suspect's eye contact is direct in meeting the interrogator's eyes. Once the interrogator has established what he believes is a known truthful response, the interrogator pairs that response with a lower possible theft figure. For example,

> *Interrogator*: Do you think the amount of money that you have taken could be as much as say $20,000?
>
> *Suspect*: Absolutely not! [*Spontaneous direct eye contact*]
>
> *Interrogator*: Great! From the investigation, I didn't think it would be anywhere near that amount. How much do you think it would be? I mean, could we be talking about say $10,000 over the entire 6 months you worked for the company?
>
> *Suspect*: No way! [*Spontaneous and direct*]

The interrogator, in assessing the suspect's truthfulness, recognizes that the behavioral response to the second amount is similar to the response to the $20,000 figure. Thus, the interrogator can conclude that the suspect is telling the truth at the second figure. That second figure now becomes a likely truthful amount and a third possible theft amount is offered:

> *Interrogator*: Okay, well, do you think you could have taken as much as $8,000 over the whole time that you have been here?
>
> *Suspect*: No way! [*Spontaneous and direct*]
>
> *Interrogator*: You're sure? You're as sure as you would be at the $20,000 figure?
>
> *Suspect*: Yes. [*No hesitation, good eye contact*]
>
> *Interrogator*: Well, would you say it's more or less than $5,000?
>
> *Suspect*: Less. [*No hesitation*]
>
> *Interrogator*: Well, do think we could be talking about say just $4,000? That's less than $1,000 per month.
>
> *Suspect*: [*Hesitates, looks away and says weakly*] I don't think so.

This same scenario can be used when interrogating a person believed to be involved in several burglaries, armed robberies, or multiple crimes.

The interrogator, using the suspect's behavior, has now identified an amount where the suspect is no longer certain. The hesitation, weak voice, and break in the eye contact register the suspect's uncertainty. This may not lead to a confession of $4,000, but the interrogator can use this information in several ways. First, the interrogator now has a point toward which he can work. This is probably the highest level of the suspect's involvement, although it is conceivable that the real amount could actually exceed this figure. However, if this technique is used in the final stage of development, after the suspect has talked through the items stolen, it is generally close to the truth.

Second, the interrogator can indirectly assign this amount of theft or frequency to the suspect under investigation. This can assist in making investigative decisions on the allocation of investigative resources on a particular case. For example, if inventory figures establish a $4,500 loss in a particular department, a suspect making an admission of $4,000 has, in all probability, been the significant problem in that department. However, if the suspect had admitted only $500, and the behavioral peak indicated that the suspect was responsible for less than $1,000, then the interrogator should continue to assign investigative resources to that department to resolve the additional shortage. In the same way, police investigators can evaluate the size of a drug dealer's business by establishing amounts and frequency of sales. This will help focus a department's investigative resources in the most fertile areas. Thus, this behavioral peak of tension can be effectively used to establish the frequency of activity, number of items, or dollar amounts that a suspect may have been involved in stealing.

This technique can also be effective in establishing a suspect's knowledge of other individuals' involvement. The interrogator asks a suspect to rank other individual's honesty from one to ten, with ten being the most honest, and begins with the most reputable people. In general, the suspect will respond to these people with the number ten. As other individuals' names are offered to the suspect, the suspect might hesitate and give a lower number, such as six, indicating that the suspect has reason to believe or has suspicions that the other individual might be dishonest or involved in similar activity. The interrogator should take advantage of this information using an assumptive question: "What is the single most expensive item that you have ever seen [name of person ranked six] take?"

The suspect will typically respond in one of three ways. First, he might respond with a particular item that he knows that person has taken. Second, he might give a specific denial, "I have never seen Bill take anything," in which case the interrogator follows up with another assumptive question: "What is the single most expensive item that Bill has told you he has taken?" The specific denial of the suspect does not deny knowledge, but rather only the actual observation of Bill's having taken something. Third, the suspect might ask if he has to answer the question. If the suspect responds in this manner, the interrogator should encourage the suspect to be truthful. The suspect responding this way is actually asking for permission not to tell. In many cases, all the interrogator has to say is, "Yes," after which the suspect gives the item or name he had been withholding.

Change of Interrogators

Generally, the primary interrogator should continue the interrogation for as long as possible. Changing interrogators before a suspect has made an initial admission of guilt only serves to strengthen the suspect's resolve. Changing interrogators is best accomplished in the latter stage of the development phase when a fresh interrogator can rework areas covered by the primary interrogator.

It might also be beneficial for the new interrogator to introduce new topics. For example, in certain types of cases, such as the theft of a deposit, an interrogator might have rationalized with the suspect that this was the first time anything like this happened. Once the suspect has admitted stealing the deposit, it is often difficult for that interrogator to expand into other types of theft activity because of the rationalization used to gain the initial admission. However, the new interrogator is not bound by that rationalization and can introduce new topics to the development process in an attempt to expand the admission.

Sometimes, suspects will withhold information simply because they are embarrassed about having lied to the first interrogator so many times: they lied and made an admission, lied and made an admission. Finally, they stonewall and will not make any additional admissions to the first interrogator. The introduction of a new interrogator at this time often results in significant additional admissions because suspects are not unwilling to make the admission but were simply embarrassed that they had not told the whole truth to the first interrogator. The introduction of a new interrogator also has the advantage of fresh patience and persistence being focused against a weakened suspect.

In some situations, the second interrogator might have acted as the witness during the primary interrogation. In this instance, the primary interrogator and witness simply switch positions. The primary interrogator is now positioned as the witness, with the actual witness taking the role and seat of the primary interrogator. The witness should be utilized as a second interrogator only when he is competent and understands the interrogation process. Allowing an unskilled interrogator to develop additional admissions often results in the suspect's recanting all or part of the previous admissions.

If, during development of the admission, the suspect increases his resistance or begins to recant his admissions, the interrogator should return to rationalizations to reduce the suspect's resistance. However, if his resistance does not diminish, a written statement should be taken immediately, before any further questioning. This way, the interrogator is assured of a document containing incriminating admissions that can be used in court or to terminate the employee.

The Use of Evidence or the Absolute Denial

Generally, an interrogator should not reveal evidence until the final stages of development. Evidence used early in the interrogation typically results in a suspect's attempt to explain it away or admitting only to what is known by the interrogator. By withholding evidence until the final stages of the interrogation, the interrogator has reduced the suspect's resistance to a confession and strengthened even weak circumstantial evidence. During the final stages of an interrogation, the suspect might make an absolute denial, which is when the suspect absolutely denies the existence of any other criminal involvement or the existence of evidence to the contrary. Usually, the suspect says something like, "That's it, that's all I've done, there is absolutely nothing else. I don't care what you or your investigations say." It is at this time that the suspect is most susceptible to the presentation of evidence. The suspect has now called the interrogator in on a game of cards and it is time for the interrogator to play his ace. By using the absolute denial, the suspect has left no room to explain any evidence presented by the interrogator.

Once the suspect has made an absolute denial, the interrogator presents a piece of evidence that clearly refutes his statement. An interrogator then often finds that the suspect is susceptible to significant additional admissions. In theft cases, it is not unheard of for a suspect to change admissions from a few hundred to several thousands of dollars simply because, at a key moment, evidence has been presented that refutes his protestations of innocence. For example:

> *Suspect*: That's all I've done; I don't care what you or your investigation says.
>
> *Interrogator*: Mark, that's just not true. I'm going to give you one small piece of evidence to show you I'm not bluffing. I'm not trying to be a hard guy or trying to trick you, but I can tell you about the money you took an hour and a half ago if you want.
>
> *Suspect*: [*Silence, withdrawn, physically shrinks as the evidence of guilt is presented*]
>
> *Interrogator*: Nobody wants to put you in a bad spot, but it is important to be truthful. How much money did you take this morning?
>
> *Suspect*: $50.

Interrogator: Okay, let's go through this again and make sure...

Interrogator returns to techniques to develop the admission.

Playing One Against the Other

One of the oldest tricks in the book is playing one suspect against another during the interrogation. The interrogator has a built-in lie detector knowing the truth has been reached when the suspects' stories match. It is much easier for a single individual to hold up under interrogation than one who belongs to a group. The single subject has all the information, while the suspect in collusion with others has to worry what everyone else is saying.

Suspects' words, when inaccurate, come back to haunt them when they don't match their compatriots'. The suspect also is forced to consider that another will somehow obtain favor and get a better deal. The advantage favors the interrogators whenever multiple suspects are interrogated separately but in the same time period. Using the story or admissions from one suspect generally encourages cooperation from the others. Collusion cases are like knocking down dominoes. The key to making this tactic successful is having enough manpower available to deal with multiple suspects at once.

Development of Knowledge

The interrogator should attempt to develop implications and investigative leads of other individuals involved in theft or criminal activity. The suspect is a font of information from which the interrogator can draw. The ability to generate implications will increase the productivity of an investigator by using the investigative resources in a direction that will prove most fruitful.

Request for Names

The interrogator should ask suspects for the names of others they know who are involved in criminal activity. Suspects might be somewhat hesitant to give information about another; however, the interviewer can overcome this resistance by offering them limited confidentiality. In addition, an interrogator who is confident and expects the suspect to give an implication is often rewarded with a name.

The interrogator should ask the suspect for implications in a way that expects an answer. If the interrogator asks, "Could you tell me about anybody else taking things?" the suspect will likely answer, "No." However, by asking the suspect firmly and confidently for a name, the suspect will often respond with one. One obstacle that individuals face in revealing another's identity is the fear of being labeled as an informant.

The interrogator should immediately tell the suspect that under no circumstances will the other individual be told of the suspect's cooperation, but this should be said only if it will be true. The interviewer should not tell the suspect that the information will not leave the room because that would be an untrue statement. The results of the information will certainly be shared with other investigators. However, if the interrogator knows it can be kept confidential, then it is proper to tell the suspect that the implicated individual will not learn of his cooperation. It is at this point that the interrogator should attempt to determine the extent and value of a suspect's information about other criminal activity.

Trading pending criminal charges for a dismissal or reduced sentence in return for an informant's help in penetrating another criminal organization is often done now. For example, two youths were apprehended with a stolen handgun. During the subsequent interrogation, they identified an apartment where gang members purchased and stored weapons. In exchange for their help in obtaining a search warrant, the interrogator offered to tell the prosecutor and judge of their cooperation in another case.

Suspects are often eager to help the interrogator solve other crimes and are full of grand promises of help. The motivation to help diminishes rapidly if the investigator does not maintain the leverage of sentencing, or a criminal complaint, over the suspect. The interrogator should work with the prosecutor before making any promises he might not be able to keep.

Once the suspect has given another individual's name, the interrogator should attempt to determine how he came by this information. It might be that he knows this information because he was also involved in the incident. The interrogator should substantiate exactly who the other individual is and the circumstances surrounding the criminal activity. This will allow the investigator to initiate a new investigation into the circumstances given or provide the information necessary to interview the new suspect. In interviewing the new suspect, the interrogator now has information to help construct either the introductory statement or the participatory accusation to begin the interrogation.

Once a suspect's name has been given, the interrogator should anticipate that there might be other suspects of whom the suspect has knowledge. If the suspect lacks direct knowledge, he should be asked for suspicions concerning others: approximately 20% of employees have knowledge of another's dishonesty at their company. In certain locations with higher theft activity, the knowledge of others might be significantly higher. In the public sector, the knowledge of other criminal activity is much more likely than in a limited company environment. The interrogator should anticipate that a suspect's friends might often be involved in the same activities as the suspect. Friends tend to associate with one another because of similar interests, values, and backgrounds.

In many cases, a suspect is reluctant to give the interrogator the names of other people involved in thefts or other criminal activity. In those situations, the interrogator should attempt to gather certain information that will help identify who the suspect knows or believes might be involved. By discovering the individual's sex, race, marital status, and position of employment, the interrogator might be able to identify the person to whom the suspect is referring. If the interviewer or interrogator exercises patience at this time, he might be rewarded with the identity of other suspects.

Substantiation of Admissions using the Polygraph

The difficulty in any interrogation is knowing when suspects have divulged all the information at their disposal. Many suspects slowly give up less important information or crimes in hope that the interrogator will be satisfied and leave them alone. Certainly, holding back information is one method of testing a suspect's level of cooperation, but this advantage might disappear if the individual confesses to what is known.

One possible solution is the use of the polygraph to test the suspect's truthfulness. A variety of possible examinations can help confirm that the suspect has told the interrogator about all the incidents. The polygraph can also be used to confirm an informant's truthfulness prior to expending limited department resources on what could be a wild goose chase.

The private sector generally is limited as to when a polygraph examination can be administered to an employee. Former employees and nonemployees are exempted from the Employee Polygraph Protection Act and may be tested whenever they agree to submit to an examination. In the event that a company wants to polygraph an existing employee, specific requirements must be followed to conform to the law. In general, public law enforcement is exempted from the Employee Polygraph Protection Act; however, state laws might prohibit certain polygraph examinations in whole or in part.

Developing an admission can be a huge return on investment. It is rare that an individual is caught the very first time he commits a crime. The interrogator, using persistence and patience, can identify the full scope of a suspect's involvement and knowledge. This careful development of admissions can allow the interrogator to clear other cases, develop informants, and recover evidence that would have been found in no other way.

During the development of the admission, the interrogator should carefully consider the consistency of the admissions and test for truthfulness of the suspect's assertions. Remember, the suspect should confirm what is known from the investigation rather than being spoon fed details by an overanxious interrogator. Determining a suspect's truthfulness is compromised when the interrogator has offered details of the case. Let the suspect offer details first; then compare them against what is known.

Part Seven

The Statement

The Statement
14

A statement is like the period at the end of a sentence — without it, the job is incomplete.

The final statement is a written document or audio-video recording obtained from a victim, witness, or suspect that encompasses the discussion that occurs during the interview or interrogation. The statement is not necessarily a confession, although, in many cases, it is. The purpose of this statement is to lock an individual into the details admitted or statements made during the interview or interrogation. Formalizing the admission in written or recorded form deters the suspect, witness, or victim from changing the story and reduces the possibility that evidence or testimony will be lost or manufactured later at a hearing or trial. For victims and witnesses, it can also serve as a means to refresh their memory at a later date.

The written statement has value in a number of specific areas. The use of the statement at a civil or criminal hearing is well understood by most people. The statement, however, also has value in union arbitrations, company hearings, unemployment compensation hearings, claims investigations, and in terminations. The private sector can use the written statement as a loss prevention tool for management. By analyzing the methods of loss, management can effectively tighten operational controls to reduce the possibility of similar future losses.

In many instances, the written statement can also be used to establish loss for insurance purposes. This is especially important in the private sector, where companies are protected by one or more types of insurance. The statement establishes that the employee breached his fiduciary duty to the company. This breach of trust is established in the statement by detailing the employee's dishonest acts. Second, the written statement also explains to the insurer the first time the loss occurred, total amount of loss, and the method used to accomplish the theft. By establishing these parameters, a company can often file a claim with the insurer.

The written statement also provides attorneys with an understanding of what a witness might testify to. These types of statements can be particularly effective in the early stages of a lawsuit, when attorneys are developing information through interrogatories or depositions. By establishing the information a witness or a victim holds, the opposing counsel can quickly ascertain the direction for depositions and what specific information can be useful.

The statement can also act as evidence, should a victim, witness, or suspect die prior to a hearing or trial. A dying declaration may be admitted as evidence if it is made by a victim who believes he is dying. These statements are often admitted even though the defense is unable to cross examine the victim because of the general belief that a dying person would not use the last breath to lie. In certain instances when a witness is dead, a statement given prior to his death may be admissible in court or at a hearing. In the event that a witness is unavailable for a particular hearing or has become mentally incompetent, the evidence provided by his statement may also have some evidentiary value.

In both civil and criminal cases, the witness, who might later be asked to testify, might have to remember an incident that occurred several years before trial. Because the memory can be a tenuous thing, the witness's statement can often help recall the circumstances surrounding the incident. Especially in civil cases where it might be 3 or more years before trial, the statement can have considerable impact on recall, and thus, on the value of the resultant testimony. These statements can also lock in truthful testimony that an individual might be tempted to change later because he was terminated or was bribed to tell a different story.

A suspect's statement can take one of two forms. The first denies any involvement but relates his alibi or the circumstances surrounding the incident. Once this information has been documented, it is difficult for guilty suspects to change their stories. Should they later attempt to change their alibi or the circumstances of the incident, the original statement can be used to discredit their newly offered information. By locking suspects into the details of their alibi or the circumstances surrounding the event, the investigation can clearly focus on proving or disproving the information contained in the statement. At trial, a statement that can be proved false has almost as much effect on the judge and jury as a confession of guilt.

The value of the written statement and its usefulness in the investigative process is demonstrated by the following case example:

Case Example

Three males in their late teens were suspected of setting fires during a single evening at three residences in the rural area of a county. The police, through their investigation, obtained a partial license number and descriptions that matched the three youths and their vehicle.

The youths used each other to establish their alibi for the evening in question. Although the investigative information was sufficient to focus suspicion upon them, it was insufficient to arrest or obtain an indictment for arson.

The three young men were interviewed separately and each was asked to give a detailed recital of the evening's activities with the other two boys. Initially, each of them gave broad, vague descriptions of the evening. However, the interviewers had each of the boys detail moment by moment where they had been, with whom they had been, and what had occurred, covering all aspects of the evening.

When the three statements were compared, it was evident that, although certain elements of the evening were consistent, the details varied greatly. The youths differed in the type of vehicle they claimed to have driven, the locations they had visited, the order of the visits, the people they had seen, and the times the events occurred. Even at points of general agreement, the details varied significantly.

These differing statements, along with the information that the investigation developed, became the focal point for the interrogation of the three young men. As a result of the pre-interrogation written statements from the three, the interviewers were able to take away the suspects' ability to use each other as alibis. This ultimately helped in achieving their confession.

The second form of a suspect's statement is an admission of guilt. The details of an admission and the elements necessary to prove the crime are included in this statement. This serves as additional evidence of the suspect's guilt. If an interrogator fails to accurately reproduce a suspect's verbal admission in a permanent record, the job is only partially completed and successful. The written or recorded admission of guilt made by a suspect has a tremendous impact on the judge, jury, or hearing officer and their corresponding belief in the suspect's guilt.

In instances where multiple admissions are made to separate crimes, the interrogator should obtain a separate confession for each crime or incident.

This is done in cases where the inclusion of other dishonest activity may bias the original confession, for example, as with a burglar who admits breaking into a home and removing cash and a TV set and who also admits stealing a car earlier in the year. The inclusion of this information in the written statement regarding the burglary might bias a jury and consequently cause the written statement to be excluded from trial.

Types of Statements

An oral statement can be put into writing in a variety of different formats. Some of these are:

- Narrative
- Question and answer
- Formal
- Audio or video recordings

The type of statement selected for use by the interrogator may be dependent on the type of case, its seriousness, the resources at hand, and the time factor.

Narrative

One of the most common forms of the written statement is the narrative. It is usually a handwritten account by the suspect, using the first person to describe his activities in the incident. This narrative is generally in the form of a series of paragraphs, written on plain paper or on a form on which the opening or closing portions of the statement have been preprinted.

The suspect's narrative describes the incident and substantiates his involvement with details. It contains the elements of the crime and, in certain cases, the suspect's personal feelings about the incident or incidents. This narrative can also incorporate information relating to the suspect's state of mind at the time the crime was committed.

Question and Answer

In the question and answer type of statement, the interviewer writes by hand or types a series of questions to which the suspect or witness makes a written response. The format allows the interviewer to ask for responses to very specific details of the incident. This format is also typically used in a recorded or formal statement.

An example of this format is provided below.

Question: On December 31, 1991, did you kill John Jones?

Answer: Yes.

Question: What did you use to kill John Jones?

Answer: A Smith & Wesson. 38 snubnose revolver.

Question: Where is the Smith & Wesson. 38 snubnose revolver now?

Answer: I dropped it down the sewer at Forest and Webster Lane in Des Plaines.

Sometimes, a suspect's written narrative statement lacks certain details or elements necessary to prove the crime. In these instances, the question and answer format can be used to supplement the written narrative statement by the suspect. The question and answer format allows the interrogator to clarify points that were unclear in the suspect's narrative statement. It is often helpful with a suspect who is evasive or who makes significant omissions in the written narrative statement.

Formal Statements

In cases where the seriousness of the incident or potential cost to a company is significant, a formal statement should be obtained. The formal statement utilizes a court reporter or stenographer to record the questions and the witness's or suspect's responses.

The use of a court reporter or stenographer in complex issues often facilitates a more detailed and complete statement. Very often, it reduces the time necessary to obtain a statement because the suspect does not have to write the information. Having suspects write can be a tedious process when they have difficulty spelling or writing. Witnesses and suspects tend to shorten statements because they are too long or difficult to write by hand. In shortening a statement, they often omit valuable information just so they can complete the statement. In complex issues, it is usually preferable to avoid the handwritten statement in favor of a formal, typed document or recorded statement.

When an upper level executive might be required to testify as a witness on behalf of the company, it is often in the interest of the company to spend the money to obtain a formal statement. Especially in civil lawsuits in which the company's liability might be extreme, the formal statement can lock the employee into his testimony. This factor becomes important should the employee leave the company or be terminated because of some unrelated issue. Any resulting dissatisfaction with the company could taint the witness's future testimony. In cases that have the potential to go to litigation, the statements should be formalized using audio, video, or stenographic recording to assure completeness.

Audio or Video Recordings

With the expansion of technology has come the ability to clearly record statements by audio or video. Many investigators successfully use these techniques to record a witness's or suspect's statement, which can later be transcribed and included in the case file. This technique is commonly used by insurance claims adjusters when they interview victims or witnesses of accidents.

Audio or video recordings of a suspect's statement or confession can make a significant impression at a hearing or trial. Because the recording shows the suspect at the time of the confession, the jury or judge is able to assess the suspect's emotional state and the voluntariness of the admission. In addition, the suspect's appearance is not polished for the courtroom but is as it was at the time of the arrest. The believability of a confession when seen under these circumstances is enhanced; the video can leave a lasting image with the court. To hear a suspect describe the incident with his own words can be absolutely chilling.

The interrogator who elects to use this type of statement, however, might also wish to take a handwritten or formal statement as well. The interrogator should consider the pitfalls in obtaining an audio or video statement. For example, interruptions of power can cause the recording to be incomplete. This stopping and starting of the tape due to electrical shortage or weakness in the batteries can cause the statement to be questioned at a hearing or in court. The statement will also have to be transcribed, which adds additional costs and time to the case.

In addition, the interviewer should consider whether the audio portion of the recording will be clearly discernible to the listener. Air-conditioning, heating, or other noises in the building can sometimes obscure the recorded dialogue. A suspect often has the tendency to speak softly or mumble when talking about the incident, which can cause the words to be garbled or indecipherable.

Voices can also become garbled if the interrogator and suspect both speak at the same time. In audio statements, it can also be unclear who is speaking and thus be confusing to listeners. When listeners have to sort out who is speaking, they tend to miss the details. For clarity, there should be only two people talking on the tapes, the witness or suspect and the interviewer, and each should be clearly identified at the onset of the recording.

Finally, the interviewer should consider applicable state laws regarding recordings and eavesdropping before recording a statement. Several states require the consent of all parties involved if the conversation is recorded, whereas some states require the consent of only one person to make a recording.

Generally for a recorded statement, the subject's permission to record the statement should be obtained. The interrogator should also note the identity of the persons present during the statement along with the date and time it was obtained. Many video recorders have a function that will allow the date and time to be superimposed on the video image. Remember that an audio recording lacks a visual sense of what is happening in the room and the body language of the interrogator and suspect. In one audio recording, a deputy was physically assaulted by a suspect who had to be physically restrained. The resulting struggle was apparent from the sounds captured on the tape and was followed by the suspect yelling that he would tell the deputy whatever he wanted to know. Certainly an attorney could allege that his client was beaten and confessed only because the deputy physically abused him. This was not the case, but from the tape alone, it would be difficult to prove that it was not so.

Interrogator Control

Regardless of the type of statement used, the interviewer must continue to maintain control to assure a usable statement from the suspect or witness. To allow a suspect or witness to proceed without direction while making a statement almost assures that it will be unusable.

Although interviewers do not dictate the statement, they certainly control the formatting of the document. Leading questions to the suspect will ensure the inclusion of relevant details necessary to prove the elements of the crime and to substantiate the admission. Interviewers should not leave the suspect alone to complete the statement because that would likely result in either no statement being written or the failure to include pertinent information.

The interviewer must sell the suspect on the need for a complete written or recorded statement. Suspects can be told that the statement will tell their side of the story and allow them to say they are sorry or to explain any mitigating circumstances. The interviewer should tell them that the written statement will accurately record the discussion between the interrogator and them.

The suspect should also be told that the statement will allow others to hear his side of the story so the others cannot blow the incident out of proportion. Similarly, a witness should be encouraged to give a statement because it can prevent his being inconvenienced with additional future interviews.

The interrogator also should consider the issue of custody. If the suspect has been in custody during the interrogation, then the *Miranda* warnings should be included in the statement along with the suspect's waiver of them, prior to the narrative or question and answer format. Regardless of the type of statement, the interviewer will find that the use of a standard statement format will enhance his ability to develop the information clearly, concisely, and in an orderly manner.

Timing of Taking the Statement

The suspect's or witness's statement should be taken immediately at the conclusion of the interview or interrogation. The interviewer has established a strong level of rapport and cooperation with the individual that should be exploited. Waiting to obtain a statement at a later date is rarely successful, and more often than not it results in a failure to obtain any statement at all. This failure to obtain a statement can impede the successful conclusion of the case when the witness or suspect rethinks the wisdom of making a written or recorded statement.

The interviewer, having concluded the interview or interrogation, should obtain the written statement without leaving the room. Once the interviewer has developed the information as much as possible, he should begin to introduce the idea of a statement. If the interrogator feels that an individual might be reluctant to write a statement, it might be prudent to have a witness hear the suspect's oral statement.

The suggestion of a written statement can be introduced to the suspect by calling it a statement of explanation. By calling it an "explanation," the interviewer reduces the formality and consequences associated with the words "confession" or "statement." This statement of explanation details what was talked about and the suspect's reasons for taking part in the incident. The interrogator might use questions that encourage a suspect to write a statement. For example, he might say, "I'm sure you'd be willing to write a statement of explanation detailing what we've talked about here, wouldn't you?" By using an assumptive question, the interrogator encourages the suspect to agree to write the statement.

Once the suspect agrees to write a statement, the interrogator should hand him the paper or forms necessary to complete it. Presenting these items, the interviewer simply states the date, for example, "Today is January 29, 2001." This statement by the interrogator encourages the suspect to place the date at the top of the paper.

In the event that preprinted opening and closing paragraphs are used, the interviewer should review the information contained in the opening. Often, these opening and closing paragraphs have been written by attorneys and contain legal terminology that might frighten the suspect. The interrogator should minimize the seriousness of these formal opening and closing paragraphs and encourage the suspect to begin the narrative of his involvement.

In the event that the interrogator has decided to use a court reporter, stenographer, or audio-video equipment to record the statement, the suspect should be sold on the necessity for them in the same way as he would have been if a written statement were used. The interviewer should briefly explain the necessity of the stenographer or recording to make sure that everything is recorded. It will also prevent the suspect from having to write all the information.

When court reporters or stenographers have been retained to take a formal statement, it is beneficial for the interviewer to brief them on the circumstances of the case prior to starting the statement. Having been briefed in advance, the reporter will be better able to follow the statement and will be less likely to be confused by names, places, or events. It is also helpful to provide the stenographer with the correct spelling of the participants, locations, or company names prior to the statement to help them accurately document the statement without interrupting.

When interrogators use an audio-video recording, they can introduce it by saying that it will enable the suspect or witness to make his explanation in greater detail without having to make a written statement. In addition, the interrogator can remind the suspect that the sound of the suspect's words will reflect the truthfulness of the admission. These recordings are often transcribed for a later signature by the witness or suspect, which allows him to correct any errors and sign the document at a later date. Often the transcription is not actually signed but is rendered in a written form for use by attorneys or investigators.

Potential Problems

Statements may be excluded from a hearing or trial for any number of reasons: the allegation of threats, use of leading questions, statements that are changed, mention of other convictions, or even the omission of circumstances favorable to the subject. Any of these can form the basis for the exclusion of a written or recorded statement. By considering and anticipating potential problems, the interviewer can prepare the statement in such a way as to avoid them.

The Suspect Alleges that the Statement Was Dictated to Him

Often, a suspect will say that the statement was dictated to him and that the suspect wrote only what he was told. This allegation might be based on the interrogator's having helped to format the statement and having used leading questions to obtain the details. Other suspects will make this allegation simply because it might seem plausible to those not present. The style of the language, use of slang, and improper spelling by a suspect tend to negate the allegation that the statement was dictated. The interviewer should avoid introducing words that would not be commonly used by the suspect. The interrogator should allow the suspect to spell and structure sentences in a way that is natural for him. This is not to say, however, that the interviewer allows the suspect to omit the necessary elements of the crime or details that make the statement complete.

The Suspect Says that He Cannot Read or Write

In some situations, a less educated individual will attempt to avoid writing a statement because he cannot spell or write well. Some individuals are, though, functionally illiterate and legitimately unable to read or write. In these cases, the interviewer might elect to write the statement for the suspect or to use a stenographer or audio-video type of statement.

When interrogators write the statement for the suspect, they should anticipate his alleging that he was asked to sign a document he could not read. In an effort to avoid or defend against this allegation, interrogators should make a number of mistakes while writing the confession. For example, they might put an incorrect street address for where the suspect resides. In the body of the statement, they might put an amount or a direction that was incorrect.

When the statement is complete, the interrogator reviews it with the suspect. When the statement is read back, the interrogator will find that the suspect will discover mistakes in the details. In the event the suspect fails to mention an error, the interrogator should point it out and question its correctness. The suspect should be asked to cross out these errors and replace them with the correct information. These corrections should then be initialed by the suspect.

When the statement has been completed, it should be witnessed by someone not present during the interrogation or interview. The statement is witnessed by having someone read it aloud, stopping periodically to question the suspect about the details that have been changed. If this method is used, the suspect will have difficulty convincing judge, jury, or hearing officer that the statement was simply presented and he signed it without knowing the contents.

The Recording of a Statement May Be Questioned

Interrogators who use electronic recording of the statement should anticipate that it might create problems in other cases. Attorneys might question why only certain confessions were documented using audio-video equipment. Although this question certainly can be handled with a simple explanation, the defense counsel might attempt to use this question to cloud the issue. Often, an attorney will allege that the interrogator has something to hide because he failed to use electronic recording devices in the present case when the interrogator had used them in previous cases. The interrogator should anticipate this ploy and be prepared with an explanation.

The Suspect Alleges that He Was not Advised of His Rights

On occasion, suspects might allege that they were not advised of their *Miranda* rights. This is more common in situations where no written waiver was obtained from the suspect. In police cases where the suspect is in custody and *Miranda* is required, it should be incorporated as part of the written or recorded statement. By incorporating the *Miranda* rights and the suspect's responses as part of the statement, the interrogator further confirms that the suspect knowingly waived his rights and the statement was given freely.

The Suspect Alleges Coercion in Writing the Statement

Many suspects will allege that they were coerced or forced into producing a written statement. This often plays on the public's fear and willingness to believe that third-degree tactics are used to obtain confessions. Anticipating this allegation, the interrogator can overcome it in one of two ways. First, in the body of the statement, the interrogator can have the suspect respond that he was not forced or threatened in any way to write the statement. In addition, the suspect should also acknowledge that the information contained in the statement is true. This, in and of itself, however, might still leave the potential for the suspect to claim that the statement was forced or coerced.

The second tactic employed by the interrogator is to use the individual who witnesses the written or recorded statement. During the witnessing, the interrogator should ask the suspect to acknowledge verbally that the statement is true, is his own, and has been obtained without the use of threats, promises, or coercion. Although a suspect might later still allege coercion or disavow the statement, it will be more difficult for the suspect to overcome the credibility these tactics provide the interrogator.

The interrogator might also have the suspect include information about his treatment during the interview or interrogation. By documenting lunch, breaks, or bathroom use in the statement, the interrogator could help deter accusations of wrongdoing. Moreover, these details help the judge, jury, or hearing officer to determine how likely it was for a coercive interrogation to have occurred. Who would serve coffee or lunch during a coercive interrogation? This tends to spoil the image of the suspect's having had a confession beaten out of him.

The Suspect Refuses to Make a Written Statement

Suspects might refuse to make a written statement for any number of reasons. Often, they are just embarrassed by their handwriting, spelling, or educational level. The interrogator, in many cases, can obtain a written statement from a reluctant suspect simply by offering to write the statement for him. If interrogators do write the statement for the suspect, they should use the preceding method to assure that the suspect does not allege that he merely signed the document without reading it.

Sometimes, however, suspects will refuse any type of written statement. Typically, they will say that their parents, friends, or an attorney told them never to write anything down. In these cases, it is critical that the suspect's oral statement be witnessed by others. It is advisable to make an audio or video recorded statement as previously discussed.

If a witness was in the room during the interrogation, that individual will be able to testify to the suspect's treatment and verbal statement. It is usually in the interrogator's best interest to have an uninvolved participant rewitness the oral admissions of a suspect who refuses to write a statement. In the private sector, this might be the company official responsible for deciding whether to terminate the suspect's employment.

In rewitnessing a statement, the witness is brought into the room and the interrogator reiterates the admission in front of the suspect. The interrogator periodically stops to ask the suspect about specific details of the admission. In doing so, the suspect is brought into the conversation and eventually the suspect re-admits to the incident in front of the uninvolved third party. The interrogator, in front of the witness, should also question the suspect regarding his treatment and the voluntariness of the confession. By having the suspect admit in front of an uninvolved witness that the statement was true and not coerced, the interrogator will help overcome any later allegations of misconduct.

In addition, this re-admission will provide the necessary information for the company official to make a decision about the suspect's future employment with the company. The recounting of details by the suspect will also enable the company official to testify at hearings should the suspect file for unemployment compensation or a union grievance.

The police interrogator might also elect to have a third party witness the suspect's confession. Depending on the seriousness of the incident, the interrogator might choose to use a prosecutor, female officer, or command personnel to witness the suspect's verbal statement. The selection of a witness in these types of situations should provide the most credible individual available to witness the admission. The use of a female officer or command personnel will enhance the believability that the statement was not coerced or forced in any way. In smaller departments where command personnel or a female officer are unavailable, the use of civilian personnel to witness the statement can be an alternative. Using a dispatcher, file clerk, or a secretary as an uninvolved third party to witness the statement might help overcome any later allegations of coercion or misconduct. The officer witnesses the statement by the method previously described and specifically asks the suspect whether the statement was a result of force or threats.

Upon completion of the oral statement, the third-party witness should make notes about the suspect's admissions to refresh his memory before testifying. These notes may be in the form of a written report or less formal handwritten notes. In either case, the notes or the report should be dated, signed, and maintained in the case file.

The Interrogator Believes that the Suspect May Be Unwilling to Make a Written Statement

An interrogator often can anticipate a suspect's reluctance to make a written statement. This belief is based on the attitude and cooperation the suspect showed during the interrogation. In cases where the interrogator believes that the suspect might balk at writing a statement, the interrogator should have the oral statement witnessed by a third party. In the event the suspect does refuse to prepare a statement, the interrogator has another individual who can testify to the admission. In addition, having the suspect make the admission to yet another person provides an effective tool to persuade the suspect to commit the admission to writing.

Another effective tactic is to have the suspect initial the interviewer's notes prior to the interrogator's requesting the written statement. The interviewer asks the suspect to verify the correctness of the notes and initial those parts that are correct. If the suspect later refuses to write a statement, the initialed notes can be introduced as evidence. The initialing of the notes makes it even more difficult for judge or jury to believe the statement was coerced or dictated.

The Suspect Avoids Admitting Elements or Details of the Crime

Sometimes suspects will attempt to avoid including the details of their admission or the elements of the crime or will not define slang terms in the body of their statement. In this event, the interviewer should prepare a supplemental statement by writing out a number of direct questions that include the elements of the crime, the details, or definitions of slang terms.

For example, a suspect might be reluctant to write or say that he killed the victim and instead says he "did him." That phrase is slang for a killing and is understood by law enforcement professionals, but it might lack the clarity necessary for an ordinary citizen to understand that the suspect murdered the victim. Using a supplemental question and answer format, the interrogator could specifically write down a question that clarifies the suspect's original admission: "On March 28, 1991, I killed Mike Smith." To this the suspect would write or respond "yes" and initial the answer. The interviewer could also define any slang term using a question: "In your statement, when you wrote, 'did him,' did you mean that you killed him?" Again, the suspect would respond "yes" and initial his answer. Used this way, the question and answer format supplements the suspect's narrative statement. It provides the specific elements of the crime and clarifies slang terms or details included in the body of the statement.

Statement Format

Interviewers should become comfortable with a format to use for each and every statement they obtain. Using the same format allows them to concentrate on the details of the incident rather than on what is going to come next in the body of the statement. In most statements, regardless of whether they are narrative, question-and-answer, formal, or recorded by audio or video, a similar format can be used.

The statement has five distinct parts:

- Part One: Introduction
- Part Two: Total admission
- Part Three: Substantiation of the total admission
- Part Four: Voluntariness of the admission
- Part Five: Signature and error corrections

Part One: Introduction

In the introduction of the statement, the interviewer asks the suspect to include biographical information himself. Asking the suspect to include biographical information is nonthreatening to the suspect and provides several benefits to the interviewer. First, it clearly identifies the suspect who is giving the statement by including his name, address, job title, and the location of the company where he is employed. Many interrogators also include information about the suspect's age, educational level, Social Security number, or other pertinent biographical information. The amount of biographical information included in the introduction is dictated by the interrogator or by department or company policy. In the private sector, at the least the suspect's name, position, assignment location, and company should be included.

The second purpose of this biographical information is to allow the suspect to get used to writing by beginning with nonthreatening information. The nonthreatening nature of the first several sentences breaks the ice and makes the suspect more comfortable with writing a statement.

When the suspect is in police custody, the *Miranda* warnings should be incorporated in their entirety into the opening of the introduction. Many statement forms have a preprinted introductory paragraph that allows the suspect to fill in biographical information. These paragraphs also often cover the voluntariness of the admission, either in the introduction or at the close of the document.

Part Two: The Admission

The second part of the statement should be a blanket admission by the suspect that he committed the crime. The initial admission of involvement in the crime contains the element of proof but lacks the details of the admission. This is done for several reasons. First, having the suspect make a total overall admission to the crime sets the stage for later substantiation. It also gives the jury or hearing officer an opportunity to hear the blanket admission first; the blanket admission will grab their attention. Second, should the suspect balk at completing the statement, the interrogator has an overall admission to the crime even though it might lack the substantiation or details. Ideally, this blanket admission should also contain the element of the crime to which the suspect is confessing. This is done by the suspect's using words that include intent — for example, "I stole," "I killed," "I robbed," that show the intent of the suspect to commit the crime. The elements of the crime necessary to prove the violation should be incorporated again during the substantiation of the admission.

Part Three: Substantiation

In this section, the suspect is asked to substantiate the admission with the details of the crime. In the private sector, these details often relate to the theft of company assets. Here, the interrogator has suspects detail the first and last time that they stole money or merchandise, the greatest amount of money or merchandise stolen at one time, the method of theft, how the money was used (including any personal details of its use), and the location of any remaining merchandise or evidence.

For the police interrogator, the substantiation will generally relate only to the details of a specific incident. The police interrogator should often begin with details preceding the crime. For example, in a rape, the suspect might be asked to identify the location where he first saw the victim. It might also include his thoughts during this first observation. Also incorporated in substantiation might be the suspect's identification of evidence, pictures, or documents. Sketches illustrate a particular portion of the admission. All these pieces of evidence should be referred to in the statement and reflect that the suspect dated and initialed the items to identify them.

The interrogator, regardless of whether in the public or private sector, should understand what will constitute proof of the suspect's guilt. In certain cases, it is necessary to include in the substantiation the suspect's mental state at the time the incident took place. Understanding what is necessary to prove the crime will enable the interrogator to encourage the suspect to incorporate those details into the substantiation portion of the statement. For example, in a homicide, the fact that the suspect had repeated arguments with the victim and had disliked him intensely for many years might provide a partial foundation for the suspect's premeditation of the murder.

Part Four: Voluntariness

Once the details of the incident have been included, the interrogator should begin to close the statement. This is done by asking the suspect if everything that he or she wrote is true. The suspect will generally acknowledge that it is the truth.[1]

Suspects should then be asked if they would include that in the statement. They should also be asked if they are making the statement of their own free will without threats or promises. The suspect's affirmative response to this question can be included in the statement by simply saying, "Why don't you put that in, too." Once this admission has been included in the statement, the interrogator, who has been reading along as the suspect writes, makes a decision whether it is necessary to use an additional question and answer statement to supplement or clarify any points of the statement.

Part Five: Signature and Correcting Errors

When the suspect has completed the narrative portion of the statement, substantiated it, and acknowledged its voluntariness, it should be signed by the suspect, interrogator, and witness. The interrogator might ask if there is anything the suspect would like to add to the explanation. Many suspects like to include that they are sorry for what they have done or the reasons they became involved in the incident. Often these reasons were incorporated earlier in the documentation while substantiating the admission. Once the suspect and the interrogator are satisfied that the statement is complete, it should be signed. The interrogator simply points to the place on the page immediately following the last paragraph and makes the statement, "Why don't you write your name here." Generally, the suspect will sign his name at the appropriate spot on the page.

If the suspect hesitates to sign, the interrogator might need to offer additional support to reduce this resistance. Encouraging a suspect to sign the statement can be simply done:

---

[1]*Note*: If the suspect hesitates to admit that what was written is true, the interrogator should return to the techniques used to reduce the suspect's resistance and attempt to develop the admissions further. Even while obtaining the final statement, the interrogator should probe for additional admissions or clarifications from the suspect. Often the suspect's final reluctance to tell the truth is overcome by the actual writing of the statement.

> *Interrogator*: Now everything that you put in here is the truth, right?
>
> *Suspect*: Right.
>
> *Interrogator*: Well, if that's the case, then there certainly shouldn't be any problem signing it because all you're doing is attesting that in fact everything in here is the truth. I mean, you said you were sorry, right?
>
> *Suspect*: Yeah.
>
> *Interrogator*: Well, then there certainly shouldn't be any problem signing it. Why don't you put your name right down there. [*The interrogator again indicates the spot on the page where the suspect is to sign.*]

Once the suspect has signed the document, the interrogator takes the last page and adds it to the other pages of the statement. At this point, page by page, the suspect is asked to initial any scratchouts or corrections made and sign each page of the statement. The suspect is told that this is done to assure that the suspect is the one who made the corrections and nobody else altered the statement in any way. At the same time the suspect initials the corrections, each page of the statement should be numbered. This is done by noting at the top of each page, "page one of three," "page two of three," "page three of three."

This page-numbering technique assures that no pages of the document are missing. Additionally, anyone reviewing the written statement immediately knows how many pages it should contain, and it is readily apparent which, if any, of the pages are missing.

Protection of the Statement

The interrogator has worked long and hard to obtain the confession and the written statement from the suspect. Sometimes, a suspect becomes reluctant to continue or will rethink the wisdom of the decision to commit the admission to writing. In some of these cases, the suspect might refuse to write any more or will attempt to destroy what has already been written. Even a partial statement by the suspect has evidentiary value and should be protected.

As each page is completed by the suspect, the interviewer should remove that page from the desk and conceal it in his case file to protect it from being destroyed. Statements left within reach of the suspect can quickly become damaged or destroyed. Interrogators who allow a suspect to tear up the statement generally allow this to happen only once in their career. In the event that the suspect does tear the statement up, the torn portions of the statement should be recovered and maintained as evidence.

On rare occasions, after beginning to write, a suspect will crumple the paper and refuse to go further. The interrogator should attempt to persuade him to continue to write. However, if the suspect still refuses, the interrogator should attempt to obtain the partially written narrative. A suspect in this state of mind will often attempt to retain the partially written document. Sometimes the document can be obtained through the ruse of offering a wastepaper basket for the scrap paper. Many suspects will, without thinking, throw the incomplete statement away. It can then be recovered later by the interrogator. When the suspect is in custody, the interrogator might be able to obtain the partially written statement prior to the suspect's being returned to the holding cell.

Generally, a suspect who begins to write a statement will complete the document. However, interviewers should protect the statement page by page. They should never leave it in the room with the suspect, should it become necessary to leave. Some suspects, upon completion of the statement, will attempt the ruse of asking to see it again so they can add something to the statement. The interrogator should never return the original statement to the suspect, except page by page for signature; instead, they should offer a clean piece of paper for the suspect to add whatever he feels necessary.

On occasion, suspects request a copy of their statement. This request can be granted unless it is contrary to department or company policy. The statement is available to the defense under discovery rules, so there is little danger of compromising the case. However, if there are other suspects to be confronted on the case at a later time, the interrogator might wish to delay turning a copy of the statement over until the other interrogations are complete. While it is not recommended to give copies of the statement to the suspect until required, interrogators intending to do so should take some precautions. Prior to delivering a copy of the statement to the suspect, they should make a copy and put on each page several unobtrusive small marks that do not appear on the original statement. They then make a copy of the modified copy. The modified copy is now saved in the investigative file and marked as the one used to prepare the suspect's copy. If copies were later made, the interrogator can now prove that those copies came not from the original, but the document presented to the suspect.

Transcription of the Statement

In those instances when a formal statement was obtained from the suspect using a court reporter or stenographer, the interrogator should have the notes transcribed for signature by the suspect. In the event that shorthand was used, the stenographer should be instructed to make several intentional errors per page on the typed document. While reading the typed statement with the suspect, these errors will be found, corrected, and initialed by the suspect.

The tapes or stenographer's notes should be maintained to assuring the accuracy of the transcription, if necessary. The stenographer should date and initial the steno book or transcript to establish its authenticity. When an audio or video recording is made of the suspect's confession, a transcription of these tapes might be made as part of the preparation for trial or hearing. The original tapes should be marked and secured in such a manner that they cannot be taped over. Court reporters, when used for statements, return a formal document that can be reviewed and signed by the suspect.

Witnessing the Written Statement

After the statement has been completed, the document should be witnessed by the interrogator and a witness. The interrogator signs each page of the statement and writes the date and time. The witness also places his or her name on the document immediately below the interrogator's signature.

If the witness was not present when the written statement was obtained, the interviewer should bring the witness into the room, first to witness the oral confession, then the written statement. The interrogator should have the suspect acknowledge that he did, in fact, write the statement, that the signature is his, and that the information contained within the statement is the truth. The interrogator also should elicit from the suspect several verbal admissions that confirm the substantiation contained in the statement. By verbally witnessing the suspect's oral statement and having the suspect acknowledge the truthfulness of the handwritten statement, the interrogator provides another witness able to testify to the suspect's admission.

Completion of Other Documents

The written statement is not the end of most investigations. It might establish probable cause for a search warrant or develop other investigative leads that need to be followed up. The interrogator, at this point in the case, might find it necessary to search the suspect's residence, business, or vehicle. Although a written statement made by the suspect might provide sufficient probable cause to obtain a search warrant, the interrogator can often obtain the suspect's consent to search his home, business, or vehicle. The consent-to-search form outlines the locations to be searched and documents the suspect's authorization for the search. Like the written statement, the suspect's verbal and written consent for the search should be witnessed.

The interrogator should remember that a suspect can give permission to search only locations over which he has control. Children cannot give permission to search the residence of their parents. However, they might be able to give consent to search only their room within that residence. The interrogator should make every attempt to recover evidence indicated in the statement. Many prosecutors will not prosecute an individual on the statement alone but also want corroborating evidence. The recovery of evidence bolsters the statement's credibility and adds to the prosecution's case.

Another standard form commonly used is a restitution agreement. Many private sector interrogators obtain a restitution agreement from the suspect acknowledging the suspect's indebtedness to the company for the amount of the admission. The restitution form also establishes a payment plan to reimburse the company for the loss. Prior to accepting any funds or obtaining a restitution agreement, the interrogator should determine whether it is the company's intent to criminally prosecute the individual. As a general rule, if the company elects to accept restitution from a suspect, it cannot also prosecute him.

Any other forms necessary to complete the termination of a suspect from the company should be presented at this point. In many cases, the company official responsible for the termination of the suspect's employment will have the suspect fill out the necessary forms. A suspect in police custody might need to complete an arrest report or other document to account for personal effects or an impounded vehicle.

The Written Report

Whenever an interrogation has been concluded, whether it is successful or not, the interrogator should prepare a written report detailing the admissions and circumstances surrounding the interrogation. Any unusual requests or problems that occur during the interrogation should be fully noted and documented. It should also be noted if the suspect was allowed to go to the washroom or was fed during the interrogation.

Any documentation of the feeding of the suspect should also be retained. In many instances, a department will bring in food from the outside. It might be beneficial to have suspects who are to be fed write their order on a menu or piece of paper and place their name on it. In this way, it can be added to the case file to substantiate that the suspect was not deprived of food or drink during the interrogation. This is especially important when the interrogation and case development takes a number of hours or even days.

The interrogator's notes taken during the interrogation should also be maintained in the case file. This is especially important should the suspect have initialed or made sketches on them. Any sketches on other pieces of paper that illustrate the method of entry or theft or any other illustration should be initialed by the suspect and maintained in the case file. Each of these can have significant evidentiary value and should be safeguarded in the same way as the written statement.

Ending the Interview

15

The only interviewer with a 100% confession rate is one who has not yet talked to enough people.

The final stage in any interview or interrogation is its close. In this stage, the interviewer's objective is to end the interview or interrogation in a professional and courteous manner, regardless of whether it was successful or unsuccessful.

Obviously, a successful interview or interrogation means that the interviewer obtained information that is helpful to the case. However, an interviewer does not always obtain the necessary information, which can create an uncomfortable situation.

The interviewer might be embarrassed or frustrated at being unable to get an admission from an untruthful suspect. The professional interviewer is the one who identifies when the process will end unsuccessfully. He then accepts the outcome, putting personal feelings aside, and changes from an accusatory to nonaccusatory tone. It is much easier for an interviewer to accept success than failure, but professional interviewers recognize that they are not always going to be successful. The only interviewer with a 100% confession rate is one who has not yet talked to enough people.

Each interview and interrogation can be a learning experience for interviewers. Assessing what they did correctly and, more importantly, incorrectly, they learn from talking with each witness or suspect. This practical experience cannot be gained in a book or classroom.

This chapter considers how to back out of an unsuccessful interview or interrogation as well as how to conclude a successful one. It also discusses the ethical considerations for the interrogator.

Professional Close

Regardless of the reasons for the suspect's lack of cooperation, the interviewer should close the interview on a positive note. By leaving the door open for future cooperation or meetings, the interviewer enhances the likelihood of gaining future information from the witness or suspect. The interviewer who fails to close the interview professionally and courteously risks the possibility of the individual's not cooperating in this or future investigative efforts.

The interviewer who talks with a suspect but fails to gain an admission of guilt might have been successful in eliciting information that can be used later to the investigator's advantage.

Interviewers should leave a card with their name and phone number and encourage the victim or witness to call them if any other information comes to mind. In many instances, victims or witnesses will recall other significant details after the close of the interview. Although the initial interview failed to obtain these details, an individual who has been encouraged to call with other information might report the details to the interviewer. The interviewer should not be hesitant to recontact significant witnesses to determine if they have recalled any other information.

At the close of the interview, the interviewer might want to take time to continue to establish rapport with the victim or witness by finding a common interest. Establishing a solid rapport often has benefits that last long after the interview has been concluded. Taking time to make the victim or witness feel even more comfortable about giving information often ensures their later cooperation when the case reaches a hearing or court. The personal relationships established between interviewers and victims or witnesses often goes a long way in assuring their continued cooperation. Many victims and witnesses who are reluctant to cooperate in a hearing may do so because they do not want to disappoint the interviewer who has shown them consideration and respect.

The Unsuccessful Interview or Interrogation

A more complex issue is backing out of an interrogation with a suspect. The reasons for the interviewer's failure vary from individual to individual and circumstance to circumstance. Regardless of the reason for the failure, the interrogator must back out of the interrogation and put the suspect back to work or release him from custody. The suspect has achieved at least a momentary victory, and the interrogator might be required to swallow his pride when releasing a suspect he believes to be guilty. It is difficult for anyone to face a mocking, condescending individual gloating over victory. It is even worse when that individual is a criminal.

In police interrogations, an abrupt halt to an interrogation comes when suspects invoke their right to silence or counsel. Other reasons to back out are the amount of time the interrogation has taken and a suspect who is able to explain away incriminating evidence developed in the investigation. Although the reasons for concluding an interrogation vary, they require that the interrogator cease the conversation and conclude the encounter.

The best interrogators recognize that not all encounters will be successful and understand that there is an appropriate time to end an interrogation. Although tempting, it is unwise for an interrogator to resort to desperate measures to obtain an admission in the closing moments of an interrogation. This rarely results in an admission but, rather, creates only an unfortunate situation. Attempting desperate measures to fix an interrogation is much like kicking a machine to make it work. Only in very rare instances will the properly placed blow result in the machine's functioning properly. Generally, when an interrogator resorts to desperate measures, the confession obtained is of questionable value. Judges, juries, and hearing officers decide on the voluntariness of a confession based upon the totality of circumstances. The interrogator who interrogates a suspect for long periods of time in an effort to obtain a confession might damage an otherwise prosecutable case.

Interrogators should be professional and courteous even when they have been frustrated and embarrassed by their inability to obtain the confession. Calling the suspect names, yelling, screaming, or otherwise threatening and intimidating him is never appropriate behavior for the interrogator. Although they might momentarily feel emotionally relieved by using these methods, they rarely cause a person to confess and are more likely to create significant problems later.

In other situations, the interrogator presses an interrogation too long and angers the suspect. It is unlikely that an interrogator does this will obtain an admission of guilt. The suspect's anger can dominate an otherwise excellent interrogator simply because the suspect becomes aggressive.

Once interrogators conclude that an admission of guilt is unlikely, they should begin the process of backing out. This process entails a subtle change in questioning that allows the suspect to enter the conversation. Interrogators might now present their factual evidence that indicates the suspect's guilt, which might break his resolve and result in an admission. However, if the suspect remains unaffected by the evidence and continues to maintain innocence, the interrogator changes direction to a secondary topic. This secondary issue could be the theft of other money or merchandise, a different crime, or the suspect's knowledge of who is actually responsible. If the interrogator obtains an admission, he begins the process of development with the suspect.

If the interrogator fails to gain an admission, however, he moves into the interview phase of the interrogation. In this phase of the interrogation, the interrogator begins to ask the suspect open-ended questions that require the suspect to talk. Many of the facts or behavior-provoking questions noted in Chapter 7 can be used in backing out of the interview. The interrogator might begin by asking the suspect if he knows or has an idea about who is responsible for the incident. The interrogation has now moved from confrontational tone to one of eliciting information from the suspect. Often, the information given by the guilty while backing out will be untruthful. The suspect might tell blatant lies while trying to cover his tracks. The interrogator should remain alert for statements that might further incriminate the suspect.

The change in who talks allows the suspect to enter the conversation. This provides several benefits for interrogators. First, it allows them to present their evidence and have the suspect make his explanation. Second, the suspect can release some of his built-up frustration at being accused. Suspects are going to want to explain their innocence. By letting the suspect talk, the interrogator allows the suspect to release this frustration. At the same time, the interrogator focuses on reasons that the interrogation took place. Finally, the interrogator shifts to asking questions that direct the suspect's attention to the future. Future-oriented questions might include the following:

- How do you see your future here at the company?
- Where do you see yourself being in five years?
- Do you have plans on returning to school?
- What type of career path do you see yourself taking?

Interrogators should not apologize for confronting the suspect. Rather, they should shift the blame to the investigation and focus the suspect's attention on other areas of the incident or the future.

Regardless of the reasons for backing out, once the interrogator has neutralized the situation by changing the interrogation into an interview, he courteously indicates that the interview is at an end and thanks the suspect for cooperation. At the conclusion of the encounter, the suspect should be told that the investigation is still open and ongoing. The interrogator should attempt to have the suspect agree to come back and discuss the case again should it become necessary. The suspect who agrees to return for another interview often does so. Many interrogators fail to obtain this agreement from the suspect and thus lose the opportunity of a later meeting.

Sometimes suspects refuse to admit anything, but the evidence alone is sufficient to terminate their employment or to prosecute. In these situations, the interrogator should still professionally and courteously close the interview. If the suspect is to be arrested, then he is detained. If the suspect's employment is to be terminated, the suspect should be asked to wait until the interrogator returns. Under some circumstances, the interrogator might offer refreshments or the use of the washroom to the suspect while the interrogator is absent. The interrogator should document the offers in his notes. This allows the interviewer time to present the investigative evidence to the individual responsible for making the decision to terminate or prosecute.

In certain situations, suspects might be returned to their jobs or be released from custody when the interrogator fails to obtain an admission of guilt. If the suspect is returned to work or released from custody, the interrogator should review what was said during the interrogation and look for new information or investigative avenues that might have been revealed by the suspect. When the suspect is to be released, the interrogator should let the suspect know that he can call the interrogator to talk. Only rarely do suspects later call and confess their involvement, but it does happen.

Sometimes suspects only need time to consider the justifications and rationalizations offered by the interrogator. After they have had time to consider the alternative, they might elect to confess their involvement. As surprising as these later confessions might be, they do occur, although infrequently. Interrogators would never have had the opportunity to resolve these cases if they had closed unprofessionally with the suspect. By leaving the door open for communication and cooperation, the interrogator achieved a successful close to an otherwise unsolved case.

Support for the Suspect

During and following an interrogation, interrogators must recognize a suspect's emotional needs. The suspect is at a low point in his life and sees no hope for the future. The interrogator must support him emotionally and attempt to focus his attention on positive aspects of the future, rather than his immediate situation. An interrogator who gloats or enjoys the suffering of the suspect is unprofessional and will not be respected by peers.

The End of the Interview

Once the suspect has given a complete admission of guilt and a written statement, the interrogator should prepare to make a presentation of the case's facts and admission to the prosecutor or person responsible for the termination of the employee. The interrogator should make the presentation of the facts and admission in a professional manner without gloating or making unnecessary harsh comments about the suspect.

Often, there is a period following the interrogation when an awkward silence between the suspect and interrogator ensues. Sometimes suspects would like to talk about something simply to get their minds off their troubles. This is an opportunity for the interrogator to develop information about the tactics and techniques he employed to obtain the confession. The interrogator has an opportunity to talk with the suspect and get insight into the techniques from the suspect himself. Many times, suspects will explain the feelings they have during the interrogation. These explanations often clarify behavioral patterns and observations that the interrogator made during the interrogation. This is an opportunity for learning that can be of immense value for the interrogator. This time also affords the interrogator an opportunity to continue to support the suspect emotionally as the realization of the consequences begins to become evident.

Final Report

Interrogators should prepare a final report regarding the interview or interrogation while it is still fresh in their minds. Waiting clouds the memory and could result in the omission of pertinent statements made by the suspect. Interviewers should clearly and concisely note the verbal statements made by the victim, witness, or suspect, as well as the circumstances of the interview. They should also note instances where the subject obtained refreshment or used the washroom. The suspect's mental state at the time of the admission can be important in evaluating the totality of circumstances. These notations might directly relate to the voluntariness and admissibility of his statements.

The report may be supplemented with notes of what occurred during the interview or interrogation. Special requests, bathroom breaks and food and drinks served can be noted. The room layout can be sketched and times of particular notifications that were made can be detailed. The interviewer might also want to note the type of accusation and rationalizations that were used along with the time the first admission occurred. The example shown in Figure 15.1 is one of many ways to retain this information.

Ethical Considerations

The interrogator should consider the moral and ethical guidelines that come with being a member of the law enforcement community. Many investigators feel a sense of frustration because they are restrained by court rulings or policy guidelines in their effort to resolve cases and identify the guilty. Often the lament, "Why should I play by the rules when they don't?" is heard. The interrogator should recognize that little separates the honest from the guilty.

WICKLANDER-ZULAWSKI & ASSOCIATES, INC.
POST INTERVIEW SUMMARY

Name:	Case #:
Address:	M ☐ F ☐ Age DOB:
City, State, Zip:	Marital Status: M ☐ S ☐ W ☐ D ☐
Company:	B ☐ W ☐ H ☐ A ☐ Other ☐
SS #:	Date of Employment:
Position: FT ☐ PT ☐	Tenure:
Location:	Salary:
Interviewer:	Witness:

Approximate Times:	Location of Interview:	Date:
Intro/Biographical	Sketch of room setting	
Begin Interview		
First Admission		
Conclude Development		
Statement Started		
Statement Concluded		
Statement Witnessed	By whom:	Comments
Police/HR Called	Officer:	
Police/HR Arrived	Officer:	
Police/HR Departed		
Subject Departed		

Describe the subject's demeanor during the interview

Special Requests by Subject	Interviewer Response w/Times
Restroom	
Food/drink	
Phone	
Lawyer/Union Rep/Parent/Medical	
Was subject left alone?	Times

Type of Approach Used	Special Circumstances
Introductory Statement	
Participatory	
Direct	
Other	

Transcribe the subject's responses to these Post Interview questions that are asked when the statement is witnessed. The interviewer and witness should then witness that the transcribed responses are accurate.

What could I have done to make this an easier experience for you?
Interviewer   Witness
How do you feel now that you have told the truth?
Interviewer   Witness
Was there anything else you wanted to say that was not in your written explanation?
Interviewer   Witness
Was there anything in your statement that was not true?
Interviewer   Witness

Figure 15.1   Form for post-interview summary.

Often, it is merely the honest individual's adherence to the legal, ethical, and moral guidelines that separate the two parties. Following the rules is difficult, especially when the interviewer has emotionally extended himself to resolve the case.

It is difficult for an interviewer to reconcile the time and effort he puts into a case with an unsatisfactory result. It is frustrating for an interrogator to see the criminal released from custody or put back to work when he knows that the person is guilty. By allowing himself to become emotionally involved, the interviewer can easily make the bad decision not to play by the rules. Interviewers and investigators must recognize that their job is to separate themselves and their work from the outcome of the case. Although the final outcome is certainly predicated on the work they have done, a court or hearing officer who does not convict the suspect is no reflection on the superb job done by the investigative community. Once they recognize that their job function is limited to the gathering of information and its presentation to the prosecution, the more emotionally secure they will be in the job they have done. The judge or hearing officer who refuses to accept the validity of the confession has to make that determination on case law and the information presented. Interrogators or interviewers who carefully prepare the case recognize the rights of the suspect and follow the legal guidelines have done the best job possible.

The interview and interrogation of victims, witnesses, and suspects can be a frustrating and a rewarding task. The success or failure of the interviewers is often a direct result of the insights and effort they put forth in resolving a case. Even a lifetime of study of the process will not enable an interrogator to have a 100% confession rate. However, by being aware of the needs of the suspect, the legal constraints, and the guidelines, the interviewer can increase the likelihood of a successful case resolution.

Part Eight

Frequently Asked Questions

Frequently Asked Questions

16

Understanding the suspect's strategy and needs during an interview or an interrogation helps in selecting the proper counter move.

Once interviewers and interrogators have experience in the process, most cases become rather routine. While the pressure of legally and successfully concluding a case is still present, interviewers occasionally run across problems they have not faced before. During our training programs we are often asked recurring questions. This chapter discusses those questions, the underlying reason for the problem, and suggested responses to the problem. Understanding the strategy of the suspect and the needs an individual has during an interview or an interrogation helps in selecting the proper counter move.

Why not just give up your evidence since that will help convince the suspect he is caught?

As mentioned in other chapters, one of the primary reasons for a confession is the subject's belief that his guilt is known. Since that is the case, why not just present the evidence of guilt and really make sure that the suspect is convinced?

Certain cases can be approached in exactly that manner when there is sufficient evidence indicating the suspect's guilt. Showing the suspect a portion of the incriminating evidence can be useful, especially with the more experienced criminal who will be skeptical of the interrogator's truthfulness.

However, a myriad of problems associated with this strategy must be considered by the interrogator:

1. The first difficulty with which to contend is that the suspect has not been offered a way to save face. The interrogator is really asking the suspect to make two or more admissions, "I did it," and "I am a bad person." The failure to rationalize the suspect's actions and allow the suspect to save face can increase resistance, even in light of the strong evidence of guilt.

2. If, during the recitation, the interrogator makes any mistakes in the presentation or interpretation of the evidence, it can undermine the suspect's belief that he is really caught. Remember that suspects are the experts because they were there when the crime took place. In many cases, the investigator is attempting to recreate the crime with an incomplete set of facts. A misinterpretation of a fact creates doubt, which can easily turn the suspect to denials.

3. Presenting evidence also allows suspects to understand the scope of their exposure in the case. Once they know what the interrogator does and does not know, they can decide what must be admitted. For example, in many embezzlement cases, there may be a number of different schemes in place to defraud the organization. Once the suspect knows which one has been discovered, he can make a rational decision about what must be admitted. This clearly will limit the suspect's admission.

4. The presentation of evidence also plays into suspects' hands by giving them something to argue about, thus delaying a confession. The legitimacy of the evidence and even what it means might be open for interpretation. The guilty will focus their attack on weaker pieces of evidence, holding them out as indicators of innocence. They may tenaciously argue over incorrect evidence even when there is other evidence that clearly establishes their guilt.

5. Finally, the innocent subject has been given enough information to make a plausible false confession using the details provided by the interrogator's factual approach. A better confirmation of guilt is to have the suspect tell what happened and, in doing so, confirm the investigative findings in hope of providing information of which the interviewer was not aware and adding further credibility to the confession.

In general, the use of a factual attack is best limited to those cases in which there is an abundant amount of evidence that becomes an avalanche overwhelming the guilty suspect's resolve. For most investigators, extra facts are a luxury not often available.

A suspect asks, "What is this all about?"

The suspect in this instance is looking to establish his exposure. Unlike the previous example, here the suspect is looking for information to identify the boundaries of the investigation: What do they know? This is the real question being asked by a suspect because the suspect has, in all likelihood, been involved in multiple crimes. Consider how many incidents the average criminal might have been involved in and it is no wonder he wants information from the interrogator.

There are several possible responses to this question depending on the goal of the investigation.

1. *Interrogator*: I wanted to talk with you about —.

This response immediately focuses the questioning on a single specific incident. Suspects can now assume what the interrogator might know or suspect. Depending on the interrogator's response, they might also be able to determine how they were discovered. There is a greater likelihood of suspects' making denials using this approach because it specifically identifies their exposure and might be viewed by them as an indirect accusation to which they must respond.

2. Did anyone tell you why I wanted to talk with you?

Suspect: No.

Interrogator: All right, well, let me get to that, right after I confirm some information. You are still living at …

This is a preemptive strike by the interrogator. By asking the question before the wary suspect can do so, the interrogator takes control of the meeting and immediately moves in a favorable direction, creating curiosity. This curiosity buys the interrogator time before being pulled into the encounter. Since an exchange of information has been promised, the suspect is also more likely to give his initial cooperation. The interrogator can now establish a behavioral norm, build rapport, and control the pace of the meeting, having extended the implied promise of future information. Anticipating the suspect's likely question allows interrogators to handle it in a way they prefer, rather than one dictated by the suspect.

3. *Interrogator*: That is what I was just going to tell you. The first thing I wanted to do is to tell you a little about what I do …

A suspect says, "Are you going to get to the point?" or "Are you accusing me?"

This conversational ploy might be used by a suspect at several points in the interview or interrogation. The goal of suspects is to draw the interrogator into a direct accusation. They can then deny involvement and learn a little more about what the interrogator might or might not know. Because there has been no direct accusation, the suspect might be uncertain of what lies ahead and is seeking information. Again, there are several possible responses to the suspect:

1. "The point is you did [*insert issue here*]." The reply by the interrogator is a direct accusation. With this response, the lines of the interrogation have been clearly drawn. The suspect now understands what the interrogator knows or suspects. The problem with this response is that it will almost certainly result in a spoken denial by the suspect, who then must use additional denials to defend his position. The advantage of this response is that it allows the interrogator to gauge the suspect's level of resistance to a confession by listening to the strength of his denials.

   With this reply, the interrogator is committed to a classic interrogation involving overcoming the suspect's denials. The interrogator has forced the suspect to lie and, as a result, that lie must be protected with additional denials.

2. Give me a minute and I think that you will see my point. There are really three things to consider ...." This response to the suspect does several things for interrogators. First, it allows them to continue with their plan of not directly identifying the suspect's crime. The suspect is attempting to identify what is being talked about to gain information and assess the amount of trouble he might be in. This reply does not give the suspect any more information than he already had. Second, the statement buys interrogators additional time to allow the rationalization process to work on the suspect's resistance. Third, the interrogator's response creates curiosity: what are the three things that are going to be discussed? how do they apply to me? While the suspect waits for the answers to these questions, the interrogator continues to use methods of resistance reduction. In general, if the suspect returns to these questions more than twice, the interrogator will have to use a direct accusation in response.

3. "What do you think I am talking about?" The interrogator might offer this response with a suspect who is more aggressive or talkative. Since the interrogator's reply offers no additional information, suspects either identify the crime they believe the interrogator might know about or they play dumb saying they have no idea. Either way the interrogator maintains an advantage. If the suspect correctly identifies the incident to which the interrogator is referring, then the investigative findings are supported, indicating the suspect's guilt. If the suspect plays dumb, the interrogator can again take control, encouraging the suspect to listen carefully.

Generally, these types of statements are a search for information, or they afford the suspect an opportunity to make a denial. Selection of the best reply depends on the interrogator's plan, the type of incident, the timing of the interruption, and the way it was said.

A suspect says, "I'll take a polygraph (lie detector) test."

The offer to take a polygraph examination is usually a stall tactic. The suspect has little to lose by agreeing to take an examination since it is unlikely that an examiner will be available at the moment of the offer. If there is an examiner available, the suspect will then suggest that he should talk with someone before taking the examination. Either way, the suspect's goal is to postpone the interrogation or interview until some later time. At the agreed-upon time, guess who fails to arrive? The suspect misses the appointment because he forgot, someone (parents, friend, lawyer) told the suspect not to take the examination, or some other contrived reason.

Depending on the examiner's schedule, the suspect might have bought weeks or even months before being challenged about the incident again. With a little luck and a busy investigative schedule, the suspect might even fall through the cracks and have this case buried under a mound of other work. The suspect has also inadvertently learned that the case against him is relatively weak and there might be some doubt about his guilt. The suspect recognizes if there were sufficient evidence to arrest or convict, there would not have been an offer of a polygraph examination.

There are several possible responses to the suspect's offer to take an examination.

1. "All right that would be great. Here, let me have you sign this polygraph consent form."

This reply is made with the presentation of a consent form for the suspect to sign indicating willingness to take an examination. The simple form consists of a couple of sentences authorizing a polygraph test. Since the suspect's offer to submit to the examination is being challenged, his behavior can be assessed by the interrogator. Guilty suspects will likely be reluctant to sign the document, or they will ask to think about it or consult with someone. They have now further confirmed the interrogator's opinion that they are involved in the incident. However, a suspect's signing of the form without reluctance and asking when the test will be administered might be an indication of truthfulness.

From an investigative standpoint, it is unlikely that suspects will appear for the examination when they delay signing the permission form. By scheduling the test, the interrogator has indirectly told the suspect there is doubt about his guilt. This then postpones the entire process in favor of the suspect and will probably increase his future resistance to a confession. Since it is unlikely the suspect will appear for the polygraph examination, the interrogator might be advised to continue the interrogation using the following strategy.

2. "I might at some point offer you a polygraph test, but I would want it to be one that you could pass. Based on the investigation, I know that you could not pass because you are involved in this situation. What I would rather do is to give you a test you could pass by asking questions like, 'Did you need the money for bills?' or, 'Did you plan this out?' so that the polygraph would show you are telling the truth and put a positive spin on this incident."

Using this response, interrogators do several positive things for themselves during the interrogation. First, they display a confidence in the suspect's guilt, which further confirms the suspect's belief that he has been identified. Second, they present the polygraph as an action capable of confirming the positive aspects of the suspect's involvement. Questions such as "Did you plan this out?" are an extension of the rationalization the interrogator was using earlier in the conversation. Finally there is the benefit of time management in the investigation. The interrogator has set aside time for the encounter and the suspect has presented himself so if it can be concluded during this single meeting there is an obvious time savings.

3. "I don't even want to talk about that."

Legal note relating to the polygraph: The Employee Polygraph Protection Act prohibits or restricts most forms of polygraph testing by private sector investigators except under certain circumstances. The private sector investigator should be aware of the legal pitfalls of this act before mentioning, discussing, or suggesting the polygraph with the suspect. Public sector investigators might also be restricted by state law or collective bargaining agreements. Many states also have enacted victim rights legislation prohibiting or restricting the polygraph testing of victims. The investigators' awareness of the legal constrains will change the possible responses to the suspect.

A suspect says, "Show me what you have on me."

The suspect is searching for information to determine what the interrogator knows. In addition, he is testing the interrogator's confidence in his guilt. Since the general strategy is to not reveal what is known about the case to the suspect, the interrogator has only limited choices from which to choose.

1. "I am not going to show you anything that we have at this point. "

If the interrogator responds in this way, the suspect is then likely to believe there is no evidence that can establish his guilt or that the case is weak. In most cases, the suspect's resistance will increase because of the belief that there is minimal evidence of his guilt.

"All right, let me show you what we have."

This reply brings us back to the first question discussed in this chapter about presenting the evidence at the onset of the interrogation.

3. "The reason we don't show our evidence is not to try to trick anyone, but rather because we have a very difficult question to answer. That question is not, 'Who did it?' That has been established by the investigation. But rather it is, 'Is he shooting straight with us?' When we say, 'Yes,' then the real difficult question becomes, 'How do you know?' The answer is, 'He told us things that we knew, confirming our investigation and that he was being truthful.' So we can also believe him when he says that the money went for bills or it wasn't his idea."

The final reply to the suspect is the best because it gives the suspect no additional information, while offering a reason for not revealing the evidence that benefits the suspect. The investigator can establish the suspect's truthfulness and put him in a positive light by showing his cooperation and by inference that other things the suspect might say are true as well.

What do I do if someone becomes angry?

Many things can cause an individual to become angry. First it might be legitimate anger because of what was being said, an intentional or unintentional slight by the interrogator. Sometimes anger can be aroused because of the individual's perception of the direction or focus of the investigation.

Guilty suspects use anger to try to control the interrogator and his plan for the confrontation. Most often, mock anger lacks appropriate behavioral clues or a logical point of origin. Many times, guilty suspects focus anger directly at the interrogator, attempting to end the conversation. They might use their anger to elicit negative emotions or statements from the interrogator to further inflame the situation. Some suspects react with anger to move the interrogator further away from them. The interrogator's response to a guilty party's use of anger has several options.

1. The interrogator returns the aggression, overwhelming the suspect's attempt to control the encounter. There are several problems with this tactic. This action burns the bridge of rapport the interrogator had initially sought to build with the suspect. Rapport is a one-way street and it is very difficult to reestablish it after using aggression. Responding with aggression also reduces the interrogator to the suspect's level of nonprofessional behavior. Rarely will this type of response be appropriate in an interview or interrogation. Further, the use of this

aggressive response by the interrogator encourages the suspect to try to move to the next level of aggression so there is a serious concern that the encounter will get out of control. Finally, this type of response could potentially coerce a confession from a suspect, making it involuntary and unreliable.

2. The interrogator moves his chair closer to the suspect. This action is unwise because the suspect already feels confined and is looking for a way out of the situation. Moving the chair closer might drive the suspect to more aggressive behavior, potentially leading to a physical confrontation.

3. The interrogator moves his chair back and shifts from interrogation to interview. This might momentarily defuse the situation but tells the suspect that the interrogator is uncertain of the suspect's guilt, which will generally increase his level of resistance. Once the suspect sees that he can control the interrogator with anger, he will return to this strategy whenever necessary to achieve his goals.

4. The interrogator uses a chair shift, gestures, and verbal redirection to defuse the suspect's anger. Note the interrogator's body position in Figure 16.1. In the first photo the suspect is attempting to control the encounter with anger. The interrogator shifts his chair to the 9 o'clock position, maintaining the same distance from the suspect. This chair movement causes the suspect to feel physically different because the interrogator's personal space is no longer directly invading the suspect's space. The position change is different from the positions most people take to argue. The interrogator feels protected, having turned away from the suspect, yet, to the suspect, the interrogator appears to have taken the position of a mediator between the suspect and some unseen adversary. The interrogator then gestures away from him toward some distant place where the adversaries await, while talking about others who might feel negatively toward the suspect. The position change allows the interrogator to remain a neutral party, not an opponent. These changes make it more difficult for the suspect to direct and sustain anger at an interrogator.

You are only saying this because I am (age, race, sex, etc.).

This tactic might be a variation of the previous example in which the individual expresses either mock or real anger. A suspect might use this type of statement for a number of reasons.

First, the suspect might be expressing his perception of reality. Minorities often feel victimized by society, and this statement is nothing more than the suspect's articulating the feeling of helplessness felt at this point in the encounter. Forget the fact that the suspect is guilty; he still feels like a victim

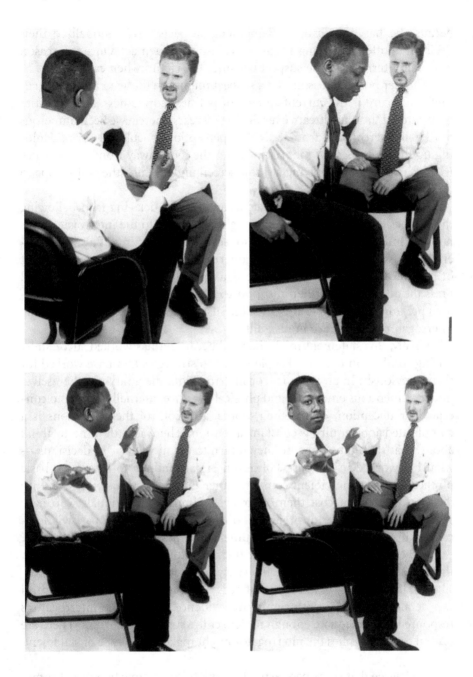

Figure 16.1 (top left) the suspect attempts to control the encounter with anger. (top right) Interrogator shifts his chair, maintaining the same distance from the suspect. (bottom left and right) Interrogator gestures away from himself toward some distant place where the adversaries await, while talking about others who might feel negatively toward the suspect.

because he has been caught. Remember, suspects have rationalized their decision to offend, creating a righteous reason for their act. Once this reason has been internalized, the suspect becomes the victim when caught.

Another possible reason that a suspect might use the age, race, or sexual-preference card is the current climate of political correctness. As minorities have entered the mainstream over the last 40 years, there have been numerous hurdles to overcome — from individual perceptions to cultural norms. Holding up the unfairness of the past switches the focus away from the evidence in the current case, supplying a smokescreen under which the guilty hope to escape.

This statement can also be used as an effective delaying tactic, allowing the suspect time to think while turning the pressure to the interrogator. It is now the interrogator who is in the hot seat defending himself against innuendo. The suspect now observes the interrogator's response to the statement of prejudice. If the interrogator shows a sign of weakness, the suspect will press the attack with further unsupported statements alleging the interrogator's prejudice. This tactic also gives the suspect an opportunity to assess the interrogator's confidence in his guilt.

Finally, this statement might be used because it has worked successfully during conflicts in the past. People return to strategies that have worked for them previously. In an interview or interrogation, the guilty put themselves under tremendous emotional and physical pressure internally. Trying to conceal their deception, censor their words, and control their emotions is a complicated job requiring constant attention. There is little time to think about what should be done, so they return to the most basic of decisions — what has worked in the past. Police officers are trained to react on a basic physical level during violent conflict, rather than making a slower cognitive decision that might cost them their lives. Similarly, individuals who have successfully used anger or prejudice to win encounters in the past will logically return to those patterns of argument in times of conflict.

If the interrogator becomes sidetracked into a discussion of prejudice, the suspect takes control of the interview or interrogation. It is also impossible for the interviewer to prove that he is not prejudiced. The loss of control can derail even a case with significant evidence because the interrogator's response was inadequate enough to deflect the suspect's assertion. There are several possible replies the interrogator might make to this type of statement.

1. "I agree that some people might think this was done because of someone's age, race, or sexual preferences. There is no question at all that some people are prejudiced and would love to act unfairly toward those people they dislike. However, in this instance, because of the way the case is supervised, developed, and documented, this could not

happen. The department demands that the personality and the preferences of the individual be ignored while only the facts, which are age-, race-, and gender-neutral, are considered. What we are really concerned about is the reasons this occurred. Sometimes, the frustrations of being held back because of perceptions ..."

This response is handled as an explanatory denial, where the suspect has offered the interrogator a reason or excuse why he could not or would not have been involved. To handle the explanatory denial, the interrogator agrees with the suspect's statement, retakes control of the conversation with this agreement, and starts a new rationalization based on the suspect's statements. In the above response, the interrogator agrees that unfairness and prejudice exist — to argue otherwise would be foolish. The interrogator then talks about the safeguards of supervision and begins to develop a new rationalization. One that would fit in the context of this statement is an individual's frustration of being put down and held back from succeeding, which might cause an individual to make bad choices. The interrogator has now taken the his statement and turned it into a face-saving device to protect the suspect's self image while also offering plausible reasons for being involved in the incident.

2. "You talk about prejudice, but you make statements about me without knowing anything about my personal beliefs."

This reply might be made if the relationship between the interrogator and suspect has been previously respectful. This response's strength lies in the relationship and rapport developed from the onset of the encounter. To advocate fairness and yet to make unfair statements about another is a difficult position to defend. The interrogator then seizes this to develop a rationalization about guessing why someone did something, and that it is human nature to think the worst about people we do not know well. Coming full circle, the interrogator ties this unfairness into a discussion of the importance in understanding why things happened the way they did, so there can be a fair assessment of the individual.

3. "My wife is (black, Hispanic, white etc.) My (son, daughter, nephew, niece) is gay. So I know personally the difficulties and emotions that they face on a daily basis."

This response should be used only when it is true. Nothing can be more powerful than a softly spoken truthful statement of having been exposed to another's experiences personally. The interrogator then expresses the feelings and emotions from a personal point of view, showing understanding and using this as another rationalization to reduce the suspect's resistance to giving a confession.

These replies are not the only ones possible, but each response by the interrogator develops the suspect's statement into a reason that someone might have made an error in judgment. The interrogator should not take the suspect's attack personally, but rather view it in its appropriate light of someone struggling to escape a difficult situation. This also provides new rationalizations that can be developed as another reason the suspect might have become involved in the incident.

The suspect says, "I am going to sue."

Suspects using this ploy are similar to the suspect in the preceding example in two ways. First, it is likely that the individual has used or observed this as a means of winning previous encounters. By threatening to sue, the suspect has frightened people into giving into his wish, and, when conflict arises, the suspect returns to the well to use it again. Second, the suspect feels a loss of control and frustration at his inability to control the situation. Threatening to sue is an attempt to hurt or frighten the interrogator. Most people who threaten to call their lawyer do not even have one; thus it is a hollow threat. The response to the suspect might be a two-part reply.

1. "I can understand the feelings that are present right now, the fear of the unknown. Uncertainty. What should or shouldn't I do?"

A big part of how people feel at this point is a result of their never having been in a position like this before. The interrogator validates the suspect's feelings, while taking no offense at being threatened with a lawsuit. The interrogator who reacts to the threat of a lawsuit emboldens the suspect to make further threats, demands, and statements. Saying, "Go ahead" to the suspect only inflames the situation and reduces the exchange to a childlike argument with a circular form: "I will." "Go ahead." "Well, I will."

Part of what we do in every investigation is prepare for being sued. What we are required to do is check and double check our facts and evidence to make sure they will stand up to inspection at trial. The possibility of an action against us is actually a good thing because we proceed only in those instances where facts are absolutely clear. But the reason we sit and talk with people after the investigation is complete is to determine if there were mitigating circumstances in their lives that caused them to make that error in judgment. The interrogator re-affirms confidence in the suspect's guilt and the completeness of the investigation. The interrogator's confidence in the correctness of the investigation addresses the suspect's need to believe he is caught before he will confess. If the interrogator shows any uncertainty relating to the suspect's guilt, it will usually result in an increased level of resistance and further denials from him.

Thus, the interrogator has let the suspect know that he has not taken the threat to sue personally and is still willing to deal with the suspect based on the facts. Without delay, the interrogator restates faith in the investigative results, which confirm the suspect's belief that he has been caught.

2. "You certainly could sue. The problem with that is it would be a civil trial where the level of proof we would be required to show is much less for us to prove what happened. For example, in a criminal trial, the level of proof is beyond a reasonable doubt, but in the civil court it is the preponderance of the evidence. The preponderance of the evidence, which is 51%, just a little over half, to win. With the investigation that we have, we are far above that preponderance and are even well beyond a reasonable doubt. What we need to do here is to find out why this happened so people can understand what was going on in your life at the time."

Many people threatening to sue have no understanding of the system and what is required to win. They believe that the mere threat to sue will scare off their adversaries. The interrogator lets the suspect know he understands the civil court system and has prepared for this eventuality. This reply undermines the suspect's hope even further. He now recognizes that even less proof is necessary to establish guilt.

3. "You could sue, but then this moment would be dragged out for years, you would be waiting, constantly, having this hanging over your head unresolved for years to come. This is a time that is unpleasant for everyone. No one wants to talk about the errors he has made in life. We all try to put those errors behind us, learn from them, and not make the same mistake in the future."

Here, the interrogator shifts to the future to show the suspect a different perspective on what he is saying when he says, "I want to sue." Having to live with an unpleasant memory is something no one wants to do. We naturally allow our minds to bury these errors, so we do not have to face them each and every day. The interrogator could illustrate this statement with a story about not letting go of a problem and having it strongly influence future decisions.

4. "You could do that. But think for a second about how problems grow. People can't talk them out, feelings get hurt, people think the worst, and the whole situation gets out of control. I think that many incidents grow worse because the people won't talk about what happened, and instead they hide behind others who might not express the feelings or

facts correctly, so the incident escalates, getting more serious than was ever necessary. It is like the old joke: there was a lawyer in town who was starving for business — he was the only lawyer in the whole area. Then one day another lawyer moved his practice to town and they were soon both wealthy. People could no longer just talk it out among themselves.

With this response, the interrogator uses the general distrust people have for lawyers and their motives. The suspect is made aware of his probable feelings for attorneys and the motives that they have while tying the suspect mentally to talking out problems so they do not escalate.

Interrogators would be unwise to challenge the suspect to sue because they have then drawn a line in the sand for the suspect to cross. This is an emotional threat made most often because of suspects' sense that they are losing control. If the interrogator handles the threat unemotionally, using a rational basis for continued discussion, he can often defuse what could be a volatile exchange.

The suspect says, "Do I need an attorney? Or, "I want an attorney."

Depending on what the suspect says and when it is said, this is either a search for information or an expression of fear. The public and the private sectors have different legal rules to apply depending on whether the suspect is in custody. Those in custody have a constitutional right to have an attorney present during any questioning if they request one. When the suspect unequivocally requests an attorney in a public law enforcement evaluation, then all questioning must cease; however, if the suspect asks a question, the United States Supreme Court has ruled that questioning may continue. If the suspect is not in custody, there is no constitutional right to an attorney. If the suspect asks for an attorney during a nonaccusatory interview, it is often an attempt to delay the interview or to intimidate the interviewer. Remember, a suspect who is not in custody must retain and pay for his own attorney. There is no obligation for the state to provide an attorney until an individual is in custody and cannot afford to hire one. For further discussion on the legal aspects of interrogation and the suspect's right to an attorney, refer to Chapter 3. The interviewer from the private sector should refer to the appropriate company policy and procedure for the proper response.

When suspects ask if they should have an attorney, the interrogator might use something like the following replies.

1. "I am not an attorney and I can't offer you legal advice. Whatever you decide has to be right for you. If you choose to get an attorney I have to stop the interview at this point without going through several important issues with you. These are things that might help you make

up your mind. I think it is difficult to know the right decision when you are not aware of all the information."

The interrogator should not offer an opinion to the suspect, rather, by pulling back and letting the suspect make the decision himself, several positive things happen. The interrogator is viewed by the suspect as being fair, which enhances the trust between the two. Second, the interrogator creates curiosity about what else is known. The suspect delays to learn what other information is in the case file and this delay allows the rationalization process to continue to reduce the individual's resistance.

2. "Isn't it interesting how things start to escalate unnecessarily? We are just two people trying to sort out a problem and all of a sudden people think the worst and ask, 'Do I need a lawyer?' Well, if you need one then we need one or two and so it goes. Costing everyone money when rational minds could have worked through the issue without any help. To make the correct decision here, one needs to understand the scope of the problem being faced, which is what we are attempting to discuss now."

Often, the question about a lawyer comes up because the suspect is frightened and the interrogator has been too direct in his statements, not sufficiently rationalizing the suspect's involvement and allowing him to save face.

3. "There is a phone right over there. Give me the number and I will put through a call for you."

Sometimes a challenge can be used to put the suspect into the position of making a decision to proceed. Most people do not have lawyers on retainer and must go to others for advice on finding an attorney capable of handling the case. The demand for a name and number will often result in an admission that the suspect does not have an attorney, in which case, the interrogator can use the preceding example to move back to rationalizations. However, there is a chance with this response that the suspect *will* make the phone call and the conversation will come to an end.

4. "You know, many times when people ask that question it is because they are uncertain and realize what they have done is wrong. The right thing to do is get this cleared up and set the record straight, showing what kind of a person you are."

With this reply, the interrogator states the suspect's "uncertainty" and moves to another implied accusation before returning to rationalization. This should not be said to an aggressive suspect, as it will likely cause denials and an unequivocal request for an attorney.

5.""I think there are three things that a person needs to consider when trying to make a decision."

Another path the interrogator could use is to ignore the question and attempt to create curiosity to divert the suspect from the question he asked."

If the suspect is in police custody and specifically asks for an attorney, all questioning must cease. However if it is a noncustodial interrogation or is being conducted by private-sector investigators, there is much more latitude in possible responses.

The suspect says, "I want to talk with my (wife, mother, father)" or, "I want to have my (wife, parent, father, etc.) with me while we talk."

These statements are a variation of the previous example and generally offered for similar reasons. If the suspect is in custody, some jurisdictions have ruled that this is the same as a request for an attorney. There are also legislated juvenile acts that might require public law enforcement to contact specific youth officers or parents whenever a child is taken into custody.

The private sector has no such constraints. There is an employer–employee relationship that does not have to allow parents or family members to be present during proprietary company meetings. This would be like allowing an employee to bring a spouse to a salary review session. If a company is bound by a collective bargaining agreement, there are usually provisions for union representation whenever there is a potential disciplinary action against an employee. The employee usually is required to ask for a union representative, and most contracts do not require the company to ask if the employee wants representation.

The National Labor Relations Board (NLRB) in 2000 expanded the ability of an employee in a nonunion company to have a representative present during a meeting in which disciplinary action might be taken against the employee. Again, the employee must request the representative, and the company is not bound to make the offer. The NLRB has flip-flopped on this issue over the years, and it bears watching to see whether they will change again. For the interrogator and company, there are no guidelines at the time of this writing as to whom the employee might select to sit in on the meeting. It is evident that a union steward would have value to the employee because of his training and knowledge of the contract, but it is unclear in a nonunion setting who could be selected and who has the right to select or object to a particular person.

Police officers acting as agents of the state are not required to abide by the contracts signed by the company. This becomes less clear with officers who have police powers and employee investigations, such as postal, railroad, utilities, and colleges. In many cases, the employer would probably have to act under the *Garrity* rule, telling the employee whether the case was being pursued as an administrative or criminal action.

A suspect says, "I want to leave."

The suspect might say this in one of two ways: a strong demand to leave or a docilely testing of the waters to determine if he will be permitted to leave. In determining what response to give, the interrogator must consider whether the suspect is in custody. If so, the answer is quite simple: "No, you can't leave. You are under arrest." Once the suspect is taken into custody by a public law enforcement officer, *Miranda* warnings come into play. The failure to Mirandize the suspect in custody can result in the suppression of subsequent statements and evidence.

If the suspect is not in custody, the interrogator may not detain him against his will; doing so might result in false arrest and unlawful restraint actions. The interrogator may, however, attempt to change the suspect's mind about leaving. Most suspects attempting to leave are in an internal panic and are listening to the most basic instinct — fleeing from a threat. The suspect is torn internally. The primitive half of the mind screams "run," while the rational half says, "Wait, I think I can fix this."

The interrogator needs to address the rational part of the suspect's mind or the primitive part will win and the suspect will flee. Most often, this can be successfully done by creating curiosity and letting suspects know that they can leave.

1. "Bob, you are free to leave anytime you choose. No one is going to keep you here against your will. This is a meeting to make you aware of certain things that will become extremely important to you in the near future. There are three things that you need to understand and take into consideration."

The interrogator uses the suspect's first name to grab his attention and draw him out of the panic he feels. He then addresses the suspect's emotions, reassuring him that there is no reason for panic and that he is free to go. Finally, the interrogator appeals to the rational mind with a promise of information that has not been relayed as yet, prompting the suspect to ask himself, "What are the three important things?" This creates curiosity and causes the suspect to delay. The interrogator then returns to the rationalization process, attempting a new rationalization because the previous ones were ineffective. The three items promised are lost among subsequent rationalizations.

2. "That's fine. You can leave anytime that you want to. No one is keeping you here. But understand, once you walk out that door, you have no control of the situation. Everything is out of your hands."

In this response, the interrogator again reassures the primitive mind that there is no reason to panic and then addresses the rational thought process. The interrogator must next address the suspect's hope: "I hope if I say nothing I won't get fired, arrested, embarrassed." This is presented by the interrogator in the third person, "Most people think that ..." For a detailed discussion of addressing hope see the chapter on rationalization and showing understanding.

The interrogator's physical actions must in no way restrict the suspect's freedom to leave the meeting. In most cases, he need not even rise from his chair to control the situation. Any request to have the suspect be seated is better made in the form of a question, rather than a command: "Why don't you sit for a second so we can talk this through?"

Do I have to read him *Miranda*?

Miranda warnings must be read only when the suspect is in custody and being questioned by public law enforcement or someone acting as their agent. Private-sector investigators not acting as agents of the police are not required to advise the suspect of *Miranda* warnings. There might be special circumstances and practices that would require the warnings be given, but as a general rule it is required only if there is police custody and questioning. Remember to know the laws in your state as well as any requirements detailed by the local prosecutor.

The subject is ready to confess, but something is holding him back.

On occasion, a suspect will have the appearance of someone ready to confess, but something holds him back. There is an unidentified hurdle that has yet to be handled by the interrogator, most likely causing the suspect's reluctance. To address, this, the interrogator must identify the problem. This could be done by randomly probing and hoping to trip over it or by using the more expedient method of asking the suspect about his reluctance.

1. "Bob, what is holding you back? What are you concerned about?"

For some suspects, this is all that is needed for them to talk about the final concern, but others might continue their silence.

2. "Bob, forget about whether you did anything for a minute. Let me ask you, if someone did do this, what do you think that person's biggest concern would be? In other words, what do you think would be the main reason they would not want to tell the truth?"

The interrogator in this instance attempts to talk about the problem in the third person, asking what that other person would likely be concerned about. This reduces the stress a suspect feels, because the suspect is not talking about himself, but someone in a similar situation. Whatever the suspect offers as the reason for the "other person's reluctance" to talk is likely to be what is holding the suspect back as well. The interrogator can now address that issue since it has been put on the table.

A suspect says, "Do what you have to do."

This statement is very similar to that of a child who is being disciplined. The child says, "Go ahead and send me to my room for the rest of my life and don't feed me. See if I care." This and the above statement, "Do what you have to do" are both emotional responses from someone who feels he has lost control. There is a fatalistic sense about this statement that indicates that the individual has lost hope and is just being swept away by circumstances beyond his control.

1. *Interrogator*: Bob, many people make statements like that because they feel that no matter what they do, they are helpless. It's like if you were a boss and saw two of your people do something absolutely wrong, no question that what they had done was incorrect. You have to talk with them. The first one says, "I didn't do anything, you didn't see anything. Do what you have to do." How would you feel about that person?

   Suspect: He was lying to me.

   Interrogator: Absolutely. You go to the second person and ask what happened. They say, "I screwed up. Let me tell you what was going on in my mind and life that got me to the point where I made the mistake." Out of those two people who would you feel better about?

   Suspect: The second one.

   Interrogator: I agree and I think most people would too.

The interrogator has helped the suspect internalize the concept that people feel differently about someone who cooperated. While not a promise of leniency, the suspect can now see that even he would feel different about the two employees in the story.

2."Before we get to that, I need your explanation for this."

The investigator can present a small portion of the evidence at this point because the suspect might be thinking the interrogator is bluffing. Besides convincing the suspect of a credible investigation, this tactic locks him into a story concerning the evidence that might prove damning later at trial or a hearing. Depending on the suspect's reaction to the evidence, the interrogator might return to rationalization to further reduce resistance and continue the interrogation.

3. "All right Bob. I had hoped we could work this out differently, but I am going to have to put you in a cell and finish the paperwork and arrest reports." (public law enforcement only.)

Contrary to the prior example, some suspects are testing to see if the interrogator is bluffing. They do not want to be locked up, but to determine the amount of trouble they are in. Unfortunately, as when teasing a strange dog, they were bitten. The suspect now has several hours to consider the wisdom of his course of action. The interrogator should do nothing to break the established rapport because the suspect might elect to talk again later.

4. "Well, Bob. I had hoped that we could work this out, but, because you prefer not to, we are going to have to suspend you pending the conclusion of the investigation. I will need to get your keys and company identification." (private sector only.)

There will always be times when no confession will be obtained. The interrogator should plan for this eventuality, having previously conferred with management, legal, or human resources to decide on a course of action. If the investigation has developed clear grounds for termination, there might be no need for a suspension and management can proceed with the firing.

Remember, this type of statement is an emotional reaction to the suspect's position. As a result of the internal sense of panic, the mind reacts emotionally, drawing on what might have worked in the past — a challenge.

A suspect says, "I think that I am having a heart attack (going to be sick)."

Be conservative in the reaction to these types of statements. Always err on the side of caution, providing medical treatment immediately. The emotional stress of being caught can create stomach upset or trigger a heart attack in someone prone to an episode. While this statement might also be an attempt to postpone the interview, it is just as likely the individual is actually ill. In one instance, a woman apprehended for shoplifting said she was having a heart attack, was ignored, and died. The liability associated with failure to provided medical assistance far outweighs the benefit of an immediate interrogation or interview. However, always recover any evidence from the suspect before he is transported.

How do I handle parents?

In the private sector, this is essentially a nonissue because it is an employer–employee relationship, with certain rights to privacy for the minor and the company. This issue continually comes up in the public sector because criminal law and state statutes specifically apply to juveniles and specify guidelines for dealing with the youthful offender. Often, these guidelines mandate notification of parents when a juvenile is taken into custody or, in some instances, when being questioned.

Investigators see variety of attitude and parenting styles. The parents are an integral part of any interaction between the police officer and the juvenile. The parents almost always want the best for their child and have attempted to be the best parents they were able to be. In the parents' minds, they have done the very best they could do. Criticizing their efforts as parents is counterproductive to the process. The goal of the initial meeting with the parents should be to win them over to join the investigator in dealing with the incident in the best possible way for the child. The parents will most often be protective of the child, in many cases because they have a fear of the unknown.

The first meeting with the parents is best done without the child present. This works well for several reasons. First, it gives the officer an opportunity to assess the parents, their attitudes, and parenting style without the child's interfering. Second, the officer's goal is to establish a trusting relationship with the parents so they understand he has the juvenile's best interest at heart. Third, the officer has a chance to talk with the parents about how he intends to confront the child and why. The entire conversation with the parents needs to be kept in a positive vein. Their common goal is to resolve the problem and get the child back on the right track. The officer should generally refrain from an in-depth discussion of specific evidence with the parents, as it could lead to arguments over the item's meaning. The result is a loss of cooperation. Finally, the officer should broach the topic of talking to the child alone and then bringing the parents in and making them partners in the process.

If allowed private time with the juvenile, the officer might be able to resolve the case more quickly. The juvenile has to wonder what has been said between his parents and the interrogator. Not having the parents present during the interrogation also simplifies the encounter by avoiding much of the family dynamics that could otherwise potentially complicate matters.

For a variety of reasons, some parents wish to be present during the interrogation of the child. If the parents are going to be in the room, the interrogator needs to decide how they can be used or ignored, depending on their attitudes and parenting skills. If the parents are more positive in nature, the room positioning of the parties should be done as in Figure 16.2. The parents have been briefed regarding what is going to be said and done during the interrogation. The officer sits facing the parents and interrogates toward them, essentially ignoring the child sitting off to the side. Because the parents are supportive of the process, the interrogator can use them and their asso-

Figure 16.2 The officer directs his comments and rationalizations directly to the parents (left) and ignores the child (foreground) until he is ready to ask the assumptive question, which is directed to the child.

Figure 16.3 When parents are angry or less cooperative, the interviewer places them to one side and slightly behind the child and speaks directly with the child.

ciated behavior to increase the power of his words. He indirectly watches the juvenile and his behavior until he believes the child is ready to confess. The interrogator then directs an assumptive question to the child, obtaining the first admission.

In situations where the parents are angry at the child or nonsupportive of the process, the interrogator positions the room in a manner similar to Figure 16.3. The parents are placed off to the side and slightly behind the juvenile while the interrogator sits across from and talks directly to the child.

In some instances, the child can be asked if he would prefer to talk alone with the interrogator because some of the things being discussed might be difficult to talk about with the parents. The goal should always be to make partners of all the participants in resolving the issue. If the officer creates an adversarial relationship with the parent, it almost always turns out poorly.

Telephone Interviewing

17

The opening moments of the telephone interview or interrogation, as well as what follows, rely on traditional skills.

The telephone interview or interrogation is similar to one conducted in person. While unusual just a few years ago, today it has become commonplace. Some companies deal with more than half of their dishonest employees using telephone interrogations. This chapter discusses what situations are best suited for telephone interviews, the skills and strategies necessary for success, and some of the lessons learned.

Why Telephone Interviews?

Times are changing and organizations need to change with them. Loss prevention investigators are catching record numbers of employees and customers in theft schemes. One has only to look at the newspaper list of area arrests to see the number of apprehensions occurring in business. More and more companies are looking at the return on investment of the investigative dollar and the way in which that money is being spent. With the advent of computerized media review, the loss prevention department can target dishonest employees earlier and more accurately.

While larger stores have a loss prevention staff assigned to their facility, smaller specialty companies might have hundreds of stores assigned to a single investigator. These stores are separated geographically, and the cost of travel for interrogations might outweigh the potential loss. The travel issue also extends the investigator further, removing him from the day-to-day tasks of auditing, training, and case development. Depending on a number of factors, an investigator can stretch both time and the investigative dollar by using a telephone interview or interrogation.

The public sector has for years used the phone as a means of doing interviews for investigative follow-up, but less often as a means of interrogation. While telephone interrogation is not the norm today, it helps sometimes to think "outside the box." The first question that must be answered is, "How important is the information that I am trying to obtain?" There is an obvious risk-versus-benefit equation to be calculated in each situation. Essentially, the investigator must weigh the potential worth of the subject's information or cooperation against time and dollars required to get it.

Disadvantages of the Telephone

Using the phone has a number of obvious economic advantages, but certainly there are also disadvantages.

- General lack of control of the interview or interrogation because the interviewer is not present.
- Communication is limited to the verbal channel.
- Unless the caller is known, the telephone can be a rather impersonal medium.
- Often, subjects are in their own supportive environment.
- The interviewer cannot tell if the person is paying attention to the conversation.
- Props or evidence are not present and their impact might be muted.
- The interviewer might be uncertain what the suspect's silence means.
- Generally, it is more difficult to develop the suspect's admission into other areas of dishonesty or criminal acts.

Each of these disadvantages can cause a catastrophe during the interrogation if the interviewer makes a wrong decision. While there are many pitfalls to using a telephone to conduct an interview or interrogation, there can be distinct advantages as well.

Advantages of the Telephone

The first significant advantage is the subject's perception that the matter at hand could not be that serious or the interviewer would be there in person. The perception fits neatly into the strategy of minimization of the issue's seriousness using rationalizations. Other distinct advantages of using the phone include:

- The suspect cannot read the interviewer's body language or expressions.
- The interviewer's physical appearance is not a factor.
- The interviewer can script the interview or interrogation and the subject is unaware of the outline being followed.
- The interrogator can refer to evidence and confirm information without the suspect's being aware of his physical movements.
- The interrogator's voice is intimate because the earpiece of the phone is held to the ear. This is a rapport-building position that is almost like having a confidante whisper in the ear, which creates a physical closeness.
- When talking on the phone, many people put themselves in a submissive head-down position to focus their listening on the conversation.
- The interviewer can react to the case immediately, while the suspect is in an emotional state following his apprehension.
- The most experienced interrogator can be used even when not physically nearby.
- The telephone interview or interrogation can be observed for training purposes, without special equipment or stressing the subject by having additional witnesses present.
- The legal liability issue of whether the suspect was being restrained or was in custody for the purpose of the interview is limited.
- There can be a significant saving of time and travel dollars.

Especially in the private sector, where investigators and resources are stretched, the use of telephone interviews can make good business sense. The investigator must pick the correct times to employ it in closing the investigation.

When to Use the Telephone

Certain cases are tailor-made for the telephone interview or interrogation. To decide to use the telephone, the interviewer must consider the importance of the information to be gained against the possibility of failure.

A positive outcome is one where the needs of the investigation are met and the truth is known. Considered within the framework of the investigation, the timeliness of the response, and the realistic probability of success, the telephone can create a strong advantage when used properly.

One instance where the phone interview or interrogation can be used effectively is when the suspect has been apprehended in the act. The emotional shock of being captured often makes the suspect willing to discuss the issue. Because he believes his guilt is known absolutely, there is no real reason not to talk about involvement. Rather than have an inexperienced interviewer conduct the conversation with the suspect, the experienced interrogator does so over the phone.

Direct evidence of the suspect's guilt can also streamline the interrogation process and encourage the use of a telephone. If the suspect does not confess, the investigation has developed such strong evidence of the suspect's guilt that the individual can be terminated from the company or prosecuted without a confession. Since the confession is less important, the phone can be used to move the investigation more quickly to a final conclusion.

Another situation that points to a possible telephone interview would be when the suspect in the case is young. The inexperience and fear of the situation can sometimes be reduced using the phone, for reasons stated above. It just seems so much less serious to them than when the interrogator is there in person.

Relatively unimportant cases might indicate a phone interview, for example, an interview of an employee of very short tenure who might even be still in the probationary period. The amount of money or product that the person could have stolen is extremely limited, so it makes no sense to expend much time and effort when those resources could be focused on more serious issues. The police officer investigating a simple theft or vandalism might take hours to arrange an interview in the station, while a simple telephone interrogation could resolve the incident in less than a half hour. The telephone interrogation does not necessarily mean that the suspect is not asked to come to the station at a later time for a re-interview, but it is a means of moving through lesser cases to allow more time for the important projects.

Finally, an assessment of the risks versus benefits and time versus costs will help determine if the telephone is the proper venue for the interview or interrogation. An important suspect or witness in a homicide, no, but a minor theft or peripheral witness, yes.

The Key Skill is Listening

When using the telephone, the interviewer is in the same position as the subject, having only the words and voice to go by. Active focused listening is the most important attribute of the telephone interviewer.

A number of barriers to being a good listener are common to most people. We allow distractions to intrude on our thought process, causing us to miss key information. Our personal biases about the case, information being offered, or the subject might cloud the correct interpretation of the information. Sometimes, the information being offered creates emotions in the listener that are counterproductive to understanding what is being said. Anger, frustration, or other feelings stop the active listening process and must be controlled so the language flows in an understandable manner.

Another fatal flaw in listening is holding internal conversations with ourselves while the subject is talking. We are filtering emotions, answering for the subject, and projecting our biases during these internal dialogues. If we then answer for the subject, or make assumptions about what is meant, we might inaccurately construe the message.

To listen to another person accurately we must consciously stay focused on what is being said. This is a complex three-part process.

1. **Prepare to listen.** Clear the mind of other thoughts, concerns, and emotions.
2. **Monitor the conversation.** Constantly focus on what is being said. This is the most important of the three parts.
3. **Correct.** If the mind starts to drift, bring it back on task. This self-monitoring role helps proctor the mind's focus and keeps it properly directed.

Assuming that the listener can control the mind and prepare it to listen, active listening takes place. The active listener breaks the conversation into four observations of the content. First, listen for facts. These are the foundation of the story being told, with the remainder being mere extensions of the structure. Second, listen for assumptions being made by the speaker. These assumptions might not be true or fit the facts being proposed. Third, listen for judgments. These judgments might not be true but are also a product of the facts and assumptions that have been made by the speaker. And, finally, listen for bias. The individual's bias can cloud the facts, creating unwarranted assumptions and judgments.

Next, capture the message by listening for key words and phrases that help identify assumptions, judgments, and biases. Evaluate the subject's response to the question that was asked. Was the answer complete? Was the question answered? Was information offered that was not asked for? Remember that, during an interview, silence is the interviewer's friend. It allows him to evaluate the subject's reply, consider the content, and filter the information provided. During an interrogation, silence is deadly, because it gives the suspect time to create a story. Furthermore, silence encourages the suspect to talk, which causes a denial if the suspect is not ready to tell the truth.

Causes of Deception and Noncooperation

A subject might be uncooperative or attempt to deceive the interviewer for many reasons. Chapter 6, on causes of denials, details why people attempt to conceal information or deceive the interviewer. The reasons for deception and noncooperation can be as varied as the subjects. In general, the cause will be found in one of three broad categories: (1) the environment in which the interview or interrogation takes place; (2) the subject himself — his strategies and experiences encourage certain responses; (3) the interviewer — the things interviewers do and say are some of the biggest causes of denial and noncooperation. The interviewer needs to pay special attention to these points during the telephone interview. If possible, great care must be taken to set up the best environment possible. Additionally, the interviewer's presentation must encourage cooperation.

Preparing for the Interview or Interrogation

The question becomes how the interviewer or interrogator can establish a mood of cooperation between himself and the subject. The opening moments of the telephone interview or interrogation, as well as what follows, rely on traditional skills.

Truth and Deception

As mentioned earlier, the subject's physical behavior is essentially useless over the telephone. The interviewer must rely instead on verbal behaviors to help make decisions during the call.

The first course of business is to establish a verbal behavior norm for the subject. Questions that are nonstressful will probably be answered truthfully. Confirming information that is known to be true is another way to clearly establish the subject's verbal patterns. Particular attention should be paid to the subject's voice range, noting the upper and lower levels. Changes in both pitch and pace have been noted to be associated with attempted deceptions.

Listen carefully to the pacing of the language during the establishing of the verbal norm. Language that slows or becomes more rapid might offer a clue to an attempt at deception. Returning to the topic or question where the change was noted allows the interviewer to discern whether the change occurs consistently, which could indicate an attempt at deception, or whether it was just a strangeness of the speech pattern.

Listen for the natural pauses that occur in conversations; the lack of these pauses could indicate a practiced story. Think of this situation as similar to giving a speech. The first time the speech is given, pauses exist while the speaker searches for the next point. As the speaker practices, those pauses diminish because he knows what is coming next. When evaluating the story, compare its telling against unanticipated follow-up questions. Are they the same or different? What might that mean? Then test for consistency.

Next, consider the timeliness of the response. Was a delay covered by a cough or clearing of the throat? The timeliness must also be assessed against the question being asked. Perhaps there should be a delay while the subject considers a reply. The lack of a delay can indicate a prepared answer for an anticipated question. Delays also can give the interviewer an indication of the subject's attitude and emotional state. A more detailed discussion of verbal behavior and subject alibis can be found in the chapter on behavior and interviewing respectively.

Interview Setting

Privacy and a distraction-free environment are critical to the process for the interviewer as well. Just as in a traditional interview or interrogation, the room should be prepared to meet the expected needs of the interviewer. Noise and distractions should be avoided so the concentration of the subject and interviewer can be focused on the conversation. Background noise can disturb the listening process of both the interviewer and the subject.

If at all possible, the interviewer should have a good quality speaker phone available. The interviewer should check in advance to determine whether the phone transmits both sides of the conversation or cuts one off when both parties are speaking. Many lesser quality speaker phones allow only one person to speak at a time, which could create confusion during the conversation. The speaker phone allows the interviewer to refer to written reports and examine evidence without juggling the hand unit. It allows the interviewer the option of picking up the handset at an appropriate time and speaking into it, creating a greater sense of intimacy, similar to that of moving closer in a conversation. There will be a noticeable change in the quality of the interviewer voice and position in the subject's ear, making it seem as though the interviewer has moved closer.

The interviewer can also have notes and case materials within easy reach. Many new interviewers can actually outline the structure of the interview, giving them a guide to follow while the subject is none the wiser. Training new interviewers can be expedited, as they can sit in the room listening to the encounter without affecting the subject in anyway.

Subject's Room Setup

If the interviewer is calling the subject at home or somewhere similar, there is little that can be done to prepare the setting. Whatever distractions or people are present generally cannot be changed. Sometimes asking the person to move to a private area can help; however, if the subject refuses, there is little that can be done except to proceed with the interview or interrogation as planned. Picking the best time and place for the phone call can sometimes avoid these types of problems.

If the call is going to be made to the individual's place of business, it is possible to have more control over the interview. The following are a few considerations:

- Prior to the call, contact the individual's manager and discuss the subject's personality, employment history, and general background.
- Discuss the necessity for confidentiality and management behavior with the subject's supervisor. This makes the management team a partner to the process.
- Identify the best method of getting the subject to the phone. Identify who will act as witness to the call at the employee's work site.
- Instruct witnesses on what you want them to do and how to observe during the phone conversation. Figure 17.1 illustrates the positions of the suspect and witness. Make sure the witness knows not to react to an admission from the subject. Let the witness know the overall positioning and structure of the interrogation that will be used during the phone call. Also let witnesses know they should not talk or counsel the subject during the process.
- Have the witness prepare the room, removing distractions in the same manner that an interviewer would if present. The witness should have a pen and paper so the subject's admission can be reduced to writing. The witness might also want to take notes confirming the times and sequence of the interview. The interviewer should be positioned off to the side and slightly behind the subject, just as if the interviewer were physically present (see Figure 17.1). The witness should limit eye contact with the subject, instead focusing on the notes. The avoidance of eye contact with the subject is a means of providing privacy during the conversation with the interviewer.

The room and the witness are now prepared for the interview or interrogation. The subject can be asked to come to the phone in the appointed location and the conversation can begin. The best way to get the subject to the phone is often the simplest; just tell him there is a phone call.

Figure 17.1 The witness should be positioned off to one side and slightly behind the suspect and should avoid speaking or interrupting the interrogator.

Conducting the Interview or Interrogation

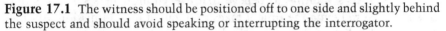

Conducting an interview over the phone relies on the traditional techniques used in face-to-face encounters. There is, however, an exception — time. If phone interrogations are going to work, the first admission is generally obtained earlier than in a face-to-face meeting. The interrogator can be more direct with the suspect, shortening some of the pieces of the interrogation and the time it takes to obtain the first admission.

The shortening of the interrogation appears to work for several reasons. The suspect is doing something very natural in his experience, talking on the phone, which makes him more comfortable. The voice at the other end of the phone is anonymous; in many ways it does not seem real, which reduces any apprehension the individual might have in confiding information. Paper-and-pencil-honesty test makers have known for years that thieves will disclose some of their theft activity in a questionnaire because it is nonthreatening. Similarly, the phone interview is also somewhat anonymous, because it is not a person in front of them asking the question.

The use of the telephone would at first seem impersonal, but with the handset to the ear it is actually quite intimate. The privacy is preserved, even with a witness in the room, because the suspect focuses on the voice that only he can hear. When the interrogator switches to the handset from the speaker phone, he or she enhances the intimacy with the suspect.

The seriousness of the incident seems also to be diminished for several reasons during the telephone interrogation. Certainly one of the most helpful reasons is the suspect's perception that, if the problem were serious, the meeting would have been in person. A by-product of this perception is a feeling of freedom because the suspect is not physically facing the interrogator. The individual's fear of consequences is diminished because it is a voice rather than a face that must be read and interpreted. The suspect's whole perception of the situation minimizes the seriousness of the incident, which is exactly what the interrogator had intended to do with the rationalization process anyway. Effectively, what has happened is that the suspect's belief system is predisposed to the process of rationalization and he has already internalized a position of minimization, which makes it easier for the interrogator to communicate the rationalizations.

The suspect's wanting to believe that everything is less serious is only one factor in reducing the time it takes to obtain a first admission. Another internalized belief of the subject is that the interrogator must have strong evidence, or he would not handle the situation in this manner. When the interrogator refers to evidence, it has even more impact because it is not visually present, because the subject commonly thinks the worst, believing it to be even more incriminating than is actually the case.

The interrogator's level of confidence in the subject's guilt is also high because of the strength of the evidence. The tone and delivery speak volumes to the suspect. The confidence of the interrogator supports the suspect's belief that he has been discovered. Just as in a face-to-face interrogation, the suspect's belief that he has been discovered is a strong component in his decision to confess. The tone of the conversation, the use of the phone, and the reduction of the suspect's fear combine to reduce his resistance and the time necessary to obtain an admission.

In a face-to-face interrogation, the suspects' first admission (if they are going to confess to a property crime) will occur between 15 and 45 minutes from the beginning of the interrogation. In phone interviews, the first admission is after 7 to 10 minutes. There is also less expansion of an admission in a telephone interrogation than there is in a face-to-face encounter in which, often, the interrogator can discover a number of other acts of dishonesty, documenting them as well. It is less likely that this will occur in a phone interrogation because of the length of tenure of the employee and the difficulty of reading behavior over the phone.

The structure of the interrogation is similar to that of a face-to-face interrogation.

- The interrogator establishes rapport with the suspect while confirming the suspect's identity and biographical information. During this stage, the interrogator establishes the behavioral norm for the suspect, speech pattern, tone of voice, and speed of delivery. This portion is often preceded by asking the suspect if anyone mentioned what the phone call was about. The purpose of this question is to create curiosity, delaying denial, and buying the interrogator time to let the structure of the interrogation work with the suspect.

- The interrogator uses the introductory statement as a starting point to convince the suspect he has been caught. Unlike the delivery of a face-to-face introductory statement, the interrogator encourages the suspect's participation and responses. This is done to maintain control and assure that he is listening to the monologue. The internal structure of the introductory statement otherwise remains the same: who we are and what it is that we do; types of losses or crimes we deal with; and how we investigate. The interrogator has spent about 4 minutes on this section, which establishes the credibility of the investigation.

- The interrogator then proceeds to rationalize why people make errors in judgment, using rationalizations that fit the suspect's background. This face-saving section is intended to provide a means of mitigating the suspect's participation in wrongdoing. The interrogator suggests he prefers face-to-face meetings with individuals who have done something very serious to further minimize the problem and reinforce the suspect's probable beliefs.

- Periodically, the interrogator might want to ask the suspect a short question, such as, "Do you see what I mean?" to assure the suspect is listening.

- The remaining sections of reducing resistance might be used or eliminated, depending on the suspect's needs. The detailed structure of this can be found in Chapter 10.

- The interrogator uses an assumptive question, either a soft accusation or a choice question, to obtain the first admission of guilt from the suspect.

- The interrogator develops the admission and obtains confirming details of the incidents. The who, what, where, when, how, and why of the case are discussed with the suspect. Once a complete admission has been achieved, it is time to document the confession.

- The final step is to secure a full documented written confession containing the admission developed during the phone call. This final step can be accomplished by asking the witness to provide pen and paper to the suspect. The interrogator then asks questions about the incident to help format the statement, beginning with questions about the suspect's background and leading to the situation in question. When the suspect replies to a question, he is asked to put that down in the statement. When completed, the written statement is given to the witness, who reads it aloud to the interrogator. The witness is instructed to have the suspect initial scratch-outs or changes in the document and sign each page. If possible, the document might be faxed to the interrogator for review, but, regardless, the witness should retain and protect the statement. If the suspect wants to add anything to a completed statement, he should be provided with another piece of paper to avoid any damage to the original.

- If there is no witness present, the interrogator might elect to record a confession over the phone. Some states have eavesdropping statutes, so the interrogator should obtain the suspect's permission to record the conversation at the beginning of the tape. When there might be doubt about who was on the phone, ask some questions to which only the suspect would know the answers. A question such as "What is your mother's maiden name?" should help confirm the identity of the individual being spoken to.

Not every case is suitable for a telephone interview or interrogation. The interviewer must select those situations where the case and the suspect lend themselves to a greater likelihood of success. Remember that the interrogation of a suspect over the telephone is not that much different from one conducted in person.

Specialized Interviews 18

The general principles of interviewing still apply to specialized types of interviews, such as field, pre-employment, or sexual harassment. Each of these different interviews has differing targets of information, but the tactics and techniques employed are generally similar.

Field Interviews

Field interviews are commonly conducted by public law enforcement and less often in the private sector. A broad definition of a field interview includes any planned or unplanned interview conducted outside the investigator's primary facility. This might include traffic stops, field contacts with victims, witnesses or suspects, or follow-up interviews at an individual's home, place of business, or hospital.

Disadvantages

The spontaneity of the interviews often precludes any type of preparation. The background of the individual being spoken to is generally not well known by the interviewer. When there is information available, it is usually only basic data, such as a driving record or computer search for outstanding warrants. The interviewer also has limited information about the subject's behavioral norm, often never having met the person before.

During traffic stops, the driver and occupants might display some initial nervousness during the interview. The driver's initial response of nervousness might be due to his attempt to avoid a traffic citation or as a result of limited experience with the police. On the other hand, the nervousness might be due to concealed contraband, outstanding warrant, or a recent criminal act. The officer, recognizing the unusual behavior, but not knowing its cause, generally extends the encounter to try to determine the behavior's origin. Truthful drivers fearing only a traffic ticket become more comfortable once the officer has made a decision to cite them for the traffic offense. While not necessarily happy about the traffic ticket, the subject has no further fear of detection, since his license and insurance are in compliance. The guilty individual's fear of detection does not diminish because he is still attempting to conceal something from the officer. Exactly what is being concealed is unknown; however, the officer, recognizing that the level of nervousness, inconsistent story, or evasiveness has not diminished, continues to probe. This only elevates the guilty subject's fear of detection and increases the leakage of behavioral changes.

Certainly, another factor influencing both the officer's and the individual's behavior could be the environment. Inclement weather, distractions from other vehicles, noises, or other individuals create behavioral distractions that can alter both the officer's and subject's posture and movement. Each of these factors can complicate an interpretation of the subject's behavior during a field interview or interrogation.

Another difficulty in a field interview is the interviewer's lack of information. Unlike an interview or interrogation following an in-depth investigation, the interviewer often has no facts against which to judge the truthfulness of the subject's story. A subject might elect to fabricate with virtual impunity during a field interview, believing it unlikely that the officer has the resources to check the story in a timely fashion. The subject might also believe that there is no available evidence that could contradict the story. During field interviews, the subject uses denial, omissions, and fabrications, challenging the interviewer to prove him wrong. Besides a difficult environment, there is also a limited amount of time over which most field interviews take place. The lack of time contributes to the interviewer's inability to detect attempted deceptions or to develop rapport. Since interviewers are unable to challenge the subject's story or facts, they must rely on the subject's behavior plus some other distinct advantages.

Advantages

The field interview has a number of real advantages for the interviewer; foremost being the spontaneity of the encounter, which, however, can be a two-edged sword. While the interviewer often lacks background information, subjects have a limited amount of time to prepare a plausible deception. Subjects have to overcome conflicting emotions while trying to keep their composure. When other people are present, the interviewer has a virtual lie detector just by comparing stories from the group. Truth is revealed by the same story's being told while deception is identified by the story's differences. The deceptions will be identified by the conflicting details that were never anticipated.

Another distinct problem for subjects is the presence of incriminating evidence that can be concealed. Such evidence increases the subject's fear of detection and results in significant and observable behavioral changes. The smell of liquor, open liquor containers, drugs, weapons, or outstanding warrants offer the officer an opportunity to search the group, vehicle, or location. Armed with the incriminating evidence, the interviewer now turns the encounter into a field interrogation. Possessing evidence of a criminal act clearly has an advantage. Most people confess once they are adequately convinced that their guilt has been discovered. With the recovery of the incriminating evidence, most individuals' resistance to a confession is significantly diminished.

The subject faces another problem during the field interview: guessing what the interviewer might know. Recognizing the interviewer's resources — communication, computer records, and another officer's memory — subjects become susceptible to bluffs, which might panic them into a change of story or an incriminating admission. The use of an enticement question that challenges the subject's story is often an effective method to detect deception during a field encounter. The enticement question is fully discussed in Chapter 7.

The field interviewer also has an advantage in knowing the patterns of criminal behavior occurring in his jurisdiction. This often allows the officer to make educated guesses about the suspect's activities. The greatest advantage to the field interviewer is experience. Practicing his skills day in and day out, the interviewer reacts with a plan in a spontaneous situation, while subjects must improvise their words and actions. The interviewer's experience leads him to make leaps of logic, tying behaviors to probable outcomes, testing the subject's action and story against both his experience and logic.

Timeframe

Most field interviews are relatively short, leaving the lengthy encounters for a more formalized setting. The short duration requires the interviewer to evaluate the subject and his fears and needs. Experience plays a large role in this evaluation and in deciding whether the person is likely to require extensive rapport building or just wants to get to the point. Rushing an interview is rarely a good thing, but using only the level of trust and rapport building necessary to accomplish the interviewer's goals is an art form. Earlier chapters discussed rapport-building techniques that are also applicable to the field interview. Behavior, language, dress, and a genuine interest in the individual will often pave the way to a wealth of information.

Reducing Resistance

A field interview or interrogation, like other forms of interviewing, might require the use of some resistance-reducing techniques. The subject, victim, or witness might be reluctant to cooperate with the interviewer for a multitude of reasons:

- Not wanting to be arrested
- Not wanting to go to court
- A desire not to be seen as an informer
- Not wanting to get others in trouble
- Financial concerns
- Relationship worries

These and other possible hurdles can hinder the cooperation of an individual. If interviewers are to elicit cooperation from the subject, they must overcome these possible hurdles. The resistance-reducing techniques can be applied to the field interview. Unlike the more formal interview, the techniques can be shortened in duration due to the limited time of the field interview. The spontaneity of the field interview and emotional state of the subject reduces his resistance because there is a limited amount of time to prepare a response. Interviewers, if they know or suspect a subject's concerns, might voice them. Addressing the individual's hurdle before he does is often an effective way to overcome resistance. If the interviewer fails to handle the individual's concern, the subject will voice fear that will hinder cooperation.

Once the field interviewer has identified the subject's hurdle to cooperation, very often, only a few sentences will reassure the subject and allow his cooperation. One common hurdle is a fear of having to testify. This might be the result of facing an unknown situation, a fear of public speaking, or even financial concerns relating to lost wages. The field interviewer can allay these fears by simply using his experience and discussing the reality of court testimony. Most investigators, except in traffic citations, do not regularly testify in court. Once victims or witnesses understand the probability of having to go to court and actually testify, their resistance to cooperation is often reduced.

Expressing understanding of the person's position initially helps establish rapport with the subject. Recognizing the fears of the victim or witness, the interviewer simply uses statements of understanding that transfer the blame away from the individual for not wanting to cooperate while making it a normal experience. The interviewer then focuses the subject's attention on resolving the problem, not referring to the fears or consequence. If the field interviewer is dealing with a suspect, he similarly transfers blame away from the suspect, using statements that rationalize his behavior. These rationalizations are covered in depth in Chapter 10. The field interviewer may blame the subject's friends, a financial situation, or impulsiveness to support his self image. Using these types of statements in an interrogation or field interrogation provides the subject with a means of justifying his behavior while not changing the elements of the crime. To support an individual's initial decision to cooperate, the field interviewer shows understanding. Recognizing and understanding an individual's mind-set and potential fears allows a field interviewer to use methods of reducing resistance to encourage cooperation.

Behavioral Considerations

The field interview is often the first performance of an attempted deception by a deceitful individual. While the subject is attempting to deceive the interviewer, most behavioral clues will appear in the first telling of the story. If the individual has prepared a story relating to his actions, it would be only in the vaguest of forms. Subsequent questions presented by the field interviewer will often reveal the individual's deception or uncertainty as he attempts to create or remember lies. During this first telling of the suspect's story, the use of neurolinguistic eye movements is most effective in uncovering deception. As discussed in Chapter 7, eye movements can reveal the internal processing of information. In the first telling of a story, alibi, or sequence of events, the individual has created an outline he proposes to use during the deception. However, the details supporting this outline have not yet been created. During the field interviewer's questioning in the initial telling of the story, these details must be created, stored, and then later remembered. The observant field interviewer can often identify potential deceptions during this creative process. As the story is retold, the subject must only remember the details and their order, showing less of the creative process.

Privacy

Like a classic interview or interrogation conducted at the interviewer's facility, the field interview is best done in a private environment. Privacy diminishes many of the inherent distractions present during a field interview. Separating the subject from a group of people enhances privacy and also reduces distractions. Many individuals are willing to cooperate but are unlikely to do so when observed by friends or relatives. During a search for a fugitive, investigators approached a number of neighbors in an apartment complex. All denied knowing where the suspect was or even knowing who the investigators were talking about. However, as the investigators walked away from the group accompanied by an older woman, she whispered that the investigators should go to a particular apartment on the third floor of the building. The woman spoke surreptitiously to the investigators because she did not want the suspect to endanger her neighborhood. However, she only offered this information when she could protect her image among the other tenants of the complex. In many communities, there is a significant stigma attached to cooperating with investigators or police officers.

Protecting cooperating individuals or confidential informants encourages their future assistance. An investigator who unnecessarily reveals an individual's cooperation may eliminate it from subsequent interviews, testimony or future investigations.

Pre-Employment Interviewing

The selection of employees is one of the most important tasks supervisors undertake during their careers. The costs associated with selecting the wrong applicant can run into the tens of thousands of dollars. Not only are the costs associated with the hiring process wasted, but the company or department might be hindered from reaching prescribed goals. There might also be issues relating to morale and associated turnover in an organization as a result of a poor hiring decision. The interviewer must select an applicant who is capable of doing the job, having the necessary skills, personality, and aptitude to be successful. In addition, the interviewer must attempt to select an applicant who will provide an honest day's work without stealing, pilfering or defrauding the employer.

Each year businesses across the globe lose billions of dollars to internal theft and fraud. A large percentage of bankruptcies and company failures can be directly related to internal theft and fraud by employees. The first line of defense in hiring an honest applicant is the pre-employment interview. When screening for an honest individual, the interviewer recognizes that most applicants will be honest and hard working. However, about one-third of applicants attempting to join an organization would steal if given the opportunity. An organization can obviously influence whether these applicants would ever steal by the level of controls within the organization. Unfortunately, about 10% of applicants will attempt to steal or defraud no matter what level of control is present within the company.

While internal theft and fraud is of significant concern to an interviewer screening potential applicants, there are other behaviors and personal traits that could lead to more serious losses for the organization. Hiring individuals with a propensity for violence or who are sexual predators increases the risks for other employees or customers of the organization. Failing to adequately screen applicants who have had a history of violence or deviant sexual behavior could create a significant liability for the organization should an incident occur. Many organizations use the pre-employment interview as their sole protection against hiring unqualified or dishonest candidates for the job.

Screening Methods

In addition to the basic pre-employment interview, a number of screening protocols can help an interviewer make correct hiring decisions. Many organizations will utilize one or more of the following tools in a pre-employment screening of applicants:

- Credit checks
- Drug screenings
- Paper-and-pencil honesty tests
- Background checks to confirm accuracy of education, employment, addresses, and professional licenses
- Criminal records check
- Driving record check
- Psychological evaluation

While each of these tools adds to the cost of selecting a potential employee, their use may be well worth the dollars spent.

The fundamental problem with conducting a pre-employment interview is the lack of information available to the interviewer. The interviewer has only the applicant's word that the information contained in the résumé or application form is truthful. Research conducted by Reid Psychological Systems, a paper-and-pencil honesty testing firm, found that over 95% of surveyed college students would tell at least one false statement to get a job and 41% had already done so. Especially during preliminary interviews when reference checking has not yet been conducted, the interviewer might be at a significant disadvantage. Even with an adequate résumé, application form and the tools listed above, there can be no guarantee that the individual hired will be a success in the position. These tools can only increase the possibility of identifying problem employees and preventing them from being hired.

Legal Aspects

A number of legal issues need to be considered before an interviewer begins the process of interviewing a job applicant. Unfortunately, the laws vary from state to state and, in some cases, even county to county. It is important that the interviewer be familiar with the employment laws in the local jurisdiction and any legal limitations or restrictions that are part of the local pre-employment process.

Significant federal restrictions relating to questioning job applicants also exist. These, along with many local prohibitions, are designed to prohibit discrimination based on race, gender, age, or disabilities. Current copies of the federal and state regulations relating to questioning of applicants can be obtained from the Equal Employment Opportunity Commission, Department of Labor, or similar state agency.

As a general rule, questions asked during a pre-employment interview should be specifically job related. Before using any question in a pre-employment setting, interviewers should ask themselves if the question is job related. Asking questions that would reveal the individual's age, such as when they graduated high school, would be inappropriate because it would tend to identify the age of the applicant. Thus, any questions that reveal information that might be used in a discriminatory fashion is generally prohibited. A wide array of areas can produce information on discrimination:

- Race
- National origin
- Religion
- Sex
- Pregnancy and childbirth
- Age
- Disability
- Sexual orientation
- Marital status
- Veteran status
- Military service
- Seeking worker's compensation benefits

Many laws protect individuals who might be perceived to fit into one of these categories even if they do not. It is also a violation of the provisions of Title VII to discriminate against an individual who, for instance, is perceived to be Hispanic but is not, just as it would be discriminatory to use this information against a person who is actually Hispanic. Specific prohibitions to certain inquiries can be found in Title VII of the Civil Rights Act of 1964. The Civil Rights Act prohibits employers from discriminating against any individual with respect to compensation, conditions or privileges of employment because of the person's race, color, religion, sex, or national origin. Title VII also prohibits sexual harassment and discrimination "because of or on the basis of, pregnancy, childbirth, or related medical conditions." Title

VII also allows for a sex-based wage discrimination claim as a result of gender bias.

The Age Discrimination in Employment Act prohibits discriminating against people who are 40 years of age or older, unless there is a bona fide occupational qualification for the position that relates to age. An employer would have to establish that a particular age was important as part of the qualifications for a particular position. If the employer could not show that age was an important consideration, he would be in violation of the Age Discrimination in Employment Act if he elicited any information that tended to identify an applicant's age.

The Equal Pay Act bars wage discrimination based on sex. Differences in salary for jobs requiring equal skill, effort, or responsibility are legal only if there is a seniority system, merit system, or measurement system that takes into account quality or quantity of work produced. The Americans with Disabilities Act (ADA) prohibits discrimination based on disability. The ADA defines disability as a "physical or mental impairment which substantially limits one or more major life activities." The definition of an impairment also includes "anyone with a record or history of such impairment or someone who is regarded as having an impairment." The ADA does not cover temporary impairment, such as broken bones or short-term illnesses. It requires that employers make a "reasonable accommodation" to enable people with disabilities to perform essential job functions within the organization.

Each of these laws as well as state and local laws is designed to assure that applicants have an equal chance for employment regardless of who they may be. The interviewer must constantly be aware of changes in federal, state and local laws that may prohibit certain inquiries from being made.

The first step in creating an adequate pre-employment interview is to identify the job description and what qualifications an applicant must have to turn in a good performance. In addition, what supplementary skills will help the applicant perform the responsibilities required in the job? Finally, the interviewer needs to identify specific personality traits that will help the applicant fit with management and other employees. In addition, evaluating successful employees who worked in the position along with those who performed at a lower than required level will help identify target characteristics for a prospective employee to possess.

Job Description

Understanding the position is essential for a pre-employment interviewer. Recognizing what the employee will do and how the job will be accomplished will help the him note traits and skills that will make the chosen applicant a success. In addition, understanding the short- and long-term salary structure and time requirements will help in selecting from among the applicant pool.

Qualifications and Requirements

Once pre-employment interviewers have identified the job descriptions, they must then turn their attention to what minimum skills are required or desired to make a potential candidate successful. In addition, what personality attributes are required for the applicant to fit in with the supervisor and existing work force? To identify such personality traits, the pre-employment interviewer should first look at the personality of management and the position's direct supervisor. Selecting a potential employee with a Type A personality might put him in direct conflict with the supervisor, who is also Type A — aggressive and micro-managing.

The philosophy of the department or company might also come into play in determining which candidate will be successful. Recognizing whether the corporate environment is one of strong central management, a looser environment allowing a more entrepreneurial attitude, or a hands-on versus delegation type of management style. In each of these environments, certain people will be prone to succeed while others will become frustrated and tend to look for other jobs.

Very often, the answer to the questions regarding a successful and unsuccessful candidate will be present during an evaluation of prior successful employees or those who did not perform. Pre-employment interviewers evaluate why an individual was not successful in a position, essentially determining what was the cause of the individual's failure in that organizational environment. Examining the individual's personality characteristics, management style, skill levels, and philosophical differences will, in all likelihood, identify previous employees who were well suited or unsuited for the position. Once this preliminary examination of the position has been completed, interviewers begin to evaluate the résumés and application forms provided by individuals interested in the position.

Evaluation of the Application Form

The first look pre-employment interviewers have at the applicant is in the form of reviewing the résumé or application form. Is the document complete, accurate, and neatly done, or was only minimal effort put into this first item of presentation?

A detailed review of the application can eliminate an applicant or focus pre-employment interviewers on particular individuals. Reviewing how the application was completed can be a valuable first observation. Were the instructions relating to the application's sections followed in the prescribed manner? Is the form completed or is information left blank or incompletely answered? What does the applicant's choice of words and spelling tell the interviewer about the person he has yet to meet? Is the application neatly done or completed in a haphazard manner?

Once this preliminary review has been conducted, a more specific evaluation is conducted looking for areas of concern. Pre-employment interviewers look for gaps in employment and employment stability. What was the nature of each job and the skills necessary to do that job? Has there been a progressions of responsibility in past positions? The pre-employment interviewer also reviews the salary history to determine whether there is a progressive increase in salary as the individual's experience and skills progress. A review of the educational section of the application helps determine whether the individual is overly educated for the position or lacks the necessary educational skills to do the job.

Pre-employment interviewers then review the application to determine the reasons for leaving previous employment. Why the individual left positions makes sense in light of the position and successive jobs chosen by the applicant. It is in this section that pre-employment interviewers might determine specific problem areas with the potential candidate. A candidate who responds that the reason for leaving was a "personality conflict" or "personal," or provides no answer, gives pre-employment interviewers areas for further inquiry. Finally, was the application form signed and properly dated and were there omissions such as failing to check boxes relating to criminal conduct that were left unanswered?

Pre-employment interviewers now compare the basic skills shown on the application form against the job description and personality characteristics required to be a success in the position. If the candidate lacks sufficient skills or other problems surface after the review of the application form, the candidate might be eliminated without even a personal interview. Those candidates, based on their application form or résumé, who appear to have the skills necessary to handle the position are scheduled for a personal interview. On some occasions, it might be that a short preliminary interview will be conducted to explore certain aspects of the application form prior to the applicant's being eliminated from consideration.

Deception by Applicants

As in any other interview, a person conducting a pre-employment interview might discover that an applicant is attempting to deceive by a variety of misrepresentations. The most likely deception faced by pre-employment interviewers is exaggeration. The applicant, in an attempt to inflate his knowledge, education, skills, and previous salary, uses exaggeration to misrepresent success. Exaggeration is also used to make false claims about qualities that are not easily verified by a potential employer, such as personality and competence.

The next two most common types of misrepresentations found in pre-employment interviewing are minimization and omission. Clearly, omission is the easiest to carry off because it requires that the applicant merely not mention certain areas where derogatory information might be found. It is much more common when an individual does mention any of these areas to simply minimize the level of problem or difficulty he had with that particular incident, personality, or task.

Many applicants misrepresent themselves because pre-employment interviewers told them too much about the company and the position at the onset of the interview. Once an applicant understands what type of individual the company is looking for to fill that particular position, he can now advertise himself as a perfect match for the skills and personality required for the position. Many times, when pre-employment interviewers spend more time talking than listening, the applicant needs to do very little to conceal portions of his background that might make him unsuccessful. When interviewers simply asks for a yes or no response to a question, they learn very little from the applicant.

Another reason applicants misrepresent themselves is their belief that they must be absolutely perfect to be hired for the position. Thus, showing themselves as anything less than perfect will, in their minds, eliminate them from consideration. What then happens is a conscious misrepresentation to conceal areas that they think might prevent them from getting the job.

Pre-Employment Interviewer Opening Statement

The opening statement made by pre-employment interviewers is designed to orient the applicant to the position and general structure of the coming interview. This opening statement also allows the interviewer to begin by reviewing general background information to which the subject will, in all probability, answer truthfully. By observing the individual's behavior during this preliminary portion of the interview, pre-employment interviewers establish a behavioral norm to which they can compare the remaining interview.

Nonthreatening

The opening should not in any way create a hostile or threatening environment for the interview, but rather be one of friendly openness:

> "Good morning, Sue. My name is _____. I am the Director of Operations for the company. I would like to thank you for taking the time to come in and talk with me today. As you know, we are in the process of interviewing a number of candidates for positions within

our organization. During our time today I'd like to review your application and learn some more about you. In addition, I hope to be able to answer any of your questions about the company and position."

Briefly Explain the Position

The pre-employment interviewer now identifies the specific position for which the applicant is being considered. In some instances, the applicant might be considered for a number of different opportunities within the organization. In that case, the interviewer should be more general in his explanation:

> "The position we are presently interviewing for is an assistant manager's position in the housewares department. The opening is a full-time position, although the hours will vary somewhat."

The interviewer might then go on to give a thumbnail sketch of the position, detailing some of the responsibilities.

Review Applicant's Background Information

With the applicant, the pre-employment interviewer reviews various biographical details contained in the application. This confirms spellings, addresses, phone numbers, best times to contact the individual, and any other basic biographical information that might be relevant.

Describe Selection Process

During this section of the preliminary comments, the applicant is told about the general process for hiring at the organization:

> "The selection process here at the company contains a number of different phases. Initially, we review the applications, which gives us an overview of the candidates applying for positions with our company. We then determine where we feel those candidates might fit with us. Each applicant is then interviewed to discuss his or her background and general experiences. Any questions that might arise from the individual's résumé or application can then be explained fully by the applicant. Following that, we will then check references and verify employment histories and dates of employment with past employers.
>
> "In addition, during the verification process, we may question previous employers about jobs listed or other information that might be found on previous application forms to determine that the applicant has consistently listed all their jobs and information. In this way, we are able to essentially determine the accuracy of the application form."

Importance of Truthfulness

The pre-employment interviewer now encourages truthful responses to questions by addressing the fears an individual might have when applying for a job. The interviewer first dispels the notion that most applicants have that they are expected to be perfect:

> "I know that when we do interviews with applicants, most people try to put their best food forward and are a little apprehensive because of the fear of the unknown. They're not sure of what they should or should not say because they do not know what the company is looking for in a candidate.
>
> "Let me assure you that we realize no one is perfect. I think that we've all made mistakes at one time or another. The important thing is that we evaluate each candidate based on the truth. The worst thing that we face is when the follow-up work finds there are some inaccuracies that raise questions or concerns that were not answered during the interview with the applicant. In the selection here at the company, we want to look at the strengths as well as the weaknesses to make sure that we make the best possible decision both for the applicant and ourselves. An applicant's truthfulness during the process is one of the most important considerations that we have."

Behavioral Concerns

Next interviewers cover the broad categories that will be discussed during the interview. As they list these topics, they observe the applicant to determine whether there are any behavioral changes in response to a particular topic. The strategy here is very similar to that used in the introductory statement, where the interrogator describes the various types of losses or crimes in which an individual might participate. This affords the pre-employment interviewer an opportunity to test various areas against the known truth of the behavioral norm, and to determine whether there is a level of stress on any of the broad categories. Should the interviewer see behavioral changes that are on time and consistent with a particular topic, he then looks to determine if, during the detailed questioning in that broad area, there is a consistent pattern of behavioral change that might indicate an attempted deception:

> "We'll be going into some detail concerning your past employment history, educational background, your experience and performance at work, as well as reviewing criminal history, drug experimentation, taking money or merchandise from companies and taking things from stores. Again, we don't expect an applicant to be perfect, but we want an opportunity to discuss this fully and openly.

The interviewer has at this point created an environment of openness and candor. In addition, by expressing his own fallibility, the interviewer has enhanced rapport with an applicant who might be at some unease because of past experiences. Here the interviewer can use a variety of different methods to determine the applicant's qualifications for a particular position.

Job History

One of the most common starting points for a pre-employment interview is the discussion of the applicant's past job history. As with other portions of the pre-employment interview, past performance is an excellent indicator of future performance with the new organization. During the discussion of the job history, an applicant should be asked to repeat the sequence of employment without benefit of looking at the application or résumé. It is common for an applicant who has omitted jobs or altered dates of employment to have great difficulty in recreating the information they put on the application or résumé. In looking at each one of the jobs, the interviewer should examine whether positions were omitted or whether the reasons an individual left make sense in terms of the explanation and subsequent employment. While discussing the previous positions, interviewers can explore what the applicant liked best and least about each job and what skills he obtained from the position.

On occasion, when it is evident that the applicant is having difficulty recreating the proper job sequence, the interviewer might utilize an assumptive question to gain an admission to the falsification of the job history. An assumptive question such as, "What would be the most number of jobs that you failed to list on the application form either because of lack of room or forgetting about them," (pause) "Was it more than five?" A denial from the subject is an indication that the individual has failed to list all jobs during the prescribed period. The denial is, in effect, an admission that it was not five jobs left off the application form, but a number somewhat fewer. With further exploration, the pre-employment interviewer can quickly ascertain what jobs were left off the application form and the reasons they were deleted. In many instances, the reason for the deletion becomes evident when it is learned that there was a termination of employment for some misconduct on the part of the applicant.

Behavioral Interviews

Another possible type of interview is a behavioral interview, which looks at the choices people have made in previous situations. Essentially, by having applicants describe their past behavioral choices, the interviewer has a window into their knowledge and skills. In an effort to predict the applicant's performance, the interviewer must not only ascertain their abilities, but also the preferences they elect to use in particular situation. Essentially, the pre-employment interviewer asks subjects to describe how they reacted in a series of similar situations to the one that they will face in the job for which they are applying. By using several situations, the interviewer can accurately identify probable choices that they would make and determine whether it fits the management style, employee base and customers of the organization.

For example, if an interviewer were to ask an applicant, "Have you ever successfully handled conflict in a position that you have held?" an affirmative answer tells the interviewer very little about the success or experience the applicant actually has had in conflict resolution. However, asking the applicant to describe in detail the situation and the choices made, the interviewer has a much better opportunity of ascertaining the true level of experience that the applicant has in dealing with conflict.

Many of the situational questions can be presented in the form of a hypothetical question. This should be based on a difficult situation that the interviewer or an employee would be likely to encounter during the job. The interviewer would then describe the situation in a very brief form and ask the applicant what he or she would do in that particular situation. The interviewer can then compare the applicant's response to the preferred course of action that should have been taken in a real situation. Unfortunately, this puts applicants with limited work experience at a disadvantage because they have little or no experience to draw on. The use of silence during a hypothetical or pre-employment interview, in general encourages the applicant to continue talking thus providing additional information for the interviewer to evaluate. In evaluating the subject's response to a behavioral situation, the interviewer should carefully listen for words that would be indicative of future-oriented events rather than incidents being described from the past. Words such as "would," "will," "could," or "often," might indicate that applicants are describing experiences never fully known and are simply creating a response they believe would be adequate. Ideally, the interviewer should look for specific responses to questions with detailed examples of what was said and how the individual specifically felt as a result of the behavioral situation that they were placed in.

On occasion, an applicant will be nonresponsive to a behavioral question. For example,

Interviewer: Tell me about a time when you had difficulty with a customer.

Applicant: That happens all the time.

Interviewer: When did it happen last? (*pause*)

Applicant: I'm not sure.

Interviewer: Did anyone create a difficulty during the past week that you had to handle?

Applicant: Not that I can think of.

Notice that on the one hand the applicant said that the situation always occurs yet, when questioned to provide an example, was unable to do so. Absolutes or qualifiers or tense changes might indicate a future event, not one experienced, and are red flags for the interviewer that the applicant is not responding adequately to a behavioral situation question.

Honesty and Drug-related Topics

Some organizations also have their pre-employment interviewers inquire about dishonesty and drug-related issues. Some human resource managers are extremely reluctant to inquire in these areas, arguing that it tends to make the applicant uncomfortable and more difficult to convince to take a position with the organization. However, inquiry into these areas does not bother an honest individual and tends to set the tone of the organization as concerned about honesty and illegal drug use by its employees. These particular areas of inquiry are often very effective in screening individuals who will be working in high-risk positions handling cash and merchandise. As with the behavioral interviewing described previously, individuals tend to perform in a similar fashion to what they have done in the past. If an organization hires an applicant who has previously stolen from an employer, one could anticipate a greater likelihood of that individual's stealing from his new employer than one who has not.

Generally, when a pre-employment interviewer covers honesty and drug-related topics, a limited time-frame is usually put on the topic to make questions relevant to an individual's current behavior. For example, asking a 35-year-old applicant if he had ever experimented with marijuana might result in an admission to its use in high school or college. The interviewer now faces a dilemma. This type of question has potentially allowed a current user to reduce his anxiety by minimizing the drug use to an earlier point in his life. The second problem is that the interviewer would be unlikely to disqualify an applicant who has used marijuana perhaps 15 years prior to this admission. It is important, therefore, that the pre-employment interviewer place limiting time-frames on the question so an applicant's actions far in the past do not cloud his current behavior.

In general, the honesty issues are confined to a 5- to 10-year period prior to the application. With drug and marijuana experimentation, the inquiry is generally limited to the last 1 to 5 years. These time-frames depend on the position an applicant is applying for. If applicants admit to being addicted to drugs and or alcohol, they might fall under the provisions of the Americans with Disabilities Act. As with any inquiry, pre-employment interviewers should assure that the questions they are using to inquire about honesty and drug-related issues are legal in their current jurisdiction. Asking about a criminal conviction is permissible, but asking about an individual's arrest record is not.

The following areas are examples of those used under the honesty and drug-related topics.

- Theft of merchandise
- Theft of money
- Shoplifting
- Criminal activity
- Buying or selling stolen property
- Use of marijuana
- Use of narcotics or dangerous drugs
- Excessive force
- Driving record

When beginning the inquiry into these areas, pre-employment interviewers begin by listing the topics about which they will be asking questions. They do this in a listing fashion, again similar to that used in the introductory statement. The purpose of the listing is to observe the subject and determine if there are any behavioral sensitivities to any of the questions being asked. Behavioral changes that are on time and immediately following the topic listed might indicate that the applicant has concealed information in that area.

In an attempt to obtain an admission, interviewers can help the applicant discuss that concealed concern in two ways: (1) by restating that neither the company/agency nor the interviewer expects anyone to be perfect; (2) by using an assumptive question rather than questions that would likely encourage the applicant to give a denial. For example, a question that would likely obtain a denial would be "Have you taken any money from a previous employer?" An assumptive question inquiring in the same area is designed to offer an honest individual an opportunity to make a denial, but an individual involved in wrongdoing is encouraged to make an admission. That question could be worded, "In the last 5 years what would be the total amount of money that you have taken from previous employers?" A typical response from a truthful individual would be a simple, spontaneous denial, "I never have." The individual who has stolen money from a previous employer generally will often pause after this question. The pause allows the applicant to consider how much money they have taken over the last 5 years and whether to make an admission. The pre-employment interviewer recognizing the pause uses a follow-up question that exaggerates the possible amount, thus minimizing any admission the applicant might make. The follow-up question might be, "You've never taken a whole day's receipts, right?" This generally will result in an immediate denial by the subject; however, it is a denial that is an admission. The interviewer then supports the admission: "Great, I didn't think it would be anything like that. What would be the most amount of money that you've taken at any single time? Was it as much as $1,000?" The applicant responds, "No." The interviewer responds, "Great, I didn't think so. How much was it?" "Five dollars." The interviewer now develops the admission, attempting to ascertain the level of theft activity that the individual had participated in at previous employers.

Creating Standards

There can be quite a variety of deviation among organizations on what level of drug usage or dishonesty they will tolerate in past employment. High-risk positions, such as law enforcement, security, loss prevention positions, and cash handling jobs, are generally the most stringently screened. However, if an individual is working on a paving crew, a company might tolerate a tarnished background.

The standards are often based on the type of business and culture of the organization. In general, drug usage and previous dishonesty would disqualify the applicant from employment in the more sensitive positions. The pre-employment interviewer develops the extent of the activities in each of the previous topics and then compares them with the established criteria. Applicants who exceed the established standards are passed over for employment while those applicants who are within the standards of acceptance within the organization are passed on to the next stage of the hiring process. This might be background investigation, reference checking, and drug testing.

Other organizations, as part of the preliminary interview, offer a paper-and-pencil honesty test to assess the individual's attitudes towards honesty; the theory here is that if an applicant thinks like an honest individual, they will be less likely to steal, while someone who thinks like a dishonest person is more likely to steal. These non-discriminatory tests have been validated over the years and have been found to be effective in reducing the level of theft activity in an organization.

Closing the Interview

The final portion of the interview affords the pre-employment interviewer an opportunity to sell the company to the candidate. There might be a discussion of benefits and a more detailed description of the job and its responsibilities. During this portion of the interview, the applicant is also encouraged to ask any questions that he or she might have regarding the position or the company. The interviewer then informs the applicant what the subsequent steps will be and a general timetable for informing the applicant of his status:

> "Well, I'd like to thank you for taking the time to come in and apply for a position with our company. It was very nice to meet you. What we will be doing in the coming days is interviewing other candidates for our opening. Once we've had an opportunity to talk with everyone, we'll begin to do reference checks and confirm other information on the application. I anticipate that that will be completed by (*insert date*). When all of the applicants and the references have been completed, we will make our final selection. We will notify you by (*phone or letter*), shortly thereafter to let you know whether we have a position available for you. If we select another candidate for the position, we will keep your application on file in case something else came up matching your skills."

Evaluation of the Interview

Once the applicant has been thoroughly interviewed, the interviewer now assesses whether the applicant meets the qualifications of the organization. If he does, the interviewer turns attention to the general skill level and educational criteria to determine if they match the position. In hiring candidates with specialized skills, the interviewer might ask a current supervisor in that area to determine the true level of skills the candidate possesses. With certain technical areas, only someone with competence in the area of specialization can truly evaluate the applicant. Finally, the interviewer assesses the individual's personality to determine if it will work with the current supervisor and co-workers. If all these areas seem to be a good match, the interviewer then moves on to verifying the individual's job history and references. In addition, any other background investigations or drug testing will be done prior to the offer's being made to the applicant.

A carefully done pre-employment interview has many positive effects on an organization. First, it selects the best candidate for the position and assures that candidates match the personality of the department to which they will be assigned. The pre-employment interview also reenforces the organization's commitment to an honest, drug-free environment. It also affords the organization an opportunity to sell itself and the position to worthy candidates. This first experience with an organization is the pre-employment interview, and it should leave both the successful and unsuccessful candidate with a positive experience.

Sexual Harassment Interviewing

During the 1990s, sexual harassment became a focus in the workplace. As more women began to take roles of management in organizations, their treatment became more and more of an issue. As the recognition of sexual harassment of women began to develop, it also expanded into the sexual harassment of males in the workplace.

There are three basic reasons for sexual harassment to occur in the workplace. The first is natural sexual attraction between individuals. As one individual tries to interest another, there might be an unwelcome advance resulting in sexual harassment. The second proposed reason is the organizational climate and authority relationship among individuals. Finally, the third proposed reason is socio-cultural, relating to the distribution of power to men in the work organization.

The media began to focus on the treatment of women in the workplace. Several major public figures were targeted for particular inquiries because of their positions in the community. The confirmation hearing of Judge Clarence Thomas was one of the first major media events relating to sexual harassment. At that time, Anita Hill made numerous allegations of sexual comments and improprieties. Other sexually related harassments surrounded President Clinton, entertainer Bob Barker and the Navy in the Tailhook scandal, as well as others. This focus on harassment also brought women to the forefront as victims of crime and physical abuse.

Forms of Sexual Harassment

There are three basic forms of sexual harassment in the workplace: visual, verbal, and physical.

Visual

Visual forms of sexual harassment generally are sexually explicit photos, sexual pinups, or sexually suggestive cartoons. In addition, visual forms of sexual harassment can also relate to a person's conduct, such as when an individual leers or stares at another. The individual might perform sexual demonstrations, such as touching his genitals, mimicking breasts, throwing kisses, or suggestively licking lips. Visual sexual harassment can also occur if an individual wears revealing clothing that causes another person to feel uncomfortable, creating a hostile work environment.

Verbal

Verbal sexual harassment can occur in the form of risqué jokes. In addition, off-color remarks, sexual innuendo, or asking about another's sexual experience or fantasies can contribute to an environment of sexual harassment. Sexual harassment can also occur if an individual offers unwanted sexual compliments, cat calls, or whistling. Excessive flirting or repeated requests for dates can also be sexual harassment, as well as unwanted propositions or repeated requests for sexual favors that are either implicit or explicit.

Physical

Physical sexual harassment occurs when there are excessively lengthy hand shakes, hugs, or standing too close to another. Sexual harassment can also occur when an individual brushes against another's body repeatedly, hangs around, or continually follows another individual. More aggressive forms of sexual harassment would be the unwanted touching of any part of another person's body or suggestive massaging of another's body. The most blatant form of sexual harassment constitutes the touching of breasts, hips, buttocks or genitals. Finally, a physical attack, tearing or pulling off clothing or exposing oneself, is the most serious form.

Types of Sexual Harassment

There are two basic forms of sexual harassment with which interviewers are concerned. First is the quid pro quo form, such as when supervisors demand sexual favors in exchange for tangible benefits. These could be a salary increase, promotion, or better hours. Supervisors, using their power, demand and exchange some benefit for sexual contact with the victims.

The second form of sexual harassment is the more common variety that creates a hostile work environment. In a hostile work environment, there is intimidating, offensive, or hostile behavior that adversely affects the individual's ability to perform work. This much more common form of sexual harassment is the result of risqué jokes, unwanted sexual comments, leers, sexual pinups or sexual cartoons. However, the hostile work environment is not limited to those just listed. To determine what creates a hostile or abusive environment, the courts have determined that looking at all the circumstances on a case-by-case basis is necessary. The courts will examine the frequency of the discriminatory conduct, its severity, and whether it was physically threatening, humiliating, or simply an offensive utterance. Finally, the court attempts to determine whether the activity unreasonably interferes with an employee's work performance. The ultimate test when considering all these factors is whether the conduct was so severe that it altered the conditions of the victim's employment.

The EEOC guidelines are found in Title VII of the U.S. Code, which reads, in part:

1. Unwelcome sexual advances, requests for sexual favors, and other verbal or physical conduct of a sexual nature constitute sexual harassment when (a) submission to such conduct is made either explicitly or implicitly a term or condition of an individual's employment; (b) submission to or rejection of such conduct by an individual is used as the basis for employment decisions affecting such individual; or (c) such conduct has the purpose or effect of unreasonably interfering with an individual's work performance or creating an intimidating, hostile, or offensive working environment.
2. In determining whether alleged conduct constitutes sexual harassment, the Commission will look at the record as a whole and the totality of circumstances, such as the nature of the sexual advances and the context in which the alleged incidents occurred. The determination of the legality of a particular action would be made from the facts, on a case-by-case basis.
3. Applying the general Title VII principles, an employer, employment agency, joint apprenticeship committee or labor organization (hereafter collectively referred to as "employer") is responsible for its acts and those of its agents and supervisory employees with respect to sexual harassment regardless of whether the specific acts complained of were authorized or even forbidden by the employer and regardless of whether the employer knew or should have known of their occurrence. The Commission will examine the circumstances of the particular employment relationship and the job functions performed by the individual in determining whether an individual acts in either a supervisory or agency capacity.

The interviewer's job in investigating sexual harassment is to resolve the case and, should it become necessary, provide a defense to a sexual harassment lawsuit. An investigator might determine that the incident did not occur. If it did, it is important that sanctions for violation of the sexual harassment policy by supervisors or co-workers be carried out and documented. In addition, the company should have developed a prompt, effective grievance procedure allowing an employee access to top management if an incident of sexual harassment occurs. Assisting in the company's defense of a sexual harassment suit by EEOC is showing that there is an existing anti-sexual-harassment policy posted at each location and a practice of informing employees of their right to work in a sexually harassment-free environment. Finally, the prudent employer also promptly investigates any formal or informal allegations of sexual harassment in its workplace, interviewing all victims, witnesses, and suspects in the incident.

Development of the Sexual Harassment Investigation Team

The sexual harassment investigations team might be simple or complex, depending on the size and resources of the organization. The investigative team needs to know the scope of authority at the outset to determine what it can and cannot do. The team makeup could be that of corporate attorney, outside counsel, human resource professional, loss prevention investigator, or outside consultant to provide the expertise necessary to fully investigate an incident of sexual harassment.

The investigation and resulting interviews become more complex as the seriousness of the sexual harassment increases. The motivational dynamics of the sexual harassment will dictate the members of the team necessary to successfully conclude the inquiry. The lesser levels of sexual harassment can generally be handled by a human resource professional and corporate counsel (see Figure 18.1).

LEVEL ONE	LEVEL TWO	LEVEL THREE	LEVEL FOUR	LEVEL FIVE
Risqué jokes, cartoons	Pin-ups, sexual photos, leering/staring	Flirting, propositions	Touches, threats (implicit/explicit)	Peeping, exposure, rape/murder
Changes in motive ➤ ------	---------➤--------	---------➤--------	---------➤--------	---------➤
Misplaced humor	Sexual arousal and fantasy	Sexual satisfaction	Power/control	Power/control/anger
		Projection of abuser's view onto victim		Fantasy/ritualistic behavior

Figure 18.1 The increasing levels of sexual harassment, with the likely morives for a suspect's actions.

The first three levels of sexual harrassment deal with sexual motivation — from misplaced humor to sexual arousal and fantasy to a desire for sexual satisfaction. In general, these levels would most often constitute a hostile work environment. As the sexual harassment moves to the latter stages of level three, four, and five, the incident of sexual harassment is more likely to constitute a motive of power and control over another. This could ultimately reach the level of a sexual assault or rape of an employee. In the upper levels of sexual harassment, it might be prudent to include a loss prevention or outside investigator more experienced in the investigation of criminal activity.

Investigative Plan

The sexual harassment interviewer begins with the development of an investigative plan for the incident. An initial review of the company or department policy on sexual harassment outlines the organization's position. The interviewer should then review applicable local, state, and federal laws relating to the incidence of sexual harassment.

The interviewer then develops background information on the parties involved, reviewing personnel files and other relevant company databases that might give insights into the work history of the complainant and harasser. It might be necessary at the outset to confer with management or legal counsel to determine the ground rules of the interview and the scope of the investigation.

The first order of business is to determine the order in which interviews will be conducted. In general, the complainant is the first person who must be interviewed. During this initial interview, the interviewer looks at the victim's story to determine whether it has internal consistency, detail, and an overall believability. The interviewer might elect to use the cognitive interview in an attempt to increase the level of details recalled by the complainant (the cognitive interview is discussed in depth in Chapter 7). The interviewer should also attempt to identify potential evidence that would corroborate either the victim's or harasser's side of the story. If any evidence is recovered, it should be documented and preserved for possible disciplinary hearings or legal forums. During the interview with the complainant, the interviewer should use exact quotes of exchanges between the complainant and the harasser whenever possible. It is also valuable to identify and view the physical location of where the offense was alleged to have occurred. This will give the interviewer a frame of reference and allow him to test the believability of the stories being told.

The next step is to interview either the alleged harasser or witnesses. The case type and development of the complaint dictate which of these is the most prudent course of action. When interviewing witnesses, the interviewer is attempting to find evidence that corroborates either the complainant's or harasser's side of the story. Again, the use of a cognitive interview might assist witnesses in recalling specific details of their observations. It might also be prudent for the interviewer to determine the alleged harasser's demeanor before and after a specific event. During these interviews, the sexual harassment investigator should also look for evidence of other possible complaints from additional victims or employees. Relevant information might also be found in exploring the relationship between the victim and harasser; it can provide a context for the events and often sheds light on the validity of the claims.

During the cognitive interview with the victim and witness, answers to the investigative questions who, what, where, when, how, and why are obtained. The interviewer should attempt to identify specific incidents, locations, and times when the incidents occurred. While doing this, the he should also look for other sources of information that would tend to corroborate the incident or disprove it.

Once all appropriate witnesses, the victim, and the harasser have been interviewed, the investigator should review the investigation to determine if there is any other information necessary to make a decision about the validity of the complaint. The interviewer should then discuss the results of the interviews with other members of the team, corporate counsel, and human resources. Follow-up reports should be prepared on interviews and on any corrective actions taken with any of the parties. There should also be a report on any appeals of corrective actions as well as a report on the final determination and final corrective action taken with the individuals.

Confronting the Alleged Harasser

If the investigation indicates that an incident of sexual harassment has occurred, the interviewer might conduct a secondary interview with the harasser in an attempt to obtain an admission. The interviewer should inform the harasser of the incident and attempt to get his or her side of the story if not already obtained.

Depending on the evidence available, the interviewer might use an introductory statement or a participatory accusation if there is some form of evidence available. The determination of which to use is generally based on the amount of evidence available and the personality of the subject. When the subject is aggressive, a participatory approach often affords the interviewer the best chance of obtaining an admission. In most instances, an introductory statement and use of rationalization is a sufficient approach to broach the initial resistance of the harasser. The most important portion of the process comes during the development of the admission. Here, the harasser offers his own explanation for the events, either confirming or disputing the story of the victim. The interviewer must recognize that individuals will often minimize the seriousness of what they have done to avoid the classic hurdles of fear of termination and of embarrassment with their co-workers.

Regardless of whether an interviewer is doing a specialized interview or a classic interview and interrogation, there are common tactics and structures in the process. By understanding the basic motivations behind the individual, an interviewer can successfully establish rapport, develop information, and gain admissions from a multitude of individuals in a variety of different types of cases. Even though some interviewers do specific types of interviews and interrogations on a regular basis, once they understand the basic structure and concepts, they can provide themselves with a format to move into areas where they are less experienced.

Index

D